TAKING CARE OF BUSINESS

TAKING CARE OF BUSINESS

SAMUEL GOMPERS, GEORGE MEANY, LANE KIRKLAND, AND THE TRAGEDY OF AMERICAN LABOR

PAUL BUHLE

MONTHLY REVIEW PRESS
NEW YORK

Library of Congress Cataloging-in-Publication Data

Buhle, Paul, 1944-
    Taking Care of Business : Samuel Gompers, George Meany, Lane Kirkland, and the Tragedy of American Labor / Paul Buhle.
        p.   cm.
    Includes bibliographical references and index.
    ISBN 1-58367-004-1 (cloth). — ISBN 1-58367-003-3 (pbk.)
    1. Labor movement—United States—History—20th century.
2. Working class—United States—History. 3. Trade-union
democracy—leaders—United States. 4. AFL-CIO—History—20th century.
5. Labor leaders—United States—History—20th century. 6.
Trade-unions—United States—Political activity—History—20th century.
I. Title.
HD8072.5.B84 1999
331.88'0973—dc21   98-47888
                                                              CIP

Monthly Review Press
122 West 27th Street
New York NY 10001

Manufactured in Canada

10 9 8 7 6 5 4 3 2 1

CONTENTS

ACKNOWLEDGMENTS

This project began with an extended essay written by Julius Jacobson on George Meany. I proposed to write several chapters around this essay, toward a jointly authored book, and I continued my end of the work, thinking of the process as collaborative. At last, the volume had so expanded and changed so much that Jacobson, no longer feeling an equal partner, reluctantly bowed out. If the phrase, "with the assistance of," did not connote a research aide, he would at least be entitled to this claim on the jacket. Still, the spirit of his work and the antibureaucratic temperament of the journal he co-edits, *New Politics,* remain herein, and I am proud to say so. He has, of course, no responsibility for the views expressed (or the errors committed) by myself along the way, but the book could not have been done without him.

I would not disguise my own predilections if I could. The needle trades bureaucrats of the 1920s who styled their left-wing rivals "*gilgul* DeLeonists" defamed the original but would have had a point with my case. At eighteen, between the civil rights movement and the anti-war crusade, I became an enthusiastic convert to the cause of the Sephardic socialist from the little Caribbean island of Curaçao. The Socialist Labor Party, a small organization made up mainly of self-educated working people, had long since lost its historic role by 1963. But leader Daniel DeLeon's penetrating critique of "labor fakirs" had a real resonance, and led to a syndicalist or Wobbly but distinctly non-Leninist way of looking at labor. I left the SLP quickly, but I have remained, in some ways, a "gilgul" (that is to say, spiritually transmorphosed) DeLeonite of old, through forty years of my own political activities involving more labor support and labor education activity, as well as more labor history scholarship, than I could have imagined.

Another experience has been, perhaps, even more important to me. My paternal grandfather, a German immigrant, was a patternmaker at the Rock Island Arsenal—the only unionist branch in a family tree made up mostly of farmers, health workers, teachers, and civil servants. But my mother, the granddaughter of an abolitionist, a proud Phi Beta Kappa, birth control advocate, and settlement house worker in her youth (also, casual acquaintance of Jane Addams) wanted badly to become a unionist with her fellow nurses in Champaign-Urbana, Illinois. A few years before I joined the SLP, she had begun to "talk union," finding none of the unions on hand at all interested in organizing nurses and soon finding herself on an unofficial blacklist. That punishment literally ruined her life, although she took real satisfaction in later news of nurses' strikes and hospital unionization. To the memory of Pearl Drake Buhle (1906-1985) and to the example of rank-and-filer Paul Andreas Rasmussen, whose faith and financial contribution helped make the publication of this work possible, I dedicate this volume.

I have a strange sort of acknowledgment to make to the late Vanni Montana, sometime anarchist, avid anticommunist, and longtime functionary in the Italian-language section of the International Ladies Garment Workers Union. Attending a fiftieth reunion of the Norman Thomas campaign of 1932, in hopes of interviewing old timers, I found Vanni, or he found me. Perhaps because he was bitter at the union's dissolution of its Italian-language newspaper, or perhaps because he wanted to unburden himself (albeit not on tape), he told me candidly about his role in the bribes, vote-buying, and assorted other blatantly illegal activities carried on by the AFL in Italy after the Second World War. After decades as a civil rights and anti-war activist interested in history of the American left, I was naive enough to be shocked by the degree of moral cynicism and outright corruption. (Earlier in the day, I'd been equally shocked to hear some of Vanni's fellow social democrats enthuse about Reaganism, but relieved to meet Victor Reuther, who had bravely exposed the CIA labor activities long denied by officials.) This conversation launched a new interest on my part, and eventually my discoveries about labor bureaucracy, going back to Gompers's secret funding by the Wilson administration to defeat anti-war movements, fell into place.

Additonally, I wish to acknowledge some of the old-time labor activists and rank-and-filers whose experiences and heterodox views conveyed to me over the decades new ways of seeing labor history: H. L. Mitchell, C. L. R. James, Martin Glaberman, Len DeCaux, Stan Weir, Mary Zackheim, Dick Powell (the president of the busted Television Writers of America, not the actor of the same name), David Montgomery, and Sid Resnick. I wish to acknowledge, likewise, those who read early or late drafts of the manuscript and made suggestions for revision: Paul LeBlanc, Frank Bardacke, Dave Wagner, Chuck Schwartz, Peter Rachleff, Jack Stuart, Dexter Arnold, Hobart Spalding, Stan Weir, Gina Rourke, Howard Brick, Staughton Lynd, Allen Hunter, and my editor at Monthly Review Press, Christopher Phelps.

Finally, I wish to acknowledge two figures in the leadership of today's AFL-CIO, Joe Uehlein and Bill Fletcher, whose insights and determination mark the path toward potential labor rebirth, and whose commitment has given me particular inspiration for finishing this book. I'm delighted to have had the opportunity to work closely with the AFL-CIO's Organizing Institute, and to draft considerable sections of *Faculty@Work*, published by the AFL-CIO in November 1998. And I wish to acknowledge those staff members at the George Meany Center, including the late Stuart Kaufman, who during the early-to-middle 1990s had the courage to break ranks and offer insights as well as damning research materials on the Lane Kirkland years, accurately foreseeing the collapse of labor's authoritarian regime and contributing in assorted small ways to hastening its end. Perhaps, in light of this book and the new scholarship more generally, the AFL-CIO will end the embarrassment of a name (i.e., the Meany Center) just as ill-suited to a functioning labor educational and organizing center as "J. Edgar Hoover" or "Roy Cohn" would be for a much-needed memorial to the victims of the McCarthy-era blacklist.

INTRODUCTION

Organized labor is currently struggling to awaken again, after a long and troubled sleep. The AFL-CIO "revolution" of October 1995, dumping a palpably incompetent and morally corrupt leadership through the most dramatic institutional challenge in a century, suggested the promise of a new, more inclusive, and more vigorous movement. Labor conservatives gnashed their teeth, and radicals of all generations responded with enthusiasm and hope. The first years after these developments have not, however, been kind to utopian dreamers.

The AFL-CIO has staged cultural spectacles, campus and intellectual mobilizations unseen since the sixties, and top leaders (especially Mineworkers' President Rich Trumka) have repeatedly made pronouncements of class conflict and progressive political alignment. The labor movement's human rights record has also greatly improved. Insiders insist that the old guard involved in human rights abuses in Africa, Asia, and Latin America, and in the overthrow of elected governments—not to mention certain acts, such as bribes, definitely illegal in the countries where they took place—has mostly been "retired," replaced with genuine idealists. But despite the sometimes powerful rhetoric, despite the new organizing staff added by a handful of internationals as well as AFL-CIO headquarters, and despite the zeal of new college-age recruits, organized labor has scarcely been able to begin the concerted effort required to replace the members lost through retirements and disappearing jobs. It has also been confounded by institutional reversals, like the election of James Hoffa, Jr., as president of the Teamsters in late 1998. As uncertain of itself and its allies as the old conservative leadership was certain of enemies (namely anti-interventionism, "extreme" environmentalism, militant anti-racism, and most varieties of feminism), labor leadership today both hesitates and diverts precious energies to the ardent support of less-than-progressive Democrats, when hesitation and diversion spell disaster.

All too evidently, the dramatically shifting workplace, with a diminishing proportion of white males and rapidly increasing proportions of women and people of color, has so far continued to leave the great majority of the union internationals behind, unable or unwilling to make the changes necessary for vitality or even survival in the twenty-first century. It takes no scholar to see that something exceedingly melancholy in labor traditions hangs heavy over a movement once known for its drama and its capacity to represent working people at large. But history is useful for the examination of dark corners, including American labor leaders' widespread participation in intelligence agency activities, coups, and assorted indignities since the Second World War, or its earlier equivalent, the AFL's determined practice of racial exclusion, gender discrimination, and xenophobia. The troubles of labor today owe a good deal to a union bureaucracy with a long record. This book studies that past through the lives and careers of major figures of the AFL and AFL-CIO.

The deepest problems of organized labor today are not mainly a matter of personalities, of course, but an aspect of a generic phenomenon. Put most simply, the postwar labor strategy of ardent support for military Keynesianism (the job-creating effect of defense spending) paid virtually all of its benefits in the short run, and to a relatively select proportion of working people. Rather than reproducing union loyalty, the defense-linked rise of Sun Belt industry created large pockets of white working class conservatism, just as big-ticket construction of suburbs reinforced racial boundaries and in several different ways greatly diminished prospects of union democracy. The environmental recklessness of everything-for-production, taken with hypocritical race policies and a staggering indifference to the expanding clerical (especially female) sectors of the workforce, made the labor movement increasingly unpalatable and unsucccessful as time went on.

At today's end of the story, the gratitude of business leaders that AFL-CIO leaders counted upon is nowhere to be seen, and the Democrats' commitment to labor's stake in society grows weaker with every administration. Entrepreneurs of high-tech industry and chain store merchandizing have less use for unions than the manufacturers who transfer ever more of their production abroad. Union leaders complain privately that a combination of automation, factory shutdowns, and conservative political sentiment have left them memberless and powerless. But they and their predecessors made the critical choices from on high, long before, closing off other strategic options with determination or indifference.

Abroad, in the historic centers of labor and socialist influence, the current crisis has been met by other traditions, with a different effect. European elections of recent years have turned out conservative parties and driven home the message of pervasive restlessness throughout industrialized societies. The actions of reformers in office has in turn pointed up the eagerness of most liberal, labor, nationalist, and erstwhile socialist or communist politicians to jettison generations-old social programs for promises of integration into the world market. Recent Asian and, for that matter, Russian movements against officeholders of various descriptions reflect a different and more stark moment of the cycle of adjustment and destabilization: across large parts of the planet, the economic and ecological limits of capitalism's latest expansionist surge are now being tested.

The structural causes of these developments can be found clearly enough in the immediate background of capitalism's apparently sudden, late-century rush. The traumatic after-effects of the Russian Revolution, including the failed revolutions in Central Europe leading to fascism, and the steadily deepening bureaucratic trough in the Soviet Union, helped set a strangely congruent pattern for organized labor across the West. Aghast at the alternatives and more than willingly accepting the limits of an expansive capitalism, key labor leaders and their political allies sought to craft a broadly social-democratic solution with economic controls and a popular safety net in the hands of the state. Business leaders in large numbers accepted the bargain, especially as relatively well-paid workers became avid consumers. The collapse of Communism (in the case of China, a steady ongoing erosion), however, reset the game, leaving profiteering all but unrestricted and unopposed as globalized markets allowed a rapid transfer of production to low-wage zones; it also negated the historic bargain and caught labor organizations flat-footed, from the West to industrializing Asia.

Behind these trends, three-quarters of a century in the making, lay another and deeper set of circumstances. The collapse of socialist and labor internationalism during the First World War ended widespread hopes (or illusions) in the steady progress of the human condition. That catastrophe alone narrowed the focus of revolutionary expectations to Red Russia, even as it soon broadened them again to include the third world. The industrial West, long presumed to be the site of civilization's next steps forward, had more than failed. True, its capacity to produce and consume continued to race upward, delayed only by a second catastrophe (of fascism and Hitlerism) resulting from the consequences of the first global war. But its social movements had possessed failings that became clearer with the passage of time. Organized labor had never interested itself particularly in the fate of workers and peasants in the colonized regions of the world. Indeed, support for empire (with a very strong race element) constituted the clearest predictive factor for the radical dénouement and the subsequent eras of reform in compact with each national capital. The labor record at home, most clearly where the racial divide had set the outside terms of class society, was hardly better.

Empire and its ideology cannot be isolated from other defining issues of the labor movement: marketable skills and the lack of them, economic militancy and quiescence, avowed socialism and political indifference, gender, ethnicity, and race. One thing is clear, however, and has been clear ever since the leadership of the AFL-CIO set itself against the progressive social movements of the 1960s and 1970s. A central experience within labor history, and a widely acknowledged problem for today's labor movement, is the suffocating authority of the labor bureaucracy. Its self-serving acceptance of existing social arrangements and the damage wrought upon lives of members might be exemplifed in one recent case. Leaders of New York City's District Council 37, American Federation of State, County, and Municipal Employees (AFSCME), in particular the union chief and the former socialist Stanley Hill, whose salary ran more than $300,000 annually, faced a perceived crisis in 1996. The first-term Republican-Liberal mayor, Rudolph Giuliani, demanded a neat resolution to the potential budget crisis to assure his re-election. District 37 leaders, eager to please the presumed future presidential contender, knew that union members would vote down a contract which offered only a wage freeze, with a promise of no strikes under any conditions, and left open the prospect of turning over union members' jobs to underpaid "work-fare" clients.

The union leadership had an all-too-familiar solution: stuff the local union's ballot box, support the mayor in his re-election bid, and trust that the anti-crime mayor would keep hands off this particular criminal behavior. As rumors surfaced, Mayor Giuliani adamantly denied wrongdoing by his labor partners. Late in 1998, the scandal broke. Without missing a beat, Hill and Giuliani insisted that the agreement made with a crooked vote was, quite remarkably, still binding.[1] As this book went to press, District 37 had been placed into receivership by AFSCME president Gerald McIntee, one of the key leaders who had had pushed AFL-CIO President Lane Kirkland out of office in 1995.

It's a powerful case in point. Without a crooked vote, a contract suitable to Giuliani would have been impossible, and the favorite Republican of labor's aging cold warriors in the Liberal Party would have suffered a black eye, if not a lost election. The story of unions, let alone the history of working people at large, cannot be encapsulated in this or any one issue. But the presence of a forceful, avowedly, institutionally, and, on a broad spectrum of issues, politically conservative leadership at the center of labor's institutions is practically unique to the United States. Like the absence of a vital labor or socialistic mass party supported by the labor movement, the tale of the bureaucrats speaks to many larger issues, in the United States and abroad. Yet only in recent decades has scholarship of any kind begun to respond substantively and creatively to the dilemmas posed by American labor bureaucracy. In eras past, a near-consensus of labor scholars, labor journalists, and others virtually across the political spectrum confined the issue in a myriad of ways.

The presence of powerful, undemocratic, and avidly anti-socialist labor leaders was first explained and praised in a literature purporting to explore the conservative character of the American worker. German theorist Werner Sombart in *Why Is There No Socialism in the United States?* (1906), pronounced abundance as the crucial source of American (he did not specify "organized") labor's acquiescent individualism. A generation later, Selig Perlman's *Theory of the Labor Movement* (1928), which could rightly be called the key theoretical document of the many-volumed "Commons school" of labor economics and labor history, confirmed the thesis that the frankly exclusionary and, in many of its component unions, frankly racist American Federation of Labor had been the proper as well as inevitable mechanism for American workers, whose material comforts had surpassed the need for all radicalism.

That these theorists ignored the sharp divisions within the working class, leaving out of consideration the great majority of American working people lacking union protection, goes almost without saying. They took as inevitable and proper the victories of craft leaders over industrial unionists and of the union machines over radicals. The spokesmen and scholars for existing labor leadership have had nothing to add on the subject in all the decades since, save to praise the AFL-CIO's formal support of civil rights legislation and to explain away its earlier (or present) behavior as a consequence of leaders democratically bending to a backward rank and file.

Robert Michels, a German theorist of bureaucracy, had offered a different explanation in *Political Parties: A Sociological Study of the Oligarchical Tendencies of Modern Democracy* (1906). Michels sought to interpret the abandonment of revolutionary expectations by German social democracy before the First World War, a political crisis that destroyed the remaining illusions in an inevitable golden socialist future. For Michels, the initial successes of the labor and socialist movements in gaining modest reforms for working people had prompted the rise of a pragmatic, task-oriented bureaucracy which accepted the permanence of class society as the guarantee of its own comfortable status. Michels was pessimistic about the possibilities of ordinary working people overturning these bureaucracies. He did not foresee the wave of strikes by unskilled workers across the U.S. and Europe during the early 1910s.

The Russian revolutionary intellectuals V. I. Lenin and Nikolai Bukharin, and their like-thinking fellow revolutionary German Karl Radek, had a more materialist perspective. The undoubted conservatism of the class of labor bureaucrats lay not in pragmatic ideology but in the real material condition of their key labor supporters, the highly-paid craft workers (the "aristocracy of labor") who by no accident formed the main body of the American Federation of Labor, the most conservative of labor movements in the West. Assorted labor critics in the United States, albeit none with a similar degree of Bolshevik prestige, tackled the same question and offered similar conclusions with additional hints of cultural and generational factors in the possible overturn of labor's conservatives.[2]

The many problems of understanding labor leadership, including the crosscurrents of radicalism among some of the most highly skilled and best-paid workers, were vastly complicated by the effects of the Russian Revolution upon radical intellectuals. Insurrectionary-minded for a few years, American Communists immediately thereafter sought to find a home for themselves close to the mainstream among workers willing to support them, emphatically including AFL members. In their optic, the blame generally narrowed to AFL president Samuel Gompers and his coterie of fellow misleaders. Meanwhile, objective differences among workers were glossed over by the categories of "advanced" (the party and its periphery) and "backward" (the unenlightened masses). Communists added important emphases upon race and racial oppression, but these additions meshed poorly with existing theories of the labor bureaucracy even as many ordinary Communists (and Socialists) acted heroically to cross the race lines and bring new blood into a tired labor movement.[3]

Labor history of every kind, for a half-century, was afterward written mostly as the heroic tale of great leaders and of the great institutions that they created. It had two distinct but not antithetical sources. The first, the "labor economics" of scholars around John R. Commons, Selig Perlman, and Philip Taft, continued to bless the moderate reformism and antiradicalism of the labor movement as properly attuned to the materialist, pragmatic character of American life. A second stream, composed of labor journalists and a rising circle of historians, elaborated the assumption that labor had succeeded in lifting up several generations of European immigrants and had now found its way into the mainstream. Along with Franklin Roosevelt's New Deal, they held, unions had given these children of suffering a better life, with ample opportunities for their children to gain an education and to rise out of the working class altogether. Offering a narrative that moved from misery to relative comfort and from exploitation to leisure, this latter history minimized uncomfortable details. Not surprisingly, many of the books that told this cheerful tale between the 1940s and 1960s were actually well-paid testimonials to past accomplishments of famous leaders, with writers' fees taken out of union dues.

It has been recognized only tardily that the leading second-generation labor analysts, often sociologists as well as historians, including Daniel Bell, Seymour Martin Lipset, and a host of others, came to labor history with an agenda of their own quite as literal as (if rather more sophisticated than) the older union-paid authors.[4] The main outlines of their views had already been suggested by Sombart and by Michels's conservative counterpart, Max Weber, but they collectively elaborated during the 1950s and early 1960s the conception that the United States had indeed been an "exceptional" society whose openness, class mobility, and prosperity had flatly ruled out labor radicalism and the class-based political parties (Labour in Great Britain, Socialist or Communist across the rest of Europe and much of the rest of the world) which unions customarily supported. A generation of liberal intellectuals thus claimed their place as philosophers of the "end of ideology" by congratulating the labor leaders who abandoned the hoary dreams of an egalitarian socialism. Cautious and conservative American unions and their leaders constituted, in this perspective, the great triumph of the American way.[5]

These views, consolidated in the high days of the Cold War as a scholarly defense of America against its enemies, found a particularly receptive audience among the readers of *Fortune*, just as one would expect. Nor was it entirely a happy coincidence that the prestigious younger scholars elaborating such views made themselves conspicuous within the Congress for Cultural Freedom, its journal *Encounter,* and its offshoot, the American Committee for Cultural Freedom, which is to say, within the key agencies of covert CIA plans and funding in the intellectual world. As subsequent scholarship revealed, even the scholarly and highly prestigious "Communism in American Life" book series which dealt widely with issues of labor, race, conservatism, and radicalism was planned by the ACCF circle, with funding for prestigious academic authors cleverly arranged through other conduits.[6] Although some of the participants later grew embarrassed at the company they kept (or rather, The Company), the milieu survived to become the intellectual backbone of neoconservatism and neoliberalism, a trajectory foreshadowed by their views of capital, labor, and American life in the Cold War era.

Not until the social movements of the 1960s had blossomed did the numbers of younger radical scholars rise to a critical mass. By the time newer generations of labor historians began to challenge systematically the assumptions and the research of their predecessors, organized labor had already suffered monumental blows to its prestige and its standing in American society. In legend at least—if not nearly so often in fact—labor had once spoken for the lowly and had gathered unto itself the idealists in society at large. Even during the early Cold War decades, unions were proudly liberal, loyal to the social reform wing of the Democratic Party, hailing (at least in self-congratulatory official resolutions) the advance of Social Security, job-creation programs, and the civil rights of minorities. As events of the 1960s eroded and finally exploded these half-mythic traditions, AFL-CIO President George Meany emerged a sputtering, foul-mouthed conservative, a bloated public embarrassment perfectly suited for newspaper cartoonists' ridicule.

Worse for the unions' reputation, official labor's aggressive Cold War posture and zeal for expanded military action in Vietnam had long since placed America's idealists and its union leaders on diametrically opposite sides. As the world watched, peace and liberation movements dramatized the role played by college students and young people of color who could not be credibly labeled "communist" and who evidently would not go away or grow silent so long as the war, racism, and poverty continued. Labor leaders, middle-aged white men by now known best for their large salaries and luxury perks, were more than furious at all this. Just as they had reached respectability by agreeing with the Establishment on the overriding issues of the day—and by helping to lift an Irish Catholic Democrat into the presidency—their image ironically descended to that of the mythic tyrannical "labor bosses" whom Republican politicians had been denouncing for decades.

Resentment against wrongful authority ran deeper in working-class life than the press allowed. But all too many younger people on the campus drew the hasty conclusion that working people were mostly Archie Bunker bigots, and that the old saga of labor heroism was finished, if it had ever existed. Not all young radicals felt that way. Thousands entered agitation around factory and community issues over the course of the 1970s. In lesser numbers, anti-war students en route to becoming professors made it their cause to reclaim the past. Along with their faculty allies, these scholars-to-be comprised the next and largest-ever generation of labor scholars, and labor historians in particular.

Their way had been prepared, although somewhat ambiguously, by a far-ranging labor scholarship focusing upon a range of issues—from cultural traditions of working-class groups to the changing structure of industry and the racial-ethnic composition of union bodies. A relative handful of older scholars, including Herbert Gutman, David Brody, and David Montgomery, all of them influenced to some degree by the work of the British historian E. P. Thompson, trained the mini-army of idealistic young intellectuals and set them loose upon a collective project of unprecedented character. Unlike previous labor scholars, from Selig Perlman to Seymour Martin Lipset, they received precious little sympathy from top leaders of the labor movement, who mostly regarded the youngsters as unwanted, if not actually dangerous to labor's prestige.

David Roediger has recently illuminated why new understandings of the labor past have emerged—and why they still meet with resistance. If "the face of organized labor is changing," then this transformation is likely to open fresh avenues of inquiry into the past. When white males no longer constitute even half of union members, as has been true since 1995, the old "naturalizing" assumptions of labor as effectively embodied within the AFL, or even the AFL-CIO, tend to disintegrate.[7] Much of the freshest research and scholarship problematizes how white, male (and for that matter, heterosexual) categories came to dominate the definitions of "worker" and "unionist" when so many exceptions and counterexamples existed from pre-colonial times onward. Other important recent work examines the often hidden racial and ethnic assumptions in scholarship which deemed exclusionary policies as being demanded by members and therefore accepted only reluctantly by benign labor leaders.[8] These are the ways that fuller pictures emerge—painfully, and without much encouragement from even today's AFL-CIO.

From the new historians' standpoint, the existing labor scholarship was not only biased regarding women, people of color, and dissenters generally. It had also simply disregarded the rank-and-file players. The older historians' obsessions with the institutions had especially soft-pedaled or ignored the social setting of union members' mostly immigrant or second-generation experiences during the crucial decades between the 1860s and 1930s.

More and more scholars of labor, women's, and social history concluded that without the tale of German immigrants in the post-Civil War labor movements, for instance, or without the saga of ordinary Jews, Italians, and Slavs, among others, in later decades, or without the stories of African Americans and Mexican Americans across the whole period, the actual history of the labor and political movements could not possibly be told. Similarly, without some understanding of off-the-job life, including the class, ethnic, and racial contestation of neighborhoods as well as factories, the supposed "working class" consisted only of pawns in industrial output with appetites for commodities. Finally, without the economic context of an emerging dual or multiple labor market, with non-whites and women locked out of better jobs (all too frequently at the insistence of organized labor), the triumph of the labor boss smoking big cigars in the limousine was practically incomprehensible.

The younger intellectuals set down hundreds of monographs and scholarly articles from the 1970s to the 1990s, filling in areas of labor's story that previous generations had never considered important enough to investigate. Documentary filmmakers and community activists staged interviews, held public meetings, and otherwise dramatized the lives of those grown old in the struggle and conveniently "forgotten" by the powerful. Traditionalists old and young who devoted fresh volumes celebrating the lives of labor conservatives Samuel Gompers, George Meany, or garment union czar David Dubinsky meanwhile continued to gain the official approval (and *New York Times* reviews) that scholars of events like the 1912 "Bread and Roses" strike in Lawrence, Massachusetts, or of the continuing left-wing role in labor, could rarely expect. Still, by force of evidence and argument as well as generational transition, the newer labor scholarship made its way.[9]

This generation of scholars—mostly middle-aged by the 1990s—along with their older and younger sympathizers naturally viewed the mid-1990s replacement of the AFL-CIO's ruling clique with special hope. With the contributions of hundreds of sympathetic journalists, oral historians and social historians close at hand, they had developed a critical if still preliminary assessment of "Gompersism," that is, the adaptation of unions to the triumph of capital and the bureaucratic mode at the expense of labor's idealists and the disadvantaged. Understanding the movements of a wider class and human solidarity that rose and fell prior to the institutional dominance of a conservative AFL also helped make sense of the repeated crisis of organized labor. In particular, the history of the Industrial Workers of the World—that most far-sighted, generous, multi-racial model of what a better American labor movement might have been—could be seen, more completely, through the common fund of labor experiences and ideas that the Wobblies drew upon, inspired, and brought together. Heroes (and of course heroines) were made, not born; circumstances and ideals could wrest unions from the shame of the recent past and make working-class movements heroic again.[10]

Only since the 1980s has the analysis of the labor movement's historic formation and development focused upon such issues as labor's response to race, gender, and law as key sources of its narrow and exclusionary outlook. What an earlier generation of scholars best epitomized by Daniel Bell praised in AFL founder Samuel Gompers's pragmatism is now seen as authoritarian, racist, and—from an early point in terms of the working class as a whole, in the long run for unions themselves—staggeringly unsuccessful.

By the 1990s, with the collapse of the Soviet Union, the decades-long ideological rationalization for labor conservatism had also lost its resonance. Not that labor's Communists received the single-minded vindication they had hoped to see, most notably expressed by their leading historian, Philip S. Foner. Indeed, the leftward turn of scholarship on issues of bureaucracy tended to indict the Party's cooperation in the "no strike" pledge of the Second World War as a world-historic blunder, and the substitution of foreign policy objectives for issues of internal democracy in many left unions as a case of oversight at best, institutional conservatism with ideological covering at worst. However, only the hidebound conservatives of the field denied the admirable and important efforts by Communists (to a lesser extent, Socialists and Trotskyists as well) to bring about a multiracial unionism; and the purge of left-led unions from the CIO in 1949-1950 is now understood to have been a disaster for labor by all but a few traditionalists.

Legal historians, meanwhile, were perhaps most innovative in confirming the overthrow of the old, rosy view of American labor institutionalism. As William Forbath has argued most clearly, the conservative intent of the framers of the Constitution carefully placed property rights above legisla-tion—in the hands of the courts. Chosen from the elites of business and the law, the judiciary (whether appointed at the federal level or elected at the state level, and usually irrespective of party affiliation) consistently defined "republicanism" in ways to exclude redistribution of power or rights to the lower classes. Even Samuel Gompers began, in his crypto-Marxist days, agitating for sweeping changes in state laws, a presumed step toward taking power away from the capitalists. Gompers and the new AFL, in this perspective, then retreated into what has been mistakenly called "volunta-rism," a minimal interference of the political state in union activities. Actually, as we shall see, the supposedly voluntarist AFL urgently sought the state's support in excluding those "lower races" perceived to be in competition to AFL members. But while the AFL was restrained from an effective legislative reform program, its left-wing labor rivals were crushed by massive injunctions and the use of court-supported police and militia. Gompers seized the opportunities offered him by the courts to legitimate a conservative and exclusionary style of unionism, as George Meany and Lane Kirkland would later use the direct assistance offered by assorted intelligence agencies to crush radicalism of all kinds at home and abroad. In this way, Gompers and his successors were less labor representatives than labor controllers.[11]

Still, even such useful explanations do not offer a theory of bureaucracy akin to that attempted by Michels or the Bolsheviks. It is striking that *Audacious Democracy*, a collection of mostly leftish essays adapted from speeches made at the Columbia University teach-in of 1996, which marked a renewed link between progressive intellectuals and organized labor, contains virtually no hint of the problem.[12] In the literature of certain neo-traditionalists, like CIO historian Robert Zieger, the high-handedness of labor leaders is still taken fatalistically, something troubling but (like general union indifference to workers outside organized labor since the expulsion of the left) a reflection of the will of generally conservative rank-and-file union members rather than tampering by outside authorities or some fundamental flaw in leadership.[13]

The forerunner of new left thinkers, C. Wright Mills, in *The New Men of Power* (1948), offered a strictly sociological analysis of the labor bureaucracy. They wanted power, these men rising from the lower classes, and had learned quickly that unions as quintessential modern organizations promoted the "organization man." Nevertheless a "strategic elite" because of their links to working people, they had the capacity to go with the main postwar drift or turn heroically against it. Mills did not, however, offer many hopes along the latter line, or any broader explanatory apparatus for the melancholy main trends.[14]

Two years later, the eclectic Marxist C. L. R. James and his intellectual collaborators attempted a rare updated theoretical explanation in *State Capitalism and World Revolution*, a rewrite of sorts of Lenin's *State and Revolution*. The crisis of capitalism had, in this view, thrown up a new, global class of bureaucracy altogether willing to abandon private ownership in favor of state ownership, so long as the rule of labor from above continued. Written polemically against the Communists' claim to "workers' democracy" in the Eastern bloc, *State Capitalism and World Revolution* had great iconoclastic power. It also effectively described some of the reasoning of left-wing American labor leaders eager to support the wartime "no strike" pledge and extend it into the postwar period. Most of all, the little volume anticipated the source of deformation in those future post-colonial societies which essentially substituted one ruling class for another, abandoning all pre-revolutionary promises of real liberation (i.e., an end to all bureaucratic as well as capitalistic or colonial rule). Socialism, in James's clear vision, meant workers' control of production and the population's clear expression of power in every avenue of life; it demanded, finally, the reconciliation of the old division between mental and manual labor.[15]

But this model, valuable for postwar Western Europe in particular, fit the U.S. experience only partially. The leaders of the American Federation of Labor harbored no such desire to replace corporate property with state ownership. Neither did John L. Lewis, or the other noncommunist leaders of the C.I.O. Very soon after the war, as capitalism regained vitality—certainly due largely to the impetus of state spending on matters related to the military past or present, from the GI Bill to Korean War build-up—the older logic of the AFL labor bureaucracy reasserted itself in force. The prerogatives of race, gender, and purported skill had never ceased to be a crucial factor, even within the most advanced and democratic unions, like the UAW. But rather than being engines of further radicalization (as James's followers and other radicals anticipated), the steady racial transformation of the workforce helped seal in the bureaucrats, supported or at least not opposed by aging white male union members. Raw anticommunism with a quest for the suburbs and racial reassurance, not anti-Stalinist radicalism, powered the further transformation of organized labor. By the time of the merger, the CIO had already capitulated to Gompersism, slightly updated to include acceptance of the welfare state and a formal, none-too-sincere aspiration for full racial equality.

To put the broader argument of this book a little differently, the carefully formulated liberal and labor-bureaucratic notion of expansive American democracy falls apart at closer examination. It always precluded European-style visions of socialism and an avowedly socialistic labor movement. But the familiar praise of "American exceptionalism," meaning the avoidance of class struggle, which was conceptually attached to a notion of the right and proper U.S. domination of the hemisphere and ultimately the planet, must now be seen as short-sighted at best. The domination of key sectors within the economy by a relatively few, immensely powerful firms able to rally the power (and allies) to crush idealistic labor movements turns out to be both consequence and cause of the imperial condition; no other modern empire, not even the British, showed the same capacity to shape its society or its labor leaders to such uniform purpose. Those outside the craft ranks suffered from the first days of bureaucratic consolidation and never ceased to suffer from the power of a conservative labor movement to work against broader forms of racial, gender, and economic democracy in society at large. America's historic labor bureaucracy is, then, finally and without doubt connected to the creation of empire. Overlaid with an array of other factors including the character of racial and ethnic hierarchies, the changing rules of industrial production, and, to no small degree, the compelling need of leaderships to put down or co-opt challenges to their authority, the steady commitment to imperial aims has demanded an "iron triangle" amounting to rules and practices *against* functioning labor de-mocracy, as well as a ferociously anti-socialist and pseudo-egalitarian rhetoric.

The demand for "more" first voiced by Samuel Gompers in the late nineteenth century as the only proper goal of American labor could not logically include the restructuring of society. It did not even include "more" for racial minorities, unskilled workers, and others similarly excluded from labor—unless "more" meant more marginalization and exclusion. Thus, the highly romantic recollection of the philosopher Richard Rorty that "America . . . was going to be the world's first classless society" and was really becoming so, thanks in large part to the AFL-CIO leaders (until the Vietnam crisis) would be laughable if it were not the bedrock belief of generations of liberal cold warriors.[16] Growing ratios between the pay of skilled and unskilled workers, economic dispossession of African Americans from large parts of the rural South, environmental assaults in all directions but especially aimed at American Indians, inner cities looted by financial swindlers, and the all-pervasive reactionary gender politics of the 1950s, not to speak of the degradation of third world life by drastically uneven economic exchanges and CIA machinations—all of these would point in the other direction, even if organized labor had done the right thing. Unblinkered observers of George Meany, Lane Kirkland, and labor's other over-fed fat cats know better.

This book is about history, but inevitably it poses a contemporary question: which way will organized labor go now, in the era of the global economy, with its back evidently against the wall? Will it return to the familiar pattern of business unionism, adjusted in small ways? Or will it move toward a new social unionism, joined to other sectors of society, the dispossessed and those eager to see life change? History lessons are useful, but working people themselves must choose. I remain, after all the social movements and defeats of my lifetime, convinced that they will choose intelligently if they have the necessary information and, even more important, the opportunity to test democratic practices in their day-to-day lives. Challenging their employers, their government, and their economic rulers, that now heavily international class of corporate giants, will demand a challenge of labor institutions as well, but it can be done. The ideals of the Industrial Workers of the World—despite vicious repression by Woodrow Wilson's war-bent administration, and despite generations of naysayers— remain at the center of labor idealism. By insisting that an injury to one is an injury to all, by recapturing the hilarious and useful Wobbly iconoclasm toward bosses and union bureaucrats, America's working people may yet triumph over cynicism and corruption.

1. SAMUEL GOMPERS AND BUSINESS UNIONISM: THE LOGIC OF EXCLUSIONISM

One of American history's grandest ironies is the role of labor leaders: through their lives and careers can be traced the fascinating pursuit of a perennial ideal, international solidarity for working-class advancement and a cooperative society—thrown into reverse. In Samuel Gompers's American Federation of Labor (1883-1926) and of the AFL and AFL-CIO administrations of George Meany (1952-1979) and Lane Kirkland (1979-1995), the key policy architects were former socialists who had learned their early lessons about class struggle within the radical movements of their time, but changed sides along the way. Gompers, an ardent socialist early in his career, himself laid down the basic lines of what has come to be called *business unionism,* running unions like a business or corporation, with dues payments as the bottom line and assorted perks normal to executives of the business world.

Gompers's circle of AFL founders, and many future leaders to follow, began with the goal of *universal* emancipation from toil and degradation. But sooner or later they staked their rising careers and historic legacies upon something very different: a fixed social order of racial, ethnic, and gender hierarchies at home and abroad. The supremacy of U.S. economic and military power across the world, with American labor's cooperation, was their way to keep the marketplace orderly. The plan did succeed in a way, squeezing human and natural possibilities into a single model ruthlessly based upon market values. But this kind of success exacted a dear price. The dogged idealists of organized labor were repeatedly crushed, their grand visions for an egalitarian, cooperative order denied and derided.

The labor movement found itself reduced, notably during the second half of the twentieth century, into a special interest group with no larger vision at all. Lacking meaningful ideals, without any visions contrary to the corporate order, it lost its ability, even willingness, to adapt to the changing labor force, and it steadily crumbled.

The story of inverted idealism begins, naturally, with Gompers himself. His keenest biographer (also the editor of his papers) acutely noted the ways in which the AFL's founding father reconceptualized what he learned from the socialist tutors of his first years in labor, and used these ideas the rest of his life.[1] Labor historians filling in gaps within a fractured nineteenth-century organizational story have found abundant similar evidence of the importance of radicalism within the largely ethnic, blue-collar life where so many modern unions had their birthplace and their pioneer eras.[2] Recent scholars point to crucial episodes of the Gompers era, such as the nation-wide 1877 railroad strike, the Haymarket events of 1886, or the Pullman Strike of 1894, and the responses of lawmakers and judges as well as voters, setting the boundaries for much of labor history to follow. In these events and in their political consequences, socialists, anarchists, feminists, and radicals of all kinds were vital, often central.

This is not to deny the considerable weight of a pre-1865 working class history, including ominous aspects such as nativist and racist sentiment. All these developments had a role in casting labor's destiny. But the legacy of that longer past can be treated relatively briefly, because so many central questions of working-class life within the industrial era came to revolve around the terms of mechanization in the later nineteenth and early twentieth century, and around the related contemporary issues of race, gender, immigration and popular culture. Here the crucial AFL constituency of craft workers faced the swift degradation of work along with loss of practical autonomy in daily tasks. Here crucial legal decisions supplied the state a battering ram against labor solidarity and offered craft leaders the rationale for a sharply conservative turn. Here, then, the dominant American business unionism was set into place. And here, too, a variety of critics and democratic activists, immigrant socialists along with a mélange of assorted others, proposed alternatives. These dissenters made their arguments heard widely through organizations and presses in a dozen languages as they organized vigorously for a way out of a dilemma that the American labor movement still faces today. They failed, but they left behind a trail of lost alternatives.

We can further trace, within the same period, the definitive development of a determined exclusionism so fateful for subsequent U.S. labor history, and the eagerness among many working men to suppress egalitarianism, to see force used against radical unions at home and against rebels threatening to American business interests abroad. Here, finally, we find the structural sources for the leaders' calculated sacrifice of union members' own interests to a share of the promised imperial benefits and to the shared psychological satisfactions of a personal superiority of the white "aristocrat of labor" over all the lowly, whether "foreign," female, or non-white.

Labor and Reform Before Gompers's Rise

The North American working popultion had never been particularly white and male, of course. Pre-Columbian peoples, the descendents of migrants from Asia, created a wide variety of communities from roughly egalitarian desert settlements, including the oldest surviving villages of the continent today, to the hierarchical Mississipian societies, with their distinct classes of artisans, priests, and rulers. Before Europeans began to arrive in significant numbers, eventually bringing destruction and death to most of these pre-existing cultures, the outstanding workforce of the colonial economy consisted in the trans-Atlantic proletariat, Melville's "mariners, renegades, and castaways" drawn from every race and corner of the globe. Black slaves, male and female, adult and child, made up one of the most productive work-communities for centuries thereafter, whole families laboring under the most extreme conditions to create the economic surplus which made the great leap into statehood and independent empire possible.[3]

These simple facts gave shape over time to a most unique working class and an equally unique set of practical and ideological conflicts. No European society encompassed a large non-white population and none saw the rise of such a profound radicalism (with many working-class roots) aimed at racial egalitarianism. Nor did any continental working class experience a widespread, popular woman's rights movement, pervaded with anti-racist (i.e., abolitionist) sentiment and sympathy for the new class of exploited factory laborer. At the same time, the potential for an aristocracy of labor, alive everywhere within industrial society, carried special meaning for a working class that defined "wage slavery" as nearly akin to the dreaded "black slavery," and that viewed the personal opportunities to advance upward, away from poverty and shame, as dependent upon the national economic expansion made possible by continuous territorial expropriations.

Despite all these differences from its counterparts abroad, the emerging American working class acted in similar fashion to others in a key respect: its labor movement strove to retain its status or to regain prerogatives threatened or already stolen by the advance of capital. Considerations of race and gender inflected the striving at each step, shaping a contradictory response to capitalism's acceleration. Amidst a world-shaking American Revolution, a quiet stability had prevailed: the bulk of production was done in small, independent shops using methods and tools little changed for generations. Craftsmen who began as apprentices moved up through the ranks, with work routines such as speed, quality, and even price set by traditions. Masters could be kind or meanspirited, but they worked alongside journeymen, provided them equipment and even boarded them at home, drawing them into mutual benefit societies and ultimately—as the master aged—selling them the business at affordable rates. The very pace of labor was leisurely by later standards, slow at the beginning of the week, faster later, but generally interrupted by conviviality and some drinking. A "moral economy" of agreed-upon fair conditions and prices was equated by these craftsmen with the fate of the American Republic. If they sought to improve their conditions, they also sought for the next century or more to restore this status, hoping that a sense of relative justice between working men and their masters would prevail.[4]

Such American workers had geography and a certain element of political change on their side. Across the first half of the nineteenth century, white working people struggled successfully—thanks to the wide expanse of American territory and the difficulty of applying European-style legal rules—to escape being "indentured" or coerced into fixed contracts, as were so many contemporary European factory workers.[5] As they resented and struggled against "privilege," as they called it, they won near-universal male white suffrage, the beginnings of public school systems, and for some lucky groups a limit to the number of hours worked, benefits little-known within the industrializing societies of Europe.

These victories came with heavy costs, some of them well-hidden, some so plain that only shared racial assumptions could hide the degree of injustice, brutality, and indeed savagery greater than any actually perpetrated by the despised nonwhites. From Thomas Jefferson to Andrew Jackson, popular leaders with strong artisanal followings insisted that Indians must die out (or be pushed out of the way) and that blacks, incapable of equality, be used as human livestock. As Alexander Saxton, David Roediger, and others have argued, the first substantial American working class achieved or rather elaborated a self-definition of citizenship by projecting "uncivilized" behavior upon such outsiders, much as the "new immigrants" from southern and eastern Europe, faced at first with racial barriers, would later in the nineteenth and twentieth centuries seek to identify themselves as "white." By this measure as well as honest and true labor, working people of the early nineteenth century entitled themselves to participation in what they deemed a free republic.[6]

Other costs were more evident in daily life. The rapid expansion of markets and assorted improvements in transportation in the early decades of the nineteenth century prompted merchants to reorganize production for cheaper goods, badly undercutting small shops. The new industrial forms springing up simplified and intensified work and precipitated the second layer of urban working people: women, recent migrants from the countryside or abroad, many laboring in America's first true factories, others producing goods at home. What these new workers had in common was bad wages—and a lack of tradition or ready means for collective self-protection.

Unrest in this society could be as distant from urban industrial life as Indian and slave uprisings, or as close as nearly modern class conflict. Artisans provided the core constituency of the Workingmen's Parties of the 1820s in New York and a few other locations, the first political parties of their kind in the world. They also established the nation's first citywide labor councils. Protests by the less skilled, from strikes to riots and sabotage (notably the torching of textile factories), lashed out against wage reductions and other worsening conditions.[7]

Cycles of defeat or demoralization and of racialized politics foreshadowed future union leaders' efforts to accommodate themselves to the winning side. A Democratic Party ideologically devoted to slavery and the expulsion or extermination of Indians swallowed up the constituencies of defeated Workingmen's Parties, appealing at once to class resentment and to race privilege. Contemporary white working class urban culture, supplying the money and the crowds for the first major expressions of American popular culture, feasted upon minstrel shows with their ridicule of African Americans, and upon low-priced commercial literature with the romanticization of Indian-killing frontiersmen as the heroes of an ever-receding Wild West. Similarly, upward-bound workingmen, most likely to be Protestants, invited masters to join their associations for temperance and self-reform, seeking to prove themselves worthy and to seal off the threat of competition from below through elaborating a vision of an American republic reserved exclusively for hard-working white people of all class origins.

The economic downturn beginning in 1837 and extending into the mid-1840s heightened the contradictions of these first stages of industrialization. As poverty spread, the pressure of employers and the courts to enforce newer disciplines upon work-life and street-life evoked heightened popular resistance in a multitude of small ways, and also created an atmosphere of reprisals against the most helpless victims. Organized attacks upon black neighborhoods which predated the attackers' own immigration blossomed, while nativist movements formed against recently immigrated "foreigners" who purportedly threatened settled ways of life.

Meanwhile, contrary forces, largely middle class but with admixtures of working-class elements and class-oriented reformers, accelerated efforts for a very different kind of republic. While the abolitionist crusade gained wider public support and more intense hatred from its enemies, South and North, early labor reformers, especially female activists, conducted a vigorous agitation in New England for shorter hours in the workdays of the emerging factory class (women and children workers in particular). Unmistakably influenced by this reform experience, a convention of women in Seneca Falls, New York, in 1848 declared a "revolution" for their sex. Meanwhile, German immigrant artisans, especially after the 1848 revolutions failed and political refugees fled overseas, formed new kinds of workingmen's societies linking abolitionism to their own socialistic understanding of labor's destiny. Thousands of Yankee workingmen, recognizing economic defeat, formed the human base of utopian socialist experiments in planned cooperative communities, unsuccessful but innovative efforts to offer model living arrangements that could eventually take the place of competitive capitalism and "wage slavery."[8] Like the spiritualist faith that swept American reform circles, preaching an ecological relation of all living and formerly living things, much of this radical activity lay far outside European political experience.

In this confused matrix of class, race, and gender, early trade unions sought to make their way. Efforts to form local and national federations of various trades repeatedly degenerated into Democratic Party factions promising legislative assistance. Typographers, the one national union able to establish itself on a permanent basis, set about improving conditions through tightening up an apprenticeship system, understandably seeking to control quality within a notoriously difficult trade of self-educated working men, but also effectively limiting job competition. With the Civil War only a few years away, some of the fledgling building trades moved toward practical rules of work, payment, and benefits—and frank exclusion of outsiders from the trade. The recession of 1857, all but wiping out labor organizations, delayed the onset of a union leadership bent upon creating an aristocracy of labor with itself in charge of arrangements. The future form of class organization remained as yet uncharted.[9]

The Civil War merged the radical egalitarian movements of the 1840s-1850s into a single crusade, grasping the opportunity for racial justice with real but little-acknowledged class content. Yesterday's reform crusaders now focused all their energies upon immediate black emancipation, urgently seeking to assist those freed and runaway slaves (Du Bois called them, with pardonable exaggeration, the participants in the largest general strike of all history) in whose destiny lay the hopes of Southern and ultimately Northern democracy as well. In so doing, the reformers ironically found themselves also supporting a vastly strengthened national state, governed by and run for the purposes of a property-owning class unprecedented in both its riches and its institutional consolidation.

The Republican Party was never far from the assumptions of Democrats and most labor leaders that without a racial limitation upon the labor market as well as a continuing rapid expansion of the economy, the nation would falter and working people would suffer. In this view, constant economic growth would postpone if not resolve the dangerous consequences of sharp class division that haunted the Old World and brought bloody revolutions.

If railroad corporation lawyer Abraham Lincoln finally came to understand that without the emancipation of slaves the Civil War would be lost, he went on believing that expansion would solve class problems by permitting able, white, male workers to leave their class origins behind.[10] African Americans could not be fitted into this equation, certainly not as free and equal citizens. Nor could women's status be raised appreciably without upsetting the assumed prerogatives of those in power, whether in the workplace or the home.[11]

The inevitable contradictions showed themselves twice over during the war. Launched largely by Irish working people, resentful that the rich were avoiding military service and making huge wartime profits while skyrocketing prices starved the poor, New York's antidraft uprising in 1863 turned days of neighborhood rioting into a racist pogrom, and then reverted to class conflict again.[12] Middle-class radicals fixed on the war and the South played no part in this ambivalent class revolt, and likewise gave scant energies to remediate a class tragedy closer to their gendered home ground: the increasingly desperate plight of seamstresses, long a uniquely plentiful (if unremunerative) occupation for women, but one undercut drastically by the widespread introduction of the sewing machine. Rising prices and vanished or maimed husbands added to the woes of this group, who along with factory operatives constituted the largest number of non-domestic, wage-earning women workers. Even the popular press recognized their plight as a new chapter in women's fate and destiny. No one seemed to know what to do for them, beyond the narrow limits of private charity.

New generations of women reformers responded gamely to the gendered side of the class issues. Little recognized at first, an emerging network of charitable efforts for working women prompted closer attention to the heartlessness of the class system. Mary Livermore, prestigious leader of the wartime U.S. Sanitary Commission, which offered indispensable logistic services for the military campaign, supplying desperately needed medicine and food to the Union Army, was typical of those prominent figures who quickly concluded—with no help from contemporary labor unionists—that capitalism lacked answers to the "Social Question."[13]

By 1865, the American working class had changed remarkably. For three decades or so after the recovery from the depression of the 1830s-1840s, the United States experienced the fastest economic and industrial growth in the world. The size of the industrial enterprise transformed the working environment, an ever-greater number of factories employing a hundred workers or more, with only a small proportion of these skilled (or paid as such). The day of the artisan producer was swiftly passing in such major commodities as shoes, tobacco, printing, furniture, and metalworking. As older artisans frequently observed, the "family" atmosphere of the boss and his handful of men all but vanished in the process. Newly organized industries like chemical producing, meatpacking, and soapmaking relied, from their inception, heavily upon unskilled workers. A rush of immigration from the 1850s-1870s, along with the entry into industry of relatively small numbers of African Americans, accounted for three-quarters of the industrial workforce.

By the same standard, the day had passed when a majority of factory workers were female and underaged; men dominated the new factories, earning almost twice as much as the women who remained numerous in certain lines such as textiles. But these men were neither the artisans of Revolutionary days, continuing generations-old patterns of labor, nor were they the masters' apprentices of the earlier part of the century, clinging to their self-definition as the foundation of the Republic.

Together with the relocation of factory districts away from rivers and other "natural" power sources of early industrialism and into the heavily proletarian cities, these developments marked the emergence of a modern working class. But it was a working class far more variegated than its European or earlier U.S. counterparts. The fledgling unions, which had maintained a shadowy existence since the 1850s and rapidly revived in wartime, set the stage for potential alliance of reform sympathizers and working people, if only the common enemy could be sighted. This alliance could be brought together only by a collective act of will, and the initiative, as so often, belonged to the radicals.

Large sections of the reform forces readied themselves for the tasks ahead. Following the Civil War, the *National Anti-Slavery Standard,* a popular weekly tabloid and former abolitionist voice par excellence, took up the issue of the eight-hour day, rallying the middle-class reform veterans to labor's cause. In 1871, it became the *National Standard,* determined to advance the rights of workers, women, freedmen, Chinese immigrants, and Indians. The same year, the National Anti-Slavery Society, renaming itself the Reform League, championed the workers' cause against, as the secretary of the new organization put it, the "growing oligarchy of railroad, financial, and land monopoly."[14] With disgust at the two major parties felt far and wide, Wendell Phillips, the greatest of all antislavery agitators, ran for governor of Massachusetts on the Labor-Reform ticket.

The simultaneous, dramatic return of the woman suffrage movement through statewide referenda battles cast further light upon possible reform alliance. The woman suffrage press, more widely read than the *Standard,* urged a far-ranging unity of women, blacks, and workers against the monopolists who had firm control of the ruling Republican Party. In 1871, Susan B. Anthony and Elizabeth Cady Stanton were voted vice-presidents of the American Labor Reform League after addressing its convention. Many of the activists who insisted upon the commonalty of labor and women's suffrage were old hands at reform, in some cases of old Yankee radical lineage. New faces were greeted as prime evidence of the great coming-together. The glamorous rights crusader Victoria Woodhull stunned Congress (and reportedly charmed President U.S. Grant in a private hearing) with her appeal for woman's vote, while declaring herself for socialism and publishing Marx and Engels's *Communist Manifesto* in English for the first time within the United States.[15]

The coalition that the revived *Standard* and assorted reformers had in mind offered great promise for labor, but one extremely difficult to achieve under the best of circumstances. Most of the potential participants hardly knew each other, had scarce communication (especially to and from ex-slaves in the South), and frequently fell prone to mistrust. Hopes soon crashed on the shoals of multiple emerging class, gender, and racial conflicts. Here, at the very point of American labor and radicalism's potentially unique contribution to a world of diverse labor movements, their need to make common cause among divergent constituencies, could be found labor's Achilles's heel, and American Marxism's signal blunder.

The traditionally Democratic (and often openly racist) leaders of crafts, like so many unionists of later generations, felt uncomfortable among woman suffragists and middle-class radicals, directing particular scorn at loyally Radical Republicans. Like the most crude New Left lambasting of left-leaning Democrats a century later, this short-sighted view willfully passed over major racial dilemmas. The Republican Party had indeed revealed itself to be the business party of the North, ruthless in its attitude toward working people in particular. But in the South, things were not so simple. Delegates to black southern workingmen's conventions held under federal occupation in Georgia, Alabama, and South Carolina during 1869-1872 (attended by ordinary artisans, farmers, and black petty merchants alike), showed a working-class potential entirely unprecedented. The efforts of southern Republicans to attract investment and build support among the moderate planter class by inviting capitalists to exploit the new pool of free labor "simultaneously politicized and restrained the action on the plantation," in the cogent phrase of historian David Montgomery.[16] Until freemen found alternative allies, the connivance of businessmen and Democratic politicians to drive them into peonage would nevertheless compel them to treat local Republicans as their only possible supporters.[17] Meaningful alliance among reformers and working people, black and white, would require both patience and understanding.

Woman suffragists faced similar dilemmas. During their last moments of potential breakthrough for a generation, suffrage forces split over whether to postpone to the future the struggle for woman's vote if only the black (male) vote could now be secured. Some of their most prominent allies began race-baiting, an impulse that grew noticeably stronger as the suffrage movement revived in later decades. Other bitter realities intruded. Susan B. Anthony answered the stubborn resistance of unions to women's presence—a refusal of the International Typographical Union in particular to apprentice women—by helping to train women privately and inviting them to take the nonunion ("rat") jobs. In 1868, her seating at the National Labor Union convention was vigorously resisted by the building trades, and the following year's convention saw her turned away. All sides could legitimately point to wrongs, without any hope of singular vindication.[18]

The immediate predecessors of both the modern socialist and labor movements took shape simultaneously within this difficult moment. An older generation of German-American immigrants, handicraftsmen and enlightened middle-class thinkers who had formed the backbone of labor support for abolitionism and created halls and singing societies that would become key transmission points for popular labor and socialist ideology, had also volunteered massively for the Union cause. Famous for bravery, they were also decimated, weary, and ready to hand on the reform baton.

But the ranks were replenished by the record flow of new German immigration during the late 1860s and early 1870s, which featured a significant radical section. These newcomers drew mainly upon the experience of European class struggle and recent political disappointment of failed American radical coalitions, forming the earliest U.S. communist clubs.[19]

Irish-Americans steeped in working-class life and politics added yet another unpredictable element to the mixture. After the Civil War, the coal miner, machinist, hod-carrier, and above all the unskilled worker of almost any concentrated industry (excepting the largely agricultural South) was more likely to be Irish than German, Yankee, or anything else. Within the working-class culture that flourished on the stage and in the streets of Philadelphia and New York for several generations, the Irish lad had been taken as symbolic representative. Depicted as rowdy and sentimental by turns, idealistic but also inclined toward racism and misogyny, he epitomized even better than the taciturn Yankee factory operative the supposed "real American" worker, internationalist (at least toward his homeland), and either politically radical, racist, or faithfully Democratic depending upon circumstances and the appeal of the alternatives. It was to him (with little concern for "her") that the socialists aimed their main working-class initiatives outside the German immigrant community.[20]

Just how ethnic socialists could remain relatively indifferent to women and nonwhite workers but view badly conflicted white proletarians so credulously—all the while fundamentally misjudging the reform and radical movements of the era—is a puzzle. One clue lies in the difficulties experienced by the International Workingmen's Association, formed in 1864 in London, which grew out of European labor organizations reviving in the 1850s-1860s from an earlier collapse. Alienated from the middle-class politics of free trade and low wages, British union leaders resolved to put forward their own international agenda. Their dramatic action during the American Civil War in support of the abolition of slavery, taken together with the support of French and British unionists for the Polish uprising, presaged a new kind of international workers' solidarity. Karl Marx wrote the IWA's inaugural address and thereafter provided the intellectual leadership, even while differing sharply on many issues from others in the IWA's governing bodies.

Just as sections of American labor intended to keep new immigrants and African Americans from competing in the labor market, British trade unionists always tended to see the International mainly as protection against the importation of continental workers to break strikes or to work by contract at lower than prevailing pay. Thus, the appeals for solidarity disguised a murkier agenda which also included greater control of available labor through encouragement of British workers' emigration to the United States, where they naturally competed against other skilled American workers.

The implied conflict of interest in labor's own forms of nationalism epitomized the dilemma of the young socialist movement. Marx himself, scarcely aware of conflicts and contradictions within the American working class, sought to use the International's general council to counterbalance the British agenda. But soon, leading British unionists who supported the suppression of the Irish Fenian rebels broke with Marx for his insistence that the Irish were victims of national oppression. Then, in the 1870s, as the Paris Commune roused immense sympathy from revolutionaries and practically none from the stodgy English union leaders, the weakened International fell upon the shoulders of outright revolutionaries. At this historical juncture, questions of American labor and the role of socialists suddenly moved to front and center, in a double symbolic sense. No European revolution followed the Paris uprising, and Marx turned his hopes firmly toward the New World. Faced in Europe with an anarchist challenge to the leadership of the First International, he also moved the headquarters of the fading organization to New York in 1873, giving it a final resting place among the badly divided working class of the world's new industrial dynamo.

The reviving American unions represented an ethnic polyglot with great promise for working-class mobilization and more than a few real achievements in institution-building, from craft bodies to a labor press and supportive societies. But they did not represent or even wish to represent that rising element in railroad and agricultural labor in the West, the Chinese, nor (it goes almost without saying) did they represent the African-American majority of the non-owning agricultural working class. The first true national federation of various labor bodies, the National Labor Union, formed shortly after the Civil War, but it hardly set an agenda beyond

educational and cooperative programs, fearing that more ambitious activities would threaten the autonomy of various crafts and bring a destructive
exodus. The NLU's member unions did share an abhorrence of strikebreakers imported from Europe, and it was on this paradoxical basis that they
turned to the International for assistance; internationalism, they hoped,
would protect them from the international labor market.

Some intellectuals of the American labor movement grasped the limitations of this perspective. One of the most admired figures of the time, Ira
Steward, father of the movement for an eight-hour workday, insisted that
immigration was a natural process of labor shifting across borders to meet
economic opportunity and escape penury. He even urged an understanding
disposition toward the much-feared Asiatic immigrants. "The misery and
the terrors that the Chinamen have already inflicted upon western America," he wrote typically, "are the moral...judgment...as retribution and
punishment for forgetting the brotherhood of the entire human race."[21]

But when Congress passed the Act to Encourage Emigration in 1865,
accelerating the use of contract labor as replacements (or "scabs") for
strikers, the issue grew more heated. By 1869, C. H. Lucker, successor to
NLU founding president William Sylvis, declared the Chinese to be "a
people so base that in California where they are known, all parties by
common consent have in their political platforms condemned them as
totally unworthy of being made citizens of the United States." Institutional racism on the part of labor leadership was off and running.[22] By
1870, the *Workingmen's Advocate* declared the Chinese to be a curse not
because of particular conditions of their employment but on strictly racial
grounds—because " 'bond or free' they are a curse to our country."[23]

This was the lamentable context which contorted the humane potential
of craft unions and threw the young socialist movement into self-contra-
diction. To oversimply the complex story of American socialism's origins
by reducing it to any single issue would be a travesty, but to minimize the
role of race and gender would be equally egregious. The early hopes for a
labor-reform alliance and the swift growth of German-language workers'
local associations encouraged the chartering of dozens of U.S. socialist
branches varying widely in political perspectives and demographic content
but uniformly zealous for labor's advance—just as Radical Reconstruction
fell to terrorist pressure in the South and anti-Chinese hatred grew in the

West.[24] The news of the Paris Commune and the rippling effects of the rapid economic downturn during the 1870s, the nation's worst depression up to that point, produced ruling class fears and social explosions with enormous potential for the labor movement and socialism. The swirling events also predictably reproduced the contradictions of class, sex, and race, rapidly undoing the handiwork of the International's initiators in the New World.

Both conservative and radical historians have, until recently, followed the line of Marx and his contemporaneous American followers on the events which offered the International a moment in the American sun, and then smashed it to bits. According to their version of events, working class (i.e., German immigrant) socialists had a grand beginning in the labor stirrings of 1870-1872, and wisely jettisoned the eccentric band of radical reformers and free-lovers gathered around Victoria Woodhull, before fading in the recession to follow. Scholars from left to right, until recently, have admitted that Woodhull and her supporters did raise public interest in socialism, but have hardly found it the right kind of interest.[25]

This narrative gibes badly with the facts. Marx himself had drafted the International's official message of congratulations to Lincoln on the president's re-election, insisting that as the Revolutionary War had "initiated a new era of ascendency for the middle class, so the American Anti-Slavery War will do for the working class," adding the famous sentence a few years later, in *Capital* (1867): "Labor cannot emancipate itself in white skin where in the black it is branded." Only four years later, in 1871, the same Marx reminded one of his German-American loyalists that the International, "founded in order to replace the socialist or semisocialist sects with a real organization of the working class for struggle," could not possibly show "partiality in favor of bourgeois philanthropists, sectarians, and amateur groups."[26] Yet the socialists who were expelled, the "American" (i.e., English-language) sections, known best for their mixture of unionists, reformers, and women of various class backgrounds, were precisely the batallion of socialism rooted in abolitionist experience and anti-racist commitments, along with the myriad of contemporary reform issues.[27]

The International's German-American loyalists had an especially telling occasion to get rid of the troublesome reformers. The English-language sections had called for the socialist recruitment of housewives—those deprived of a right to labor—on a parity with wage-earners. These radicals had clearly in mind the kind of broad social movement that would push democracy radically forward on many fronts of class, race and gender simultaneously, not in narrowly industrial confines. The very success of these sections in recruitment and local activity demonstrated a growing danger to the German-American leadership. Indeed, at the head of the huge parade down Fifth Avenue in support of the Paris Communards were none other than the charismatic Woodhull and her sister Tennie C. Claflin, along with African-American war veterans in uniform, a demonstration viewed by German leaders as mere public theatrics and a detour from serious union organization.[28]

But for their expulsion from the International in 1872, the American radicals might possibly have created an unprecedented kind of socialist movement, effectively egalitarian in gender and aggressively anti-racist. (By summer of that year, Woodhull ran with Frederick Douglass for the nation's highest offices for the "Cosmo-Political Party.") That the German leadership around music teacher Friedrich Sorge obtained Marx's written consent for the expulsions but lost the majority of socialist sections in the process, bespoke the contradictions between dogma and life that would repeatedly rend American left organizations and strand labor institutions without a fund of idealists.[29]

From the viewpoint of Marx's uncritical partisans, then as now, this conclusion stood facts upon their heads. An elderly German-American socialist newspaper editor, reconstructing in 1918 a careful history of the Internationalists' saga in the United States, had no doubts that the reformers had tried to make over the socialist sections into a bourgeois movement and that, as in their various labor reform organizations, they threatened to pollute and disorient the proletarian character of socialism.[30] But if radical reformers had an excess of enthusiasms, their opponents suffered from a political myopia in which a thin strand of the labor movement—the most skilled and effectively organized, also the most determinedly exclusionary—stood for the whole, and in which considerations of race and gender were thrown over wholesale as unimportant to working-class progress. Those excluded had their own important contributions to make, not to be ignored or shunted aside as mere annoying and destructive hobbies.

Revealingly, young Samuel Gompers shared the International leaders' bias. Recalling the scene from fifty years later, Gompers described the dissidents as "a brilliant group of faddists . . . and sensation-loving spirits" who were not really "working people and treated their relationship to the labor movement as a means to a 'career,' " adding that they innocently "did not realize that labor issues were tied up with the lives of men, women, and children."[31] These rationalizations conveniently ignored both the larger history of conflicting interests among various strata of working people and the special contributions of the radical reformers. Neither Gompers nor the immigrant leaders of the International in the United States had any interest in assuring women the right to work or helping them (in the other contro-versial issue raised by Victoria Woodhull) to claim rights upon the use of their own bodies. Gompers also conveniently dismissed the ominous implications of bureaucratic measures directed against "outsiders" per-ceived as harmful. In the decades to come, AFL and AFL-CIO leaders articulated similar logic to define the labor movement in the narrowest possible way and to jettison "troublemakers" without recourse to demo-cratic niceties.

Nor was such scorn limited to the middle-class radicals. German-Ameri-can leaders of International sections also sought to dampen the emergence of the mass movement of the unemployed in New York City during the early 1870s, notwithstanding its largely Irish-American and unimpeach-ably proletarian character. Bringing together unemployed unionists with a large section of the hapless poor meant mixing with an undesirable and unpredictable underclass. In short, *anything* which distracted from union efforts among eligible craft workers was viewed either as flatly unaccept-able or inappropriate given the limited resources of unionists to tend to more than their own business affairs.[32]

The Internationalists, in the long haul, mistakenly had contributed to the defeat of dissent after the Civil War. The swift erosion of Northern liberal commitment to freed slaves, the collapse of the National Labor Union, and the splintering of the woman suffrage movement left reformers as well as labor radicals trapped in their own separate milieux. The great moment of opportunity was passing quickly. Against these large developments, the collapse of the U.S. wing of the First International was hardly noticed. And yet it had its own lasting significance. Confident of an approaching world proletarian revolution, Marx generally regarded specific forms of national and racial oppression mainly as impediments to the self-conscious activity of the industrial working class itself. Not that he brushed aside human misery. He knew perfectly well that so long as organized labor remained deluded by a sense of superiority to an oppressed people, it would remain unable, perhaps even unwilling, to free itself. But all too certain of the proletarian march and obsessed in his correspondence with his American supporters over the conflicts rending the International, he could not imagine a different approach toward socialism. That is to say, he could not imagine the paths that Americans would use most often and most effectively to create vibrant radical movements based upon the complex legacy of the world labor and the vision of a larger egalitarianism.[33]

The Knights of Labor and Their Undoing

It was by no means foregone, even under the most unfavorable circumstances, that the American labor movement would take a definitive exclusionary turn. In the fading National Labor Union of 1870, egalitarianism coexisted with racism, and ugly sentiments toward Chinese were offset to a degree by an eagerness to protect and to take in African-American workers on an equal basis with whites—even by many of those, including William Sylvis, who were blatantly prejudiced. Not until the American Federation of Labor was created fifteen years later were the labor movement's tendencies toward racist absolutes ratified and institutionalized. Why did the labor leadership take this road and why did it succeed?

Part of the answer lay in the continued political disappointments of the left during the depressed, tumultuous 1870s. New York City's Tompkins Square Riot of 1874, which reputedly terrified young Samuel Gompers into a sober labor conservatism, was in reality a police riot against a basically peaceful assembly of unemployed men and women desperate for jobs or food. Small-scale civic uprisings, demonstrations, and electoral upsets continued for years against corporations perceived to be destroying workers and small businessmen alike in the industrial towns of the East and Midwest. Far from being aimless rioters, the crowds and their leaders frequently evoked Christian ideals and older community ways against the economically immoral and intrusive capitalists.[34] During 1877, Americans experienced their first massive, violent *national* episode of class struggle, a railroad strike which spread from West Virginia to cities from Pittsburgh to Chicago and St. Louis, bringing a week of riots, police and vigilante action with dozens dead and hundreds wounded, and a short-lived "commune" in St. Louis where socialists presided over a workers' government (minus black participation, greatly feared by whites of all kinds, including local socialists).[35]

Out of the maelstrom came a reform impulse carrying a handful of socialist candidates into state governments and local office, especially in Illinois, and raising wider working class hopes for a new class-based party of workers and farmers. By 1880, the movement had faded, for some of the reasons that reformers a century or more later would easily recognize. Votes were stolen by the thousands, and the Democratic Party in particular made bribes and offers of personal advancement to popular socialists, while encouraging the racial meanness settling over the landscape. Indeed, a section of the same loyal Missouri troops which had left the South in 1876, abandoning African-Americans to unabashed racism, put down the St. Louis strikers. The symbolism was unmistakable.

Despite all this, no AFL yet existed to stifle egalitarian alternatives within labor. The Knights of Labor, a new federation, arose out of the ashes of the National Labor Union. Beginning in secret circles of fraternalism among Philadelphia carpet weavers and growing into a powerful movement of wildly heterogeneous composition, from local bodies to craft associations, the Knights assumed the shape of assorted reform impulses within and around the working class. Organized against the chaos of the market and the cruelty of monopolies, as beloved New York labor editor John Swinton put it, the Knights held the "key that unlocks the portals of that mysterious, majestic temple of the future, into which who so enters has felt the touch of the ultimate ghost."[36] It was the key of human solidarity later to be championed by the Industrial Workers of the World and by the Congress of Industrial Organizations at its best, early moments.

Strenuously opposed to contract labor and inclined, especially in the West, to condemn "coolie" labor, the Knights nevertheless affirmed a human solidarity based upon common toil and rooted in working life. Only liquor dealers and lawyers were constitutionally forbidden membership. Leading a strike against a hated railroad monopoly in the Southwest in 1882, the new organization gathered membership from the remnants of the older radical reform and shorter-hours movements alike. Soon, the black working class in some of the industrialized South (Richmond, Virginia, in particular) flowed into the Knights' ranks. Likewise, Mexican-American movements against whites' land-stealing allied themselves with the Knights as they cut through the barbed wire of offending settlers. Assorted trade union organizations of the skilled workers came in as well, though the largest section of Knights' membership came from the mainly unskilled sections of Irish-American working class. In 1886, the Knights numbered more than half a million. The strikes that they and the unions in the fledgling, and much smaller, AFL led that year brought out some four hundred thousand workers, more than in any previous year of American history.[37] As labor historian David Montgomery notes, the unionization of unskilled workers, women in particular, had the effect of radicalizing the surrounding craft workers, because "it closed the door decisively both on employers who wished to compensate for higher wages paid to craftsmen by exacting more from the unskilled, and on craftsmen who were tempted to advance themselves by sweating others."[38]

Refusing to organize themselves along craft lines, the Knights met on a factory-wide or even a neighborhood or regional basis. Their leaders, uncertain about a proper course and overwhelmed by the massive popular response to the organizations, usually disapproved of strikes as futile and harmful to hopes of social reconciliation. Moderation in tactics sat paradoxically and uneasily with revolutionary ambition. They firmly believed that the clock could be turned back against the advance of the wage system as society was moved onto another track, toward a voluntary cooperative order.

During the early months of 1886, the movement seemed vast and unstoppable. Seen less optimistically, members and leaders lost track of each other. At the Knights' strongest points of influence, they simply took over factories, reorganizing production logically and democratically—without the interference of management. Elsewhere, their meetings seemed to substitute for town government, so massive was the outpouring and so eager the sympathetic lower middle class of small merchants and professionals to see a new society based upon function and popular participation rather than upon profit. In a few short years, the Knights also precipitated a rich culture of communitarian rituals including picnics, marches, poetry, fiction, and song.[39]

Never had industrial democracy marched forward so swiftly in the United States, and not until the Industrial Workers of the World and the Congress of Industrial Organizations would it do so again. In the arc of the 1880s struggles, as strikes accelerated in response to employers' moves to recover control, and as newspapers warned hysterically of violence and revolution, the Knights leaders' collective nerve failed. Badly shaken, calling off key strikes despite workers' determination to hold out, denouncing courageous local leaders as unfit even to be Knights, they sabotaged their own movement at its moment of truth. Almost overnight, the movement dwindled to less than a hundred thousand. It was still more than the thirty thousand or so that AFL claimed. But the Knights never recovered.[40]

The failure of the Knights was not, as business-minded labor historians would later claim, because the AFL was "realistic" and properly adapted to modern society while the Knights were hopelessly backward, but because of the limits of vision and will in the Knights' leaders, because the power of American capital placed unendurable stress on the fragile movement, and because of the creation of an AFL eager to take labor in a narrower direction.[42] That is why in 1886, recent scholars argue, the U.S. truly became an "exception" within Western industrialized society, with a conservative winner among organized labor disdaining a labor or socialist party of its own class in favor of existing parties.[42] In an ironic footnote to history, the charismatic leader of the Knights, Grand Master Terence Powderly, left the labor movement behind and later found himself at the head of a federal agency responsible for assisting new immigrants to find work. His and his constituencies' most formidable enemies were, by no surprise, the same as they had been in his Knights' days: the leaders of the American Federation of Labor.

But the destruction of the Knights alone would not have been enough to guarantee the supremacy of the new American Federation of Labor. Chicago, known in these days as "Little Paris" because of the frequent strikes and the revolutionary temperament expressed in strikes and meetings, had seen the rise of a working-class culture more protracted and intense than that of the Knights. Mostly German and Bohemian, but touching Irish and assorted other workers, a network of cultural associations, gymnasiums, schools, newspapers, and theater carried the message of socialism and struggle far and wide. More Chicago radicals enlisted in the AFL than in the Knights, but they combined to lead the movement for a universal eight-hour day. At the peak of this movement, on May 1, 1886, police rushed a crowd dispersing from a rally in the Haymarket district, and a bomb was thrown at police, who fired on the crowd, killing and wounding far more than suffered from the bomb.

This was the signal that the authorities had awaited (and actually, many believed, prepared). A full-scale red scare allowed police in Chicago and many other locations the opportunity to break into fraternal and newspaper offices, smashing equipment and breaking heads, and permitted employers to "blacklist" from employment in the district all those who could be identified as radicals. Eight avowed Chicago anarchists went on trial for the Haymarket bombing, accused of not of direct involvement with the incident but of possessing dangerous ideas. Four died on the gallows, one committed suicide, and the last three were pardoned years later.[43]

The wave of class-conscious sentiment had not yet died down. The elections of autumn 1886 brought a dramatic if brief success for local labor politics. Hundreds of thousands of votes for ad hoc labor parties and the election of a smattering of candidates might in other times have seemed a promising beginning. In this climate, however, hopes for an independent labor politics quickly dampened as the blacklisting continued and the newspapers cried for punishment of "foreigners" making trouble. Democrats once more picked up the pieces, relying especially upon Irish working-class loyalties.[44]

Only these combined defeats allowed the consolidation of the Knights' institutional competitor within the labor movement. The craft unions gathered in the Federation of Trades and Labor Unions of the United States and Canada in 1881-1882 were reorganized, under the control of Gompers, as the American Federation of Labor in 1886. Gompers recalled proudly that his forces had "roused the trade unionists of the country to an understanding of the menace which the Knights interposed to trade unions."[45] But this claim should not be taken at face value. Conservative labor historian Selig Perlman more correctly called the assault upon the Knights by the AFL a clash "between the solidarity of labor and that of trade separatism" or "between the unskilled and skilled portions of the wage-earning class."[46]

After a rapid increase in the number and size of strikes up to 1886 came a rapid increase in a particular kind of strike: not spontaneous strikes (as so often the case with the Knights) but strikes officially called by union locals, less often about wages than about union recognition and union rules. "Sympathy" strikes in which fellow craftsmen refused to cross picket lines played a key role in enforcing union jurisdiction and preventing employers from using one set of workers against another.[47]

These efforts brought success. The eight-hour movement went ahead full-steam by the end of the 1880s. Hundreds of mass meetings and demonstrations, held simultaneously on July 4, 1889, carried the message. The next year, the carpenters took the lead in demanding eight hours, and the miners were slated to follow, but Gompers abandoned the vision of a coordinated movement thereafter. Nonetheless, the strongest unions succeeded on their own: carpenters, typographers, granite workers (who obtained a nine-hour day), and others won victories, bringing a flood of new members. Many local central labor federations, brought into existence in the rush of Knights' enthusiasm, essentially continued to build upon the momentum, albeit for the trades and with frequently voiced aspirations for a wider movement. Gompers himself made vague statements about the need for solidarity among men and women, skilled and unskilled, while hardening in practice the existing and uneven lines of union development.[48]

Union success was, moreover, a two-edged sword. Nowhere were "sympathy" strikes were common than in the construction industry. And nowhere else were these reputed measures of solidarity used more to build personal followings behind union leaders, to demand payoffs from employers, and to exclude unwanted workers. The home unions of future AFL-CIO President George Meany and of organized support within labor for the Vietnam War, the construction trades, especially in New York, epitomized the ways in which organized "solidarity" could be made into something very much like its opposite. In a larger sense, precisely because the emerging leaders of the AFL quickly came to regard other struggles as mere diversions and had scorned various efforts to press the inclusion of women, blacks, Mexican Americans, Chinese Americans, or (in most instances) unskilled labor of any kind in the labor movement, they gave shape to an exclusionary movement. To do otherwise would have meant difficult struggles for solidarity at great risk to modest potential gains within the emerging system. It would also have meant association with the lowest ranks of society, threatening the loss of "respectability" and even of "manhood" in existing terms.

The Formation of Gompers's Ideology

The circuitous route by which Samuel Gompers arrived at the position of chief race-spokesman for white male labor against Chinese-American competitors is a fascinating and important one. Born in London's East End in 1850 to a family of Dutch-Jewish immigrants, Gompers grew up across the street from a silk factory, with his grandparents and five of their children just one floor above in the tenement. Other branches of the family had prospered as merchants, publishers, and rabbis; his grandfather, an antiques salesman, was a bit of a dandy. But bad luck befell these Gomperses, and Sam left school at the age of ten to apprentice to a shoemaker, then to a cigarmaker. It is said (although perhaps the details were embroidered later for their effect) that while at the bench he would sing a protest against slavery, "The Slave Ship," among other popular tunes. The family left for the United States in 1863, thanks to the Cigarmakers Society's emigration fund—quite an irony given Gompers's later vociferous hostility to immigrant labor.[49]

For the next twenty years, off and on, Gompers worked at his trade, heavily German in the makeup of some of its more skilled sectors, and deeply influenced by immigrant socialists. He also made himself a "joiner," mainly of fraternal clubs at first, like the Independent Odd Fellows. These offered a way of making friends and useful connections, an enthusiasm he easily transferred to the union movement. At seventeen, he married a sixteen year old cigar-stripper of similar background, and their son was born the following year.

Cigarmakers, like many other immigrants toiling in misery at low wages, faced several special problems. Capitalism's mechanical advance was full of regressive pockets, as it would continue to be long after the industrial revolution. The "sweated" system of cigarmaking depended upon families working in their tenements for subcontractors, often fellow immigrants one step up who offered pitifully low piece-rates and squeezed out the difference. Newer workers, from Asia (on the West Coast) or Bohemia (in the East and Midwest) offered themselves at the lowest wages.

To make matters worse, but in a way more simple, the cigar mold mechanical press permitted manufacturers to dispense with many of the skilled workers for less expensive cigars.[50]

At first, Gompers viewed the competition of unskilled workers with a certain ambivalence. As early as 1870, the Cigar Makers International Union prohibited members from working with the impoverished involved in bunch-making, thus limiting the introduction of the cigar mold in some sections of industry. As late as the early 1880s, Gompers organized politically to banish manufacturing in tenement dwellings. A victory in 1884 in New York State law roused the cigarmakers' confidence in effective political action and prompted a jubilant demonstration at Cooper Union. New York courts struck down the decision the following year, on the basis that "free labor" included the freedom to be a tenement-house worker—"an unconscious parody," as legal scholar William Forbath says, "of the values and fears of mid-nineteenth century artisans," but a fair prediction of the court cases ahead.[51] But militancy about tenement exploitation did not indicate radicalism, by any stretch. Gompers had, after all, played to Democrats mostly (potentially favorable Republicans as well) as part of the strategy he had already adopted within the craft federation, rather than building up a potential labor or socialist opposition to sweated labor, as European labor activists were doing. Second, Gompers really sought to abolish competition to his factory-worker union members because few of the tenement house workers were likely to ever achieve factory employment and union cards.

On the verge of launching the AFL, Gompers had already come a long way from his socialist days a decade earlier. When his lieutenant Adolph Strasser voided the election victory of a left-winger to the Cigarmakers' largest local in 1881 and appointed a Gompers (and Strasser) stooge, Gompers had come a long way from labor democracy, too. In this transformation, race and gender, the familiar challenges to American labor, played a prominent role.

Gompers met his socialist mentors in 1873, working in a shop owned by a political emigré from Germany. There, he came into contact with the Economic and Sociological Club, composed of self-taught workers, German and Irish, who regularly met above a nearby saloon to discuss social questions. As he later admitted, he then read the *Communist Manifesto,* learned the gospel of unionism from First International veterans, and believed, at least for a time, in a great socialistic future for the world's peoples. But his elders were also "practical" men.

To their credit, they sometimes showed flashes of idealism before drifting into exclusionism. Adolph Strasser, later to become one of Gompers's fervently anti-socialist aides, determinedly attempted at first to guide the United Cigarworkers, a wing of the CMIU, into unionizing the unskilled cigarworkers heretofore forbidden by absence of skill from CMIU membership. The UC's model clause, promising membership to all "regardless of sex, method or place of work, or nationality," could have been a union provision of a democratic labor organization, at least within the framework of the factory, if not beyond. But in the face of the depression of 1873, the effort failed, and two years later, the rising local leader Gompers folded the United Cigarworkers into the CMIU outright, eliminating the unskilled.[52] Similarly, during the great railroad strike of 1877 Gompers himself joined a cooperative cigar shop to raise money for the strikers (suffering a brief blacklisting as a result). But he had by this time set his basic direction. When one wing of the disbanded First International relocated itself to Fall River, Massachusetts, to unionize textile workers (at that moment the largest single industrial workforce and the most female), Gompers drew the opposite conclusion. As he recalled in his autobiography:

> In 1878, of forty thousand cigarmakers in the entire country at least ten thousand were Chinese employed in the cigar industry on the Pacific Coast. Adaptability and power of imitation soon made skilled workers of the Mongolians. As their standards of living were far lower than those of white men, they were willing to work for wages that would not support white men. Unless protective measures were taken, it was evident that the whole industry would soon be "China-ized." The Pacific Coast white cigarmakers at that time organized independently, were using a white label to distinguish white men's work done under white men's standards. But local organization was an inadequate protection against the strong tide of Chinese immigration that threatened to flood the West.[53]

In short, a national movement was required to exclude Asian-born workers *precisely because they were able to learn skills*. Craft unionism was not necessarily based on craft at all, but on other types of preferences.[54] Gompers could take solace in his racism from Marx's disciple Friedrich Sorge, who personally expressed his solidarity with the anti-Chinese movement of the West Coast, tragically repudiating not only the non-Marxist reformers of the First International who made a point of defending equal rights for Asian immigrants but Marx's own anti-racist outlook.[55] In any case, Gompers helped refashion the craft labor movement from its ambiguous but frequently egalitarian origins into something very different.

Sympathetic scholars have offered a different reason for Gompers's increasingly vivid racism and xenophobia. Immigrant labor leaders, according to his defenders, badly wanted to be accepted as Americans among Americans, and that meant being accepted by leading Americans. The businessmen who could come to an agreement with unions had, in effect, accepted Gompers and his legions into an American compact. Foreign-born workers who rejected his leadership automatically proved themselves in his eyes to be un-American, undeserving of American privileges.[56] This ideological turn or hardening was, by this explanation, part of a national rather than class definition of the "American standard of living" or "American wage," as defined by the AFL later in the nineteenth century. The "American" in the equation corresponded to the notion of "living wages" rather than "slave wages," the right to something approaching middle-class levels of life-expectations and consumption rather than the "wage slavery" denounced by the Knights of Labor as the essence of an unfree condition. The living standard of a civilization, Gompers and other AFL leaders made clear, precisely differentiated white, male workers from the likes of Asians and of women who had, by definition, no standard of living because they were part of the family wage defined by its male earners.[57]

This logic genuinely helps explain, if perversely, the correspondence of Gompers's support of anti-immigration bills in Congress with his failure to contest Jim Crow provisions within unions and the outright exclusion of women from numerous trades. The rise of lynch law in the South found him unmoved—or rather moved to sympathize with the exclusionists, if not the lynchers. Respectability, as defined by the white Anglo-Saxon Protestant upper class of the day, barely included even white male Catholics. Labor leadership took the shape of the business class that it opposed but also in many ways admired.

As late as the early 1890s, Gompers did occasionally encourage the organization of black and white workers together in the South, as a practical matter of union efficiency. Intermittently, he favored particular local formations of women workers within unions. Far more typical was Gompers's devious approach to the issue of "whites only" clauses in union bylaws. He urged the lily-white Locomotive Firemen to join the AFL in 1895 on the basis devised by the Machinists: membership remained formally open to all races, but only whites could pass through the initiation rituals. If AFL unions could not properly exclude members because of their color, he added, they could exclude individuals for a variety of reasons, such as the probability that if some blacks served as strikebreakers, then all could be excluded on principle.[58]

Gompers's exclusionary attitudes and actions steadily deepened over the years as the AFL grew at once more rigidly bureaucratic and seemingly, at least in its own narrow terms, more successful. Challenged from the left by socialists and radicals of various tendencies, Gompers also moved rightward within labor, taking for his allies the most unembarrassedly racist, xenophobic, and otherwise exclusionary unionists. They, too, in that day represented the respectability that Gompers sought for himself and the AFL.

In the late nineteenth century, similarly, an understandable concern with contract labor (that is, workers brought overseas to fulfill a specific contracted time or job, normally at very low fee set in advance) quickly deepened and expanded into xenophobic opposition to all immigration that might weaken the craft movement. In 1882, just as the AFL's predecessor organzation was formed, the Chinese Exclusion Act successfully passed Congress to Gompers' great satisfaction, and the AFL would over the next decade repeatedly insist upon the Act's more complete enforcement.

By 1889, the AFL, meeting amid widespread unemployment of its members, debated its first (and unsuccessful) resolution to demand a halt to all immigration. Two years, later Gompers spoke for a similar motion, this time successful, insisting that restrictions were intended not merely to protect American craft workers but to aid Europeans to run their own affairs as well. By 1892, Gompers condemned philanthropic groups such as United Hebrew Charities which were assisting the immigration of their peers. By 1894, Gompers asserted that the Chinese had "allowed civilization to pass them by untouched," thereby menacing "the progress . . . of the workers of other countries, and cannot be fraternized with."[59] Three years later, the AFL's executive council, under Gompers's firm hand, reported that a majority of unions favored more severe immigration restrictions at large. A resolution was approved overwhelmingly urging a literacy test, the means notoriously used in the South to prevent African Americans from voting.[60]

In reality, the charge of immigrant responsibility for the decline of labor's conditions was based upon prejudice rather than experience. As statistician Isaac Hourwich conclusively demonstrated in the 1910s, newer immigrants took over rungs unoccupied by craft unionists or already abandoned with the changes in production.[61] AFL strikes even in the midst of the severe 1893-1897 depression were rarely broken by immigrants. But as continued improvements in mechanization gradually (in some cases, not so gradually) undercut the craft worker, AFL leaders had to choose strategically between an all-inclusive movement and a circle-the-wagon movement of relatively privileged workers, the "aristocracy of labor."

Gompers had no equivocation on that score. The Progressive Cigarmakers Union of the early 1880s, which had sought to offer alternatives to the mainstream AFL's political timidity and its racial or ethnic particularism within Gompers's own trade, was ruthlessly stamped out as a socialistic menace, a "dual union." Gompers applied the same narrow principle to nearly all efforts to organize across nominal class and skill lines and bring workers into a common industrial union—except those blessed with precedent, like the United Mine Workers and United Brewery Workers which inherited a model of all-inclusive unionism from earlier nineteenth century practices.

The very anti-imperialist movement which brought Gompers to the forefront briefly as the opponent of military interventions in Cuba and the Philippines at the end of the century also propelled him toward a more definitive racist expression. Like the "respectable" figures he hoped to be embraced by, he warned against empire precisely because it invited the yellow race onto American shores. The degree of good-willed pacifism (or isolationism) in his perspective could readily be separated from this racist element, and his anti-imperialism in time disappeared as he aspired to play a major role in the government's decision-making process.

Gompers urged another crucial shift upon the labor movement in these years. According to most early labor leaders, as well as radicals of all kinds, the inequity of capitalism and the wage system was based on exploitation:

not the poverty of workers as such but the theft of most of the product that, in one way or another, they had created. The essential experience of American workers as a class, founded on the reality of wages (rather than goods bartered from another tradesman), allowed ambivalent possibilities. The idea of a "living wage" for the creators of wealth went back to the 1820s-1830s, and was expressed in one way or another by an assortment of union officers and intellectuals sympathetic to working people who believed that the freedom could be found within a thriving market economy. Catholic prelates, seeking amity between labor and capital, likewise blessed the idea of the "living wage" as proof of employers' good intentions. It proved good as a slogan and demand, and has remained so since. But something within working-class life also resisted the notion that, as Gompers famously put it, the worker had no right to "demand more than an equivalent for his services," the word "equivalent" being something less than the value realized by the capitalist.[62]

With the passing years the ideal of the "living wage" came to reinforce racism and hostility toward lower-paid, less-skilled workers. "We are not going to let [the Caucasian] standard of living be destroyed by negroes, Chinamen, Japs or any others," Gompers asserted in 1905, and the principle extended in all racial directions.[63]

Labor Idealism and the Craft Worker

The Gompers view did not, of course, represent the entirety of the AFL. Repeatedly from the 1870s to the 1910s, considerable sections of craft labor found AFL policies incompatible with their own needs and interests. Large numbers of skilled workers practiced solidarity not only with each other in various ways, from refusing to cross picket lines to boycotting non-union products, but also (often with left-wing leadership) in solidarity with unskilled workers and the assorted victims of American empire-building. Some socialists and those whom scholars call anarchists (they usually called themselves "revolutionary socialists") influential within the labor movement, especially in Chicago, espoused egalitarianism and internationalism as the core of their belief. These idealists kept labor's highest aspirations afloat as they fought a backstairs struggle against the AFL's drift toward an exclusionism increasingly apparent in its determination to lobby for restrictions on immigrants from Eastern and Southern Europe as well as Asia.[64]

Nor were they alone. The heavily Germanic brewery workers, heir to European traditions generations old, practiced their own brand of industrial unionism. So did thousands of textile workers and shoe workers, especially in New England, faced with the crises in their trades. Even within demonstrably undemocratic unions, like the United Mine Workers, glimpses of militant activity, multi-ethnic solidarity and even multi-racial efforts frequently defied the general drift within the AFL. Beyond these specifics, a rich labor culture congealed in many working-class communities. Epitomized in the widely-published "song poem" or lyric labor verse of the decades after the Civil War, the sentiments were sometimes narrowly devised in ethnic, regional, or occupational terms, but more often described an egalitarian and inclusive labor vision. Labor newspapers, representing ironworkers (who had their special songsters), outside laborers like granite cutters (who reflected frequently upon the natural surroundings they observed), and trades heavy with immigrant workers bearing European folk traditions, devoted considerable column space to such lyrical visions of a better sort of order bound to come.[65]

Yet labor's internal conflict also continued. Socialist idealism had mixed freely with local anti-corruption impulses of the 1870s-1890s which took hold among German-dominated crafts especially, often leading to the creation of parallel bodies of city central trade organizations. The local AFL's tendency toward moral and pecuniary corruption, an essential cog in the Gompers machine (and every subsequent bureaucratic labor leadership), reminded idealistic Germans that local trades groups had organized in the first place for solidarity and not for graft. Some of these highly democratic counter-institutions eventually rejoined reformed city federations, while others remained stubbornly independent. Independent-minded local unionists resented nothing so much as Gompers's stiffening determination to refuse recognition to city federations which included local unions that had fled or never joined the AFL internationals; they rightly suspected him of bolstering his personal machine and tightening the noose around any and all opposition.[66] But such localized opposition to Gompers and the AFL leadership grew more difficult as the AFL gained more affiliates and acquired the strength to reward friends and punish dissenters.[67]

Recent labor scholarship, broadening the social histories of occupational
and local populations, further explains the strengthening of Gompers's
hand against reformers and radicals. The "factory artisan" of the 1880s, a
key figure in the transition to ever-larger shops, was highly skilled and paid
relative to the unskilled workers around him but lacked anything resem-
bling the independence of the worker in the bygone smaller shops. More
and more, he had a supervisory role, sometimes over semi-skilled women,
often over workers from another (and more recent) immigrant group.[68]
Some, notably the skilled woodworkers at the heart of Chicago's revolutionary socialist milieu, struggled forcefully against the loss of craft and
autonomy. Others more numerous sought to use the advantages of their new
position over the less fortunate around them, from the workplace to the
neighborhood.

It was not only the supervisory role and financial benefits which marked
the emerging aristocrat of labor. To take an extended example, the overwhelmingly Irish-American trolley car conductors of the late nineteenth
century, a group frequently at the center of citywide general strikes, were,
like automobile workers decades later, at the transportation hub of an
expansive society. The displacement of horse cars with electronic ones and
the building of far-flung railbeds (especially running out of large Eastern
cities) created the first suburbia of the working class. In many cases, the
new inhabitants had no choice but to move, as their old urban neighborhoods were torn up for city centers with administrative and financial
specialities. Their good pay, however, also enabled many trolley drivers to
become homeowners for the first time, in the newly expanded sections
bordering upon farmlands and, in some cases, upon expansive city parks
within a transformed (and not yet tragically degraded) urban ecology.

This was the good life for the skilled worker, always within limits. Ill
health or personal tragedy could erase its benefits overnight. Erosion of
skills by new productive processes also perennially threatened. Renewed
depression, like the severe downturn begun in 1893, or corporate managers
could undermine any personal advance and provoke heretofore conservative workers into unanticipated militancy. But it was also undeniable that
such skilled workers enjoyed many of the advantages of middle-class life,
from Belgian carpets to vaudeville shows.[69] Their geographical separation

from the rest of the working class, emphatically including their worse-off relatives, marked off different worlds.

The "new immigration" which brought millions of Eastern Europeans to American shores and met the demand for severely underpaid industrial labor further dramatized the difference between the aristocrats and serfs of the working class. By this time, United States had the largest ratio of wages between best-paid and worst-paid workers within any Western nation.[70] Better-off workers, even many of those with socialistic leanings, would do almost anything to preserve these privileges for themselves and their families. The fondness for the Democrats within much of the AFL bonded local unions to their only powerful political allies, including city officials who refused to break strikes, but bonded them also to a national party that hailed itself the enemy of the black man (and of woman's suffrage) with the same energy that it proclaimed itself the friend of the working man.

Faced with complexities unseen in Europe, punished by the defeats of the middle 1880s, the opposition to Gompers lacked the capacity to sustain itself let alone grow like the socialist parties around European labor movements. Groups of radical craftsmen distant from New York's thick socialistic milieu typically went through phases of activity and then disappeared organizationally until another upswing brought new faces and fresh energies. By the later 1880s, the socialist critics of Gompers were caricatured as *alte Genossen,* "old comrades" too hard to be broken by repeated painful contact with the stone walls of a strange land. When a small rebellion of the (German-language) Socialist Labor Party weekly newspaper editors against the AFL's presumed leadership of the working class was nipped in the bud through the manipulations of Manhattan SLP leaders, the avowed party of American socialism sank out of sight, into the local singing societies, picnics, and committees supporting homeland socialists from afar. This was the laconic prototype, in many ways, for future political movements within labor, from Communism to Zionism, which came to place their hopes abroad while accepting the bureaucratic conservatism of their own labor institutions as regrettable but inevitable, and possibly better than uncertain alternatives.

Gompers himself, meanwhile, made highly selectively use of other foreign "models." He drew conclusions from the organizational successes of "new model unionism" in Britain. Adopting high dues by the standards of the day and offering high benefits, restricting membership to the so-called aristocratic section of labor, all made craft workers' own solidarity in a strike situation more practical. Strongly centralized leadership (long urged by German socialists) presumably gave unions the power needed to conduct vigorous strikes and organizing campaigns. It also, however, gave elected leaders enormous tactical advantages over internal opposition and transformed the most influential of them into highly paid public figures more attuned to the admiration of their business counterparts and the press than to the needs of workers in their own organizations.

Gompers would shortly need all the organizational muscle he could bring to bear against the multiple crises facing conservative craft unionism and the unexpected revival of labor's left. The massive depression of the 1890s convinced many workers, including some of the most skilled and highly paid, that the last days of capitalism were surely near. Simultaneously, the ranks of American socialism were transformed by the arrival of new waves of radical immigrant working people and intellectuals from Russia, Poland, Italy, and other exotic places on the world map.[71] A relative handful of these immigrants would supply future layers for the labor bureaucracy; others more numerous would provide the shock troops for union democratization.

Gompers and the Renascent (Mostly Jewish) Left

In an atmosphere of widening radical prospects marked by major events like the violent Homestead strike of 1892, the transracial New Orleans general strike of the same year, and the Brooklyn trolley strike of 1894, the advance of "industrial armies" of the unemployed upon Washington, the appearance of planned utopian colonies, the emergence of widely-read grassroots radical newspapers, and above all the rapid rise and fall of the multiracial populist movement, the opposition to Gompers suddenly took on new life. New recruits, both native- and foreign-born, most intensively in New York but also scattered through virtually city and industrial village outside the South and in new ethnic ghettoes virtually pressed themselves upon the insular Socialist Labor Party. Easily the most important new bloc was Jewish, and the radicalized immigrants quickly raised their own challenge to bossism within the consolidating AFL machine, a challenge as serious as local German radicals had posed during the 1880s.[72]

To be sure, there were important differences between the German immigrants and the immigrant Jews as bearers of labor idealism. German attachment to craft skills helped some families move out of the working class rapidly, and others (including a loyalist socialist contingent) to cling to specific sectors of industrial production for decades. Neither geographically nor culturally, however, did one industry play for Germans the role that the needle trades played for Jews. For almost a half-century, American Jewry at large, indeed, was inseparable from the needle trades—and also from the increasingly conservative labor bureaucracy that at the end of the twentieth century had doggedly outlasted by generations the presence of Jewish workers in the relevant industries.[73]

The rise of industrial capitalism's consumer outlet, the ready-to-wear garment market directed first at the new middle classes but also at the working class, created new demands for wage laborers, and made mass Jewish migration to the United States from Eastern Europe feasible. Increased persecution in the Old World, alongside the more familiar poverty, made it increasingly desirable. As recent scholars have emphasized, industrialization and urbanization had already begun the erosion of the old elites in the Jewish pale, the rabbis and the merchants. The population shift to the New World accelerated the process.

The very character of the needle trades with their sub-contracting system of extended family labor lent itself to new twists upon Old World *shtetl* or village ties. *Landsmanshaften* sickness-and-death benefit associations of immigrants from the same districts eased the way for the *Arbeter Ring* (Workmen's Circle) to be founded in 1892. Imitating and self-consciously building upon the success of the German immigrant fraternal bodies, the *Arbeter Ring* ultimately became the most enduring of all the left-led immigrant benefit societies. For a Jewish community still constrained by a conservative religious elite, it provided an independent center of secular, socialistic working-class self-education, sometimes allied with AFL leaders and sometimes forcefully against them.

The arrival in the 1890s of tens and then hundreds of thousands of impoverished Jewish immigrants to New York and a scattering of other cities also coincided with the shattering economic crisis. Driving already low prices for finished goods downward, and prompting near-total unemployment during the "slack season," the depressed conditions of 1893-1899 meant that a diasporic Jewish sense of homelessness combined with acute awareness of the ruthlessness of capitalism. The spread of tuberculosis—the *proletarishe krank* ("workers' disease") well-known to come from the bad air circulation and the starvation diets of ghetto dwellers—only deepened the desperation and rage.

Neighborhood sentiment against the horrors of tenements reinforced a class sensibility. The bosses and slumlords were often enough Jewish, too, clawing their way to the top over the bodies of their fellow immigrants, craving both assimilation into American capitalism and (especially later) an identity such as Jewish nationalism suitable to their own notions of power and authority. In this climate, poor Jews easily sympathized with the non-Jewish workers who did not stigmatize them, and simultaneously utilized their ethnic communitarian traditions against Jewish capitalists who exploited their own. Nascent labor leaders often sought to have it both ways: to uplift the Jewish working class through a radically democratic movement of working people, and to uplift themselves. Revolutionary sentiment pointed toward the dream of proletarian autonomy, while pragmatism impelled immigrant labor leaders to work with any available authority, including state officials and far-sighted industrialists who sought for their own reasons to guarantee a stabilization of the market through a limited cooperation with unionists in "fair" commerce with greater public respectability. The United Hebrew Trades, launched in 1888 by Jewish socialists, quickly offered strong hints in both directions.[74]

The presence of European-trained radical intellectuals, themselves thoroughly proletarianized by their conditions, gave definite and unique voice to the sense of mass urgency and hopes for release. Exemplary Jewish labor poets—whether anarchist or socialist, invariably revolutionary-minded before the turn of the century—met the Jewish masses' strikes and suffering with voices of millennial inspiration. This emerging radical intelligentsia also made clear that it to spoke in a cultural voice and with a Jewish accent. The famed Morris Rosenfeld, "teardrop millionaire" Yiddish poet, wrote lyrics that apotheosized labor's suffering, making Yiddish culture itself a sort of imaginary homeland of a people who could not imagine a secure home without the victory of the cooperative commonwealth.[75]

Tragically, prospects for the alliances that this would require in the rest of America did not look especially bright. Various local and state labor parties of the early 1890s, supported by many AFL locals, were still-born, unable to make headway against Republicans and Democrats. Even when led, as in Chicago, by great contemporary reform figures such as Henry Demarest Lloyd, they could not successfully bridge the gaps between middle-class reformers, craft unionists and the unorganized, frequently voteless, new immigrant masses. At a state and national level, the insurgent (and at points, racially egalitarian) People's Party peaked in 1894. Fearing marginalization and faced with repeated incidents of intimidation and vote-rigging, the populists merged with charismatic Democrat William Jennings Bryan's presidential bid in 1896. Gompers supported Bryan as well, cashiering a popular secretary-treasurer who complained that the AFL president had thereby violated his own grand (and in practice, anti-socialist) principle of nonpartisanship.

The joint ticket was a disaster. Most state Democratic machines refused even to accept Populist Tom Watson as a legitimate vice-presidential candidate. Bryan's defeat by Republican William McKinley, the continued repression against Populist voters in the South, and, most of all, the logic of the fusion process itself eviscerated the Populist movement. Meanwhile, membership in the existing national labor organizations hemorrhaged severely as unemployment spread. Demoralized, key affiliates of a briefly powerful AFL seemed on the verge of collapse, following the badly reduced and staggering Knights.

Leaders of the resurgent socialist movement looked hard for strategic solutions to the puzzle. Without a political arm, they concluded, a labor-socialist movement had little chance of lasting influence on American life. The efforts of German, Irish, and American-born socialists of the 1870s-1880s had palpably failed to build electoral organizations as socialists had done in Germany and as the Yankee reformers had successfully done in the Republican Party only thirty years or so before. But perhaps the idea of a party had not been wrong after all, merely the time not ripe. They knew that a political movement could not be built overnight. But they looked suspiciously at labor leaders who claimed to be socialists or sympathetic to socialism but who determinedly buried left-wing political projects in the exclusive name of trade union work.

Socialists and assorted radicals within labor therefore took Gompers's refusal at the 1890 Detroit AFL convention to seat a delegate from the socialist movement—a standard European procedure—as a straw in the wind. Arguing that only bone fide unionists were eligible to participate officially, Gompers had framed the issue as narrowly as he sought. "No politics in the union," became in practice "no *socialist* politics in the union," the refusal to treat socialists as organic members of the movement and refusal to endorse of socialist candidates in political contests. Endorsements were being given freely on all sides to friendly Democrats and the occasional Republican willing to deliver on national issues such as protective tariffs and immigration restriction or else to supply local patronage, such as jobs and payoffs for a labor leader, his friends, and family. As with the questions of race, in which explicitly segregationist locals and internationals were casually accepted, Gompers's policies bore the simple logic of exclusionary business unionism.[76]

Gompers and other leading business unionists rationalized their caution and wooing of major party politicians as due to the "government by injunction" era which emerged with the social restiveness and, in particular, the rise of sympathy strikes and boycotts. Here, at least, they had a point. From the later 1880s, as unions sought to establish themselves by announcing boycotts of non-union goods (not so ironically including goods produced by Asian labor), the courts ruled repeatedly that such unwarranted interference in private property constituted criminal activity. The Pullman strike of 1894, in which Eugene Debs led a vast movement of western railwaymen in a sympathy strike for the Pullman workers in Chicago, precipitated the use of injunction by bayonet, i.e., federal troops against strikers (and arrest of their leader Debs, who according to legend became a socialist while imprisoned). Gompers and supporting craft unionists viewed this dramatic development as vindication of their caution; Gompers's opponents saw it as proof that nothing less than a political challenge to the state could meet the challenge of a business-governed society.[77]

Evidence could be argued on both sides of the case for hopes to overcome the courts through national and state legislation or protective efforts. Starting in 1888, the Illinois Women's Alliance, middle-class reformers and socialists of Chicago, vigorously conducted a campaign of investigation into factory conditions and the use of child labor. In cooperation with the socialistic Chicago Trades and Labor Assembly and Hull House, the IWA eventually sponsored a successful state legislative bill prohibiting the employment of children younger than fourteen and appointing women as factory inspectors. Compared to this grassroots effort, the Erdman Bill passed by Congress in 1895, which commanded strike arbitration between railroad workers and corporations, was essentially a top-down effort to defuse strike violence by imposing solutions. (The AFL opposed it as wrongful mandatory compliance.) In 1897, Congress passed a bill to create an industrial commission, which was finally accepted in 1898 by President McKinley as a forum for public opinion and, above all, corporate opinion-making. Federal judges, meanwhile, as much as overruled all rights to picket and boycott unfriendly employers. AFL unionists who felt they could achieve aims through politicking were disappointed again and again.[78]

But there were other and more important reasons for local politicking, most especially for the skilled workers of the construction trades. During an era of vastly expanding political machines and lucrative public works projects that lasted even into the depression years, the institutional logic of steering particular projects toward particular groups of workers possessed an almost irresistible appeal, and not only to the upwardly bound national union leader. By 1880, for example, one out of every eight voters in Manhattan appeared directly or indirectly on government payrolls. Even a craft union born in radicalism, with a socialistic founder, might turn conservative as the goodies multiplied. For example, carpenters' leader P. J. McGuire, an ardent First Internationalist in his youth, had become the disciple of the hierarchies and rigid exclusionary provisions that marked mainstream organized labor from the late nineteenth century forward. If during the 1880s erstwhile radicals like McGuire had retained a certain socialistic perspective as they fought the Knights, by the end of the century they had devolved into pure and simple bureaucrats—or, as in McGuire's case, yielded unwillingly to the younger, ungrateful, and markedly unidealistic generation whom the founders had prepared to take the increasingly lucrative top jobs.[79]

Even so, this drift toward conservatism was far from universal. As the depression of the 1890s deflated AFL leaders' claims that union membership raised or at least upheld proper wages, appeals for labor solidarity expressed something of a special quality. Solidarity of one craft for another, one ethnic group for another, and occasionally one race for another, emerged unexpectedly in many strike situations. Unlike the unskilled, craftsmen could hold their positions and sometimes win or at least fight to a draw. It was not difficult for visionaries to conclude that working people wanted something more than the existing labor leadership and that, given the chance, they would fight for it. The opportunity to present workers with a real alternative loomed in a strange conjuncture of institutional labor crises.[80]

The Knights of Labor, increasingly a rural organization of perhaps twenty thousand members but with significant pockets of working-class affiliation remaining here and there, underwent one final major effort at renovation. At its center was New York's District Assembly 49, which had long been a center of radical politics, including a militant anti-racism. When even the Knights (who welcomed blacks to their ranks) disdained Chinese labor during the 1880s, some of the most prominent D.A. 49 leaders had insisted upon the oneness of all toilers and sufferers without exception. The same D.A. 49 had become by the early 1890s a debaters' center for middle-class women active in the mobilization of their less fortunate sisters. The deputation of radical leaders from D.A. 49 to the national Knights was, then, a natural step. Maneuvering to secure the editorship of the *Knights Journal* for Lucien Sanial, a former French naval officer who had shortly before begun editing the new English-language weekly *The People,* socialists believed they could foster a Knights' revival along socialistic and industrial rather than cautious, uncertain, and increasingly rural lines.[81]

The AFL, with a claimed (but considerably exaggerated) membership of a hundred thousand, looked just as promising politically, for an extended moment, as socialists within it advanced a "political programme" at the 1893 convention. The left advocated independence from the two conventional parties and a series of immediate demands such as the abolition of sweatshops and the municipal ownership of public utilities. These were modeled after demands put forward by Britain's Independent Labour Party. Clearly on the defensive, Gompers was quoted by the press as saying he agreed with "almost everything." The program was approved in convention virtually without alteration. But Gompers had a scheme to nullify the leftward turn. When the executive council submitted the program to affiliated unions, it demanded a separate vote on each of the sections, purportedly to prepare for a ratification at the 1894 convention. Gompers then went all out, lining up the opposition. Former socialists Adolph Strasser and P. J. McGuire led the successful effort on the convention floor to vote it down, piece by piece. Infuriated, the socialist bloc joined other discontented unionists in replacing Gompers as AFL leader with United Mine Workers President John McBride.

The victory over Gompers was dramatic evidence of unionists' attitudes toward him, but pyrrhic. The cautious bureaucrat McBride, all but inviting Gompers's triumph in a rematch, urged abandonment of the very same political program as a necessary step toward unity. Thoroughly disgusted by this latest development, and in some cases actually resigning their elected positions in the AFL's executive bodies, socialists effectively removed themselves from the picture. At the 1895 convention, Gompers retook the presidency. Throwing a bone to the loyal opposition, he approved as delegates passed a vapid resolution urging "the duty of union working-men to use their franchise so as to protect and advance the class interests of the men and women of labor and their children," including "more independent voting outside of party lines." Triumphantly tightening his leadership, Gompers was never seriously threatened again.[82]

He had also begun to complete a pattern of leadership styles around him. Between 1870 and the year Gompers regained the presidency, a typical leader of a national union remained in office only a year or two, returning to lower levels of bureaucracy—even to the shop floor (especially in smaller unions). In the next twenty-five years, half the national labor leaders held their offices for at least fifteen years. Top-down unionism was on the verge of consolidation.

When the ailing Knights' leaders reneged on promises to open up their journal, insurgents felt they had little choice but to seek real unity of labor in their own way. If the AFL had beaten the Knights only a decade earlier—as the thinking went—and itself now seemed close to ruin, organized labor might best protect itself by once again broadening its ranks through creating a new institution. By mobilizing committed unions and organizing unskilled workers, they could surely pull back from the brink. At any rate and arguably with the same justification, the radicals felt that they could wait no longer without losing their own real and envisioned constituencies.

The formation of the Socialist Trades and Labor Alliance (ST&LA) in 1895 has invariably been cast by orthodox labor historians as both a political invasion into labor ranks, and an invitation to destructive jurisdictional disputes. Indeed, competing unionists certainly traded insults and sometimes treated rival groups to real strikebreaking—just as the AFL had battled the Knights, the IWW would battle the AFL, the AFL would battle the CIO, and individual unions would continue to raid each others' memberships on a casual basis almost to the end of the twentieth century. Partisan scholars of the AFL nevertheless cast the Gompers loyalists as the injured party and the socialist insurgents as mere fanatics. From the standpoint of largely female New England textile workers and other survivors of Knights unions, or the unskilled garment unionists ignored by the AFL unions, the scene looks entirely different. Recuperating, it seemed at first, the legacy of the NLU and Knights in a half-dozen major industries, the new social movement could—in the members' minds eye—easily become the comprehensive organization that Gompers foreswore.[83]

The ST&LA began with perhaps more than half the remaining Knights' national membership behind them and the cream of idealists from the defecting AFL locals. By ill fate, they came a few years too late for the most militant efforts of the needle trades, virtually finished off in the depression, and a few years too early for the next radical federation, based in Western mining camps and organized at the turn of the century.[84] Enthusiasts of the ST&LA could not have foreseen the total defeat that faced them. The depression had severe effects upon strikes and organization, the AFL was effective in its hostility (including collaboration with the commercial press, police and employers against the new union), and the ST&LA's socialist savants were increasingly heavy-handed in their insistence upon political loyalty tests. They made valiant efforts nevertheless, and many of their would-be recruits were non-candidates for AFL membership in any case. These workers had little to lose, and the wrath of the Gompers officialdom could not worsen their condition.[85] Lose, however, they did. By 1899, when the Socialist Labor Party that had inspired the ST&LA split into two hostile factions, the ST&LA had become only a shell of political loyalists. For a second time, the AFL had knocked out its egalitarian-minded competition.

The impact upon the Jewish labor sector was decisive and traumatic. Political war within the ghetto practically isolated the followers of the

Socialist Labor Party and the ST&LA, as erstwhile anarchists lined up with the AFL and a split-off group of socialists joined them. Garment unionism virtually died for the time being, especially outside the skilled trades. But more moderate socialists triumphed through the creation of a new daily newspaper, *Forverts* (the *Jewish Daily Forward*), and the capture of assorted institutions like United Hebrew Trades and the *Arbeter Ring*. This moderate wing, whatever fault it found with assorted AFL policies (such as the intended exclusion of new immigrants), remained firmly supportive of the institution and bitter opponents of alternatives. Only under the most unusual circumstances could they be defeated on their home ground. Those who had joined the AFL machine in search of careers got their wish. Philosophical anarchism, even a moderate socialism, could flourish in the minds of those who could be relied upon to do Gompers's bidding.[86]

The dream of a new Knights or a European-style socialist labor union federation was therefore beaten by a triumphant AFL. But it did not fail to leave behind some important lessons. Observers began to perceive, behind the perfidy of Gompers's attacks and the assorted failures of the rebels, the shadow of an internal class struggle within labor's ranks. Not for nothing would Joe Ettor, a hero of the 1912 Lawrence strike, write later in a serialized history of American class conflict that as far as the new immigrants were concerned, no real American labor movement had existed between the Knights and the Industrial Workers of the World. Not for nothing would future black labor leader A. Philip Randolph call the AFL the "American Separation of Labor" and label it "the most wicked machine for the propagation of race prejudice in the country."[87] In its triumph over the ST&LA, the AFL had become more than ever the face of an exclusionist labor minority fearful of losing its status as a special interest group somewhere between the middle class and the working poor.

The socialist opposition to Gompers had framed the decisive issue poorly as one of reform (which would benefit labor leaders only) versus revolution (which alone could improve conditions of all). The logic of SLP leader Daniel DeLeon's famed series of ringing addresses about the class struggle during the 1890s rightfully pointed to the necessity of connecting local struggles with a national and international perspective. But DeLeon assumed mistakenly that since capitalism could not recover, neither could unions ever again raise wages. The militants of the day would have done better by far to base themselves upon the principle of solidarity and the promise of industrial unionism (or social solidarity), as the Knights had done and the Industrial Workers of the World soon would do. And yet, despite false estimates and despite a political rigidity that alienated him from many sincere union activists and more reform-minded socialists, DeLeon had keenly identified the character of Gompers-style union "adjustment" as one suited to the particulars of modern capitalism.

The class of working people, DeLeon would argue more fully a few years later, was potentially capable of transforming society at large, but it lacked a material base of the kind that capitalists possessed when they had overthrown their predecessors, the aristocracy. Workers were more susceptible, therefore, to the lures of the powerful, who could evoke the power of the state against them. Labor "fakirs," as he called leaders emulating Gompers, had become an intermediate class of sorts, a bureaucracy which arose within labor itself. Its clearest manifestation was the regularization of the day-to-day working relations between themselves and the employer. Even socialist-led unions, despite intermittently urging members to vote socialist, enforced and codified existing arrangements. At this stage, DeLeon was sure that socialists had done better in Europe and that Gompersism, which represented the frank acceptance of capitalism as the proper organizing force of society, was a peculiarly American problem. Soon he began to suspect that despite the absence of a large and cohesive socialist movement, American workers were not so backward after all.[88]

Others besides DeLeon were finding it necessary to challenge Gompersism and its limitations. Colorado populists, in cooperation with the state AFL of the 1890s, successfully pushed through legislation specifying an eight-hour day for all mine, mill, and factory workers; but the state supreme court twice ruled the legislation unconstitutional, an indefensible invasion of a worker's right to work for as long as he wishes. Gompers considered these decisions proof of labor's need for caution—his colleague Strasser sneered that genuine skilled workers could gain their own eight-hour days, without legislation—while Colorado miners themselves looked to direct action and solidarity of a markedly different kind. If Gompers sought adjustment, the miners sought a new industrial democracy.[90] The rise of the Western Federation of Miners and its creation, the Western Labor Union (WLU), at the end of the century, grew out of the frequently violent struggles of the Rocky Mountain West. Not initially political (or socialistic) in any of their claims, the miners and associated unions returned simply but emphatically to the Knights' vision of real labor solidarity. They could find it nowhere in the American Federation of Labor, and in 1902 they audaciously transformed their own regional movement, the WLU, into a would-be national entity, the American Labor Union (ALU). Viciously attacked in Gompers's circles, the ALU could not compete outside the mountain states. But its existence indicated once again the urgent need for a new kind of national labor movement.

Socialists and egalitarian unionists had still other reasons to be suspicious about the drift of a privileged labor leadership. Just before the end of the century, the reformist *Jewish Daily Forward,* which swiftly became the largest-circulation Yiddish-language newspaper in the world, had put itself at the head of an orchestrated Lower East Side enthusiasm for the Spanish-American War. The *Forward* urged revenge against the Spanish for wrongs done to Jews four centuries earlier. But this was mere rationalization: it noticeably revelled in the military victories of American expeditionary forces, indifferent to the real fate of those killed or placed under American domination, whether Cuban or Filipino.[90] This enthusiasm for military conquest offered the grim prospect of socialists vicariously sharing in the spoils of empire—even those who, like Jews in desperate need of international sympathy and solidarity, had nothing to gain and much to lose from the global spread of brute militarism and imperialism. Once more, and this time among immigrants who might have known better, expansion and race privilege offered psychic benefits linked to a rising labor bureaucracy.

Gompersism, the Industrial Workers of the World, and Hope for Industrial Cooperation

In 1903, United Mine Workers President John Mitchell declared revealingly, "The trade union movement in this country can make progress only by identifying itself with the state."[92] Mitchell provided his own best evidence when he identified the labor movement with himself. A poor, orphaned boy from a coal mining town, he followed his family into the mines at a young age, traveled the west, and quickly advanced as a local politician in Spring Valley, Illinois. An organizer during the vivid 1897 strike, he advanced by siding with the United Mine Workers leadership against his own fellow unionists, who had voted to continue the strike. For him a strong national union became both means and end, and through the backing of powerful figures, he became a "boy president" in 1899, promising that the assistance of government would make coal mining a safe and well-paid occupation. By 1904, and largely thanks to the dedication of ordinary miners, the UMW had indeed grown to more than a quarter-million members out of the 1,676,200 claimed by the AFL in that year.

Within a year of his election to the UMW presidency, Mitchell could be seen flashing diamond-studded jewelry and expensive suits, signifying his successful effort to use his position to acquire businesses and to invest in real estate. Busily organizing a far-flung bureaucracy, he quickly made himself an enemy of the union's radicals and a social friend of coal operators. He had adopted, an otherwise sympathetic biographer says, the "culture and attitudes of the employing class."[93] He naturally became a key labor representative to the new National Civic Federation, which sought to promote labor peace (on the terms of the employers, critics claimed) and to make class consciousness and class struggle obsolete. In the following decade or so, Mitchell repeatedly joined Gompers in seeking the good offices of government and in cementing an alliance with the Democratic Party.

But all was not well. When union growth slowed after the first years of the century and employers put out of their minds the frightening social disorder of the 1890s, an open shop campaign suddenly opened, with industrial spies and blacklists used extensively against even the most moderate unions. Worse was a concerted legal attack. Restraining orders were issued against strikes, and in the Danbury Hatters case of 1908, the Supreme Court ruled that unions could be prosecuted under the Sherman Anti-Trust Act and union members made personally liable for supposed restraint of trade.[94]

Outraged by these betrayals of class harmony, Gompers and his circle vowed to even the odds at the ballot box. Ruling out support for socialists, Gompers returned to William Jennings Bryan, who led a Democratic Party that stood for weak central government and autonomy of southern whites (the most cohesive section of the party) to act as they wished toward African Americans. While as racist as Gompers, Bryan embraced reforms of various kinds far beyond Gompers's own perspective: the elimination of monopoly, the abolition of the Senate and even the government ownership of railroads. Bryan's failure in 1904 prompted AFL leaders to launch a more vigorous political campaign in 1906, and to redouble their efforts in 1908. Dozens of AFL staffers devoted themselves to political campaigning for Democrats in New York, Illinois, and Ohio, in particular (by no accident, large centers of the competing Socialist Party). At first, they urged electing union men to office, but the tactic switched quickly to the modern position of winning endorsements of the AFL program from any and all Democratic candidates. (AFL allies in Congress often proved their loyalty by arguing labor's conservatives should be promoted by businessmen and politicians so as to ward off labor's radicals.) Likewise, the AFL campaign by 1908 became highly centralized, as Gompers and his lieutenants felt a need to prove to Democrats that their organization was solidly behind their choice.[95]

Democratic partisanship was never an automatic course for labor. Republicans, maverick voters following newspaper publisher William Randolph Hearst's Independence League, and, of course, the Socialists challenged the right of the AFL to speak for working people. The charge hit home against what many union members properly concluded was Gompers's own autocracy. William Howard Taft easily bested Bryan for the presidency, but in the context of a shifting urban machine politics, the embrace of the Democratic Party by the AFL had a meaning that Gompers had never intended. By nature cautious about political commitments beyond the state or local level, and still largely faithful to the idea that a movement of skilled workers could win immediate reforms best through their own action rather than political reforms, the AFL had indirectly endorsed (or even created, willy-nilly) the welfare state vision that gradually emerged within the modern Democratic Party. But there was a price. Labor Democrats naturally accepted the racism of the Democratic Party as a given, even as they sought to mobilize Irish-Americans in many places, Jews in a few key districts, and assorted other ethnic working-class populations where their votes would count.[96] Indeed, the stark decline in African Americans' working and living conditions in many northern urban areas during this period, including the loss of jobs and neighborhoods yielded to white ethnics, grew up in conjunction with the rise of so-called "progressive" politics bearing a racist edge. These initiatives were both the seedbeds of the New Deal and its deeply regressive side.[97]

From a pragmatic and more immediate viewpoint, the indifference of most workingmen to the AFL's pleas for a favorable presidential vote was sharply disappointing. Powerful labor leaders made their own deals, John Mitchell supporting his friend, the outgoing President Theodore Roosevelt, who stumped for William Howard Taft, while the longshoremen's president angled for a lucrative Republican appointment as commissioner-general of immigration. Predictably, Gompers turned his rage instead toward Eugene V. Debs, the Socialist standard-bearer, broadcasting the ridiculous charge that Republicans (he obviously didn't mean his own colleagues) financed the Socialist campaign. Socialists were quick to note that the allegiance to the southern Democrats directly allied the AFL with the practices of convict labor, child labor, and casual strike-breaking. *The Seattle Union Record* accurately labelled Gompers's complaint against socialists "the whine of a pettish, disgruntled old man," but did not accurately measure Gompers's ability to bounce back and take revenge.[98]

Gompers's challengers went two very different ways. After the disappointments of the 1890s, many unionists concluded that the effort either to take over the AFL or to push out Gompers was a Sisyphean task. Perhaps a labor-socialist party could not be built to elect a majority of congressmen or a president, but socialists could educate every potential convert, from the working classes to farmers and the middle classes, to face the moral crisis posed by capitalism and the salvation of civilization in socialism. This was a deeply ethical view, backed by the observation that the economic-financial consolidation of capitalism apparent to contemporary observers in the growth of banks and giant industrial empires would continue along with periodic recessions and the threat of total economic breakdown. For the optimists, the formation of great trusts within an uneven economy presaged the possibility of democratic revolution, in one way or the other, while unions either held onto their flocks or, at worst, failed and collapsed.

Within a few years, hundreds of Socialist Party candidates, nearly all of them elected by solidly working-class constituencies, actually took office, with high hopes. Behind these successful candidates stood dozens of local and national socialist newspapers and magazines in nearly every industrialized district of the country outside the South (as well as many rural zones) and in more than a dozen languages. The maximum educational campaign featured titular Socialist leader and perennial presidential candidate Eugene Debs, granted a sort of sainthood among large sections of the working class. Despite occasional setbacks, the Socialist Party swelled to a hundred thousand members with a following perhaps ten times that size, especially influential in Oklahoma, parts of New York, Illinois, Pennsylvania, California, Washington, and Wisconsin (including Milwaukee, which sent the first Socialist to Congress in 1910), and among a scattering of European immigrant groups including Hungarians, Lithuanians, Slovenians, Ukrainians, Germans, and Jews.

Socialist electoral hopes were badly eroded, if not dashed, after 1910 with the rise of a progressive movement bearing its own candidates (whether Democratic, Republican, or non-partisan). Middle-class reformers with credentials and financial backing to carry through reform measures like improved city services and even the municipal ownership of utilities, along with the regular benefits provided for working-class voters by urban machines, both stole the issues that previously only socialists had urged and also siphoned off the job-hungry. Many Socialists elected to local office were also defeated after a single term by coalitions of Democrats and Republicans determined to freeze out all third-party competition. In one-industry factory towns especially, but also in assorted locations, Socialists nevertheless held on, still expecting hard times for capitalism and a larger turn of working-class voters toward the left.

Other radical and socialist opponents of Gompers went a very different way. Around the turn of the century, a handful of labor thinkers, some of them close to European currents and some not, began to conclude that the industrial golden age of the future was not likely to be reached, at least not in America, by appeals for political support of socialism and patience with a socialistic labor bureaucracy. European socialists had grown powerful through attacks on the privileged remnants of feudal society, the absence of which at least partly explained the weakness of socialist politics in the United States. The class struggle in the United States seemed to have skipped stages to become mainly a direct struggle over power within the production process rather than the electoral process. According to this argument, the United States was the one place on earth ripe for the spirit of potential industrial solidarity to lead to its logical conclusion: a society without the coercive state apparatus in any of its possible forms, capitalistic or state-socialistic. The actual agency of revolutionary transformation, preparing the society to come, might well be the all-inclusive union—one organized on entirely different principles from the AFL.

The founding convention of the Industrial Workers of the World in 1905 declared the formation of the "Continental Congress of the Working Class," a class now ready to create its own industrial theory and political program. This message had, in a broad sense, been awaiting recuperation since the Knights of Labor. But DeLeon's "Preamble to the IWW" (an address delivered in Minneapolis on the eve of the Chicago convention and later distributed widely as a pamphlet, *The Socialist Reconstruction of Society*) captured the thought with an admirable intellectual sweep. Delegates roundly greeted the man who had explained to them that they were preparing to reformulate the very basis of modern society, elevating humankind to a higher form of the once-universal communality that anthropologist Lewis Henry Morgan had analyzed in the surviving American Indian tribes that he had encountered.[99]

In its vision and practice, the IWW was everything that the AFL refused to be and did not wish to be. It sought to live up to its internationalist ideals by organizing those workers (Japanese Americans, Chinese Americans, Filipinos, Native Americans among others) explicitly excluded by the AFL, it proclaimed the inevitability of class conflict, it derided any "fairness" with business and government as an illusion, and above all it carried itself with the dignity of the ordinary Joe. The Wobblies' songs raced around the English-speaking world, and their cartoons caused working people to laugh out loud, while the AFL could not claim a single cultural contribution of note.[100]

Nothing in the IWW, however, went according to theory. The great bulk of the older unions headed by socialists—most notably the Jewish needle trades unions but also the brewery workers, machinists, and others—remained within the institutional security of the AFL. Locals within various craft unions, whose restless members deeply wanted a radical alternative, were held tightly in check. Socialists who had risen to the apex of AFL local bodies and staved off attacks of ST&LA unionism during the 1890s often proved among the most vociferous opponents of the new industrial unionism. In turn, major failures to attract support highlighted serious internal divisions among Wobblies, prompting the departure of the Western Federation of Miners in 1907, which left the Wobblies without the bulk of their founding membership. The IWW of subsequent fame and legend nearly collapsed during the deep recession of 1907-1908. Unlike the crushed Knights and the failed Socialist Trades and Labor Alliance, however, the IWW possessed a large saving grace: an enduring labor culture of individual and collective rebellion, American to the core, rooted most especially among itinerant workers in the extractive industries of the West and capable of sustaining an ethos even on the thinnest material base.[101] And yet no one in the IWW could see a clear way past the stranglehold that the AFL had on American labor's potential.

The Wobblies and the electoral-minded socialists alike—to say nothing of Gompers and his circle—were stunned by the sudden industrial uprising of the unskilled, impoverished, and foreign-born working class. From the strike of a largely Slavic workforce in McKees Rocks, Pennsylvania, in 1909, immigrant workers of various kinds swung into action for most of a decade. The shirtwaist strike of New York women (mostly Jewish and Italian) that same year, overriding the pessimism of Jewish union and socialist leaders toward the capacity of such women to sustain themselves, shocked socialists into vigorous support action. A wide variety of other such strikes, most of them unrepresented by any existing unions, climaxed in the Lawrence, Massachusetts, textile strike of 1912, where the IWW valiantly and with scarce resources worked to unite some sixteen nationalities into a single fighting force. America, including its middle classes, suddenly seemed perched over a proletarian volcano.[102]

Wobbly editor (and former DeLeon protégé) Justus Ebert penned the basic IWW document of Lawrence, starkly titled *The Trial of a New Society.* Drawing quotations from the court proceedings indicating a frame-up against the strike's organizers, Ebert carefully argued that a new society already formed within the old one had socialized itself to do the work that needed doing. This impoverished crew, Ebert wisely added, needed only the opportunity to show itself as the real America. A current DeLeon protégé and SLP newspaperman, the nineteen-year-old Louis C. Fraina, reported from the strike scene at Lawrence that the solidarity and spirit of the immigrants made one wish that all American labor were fresh off the boat. It was a line of thought that neither DeLeon nor anyone else had applied to the vast, still overwhelmingly agricultural African-American workforce. But DeLeon's assessment of a labor bureaucracy contained within it the notion of a counteractive force to modern capital, a layer of new, rebellious workers at the bottom of the heap. In speaking out against the conservative tendencies of existing unions and labor leaders, Ebert had nearly identified the potential pursued by future labor radicals seeking to embrace minorities and women into the union movement. DeLeon, along with IWW representatives, had been among the earliest in the contemporaneous socialist ("Second International") congresses to decry measures for immigration restriction, and he had as much as anticipated the notion of mass worker rebellions outside the craft labor network.[103]

In that same 1912, moreover, nearly a dozen ethnic socialist groups with their own extensive working-class followings pressed themselves upon a rapidly diminished Socialist Party. Some were fixed upon European events (not surprisingly, with their relatives and comrades about to be swallowed up by war and potential revolution), but their "language federation" Socialist Party affiliates embraced the strike waves and constructed branches, fraternal societies, and clubhouses across large parts of urban America.[104] Among the diverse radical milieux, the thought spread that perhaps the key questions of socialist strategy had been phrased incorrectly all along, or had changed remarkably with circumstances and potential constituencies.

At the theoretical level, several key thinker-activists took the first steps toward a structural interpretation of the sharpening conflict within the middle and working classes of society. Austin Lewis, an English-born intellectual who served as lawyer for unskilled workers on the West Coast (and also translated the first English-language version of Engels's *Anti-Dühring,* which predicted an "invading socialist society" within the shell of the old), reported on strike outbreaks of the unskilled, and drew startling but increasingly familiar conclusions.

From Lewis's philosophical perspective and intimate observations, the craft workers' skills were not products of the modern socialization of labor so much as the "small property" of handicraftsman carried into the modern age. The modern factory system had steadily eroded the power and influence of the craftsman, who along with the fading middle classes of small entrepreneurs looked to various protest movements (including the Democratic Party and the socialist movement) for redress. The craftsmen's conservative leaders personified and frequently articulated the distance

AFL members had marked off from the life of the ordinary worker. But the same process had also created a class of modern proletarians who "have nothing in common and have never had anything in common except the fact of common environment to the machine industry."[105] Made radical by their environment and their own experience rather than by propaganda, they embodied the "growth of solidarity and discipline, self-restraint and practical efficiency" that would be the proper legacy of the machine age to the future industrial democracy.[106] But the labor and socialist movements had to transform themselves, to learn the nature of craft unionism's inherent bureaucracy and how to overcome it with mass unionism, so as to help facilitate that process.

If overdrawn in several regards, Lewis's view had the merit of pinpointing the centrality of the unskilled worker within the newer production processes and, as counterpart, the eroding status of the craftsman. Louis Fraina, an Italian immigrant boy who dropped out of school to support his family and became a teenage socialist street orator, delivered the fullest version of this notion, international in scope and philosophical in content. He had the advantage of writing a few years later than Lewis, after the consequences of bloody world war upon capitalism and the labor movement had grown clearer. He also had the opportunity to mingle with Greenwich Village currents and conceptualize a *cultural* counterpart to the notion of a new working-class counterforce to the AFL and its labor bureaucracy.

Fraina argued that what he called "state capitalism," an expansive capitalist state embracing administrative centralization and militarization, had rendered the old socialist expectations irrelevant. Liberalism, as it had taken ideological form (Fraina found fault in the philosophy of pragmatism), now offered the intellectual counterpart to AFL unionism, narrowing the range of radical thought, aiding and assisting the upper classes and upper strata of labor against the threat of the "irrational" lower classes and of the world's suffering peoples at large.[107]

Fraina directed the sharpest of his polemics against William English Walling, a renowned socialist intellectual en route to becoming an AFL spokesman. Walling had observed shrewdly that socialists had been blind to the inner strengths of capitalism, "the increased power and strength that it will gain through 'state capitalism' and the increased wealth that will come through a beneficent and scientific policy of production." Better regulated, the system would be successively transformed by the mechanics of a complex struggle: a state capitalism under the hegemony of big and petty bourgeoisie would be supplanted by a "state socialism" under the petty bourgeoisie and the skilled workers. In the process, the allegedly messianic character of socialism would fall away entirely, and the social question would become no more than "the struggle by those who have less, against those who have more" in "matters of income, hours, leisure, places of living, associations and opportunity."[108] Such a struggle could be properly ordered, guided by reform through existing institutions. The *disorder* implied by the ideas and very constituency of the IWW was, finally, a danger to the social détente which could make this benign process possible.

Even in AFL circles, confidence in such a benign outcome wavered. As the class conflicts of 1909-1913 took shape, skilled workers once again began to perceive that the emerging system often delivered fewer benefits for them than thinkers like Walling predicted. Solidarity campaigns of mutual support in strikes, like a dramatic one by railroad workers over several years, violated the AFL norm of workers with union contacts crossing picket lines and in effect scabbing on those still striking. The attempt at coordination by railroad brotherhoods, the appearance of metal trades councils, and (by the time of the war) the appeal for solidarity among the skilled and unskilled often bypassed the idea of political or electoral "socialism" altogether for a more popular American idea: *workers' control of production*. Many local AFL members and even leaders unmoved by socialism mulled the idea, while Gompers's circle rejected it out of hand as impossible and undesirable, an erasure of the line between labor's prerogative and capital's rights.

Conservative chiefs of AFL unions ranging from the hatters and pattern-makers to tailors, sheet metal workers, carpenters, and machinists, all lost their offices to socialist-backed candidates during 1911-1912 on grounds of solidarity versus conciliation with employers. A combination of administrative manipulation, political alliances with Democrats inside labor, and forceful support of labor conservatives by the Catholic Church was required to bring anti-socialist functionaries back into union office.[109] The renewed victory of Gompers was sealed by the events of the First World War. As labor surged forward, anti-war ideas were in many parts of the country forbidden in published or spoken form, and those who voiced them faced deportation, arrest, beatings by vigilantes, and even lynching. The IWW, which carefully refrained from any political statements, was nevertheless suppressed in a fashion unknown hitherto in the United States, save perhaps for the attacks on Reconstructionist radicals in the post-Civil War South.[110] This time, the modern version of the Ku Klux Klan had the presidential seal of approval and top labor leaders' avid cooperation. Gompers demanded political acquiescence to the war, or at least silence, as the price of admission for newcomers to the AFL's own swelling wartime bureaucracy. Upwardly mobile intellectuals around labor, like Walling, made their contribution by insisting that the U.S. economic empire that had expanded dramatically in wartime was benevolent, and that the leaders of the AFL, in their appeals for loyalty to government and indifference to those suppressed, accurately represented the interests of the working class.

Regulated "state capitalism" did indeed take shape, even by 1917, though it more resembled Fraina's nightmares than Walling's dreams. As newspapers were suppressed, Socialist Party offices destroyed, and local and national anti-war spokespeople, including Eugene Debs, sentenced to long terms in prison, Fraina acutely observed that the newly regulated system included "the extension of the functions of the federal government, regulation equally of capital and labor, the Strong Man policy of administrative centralization," and "the mobilization of everything by a national administrative control of industry." Having failed to organize an international system to regulate the transfer of profits among ruling groups, capitalism now rended the world, and (as Fraina correctly anticipated the worse horrors to come in the next world war and after) prepared the basis for future global conflicts.[111] In that process, Fraina argued, leaders like Gompers could be depended upon to serve their true masters, while former socialists like Walling would tag along and rationalize the process—as perhaps temporarily dreadful but inevitable, and ultimately beneficial.

Capitalism's brutality and mainstream labor's complicity had within a few years already discredited, even for the initially enthusiastic, any notions of easy progress through governmental expansion. Socialists and unionists learned that they would be compelled to argue more vigorously against the growing tide of racism and nationalistic hatreds, and for the democratic federation of nations and peoples in a transnational, transracial world society.[112] They would face a labor leadership empowered against militant workers by federal military assistance and city police "red squads."[113] The problem was not strictly political. In Fraina's reasoning of the 1910s, radicals also had to cast off the dead weight of philosophical fatalism so deeply associated with acceptance of the labor bureaucracy, to dedicate themselves to heighten mass consciousness, to create a resistance movement more attuned to what he called the "spiritual reality of life." Outside the courageous, left-wing (Communist or other) sectors of the ethnic labor movement, this admonition would be lost for a generation.[114]

Cultural changes within working-class life were coming fast and furious. Even as millions of workers won small but important victories in shorter hours, making leisure time possible, the youngest generation among them and their siblings responded, especially in the big cities, to the world of entertainments and accelerated socialization opening around them. Genteel observers, noting young people's participation in dance halls, amusement parks, beaches, and city parks remarked with a sense of mounting horror at their open sexuality in particular and their general eagerness to grab life in front of them.[115] Fraina himself had joined the staff of *Modern Dance,* while continuing his writings on anti-colonialism and the struggles of the unskilled. The younger working class, he insisted, was undergoing a revolution off the factory floor at least as much as on it. Jazz dancing, as women's historians would recognize decades later, symbolized the growing freedom and subjectivity of big-city youth. From Fraina's point of view, it showed the possibility of a new multicultured and multiracial people, free from the prejudices and backwardness of their European and African predecessors. It was this new "race" of people who were fitted to transform America and make democracy real.[116] Fraina similarly saw gendered issues in the blue-collar bohemianism of the flapper, including her use of birth-control equipment—a search for personal, gender, and class self-fulfillment. As he put it in *Modern Dance,* "The community is finding a collective artistic expression, and communal activity is becoming a vital factor in the advancement of civilization."[117] Fraina's dream was one of approaching working-class self-realization based upon real developments, even if it proved unrealistic given the circumstances of war and repression.

Gompers's Wartime Triumph

Before the 1910 election campaign, a swell of local and state enthusiasm for independent labor parties had seemed for a moment almost to sweep the AFL away. Actually, Gompers had no intention of allowing such a development. Amidst a racist fever that spread from the old South to the border states and received the indignant defenses of Democrats against "interference," Democrats elected thirteen union members to Congress in 1910, and managed to get the Democratic Party leadership to usher through various bills, including one forbidding most anti-labor injunctions. None of these measures surmounted a hostile Senate and President Taft's vetoes, though during the last days of his administration in early 1913, Taft made a gesture to the AFL, signing a measure establishing a Department of Labor.

Southern-raised Democrat and Princeton College President Woodrow Wilson, elected in 1912, regarded the unions as the enemies of economic free choice and himself "a fierce partisan of the Open Shop." Saddled with labor's support and a thin coalition, however, he appointed a former UMW official as secretary of labor and permitted a United States Commission on Industrial Relations (some of its members definitely pro-labor) to hold wide-ranging investigative hearings. Socialists warned that all such progress could be wiped out overnight, and they were correct. But an airing of the labor case, stated even mildly, was something new in mainstream politics.[118]

The AFL moved on the legislative front to add a rider to a bill prohibiting the Justice Department from using money from the Sherman Act to prosecute labor or farm organizations; Wilson signed the bill, but declared that he would find the funds whenever he considered the prosecution of unions necessary. The Seaman's Rights Bill, mandating improvements in the working condition on ships, was passed despite Wilson's opposition and the president reluctantly agreed to sign it. After much congressional wrangling, another bill emerged in 1914 limiting under certain conditions the use of injunctions against strikes, and allowing that farm and labor unions should not be considered illegal combinations when they engaged in strictly legitimate acts (thus leaving aside many standard strike tactics considered non-legal). This compromise seemed so weak that several labor congressman threatened to combine with Republicans to kill the measure entirely.

Seeking vindication of his strategy, Gompers quieted opposition, adding only that workers would respond at the polls to anti-labor politicians.[119]

The Clayton Anti-Trust Act passed in June 1914 did not satisfy in any meaningful way the twenty-year AFL lobbying against judicial harassment, but Gompers urged passage and with his allies managed to get wording added, at the last moment, specifying "the labor of a human being is not a commodity or article of commerce." Employers gained more important changes rendering, in the phrase of a recent historian, "the bill nearly meaningless for workers' rights."[120] Undaunted, Gompers pretentiously described the Clayton Act as "Labor's Magna Carta," pronouncing his own lobbying activities a resounding victory for labor. The other major labor congressional victory, the Keating-Owen Child Labor Bill, was passed in the eve of the 1916 elections, along with a model workmen's compensation bill, in a mini-flood of regulative legislation.

Ironically, the most concrete and effective congressional legislation of the Wilson administration was stoutly resisted by Gompers and his circle. The Adamson Act, signed by Wilson in 1916, successfully established an eight-hour day for the most aristocratic of American workers, locomotive engineers. Prompted by Wilson's determination to avoid a nationwide railroad strike, with the Pullman strike boycott led by Debs a vivid precedent for what the railroaders could do, Wilson took the judicious road. For Gompers, the regulation of hours by legislation was anathema, removing from the AFL the prerogative to set that decision with the employers. Nevertheless ensuring the railroad men's cooperation in efficiency for the war-driven boom and the coming American participation in fighting, Wilson outfoxed the labor leader and pushed him out of the headlines for Frank Walsh, the Senatorial progressive responsible for the drama of the earlier industrial hearings.[121]

The key developments in labor actually took place off the political field, within revived older unions and new ones which sprung up shortly before or during with the war. The shortage of workers (thanks to booming war orders and a cut-off of new immigration) placed them into a sellers' market, prompting record strike levels for every year from 1915 to 1919. Union membership rose from 2.7 million in 1914 to more than 5 million just six years later; AFL unions alone gained a million members. Many socialistic ideas suddenly became widely popular, and radicals of all kinds found themselves elected to union office, running organizing drives, beloved not so much for their political views but for their willingness and capabilities to organize to fight the bosses. Contrary to Gompers's expectations, nearly all of the new and revived unions drew, to one degree or another, upon radical traditions. Contrary to radical hopes, they left behind the shrunken and suppressed IWW. The Amalgamated Clothing Workers, largest of the new bodies, mixed left-wing political education with practical industrial unionism, including a stress upon workers' own control of their machine process, in Knights of Labor style. In jewelry, auto, textile, and other sectors, workers, although armed with socialist or formerly Wobbly activists urging mass mobilization, were tolerated for the moment by an AFL leadership eager to expand its membership base and confident of neutralizing political challenges from below. Only a new mood, at once militant and generous, could explain proud New England machinists threatening to strike until all the underpaid women of the department stores were organized.[122]

Were it not for socialists in the AFL as well as independent unions, the expansion of the organized labor movement by more than 50 percent of its pre-war levels in 1919 would have been inconceivable. Yet Gompers and his leadership made themselves the chief beneficiaries of this activism. For Gompers in particular, union growth had become a stepping stone to the pursuit of his secondary career as a public personality. Renouncing previous opposition to war in 1916, he eagerly joined the National War Labor Board, whose chief purpose was the eradication of strikes for the duration of the armed conflict. Gompers thus became an inside-the-beltline figure, the first labor leader to substitute lobbying for organization. He made a point of announcing his loyalty before the National Civic Federation and the elite League to Enforce Peace in 1916, pronouncing a firm notion of labor's future under his very own guidance and American hegemony.[123]

Until the First World War, foreign policy had been beyond the scope of most unions except those craft bodies which pressed for tariffs to protect their manufactures or, far less benignly, pressed (with Gompers's zealous support) for restrictions on immigration, Asian immigrants in particular. In 1914, European socialists at the head of their respective labor movements, promising to resist war, caved in even before the guns started firing, especially with unionized munitions jobs at stake. In the United States, the

European war brought popular revulsion against conservative and government moves toward "preparedness." Labor pacifism or anti-interventionism was stronger than it would ever be after 1940, when millions of jobs came to depend permanently upon war or the threat of war. Jewish working-class opinion, for instance, held overwhelmingly that military involvement could bring only suffering to Eastern Europe, recalling subjects' long history of being forced to fight for one ruler against another. Similarly, few German Americans favored the Kaiser, but even fewer could see sense in any kind of war. Irish Americans generally regarded potential European warfare as an opportunity for their American rulers to join hands with the English oppressors of the homeland. These groups, along with a variety of Christian pacifists and plain enemies of war, were near the center of American labor.

The Chicago Federation of Labor (CFL), disproportionately Irish and led by the mercurial John Fitzpatrick, was a typical combination of craft privilege and social idealism. Ranging politically from progressive to outright socialist, CFL members fought for unionization of Chicago and simultaneously against the national centralization of unions which Gompers craved as a means to expand his influence and clamp down on dissent in advance. The 1916 Easter Rebellion in Dublin, with a martyr's death for syndicalist James Connolly (who had, for some years, worked in the American SLP), inspired the CFL ranks along with many other unionists. At least among sections of the working class, an awareness dawned that rebellions against empire were a part of the world class struggle. "We feel and believe," read a typical CFL resolution in response to Woodrow Wilson's preparedness campaigns of 1915-1917, "that wars are unnecessary and caused by the exploiters of labor for the express purpose of advancing the portion of large capitalists." The CFL called "upon the working people of America who must do the fighting if war occurs to register their emphatic protest. . . ."[124] As U.S. entry into the war neared, the CFL sought a congress of labor groups to vote on workers' positions, a notion doubly repugnant to Gompers: politically unwanted and overly democratic. Local activists formed Labor's National Peace Council, enrolling more than a million members before indictments were handed down on charges of conspiracy to prevent shipment of munitions to the Allies. Bit by bit, Woodrow Wilson was showing the mailed fist, and Gompers was eager to see it used. The CFL, like a large section of the anti-war Socialist Party, struggled bravely on, with massive peace education, anti-preparedness parades, and attacks on the sensationalist press. Gompers cleverly invited Wilson to attend the 1917 AFL convention and appeal to the delegates personally.

In hoping to neutralize traditional government hostility toward unionization in return for AFL support of the war, Gompers invited government repression of his radical opponents in the labor movement, most especially the Industrial Workers of the World. Resisting Latin American unionists' appeals for the U.S. government's release of IWW prisoners, he declared Wobblies to be "enemy of unionism." The AFL president had meanwhile already quietly laid out plans for a business union internationalism. Endorsing the "ward" status of U.S. rule in Puerto Rico and the Philippines, he insisted upon the right to create AFL-style unions in such places as the U.S. conquered. He rationalized that colonial status would give workers the high wages to buy American products and simultaneously make products manufactured in these places sufficiently expensive that American capitalists would become uninterested in exporting jobs there. Gompers, like Wilson, dreamed of what historian William Appleman Williams would later call the real "open door" for the hemisphere—that is, imperial economic control of the Americas. Unions would spring up from Canada to Chile, guided by the cash and the influence of Americans like Gompers himself. That, he argued, would discourage the spread of socialism, anarchism, aggressive nationalism, and other popular beliefs that might inhibit U.S. interests.[125]

Much as it did for the intellectuals like Walter Lippmann and John Dewey around the *New Republic,* the First World War offered labor leaders a short cut to a national government of bureaucratic partners and their advisors, a large and permanent role in the public order. President Wilson's reform program provided a model of business and labor leaders exploring their common interests, focusing on economic growth and forestalling threats such as the radical redivision of wealth.

The Pan-American Federation of Labor (PAFL) was the perfect vehicle for the institutionalization of such perspectives. In 1912, Gompers and Mexican labor officials moved toward an all-American conference on labor, a counterpart to the business forum held in the wake of the hemisphere-wide shipping through the Panama Canal. At first, the new organization seemed intent upon actual labor objectives, although Latin American unionists (responding to a questionnaire distributed by the Americans) had the definite misimpression that Gompers shared their socialistic or anarchistic views. In the early days of PAFL, Gompers himself signed on to a protest against the extradition of the Magón brothers, Mexicans who had agitated on the north side of the border and were sought by their home government. As war approached, however, the real aims of the organization became clearer. A manifesto hailed hemispheric unity against the "military" dangers of German influence. Soon, the PAFL was to be strictly subordinated to the war effort, although not without subterfuge and resistance. A resolution to appeal the U.S. government's jailing of labor leaders was defeated at the next PAFL congress, as Gompers denounced the hapless IWW. On the other hand, Mexican unionists who questioned American labor's exclusion of Mexicans from U.S. unions were politely told that internationals made their own decisions, over which Gompers and other officers had no influence.[126]

On the home front, socialists formed an influential "front," the People's Council of America (later, the People's Council for Peace and Democracy), with Sidney Hillman its outstanding public figure. The administration promoted an ostensibly nongovernmental alternative, the American Alliance for Labor and Democracy (AALD), secretly funded by the Committee on Public Information. Like future organizations of erstwhile socialists proclaiming their moral independence while taking secret funding and vigorously supporting U.S. foreign policy, the AALD had few members but an outsized treasury. Ironically, Woodrow Wilson had wanted to make the financial arrangement with the turncoats public; the wily Gompers, anticipating socialist charges of a sell-out, insisted upon secrecy, just as Meany would do after him.[127]

In May 1917, as the president's press secretary warned darkly of the "contagious effects" of socialist propaganda on the war process, the AALD moved into an attack mode. Former syndicalist Walling and former socialist John Spargo among other "paytriots" (as the radicals jeeringly called them) recognized the impossibility of converting the Socialist Party majority to a war program. Instead, they sometimes urged, sometimes quietly endorsed, and generally declined to protest the growing government persecution of the dissenters.[127] The 1917 October Revolution in Russia threw the foreign policy elite and its *New Republic* intellectual allies into a tizzy. Former Secretary of State Elihu Root cursed the IWW for supposedly acting as German agents through peace agitation, urging "instant and severe punishment" for radicals. Wilson's Secretary of State Robert Lansing, who had welcomed the Kerensky government's enlistment in the war, announced a refusal even to recognize the Bolsheviks or their proposals to end the conflict. By February 1918, as Wilson considered his alternatives, including a possible recognition of the Bolshevik government in order to entice its new rulers back into the war, he digested a fresh memorandum from Gompers and Walling, warning more direly of "war weariness accompanied by Utopian dreams." The "very grave danger" of strike waves in France and Italy haunted them with the prospect of similar strikes in "foreign industrial centers" like Chicago and New York, where immigrants dominated the workforce. This was, as a scholar notes, the forerunner of the "domino theory" invoked by conservatives, liberals and labor leaders to justify U.S. presence in Vietnam. Indeed, among the underlings attempting to carry out Wilson's Russia policy were the Dulles brothers, John Foster and Allen, and young intellectual Samuel Eliot Morrison. The Dulleses would carry out diplomatic and CIA intrigues of the Cold War, and Morrison would recast all American history in this imperial light.[128]

Inevitably, the fear of foreign radicalism and of the swarthy immigrant fed anti-Semitism as well as generalized xenophobia in Wilson's WASPish circles, just as Gompers, the Germanic Jews of the *New Republic,* and even the leaders of Jewish anarchism went all out on the war (and against the new Bolshevik regime) in order to prove their loyalty. In 1919, Wilson himself described a "hyphen" (as in "Italian-American") as indication of as the most "unAmerican thing in the world," a dagger wielded by those who were "ready to plunge [it] into the vitals of this Republic." As Lansing's office circulated charges that Lenin was the only gentile among the Jewish Bolshevik leaders, Secretary of War Newton Baker warned of similar stirrings "among the negroes," financed by Bolshevik agents. Even the rise of premarital sex in the person of the flappers seemed connected to the Russian attack on what Wilson regarded as his own Puritan tradition. The wild ideological attack on Bolshevism was secretly accompanied by some fifteen thousand U.S. troops invading the Russian north and east, the

blockade of desperately needed food supplies, and U.S. arms shipments to
White armies, not excluding the justly feared anti-Semites. The Cold War had
begun, in secrecy, hidden behind presidential blather about world democracy and armed with just the kind of brutal allies the United States and its
labor leaders would count upon repeatedly in the future around the globe.[129]

The East St. Louis race riot of 1917, a pogrom against African Americans, drove home a similar point for Gompers. If Chinese immigrants had
been despised for their putative willingness to live on too little and thereby
lower working-class wages, African Americans were accused by the press
and by Gompers of the opposite, a primitivist overconsumption. He as-
cribed the riot to a racial "clash of standards" following the boom economy,
in which, he stated, "East St. Louis became a sort of convention center for
excited undisciplined negroes who were intoxicated by higher wages than
they had ever known," wages for which they were "totally unfitted by
experience." Though blacks might make more money than in the past, they
were inherently and properly "low wage" workers with no place in organized labor.[130]

Gompers himself was doing quite well, meanwhile. His enthusiasm for
preparedness paid heavy dividends. He gained a position on the Civilian
Advisory Commission of the Council of National Defense in 1917. An AFL
convention shortly afterward endorsed the official resolutions that his
aides crafted, and historians have often mused about how the outspoken
resistance of so many labor leaders to giving government policy a blank
check had disappeared so quickly. Briefly, Gompers successfully smeared
opponents as German agents and would-be saboteurs, denied them any
positions on convention committees (which he personally appointed), and
strong-armed others with the combination of threats and bribes that have
characterized labor officialdom's foreign policy tactics ever since. It should
be added that some of the key labor war opponents, such as the Amalgamated Clothing Workers' leader Sidney Hillman, abstained from directly
challenging AFL positions because they, too, saw in the opening of war
markets an economic bonanza. Others simply chose to stand pat rather than
threaten their good standing with Gompers and Wilson.[131]

Wilson himself moved to create enough government subcommittees to
include a number of additional labor leaders in respectable positions—just
as Franklin Roosevelt would promote former strike leaders into "labor

statesmen" during the Second World War. By agreeing to approve the labor side of military-related projects, Gompers and his peers gained a temporary but nominally awesome influence. In turn, the National War Labor Board formed in 1918 mediated between business executives and unions in order to avoid strikes—not quite what had been promised. If at first the Board seemingly tilted toward favoring union reconition, it soon turned toward an "arbitration" which muted the effect.

Gompers also quelled international labor initiatives for an early peace, urged especially by British labor leaders facing rebellious workers. As the AFL president famously put it, "one had to be an effective nationalist before one could be an effective internationalist," implying that such labor calls for early peace must have been inspired by the Germans rather than arising from ordinary Americans.[132] The European socialists sought, as a recent scholar puts it, to "make labor an international force in its own right."[133] Gompers wanted only labor participation with business and government leaders in decision-making councils. Indeed, by siding with British political leaders against the British unions, Gompers managed to derail any effective labor internationalism. When European delegates finally gathered for a labor peace conference in January 1919, many of them determined to take an independent position on war and its roots in capitalism, the effort was too little and too late for decisive action.

Local unionists in Chicago, as local unionists in so many places during wars to follow, learned that popular protests registered no effect within national union headquarters except to evoke a well-organized counterforce. The CFL continued gamely, charging rightly that Wilson and Gompers had become agents of business interests, heedless of the untold human costs of war, and that their high-handed maneuvering violated any sense of union democracy. When the CFL brought to the floor of the 1918 AFL convention a resolution on Irish independence, Gompers's henchmen prevented a vote. When the CFL demanded that labor delegates to peace commissions be democratically elected instead of hand-picked by Gompers, the AFL leader sent out an AALD "truth squad" to "investigate" elements of "Bolshevism" and "Fenianism" in Chicago and elsewhere. Meanwhile, the AFL president carved out a place for himself on the Commission on International Labour Legislation, creating the International Labor Organization (ILO) under the League of Nations. He opposed any effort by ILO officials to make international law, insisting that the United States would never tolerate that kind of internationalism. His hopes to create a nominal international labor bill of rights fell on deaf ears.

Gompers did have a global vision, albeit one with no place for socialist or revolutionary governments abroad. He fiercely opposed any violation of the sanctity of capitalist property, and he accepted the arguments of his war board partners that material progress for AFL members depended upon industrial efficiency and growing markets for American goods. The "free" international marketplace became the engine for economic growth and universal happiness.[135] Efforts to interfere in some substantial way, anywhere, meant a less effective world economy to benefit white, male American workers. Did Gompers understand that such a globalization, well underway even in the later 1910s, would work to the distinct disadvantage of "undeveloped" countries and continents, leaving them as suppliers of raw materials at low prices and oceans of mass poverty? Possibly, since the fate of people of color had been no concern of his.

At war's end, union leaders learned that the sacred right to collective bargaining had in no way become accepted. Leftish labor leaders stalked out of Wilson's Industrial Conference of 1919, convinced that Gompers would now come to his senses. Instead, Gompers seized the opportunity to explain that the "responsible elements" were now completely in charge of labor, voicing total support for the winner-takes-all Versailles Treaty. Wilson quietly dissolved the war boards, leaving labor bereft of those agencies which, Gompers had hoped, would guide postwar negotiations. With dogged loyalty, Gompers organized the AFL Nonpartisan Political Campaign—to support Democrats running for office.

After the War

Other observers spoke of labor coming into its own in very different fashion. As disillusionment with Woodrow Wilson's war spread and a Socialist Party diminished by repression showed signs of a comeback, electing fresh candidates to office in several states, huge labor parades of 1918-19 seemed to predict dramatic postwar events to follow. The 1919 Seattle general strike, effectively tying up the city for nearly a week, offered strikers' committees handling all the necessary details of a countergovernment. Meanwhile, a nationwide steel strike involving a quarter-million workers appealed to ethnic groups of virtually every kind before being crushed. And the Chicago packinghouse unions brought together black and white workers in an unprecedented show of racial solidarity. The Russian Revolution's soviets (or workers' councils) seemed to many to speak for labor's future everywhere, even its future in America.

The widespread public disillusionment with the "Great War" meanwhile offered the mainstream labor movement a last, crucial opportunity to effect an alliance to protect wartime gains. Delegates from the labor party organizations in a half-dozen states along with "Committee of 48" remnants of the earlier Progressive Party rallied in Chicago in July 1920, reconstituted themselves the Farmer-Labor Party, and nominated Utah lawyer Parley P. Christensen and veteran AFL unionist Max Hayes as candidates. Despite lack of formal support from the AFL and a general absence of funds, the FLP garnered more than a quarter-million votes in eighteen states. (Socialist leader Eugene Debs, campaigning from behind prison bars, where he sat for opposing the war, rolled up nearly a million votes himself.) Dozens of AFL locals and city federations registered their enthusiasm for a 1924 farmer-labor ticket of some kind as the conservative drive for the open shop (restyled the "American plan") swept across the nation, anti-strike injunctions proliferated, picketing was forbidden, and union membership fell—from 5 million in 1920 to 3.5 million just three years later.

Emerging from the Socialist Party, a new Communist movement met this drift with the Trade Union Educational League (TUEL), an organization rooted in assorted AFL locals which urged organization of the unorganized, more rank-and-file control of unions, federal unemployment insurance, and support of socialism. Led by William Z. Foster and unequivocally repudiating alternatives to the AFL (rejecting, to be specific, the IWW), the TUEL had strong support among miners, textile, and needle trades workers, and attracted a scattering of small, avowedly left-wing unions. For a moment, in 1922, it seemed capable of far-reaching influence, if not the ability to overturn Gompers's rule; afterwards a furious attack on TUEL members, and the drift of labor to the right, isolated the TUEL to the margins.

Meanwhile, a remarkable movement of workers' education had grown up out of the remnants of the Socialist movement, the experiences of early "labor schools," and the thirst for self-education among many working people. City labor councils and some state federations eagerly supported these experiments, and a Workers' Education Bureau served as a sort of clearing house for assorted activities. Tentatively approving the experiment, AFL leaders quickly grew anxious about the consequences. Gompers himself warned that advocating socialism or industrial unionism would be "hurtful and dangerous." Forcing the WEB to purge from membership local schools not directly affiliated from the AFL, Gompers sought to kill or tame the movement, and he succeeded in blunting its development.[136]

Despite such setbacks, a third party breakaway for labor still looked possible as of 1923, and the Chicago Federation of Labor took the lead. But different assessments of the prospects for a full-blown national party, combined with the flagrant influence of Moscow upon Communists deeply involved in Farmer-Labor activities in Minnesota and the Northwest, prompted the CFL to withdraw from election plans, at least for 1924. (Communists and their allies, including the aged Mother Jones, at first launched a "Federated Farmer-Labor Party," then abandoned the effort.) Progressive Party candidate "Fighting Bob" LaFollette, who had been passed over for Teddy Roosevelt in 1912 and courageously opposed the U.S. entry into war from his Senate seat, was backed by a coalition of liberals and socialists as the logical alternative. He offered labor a strong national platform if not a nationally organized third party. The indifference of Democratic candidate John Davis to labor's plight (or more to the point, the AFL's legislative agenda) prompted warm support for LaFollette, especially among the railroad brotherhoods. But the Wisconsin senator's opposition to Wilson, the abandonment of his solid middle-class Wisconsin constituency for a radicalized following of workers and farmers, made him not at all the sort of person that Gompers could trust or control. Quietly, without any major pronouncements, the AFL leadership pulled back from LaFollette in the months before election day.

Gompers had his own answer to the Progressive vision. The overwhelming Republican victories of 1920 left him fewer political cards to play at home, but the AFL leader developed a lively international agenda. The story of the Pan-American Federation of Labor, foreshadowing the failure (in at least labor terms) of future collaboration of labor leaders with the State Department and the Central Intelligence Agency, offered a case in point.

Chester Wright, a former editor of the Socialist Party's *New York Call,* became PAFL's secretary, and the organization (as its historian says) had "few occasions to aid the labor movements of Latin America" but many occasions to sound the AFL perspective.[137] It embarrassed itself especially in regard to immigration issues: American labor leaders made clear that they wanted no part of any further immigration. Gompers's death reduced the organization to a cipher, temporarily rebuilt in order to oppose the Mexican government's nationalization of U.S. corporate oil holdings in the later 1930s. The PAFL had never been indigenous to Latin America, just as the AFL and AFL-CIO's other foreign endeavors would always bear the marks of the U.S. "model" and U.S. control. Trustworthy and conservative Latin American unionists were nevertheless invited north, wined, dined, and otherwise rewarded during Gompers's last years. Revolutionary movements anywhere (except, of course, against Communist governments) were, naturally, opposed on principle. Quite openly, the AFL's diplomatic power depended on demonstrating to the American government and business allies that its leaders were invaluable allies. They could be truly valuable only in a "stable" world, "stability" being something very much like business-as-usual. Protection of American corporate interests would invariably define the accepted limits of political change.

After the 1924 election, AFL leaders predictably renounced third party politics once more in favor of the old reward-your-friends policies. By that time, the PAFL's business-unionism-in-one-hemisphere was Gompers's chief accomplishment of recent years. Its activities offered him a last opportunity to travel abroad, denounce radicals, and praise the "constructive" business unionism that he had successfully forced upon all those within his reach. On a train ride back from Mexico City in 1924, the old authoritarian died peacefully, in his sleep.

Gompers's AFL was by this time badly diminished, but his ideas lived on. William English Walling's *American Labor and American Democracy* (1926), articulating a corporatist version of Gompers's and Walling's own earlier theories, welcomed private capital, profits, and economic expansion as the inevitable and proper basis of society. As critics pointed out, something was badly missing from Walling's equations. Not only the unskilled worker but non-whites in general, together adding up to a majority of the working class in the United States, had become invisible in

Walling's account. Walling had also lost sight of the assorted victims of empire abroad, and made no mention of militarization and war as necessary consequences of national economies competing on a world scale. His was a utopian capitalism, one with no down side, too obviously the intellectual construction of a career-minded former idealist.[138] This dénouement was shared by many union staff intellectuals in the 1920s, stunned by the collapse of the socialist movement and the global triumph of American capital. Not only did they fail to calculate the costs of empire, historic and contemporary, upon those most heavily weighted down by them, but working people themselves now disappeared as a potential emancipating force. By assuming as proper and permanent a union chain of command that placed at the bottom, former socialists and others never bothered by Gompers's style weighed in heavily against the revival of labor democracy in the next era.[139]

Nowhere was the distance more marked between continued rank-and-file enthusiasm on the one hand and bureaucratic encrustation on the other than in the needle trades, heavy with Jewish workers of earlier and more recent immigration. Often veterans of the Jewish Labor Bund in Europe, union leaders in these quarters had almost uniformly begun as socialists and reminded union members frequently of their youthful sacrifices. During the first decade of the century, this older generation had first experienced disillusion with the pace of change, tasted the perquisites of officeholding, and diluted their youthful ideals. By the 1910s, amid a new wave of labor insurgency, some held on to their positions by meeting the revolutionary enthusiasm of Russian-inspired youngsters with blunt denials of union democracy. Quick to point to Communist sins, they rationalized their own as "saving the union," with themselves (still nominally socialists) in charge. Notwithstanding their sentimental attachments to old ideals, they steadily gave way in daily matters to the permanence of authoritarian giants such as the ILWGU's David Dubinsky, who came to dominate the world of Jewish labor and socialism while supporting the conservative factions in American labor at large.

The intra-class conflict between the bureaucracy and the lowest levels of factory workers—a familiar theme of the most acute theorists since DeLeon's time—took new forms in the 1920s and after, with political splits in unions, fraternal associations, workers' theaters and even summer camps. Ordinary Communists, discouraged by the factional wars and diminishing democracy within the Communist movement itself, held to the ideals of genuine working-class internationalism, free of racial and imperial privileges. Often the more recent immigrants and most disadvantaged workers, they could easily feel the pain of others. But they were helpless to prevent the contribution of their own party's bureaucratic leadership to the top-down styles of labor. Even the valiant efforts to organize industrial workers, the greatest accomplishment of Communists during the era, were marked with the assumptions of worker apathy and the need for tight command structures.

Communists usually found common ground with Sidney Hillman of the new Amalgamated Clothing Workers of America (ACWA), who more successfully rode the waves of militancy, modulating the challenges by embracing or coopting erstwhile leftists (including Communists) who saw the successful mobilization of labor as the great possibility of the time. But the problem was never simply one of flexible and inflexible leaders. By the 1930s, the Jewish-led unions, especially the ILGWU and ACWA, had the requisite strength and energy to establish a framework for the emerging industrial labor movement. Located in the regions somewhere between liberalism (or the liberal socialism of the "mixed economy," a phrase invented by an ILGWU educational director) and conservatism (including quiet acceptance of a prevalent racism), this style of unionism placed heavy emphasis upon maintaining the support of government allies—first in Albany, then in Washington. These two unions, the ILGWU in particular, had played no small role in isolating the Industrial Workers of the World, before the decisive federal government crackdowns on the Wobblies. The ACWA would play a very large role in strategizing a CIO path mediated with government functionaries and political leaders, sans the participation of ordinary workers or systematic regard (rhetoric apart) for the fate of racial minorities and others left out of the compact.

In these ways, the combined weight of industrial unionism's defeat during the 1910s, the Wilsonian political repression of the socialist and syndicalist left, and the victory of Gompers-style imperial unionism continued to count heavily in labor for the rest of the century (and not only in the United States). Left-wing opposition, faced with daunting odds and often hamstrung by the Communist Party's own bureaucratic forms and accomodations, struggled to offer desperately needed alternatives.

Gompers's Legacy

Advanced business leaders in American industry met Gompers's conservatism halfway in the 1920s, but with the intent of eliminating unions altogether. The "welfare capitalism" of many corporations during the 1920s promised (and sometimes delivered) greater job security and health insurance. The companies donated considerable funds to neighborhood churches and other agencies assisting the poor. They sponsored sports leagues, appealed directly for individual loyalty and potential promotion over ethnic clannishness, and even held human relations classes to improve foremen's factory demeanor. Academics like famed Harvard Business School professor Elton Mayo conducted experiments to learn "what the worker thinks" and how grievances could be minimized. Not so different from Gompers in some key respects, they promised to achieve the goal of harmony between capital and labor. Some companies even called their practices "industrial democracy," stealing a march on the reorganized socialist educational bureau, the League for Industrial Democracy. (Not that repression was set aside completely. Some of the same firms regularly checked absences on May Day or during an event like the execution of anarchists Sacco and Vanzetti in 1926 to pinpoint "reds" and insulate other workers from their presence with firings and industry-wide blacklisting. Less gentle employers in many regions of the country depended upon mobs or the Ku Klux Klan, at its high tide during the 1920s, to threaten, harass, or brutalize radical unionists.)[140]

Gompers seemed to be genuinely surprised at the combined sophistication and viciousness of the campaign to replace unions. The arrangement that he had made (or thought that he had concluded) between government, business, and the AFL during the war came apart and continued AFL lobbying in Congress had little effect in bringing it back together. Democrats drifted rightward, as they would again and again after the consequences of wars had disillusioned the public and after labor officials were no longer needed to ensure productivity. (On race issues, which hardly concerned the AFL, they continued the lily-white impulses of Woodrow Wilson or went over, in some districts, body and soul to the KKK.) The

Republicans, for their part, fed off the disillusionment with big government, adopted a less interventionist internationalism (to call it "isolationist" would be a familiar exaggeration intended to boost the interventionists' case), and openly praised big business. Only in one major regard did Congress satisfy the AFL, by shutting off immigration in 1926.

Working-class life did change, especially for younger working people who went to silent movies, danced to jazz tunes, necked, and sought a different and far freer life than their parents had enjoyed. Even the flourishing ethnic halls, Yiddish theater, and the Harlem Renaissance registered shifts of concern that Louis Fraina would have recognized. For that matter, a fair number of craftsmen enjoyed good enough wages during the generally prosperous 1920s to buy Model-T Fords and enjoy the equivalent of a middle-class life. But for most working people, the quest for a different life ran into sharp limits. They might *feel* differently (as many Americans of all classes did) than their predecessors had before the world war, more detached from a European or rural American past, more part of an exciting metropolitan culture. But the reality of life and labor continued to defy the glamor of the movie screen and radio commercials. Crucial industrial zones of the country, including the textile and coal districts, were already in serious recession before the stock market crash. "Progress" came to a screeching halt on Black Friday in 1929.

By this time, the assumptions that prevailed within the world of Gompers had disappeared, quite as much as the innocent hopes of the Socialists to educate workers into socialism, or the IWW's expectation of the triumphant One Big Union not far ahead.

If Gompers had known that his style of labor politics would bring the AFL to the verge of ruin by 1930, might he have ruled labor differently during his glory years? Not likely. Gompers had chosen privilege and self-importance, his acceptance by business and government leaders, over labor democracy in every instance. He never lost the aura of his own importance, even as the labor movement sagged at the end of his life. With a personal machine of 2,000 organizers and 125 paid functionaries, the AFL aura had not disappeared for him. He believed that, in the long run and despite much contrary evidence, corporations and politicians would repay the AFL for his own personal loyalty to them. As an early prototype for the Cold War liberal politician and hawkish labor leader, he so believed in his own capacity to manipulate institutions and individuals that he brushed aside all unpleasant consequences for others. By the time of his death, he was nearly the caricature of labor leadership that George Meany and Lane Kirkland would realize more completely in their own eras.

2. MEANY TAKES COMMAND

In a 1966 talk to the Businessmen's Committee on Latin America, George Meany professed that labor leaders like himself fervently believed "in the capitalist system and . . . are dedicated to the preservation of this system, which rewards the workers." For their trouble, he said, "the investors of risk capital must also be rewarded," obviously including the investors in the room. In 1977, the same Meany was officially presented the highest award of Social Democrats, USA, by philosopher Sidney Hook, who had over the decades shifted his allegiance from the *Communist Manifesto* to the manifesto for Richard Nixon's re-election in 1972. The symmetry is right: the leading labor apostle of capitalism, of business unionism, and of the CIA's righteous role against threats to private property worldwide, testifies at a ceremony sponsored by a group now remembered best for its avid support of the Vietnam War and its clandestine activity around Ronald Reagan's foreign policy apparatus.[1]

All perfectly normal so far, in the neo-conservative and spy-heavy atmosphere of the later Cold War. What gave the event the unintended character of political satire was the nature of the accolade to Meany: a Eugene V. Debs Award, named for the uncompromising socialist who despised business unionism and pronounced capitalism "inherently a criminal system . . . based upon the robbery of the working class and corner-stoned in its slavery," a figure who represented everything that Meany opposed and sought to suppress from union ranks. Undaunted by this all-too-evident contrast, Meany's admirers sought to add a touch of glamor to his colorless record by virtue of an award whose symbolic significance asserted a mythical continuity, the common denominator that could exist only in the imagination of the sponsors.[2]

Making of a Bureaucrat

The history of George Meany is a success story, a labor variation on the American Dream. A youngster not conspicuously bright or mechanically talented rose from relatively humble beginnings as a tradesman to president of the American Federation of Labor and then the AFL-CIO, nearly thirteen million strong by the time of the 1955 merger. Such dramatic social mobility has not, in recent generations, been confined to those gaining entry into the upper business or professional classes. Personal success for Meany, as for so many in the upper ranks of union officialdom, brought prestige, power, and privilege: a chauffeured limousine, a healthy expense account, an official salary that reached six figures by 1977, two homes, and membership in exclusive clubs, where he maintained cordial relations with legislators, governors, cabinet members, presidents, bankers, and industrialists.

Just as neither modesty nor principles inhibited Meany from accepting what he had earned the hard way, he could see nothing amiss in the lavish union conventions and council meetings at posh hotels and spas, or in the construction of a marble edifice in Washington, DC, as national federation headquarters. These constituted the emoluments of power. Anyone who questioned the wisdom or propriety of such displays of affluence by workers' representatives, even in times of economic hardship, was dismissed with the special scorn of the powerful toward the impertinent.

Union power also allowed Meany to meet his responsibilities as a devoted family man, which is to say a good provider, rewarding each of his three sons-in-law with a kind of dowry: a handsome job. No wonder Ernest S. Lee said of Meany: "There is a great warmth about the man that I don't think the general public sees." It was easy for Mr. Lee to see because he was himself a Meany son-in-law, awarded the job of AFL-CIO Director of Foreign Affairs—one of Meany's perennial special interests—when Jay Lovestone retired from the post in disgrace in 1974.

If this appears to be a personal or narrowly biographical note, such appearances deceive. Inflated salaries, large expense accounts, nepotism, and ostentatiousness indicated and reinforced, from Gompers's time to the Meany era and beyond, the wall that divides union officialdom from the rank-and-file. A bureaucratic, self-perpetuating ruling group within trade unionism, with its own ideological pretensions, interests, and rewards, had expanded rapidly and fattened measurably. Below, members grew steadily more alienated not only from the "efficient" and "automated" corporate workplace but also from what was theoretically "their" union. Samuel Gompers had presided over the gestation of American labor autocracy; George Meany strengthened its reign; Lane Kirkland would wear out the seat of power. The irony of the American worker reduced from subject to object in an organization based on his or her class is as old as the style fostered by Gompers, and, despite glamorized histories, typified even most of the CIO even in its best days. But this long-existent, internal bureaucratic encrustation stifling union democracy and the union movement proper were decisively widened and hardened through the rule of Meany and what can properly be called "Meanyism."

Born to Irish immigrant working-class parents in 1894, the second of ten children (two of whom died in infancy), George Meany began life in the predominantly Irish-American section of Harlem. The Meany family soon moved to the South Bronx, where George grew up. The father, Michael, was a plumber by trade and president of his union local. Like many an American father, Michael nurtured "higher aspirations" for his son. George, however, had no academic or intellectual interests, dropped out of high school after one year, took on marginal jobs for a while, and at age sixteen, without parental consent, went to work for a small plumbing concern. Disappointed but resigned to his son's aversion to higher learning, Mike Meany wisely insisted that young George attend trade school to prepare him for a journeyman's examination. After three years of trade school came the craft test, the moment of truth. The young man failed. He tried again in six months and this time passed, perhaps with a little informal assistance. A probationary member of the Plumbers Union, he finally, in 1917, attained full fledged membership in Local 463—his father's local. The elder Meany died in 1916, and George's older brother, incapacitated by wounds suffered in France during the war, died in 1920. In the face of all-too-typical working-class tragedy, George became the family's financial mainstay. [3]

Meany began to envision by way of his father's example an escape from a lifetime of manual labor, mounting bills, and responsibilities. He felt intuitively at home in the tradition of Gompers, a man he both studied and admired. The impossible image of Meany appealing to Lenin against sectarian Communist designs on the New York City Building Trades Council is enough to show that Meany was never the sort to spend time reading Marxist (or any other) theory. While Gompers had fallen away from radical or progressive ideas, Meany never rose to them. Perhaps this explains why Gompers at his miserable worst, castigating "niggers" and conspiring against socialists, never fell as far as Meany with his trademark gay-baiting ("people who looked like Jacks, acted like Jills, and had the odor of johns about them") aimed at the likes of Democrat George McGovern's supporters in 1972. Not only was he anti-intellectual, but he was famous for leaving his work "at the office" and devoting his leisure hours strictly to—leisure.

Unlike Gompers, who had personally known grinding poverty, Meany was merely insecure. He was also remarkably indifferent in his younger years to the labor radicalism swirling around him. If Meany had any reaction, similarly, to the lynchings and Negrophobia that swept the south, climaxing in the Brownsville Riot of 1919 and a subsequent rise of the KKK, or to the interracial unionism that flared in Chicago's stockyards and the Garveyism that briefly took root in black working-class life, he kept no record. He seemed unaware of the grand contemporary experiments in labor's public voice, like Chicago's radio station WCFL (for the Chicago Federation of Labor) or New York City's WEVD (for Eugene V. Debs).[4] Already in his mid-twenties and beyond, Meany had his eyes firmly set on other matters.

Meany rose within and would always identify with a sector of the AFL—the building trades—so notoriously corrupt and clique-ridden that in many circumstances even to call them "unions" at the local or neighborhood level is semantically doubtful. Their consolidation dated back mostly to the 1880s-1890s. Blessed with the power to shut down an urban construction job at will, the building trades outsurvived other unions during tough times by relying less upon class sentiment or solidarity than upon family connections, vote-getting influence on the nearest political machine, physical threats, and the estimable power of the well-placed bribe. Each construction union local guarded its own fiefdom and nearly every one staged at least occasional raids upon rival territory. This permanent jurisdictional warfare brought forth leaders who negotiated with money and muscle the prerogative of what classification of worker would cut the threads on pipes and install them, or plaster what and where—plumber, pipefitter, electrician, boilermaker, or carpenter. "Skills" were frequently fictitious, the inheritance of a bypassed technology, or at any rate no more demanding than for "unskilled" production work of non-unionized workers, and, like most of these, learned on the job. Entrance into the trade, as in Meany's own case, was due less to passing tests than to family birthright. Strikes, which took place sporadically, were as likely to be directed against another union as against an employer. Above all, "outsiders" like people of color or women knew they were excluded from these jobs on principle. Altogether, the atmosphere evidently instilled in Meany a definite social vision or, rather, a perfect absence of it.

Building trades unions necessarily entered into special agreements with contracts and builders whereby only union labor could be used on a job and the unions would only work for those who accepted such a double-ended, closed arrangement. That way, the craft union worker could get his "more," since the compliant contractor could bid higher on a job than the contractor who was not party to the deal and still be awarded the work, assured of a skilled workforce. The interested parties passed the extra cost on to the tenant—often driving the independent contractor out of business, and in later eras, toward the use of non-union workers. From the modus vivendi of traditional union and contractor collaboration, a modus operandi followed of graft, corruption, racketeering, and violence by all parties in the building trades. Shoddy materials, tenement design to cram more families into less space, evasion of all manner of city building codes, kickbacks, no-show paid employees, double-dealing, protection, beatings, and blacklisting all took their place as elements of normal procedure. From time to time, urban reformers managed a clean-up of some proportions, usually trapping the smaller fish (or the unreasonably greedier ones) in legal nets. Then things went back to their usual ways.

Meany's autodidactic learning seemed perfectly suited to the task at hand. He became known early for expert on-the-job inspections for the fulfillment of union prerogatives, especially his encyclopedic knowledge of work classifications such as proper ratios of helpers to journeymen and the often highly imaginary (for that reason all the more tightly regimented) demarcations between different trades. He had the aptitude of a foreman, and he quickly became one, with a master plumber's license. Often his strongest motive and his most notable accomplishment was, simply, to take the work away from non-union workers within union jurisdiction. Under his rule, because those entitled by birthright or favor gained the privileges, other workers were merely in the way, unwanted even as potential new union members. "For our part," he later quipped, "they could drop dead."[5]

A Labor Conservative in Tumultuous Times

In 1917, Gompers and carpenters' leader William Hutcheson decided that the time had come to organize a New York City Building Trades Council. Gompers was evidently anxious to have a working body to counter the influence of the Central Federated Union, then regarded as a threat— just as socialist-dominated and mostly German-American local federated bodies had repeatedly been earlier when they sought to shake loose from AFL conservatism and corruption. Hutcheson, deeply corrupt, had his own designs: city-wide supremacy for his carpenter locals within the construction industry. To help in this cause, Hutcheson and Meany called upon the varied talents of Robert Brindell—a notorious labor gangster of the dock and pier carpenters union—to enforce the new arrangement. By 1920, however, Brindell was convicted for three counts of extortion and sent to Sing Sing. Yet he had managed to do the task that the AFL leaders set out for him, the creation of a Building Trades Council which could be safely dropped as an embarrassment and replaced with another of similarly conservative posture but better public reputation. Meany had the great luck to be in the right place at the right time. In 1919, he ran for Local 463's executive committee and won, by his own account, "because my name was Meany," the son of a respected, deceased local president. That very year, the New York state legislature assigned the Lockwood Committee to look into corruption in the construction industry. When Brindell took the fall, many of his lieutenants went with him. One of them, the business agent of 463, suddenly faced an unstoppable re-election challenge from George Meany. Now the young man was really on his way.[7]

In the 1920s, as leading labor figures struggled to broaden and redefine their purposes into a public engagement beyond the workplace, Meany moved from business agent to office of the president the New York State Federation of Labor. His admirers hailed him at the time as a source of new blood, a young and vigorous unionist. There was some truth in this boast.

At age forty, he became the youngest member of the AFL's New York state executive board. But so hardened had the craft leadership become by this time that anyone under fifty was a stripling, and anyone with ideas regarded as an intellectual dynamo. Meany thrived by challenging no principle or personality of the operation. Unionism at large was fighting furious back-stairs struggles in many trades, but Meany led no strikes and appealed for no mass actions. City unions, dominated by the building trades, were in any case more concerned with the politics of Tammany Hall than with the fate of embattled craft unions elsewhere or the organization of the mass of mostly unorganized and unskilled workers. Meany's promise brightened when, in 1923, the new citywide Building Trades Council was chartered by the Building Trades Department. Untainted by the current scandals and blessed with his father's name, Meany was a natural for council secretary. He retained his position as plumbers' business agent, but he moved up to take responsibility for sixteen craft organizations. He had the task of settling the perennial jurisdictional disputes and dealing with employers on an industry-wide basis. This shift brought him in direct contact with important union leaders, including Joseph Ryan, magnum gangster unionist of the waterfront and a formidable power in New York City politics.

In New York, the labor officialdom was tied firmly to the Gompers strategem of alliance with the Democratic Party, and Meany was a diehard supporter of the approach. Even in 1924, when Robert M. LaFollette's third party candidacy for president was enthusiastically backed by many public figures as well as the fading Socialist Party and thousands of ordinary unionists, and armed with the formal endorsement of the national AFL, Meany joined the New York State AFL, like the city's central trades and labor council, in remaining unmoved. Henceforth, despite the electoral campaigns of Socialist Norman Thomas—an occasionally important factor in New York labor politics from the middle 1920s until the middle 1930s—no one would seriously threaten the national loyalties of AFL leaders in New York.[7] This often meant supporting Democrats over candidates with better labor records. In the New York mayoral election of 1933, for example, a maverick Republican (and fusion candidate) Fiorello LaGuardia ran with the support of reformers and erstwhile socialists. Never mind that Socialist Party veteran Morris Hillquit was making one last, dramatic bid for the office, running against capitalism in the depths of the

Depression. The more threatening candidate was author of the Norris-LaGuardia Act of 1932, which severely limited the use of crippling anti-labor injunctions. This achievement was hailed more than a little self-proudly by the AFL's Executive Council as "the outstanding legal accomplishment of the American Federation of Labor." Meany nevertheless viewed LaGuardia as a politically suspect radical. Besides, Tammany Hall beckoned. LaGuardia received no AFL support.[8]

Meany had personal reasons for such Democratic Party loyalty besides his cosy relations with New York politicians. As the Depression steadily deepened, AFL traditionalists at first held firm to their laissez-faire or "voluntarist" stance on social welfare legislation. Union leaders bitterly opposed state unemployment insurance plans or broad minimum wage laws as examples of government interference into the natural jurisdiction of unions. It was not a persuasive view—neither for members that the weakened AFL had failed nor for the large majority of workers beyond the AFL pale. Slowly, over the course of the 1930s, partly because of the growing popularity of Franklin Delano Roosevelt, AFL leaders warmed to social legislation. But Meany opposed even minimum wage legislation until 1937, on the basis that it would usurp the special privilege of unions to establish proper rates for their members through collective bargaining.

All this stood in stark contrast to the realities of life in the Great Depression. As labor historians have detailed in recent decades, virtually all the social welfare promises made by corporations during the 1920s—some of them actually realized for better-off workers—went rapidly down the drain. The material advances for the fortunate, such as modern appliances, better housing, and medical care, had largely swallowed up wage increases even before the Depression (and drove many wives to work in bad factory conditions). The all-important ethnic communities that had raised themselves up through fraternal financial associations and multiple family jobs at poor wages saw their savings wiped out in the economic crash, their half-purchased houses repossessed or rent unpaid, and their worldly goods moved onto the street unless "reds" halted the police and "renegotiated" with the authorities and landlords. Churches, which had often filled the gaps temporarily for the most hard-hit ethnic and black or Mexican families, quickly ran out of available resources and appealed desperately for government assistance.[9]

A popular sense emerged that "the system" had failed and something dramatically different was needed. Neither "socialism" (presented as government ownership, or in the case of the Soviet model a "workers' paradise" of collective workers' dictatorship through the state) nor modified welfare capitalism had broad appeal in the immediate crisis, in part because of the effectiveness of the repression of the First World War and red scare. But in the early 1930s, skilled organizers from the re-energized Communist or Socialist parties (or any of the half-dozen, smaller groups on the left with spirited followings), speaking to public frustrations, made headway on issues through direct action. Massive movements of unemployed workers rallied tens of thousands under banners demanding dramatic and unprecedented government assistance. "Rent strikes" (collective nonpayment to tenement owners), "farm holidays" (refusal of farmers to make payments to banks or deliveries of goods), marches for bread, and literal rioting for relief funds helped break the mood of apathy and despair. Repression followed, but so did concessions.

The sense of crisis propelled Congress into unprecedented action on many fronts. Even before the 1932 election ousted Herbert Hoover for Franklin Roosevelt and a strongly Democratic congress, the Norris-LaGuardia Act essentially delivered what the Clayton Act of 1916 had promised: relief from injunctions issued for decades against strikers. Finding that no liberty of contract actually existed between the individual worker and his employer, the act legitimated collective bargaining, preventing it from being assessed a restraint of trade, and outlawed (at least in theory) the "yellow dog" or anti-union contract with employees.[10] The passage of the National Industrial Recovery Act (1933), written in consultation with AFL officials and Sidney Hillman, enacted codes for industry and labor, including the famous Section 7(a), abstractly stipulating the right of workers to organize. But the National Labor Board could not impose the will of the government, because employers had no duty to accept collective bargaining. The passage of 7(a) only helped marginally to level the playing field until the Supreme Court ruled the NIRA unconstitutional in 1935. Bitterly anti-labor employers continued to resist, and the officials adjudicating disagreements sided more and more with business.[11]

If the New Deal made an important contribution to labor at the depths of the Depression, then, it was indirectly—through public disillusionment with NIRA and the rage that spilled over into a live-or-die determination among many thousands of ordinary working people. Three remarkable local developments in particular made a revival of the old Wobbly dream, solidaristic industrial unionism—the antithesis of Meany-style unionism—well-nigh inevitable. During 1934, city-wide strikes occurred in Toledo, Minneapolis-St. Paul, and San Francisco, all led by radicals, though different groups in each case: the first by the followers of labor educator A. J. Muste, the second by the American followers of Leon Trotsky, and the last by Communist Party regulars. All seemed to demand, albeit more symbolically than in rhetoric, more than a contract settlement, something closer to a new way of life. Each demonstrated, in its own way, the powers of solidarity in the face of brutal but unsuccessful employer and police response. According to recent scholarly treatments, these events were more deeply rooted than the conservative federation's leaders could have imagined in local AFL unionists' bitter experience and thirst for revenge against the anti-union atmosphere of the 1920s. They had learned a degree of solidarity through grasping the precariousness of their own status.[12]

In a larger sense, what historians have called "solidarity unionism" repeatedly swept working-class communities from 1933 through 1938, often bypassing the hidebound existing union bodies in their tactics, organization, and community support-building. The mass-production industrial town of Barberton, outside of Akron, Ohio, provides an exceptionally well-studied case in point. A heavily immigrant working class made up of Slovaks, Hungarians, Poles, Croatians, and Serbs, plus thousands of southern white Protestants and smaller numbers of African Americans toiled in Barberton, making electrical parts, tires, and marine boilers. A town which had in earlier decades sometimes mustered a 25 percent vote for Socialist candidates, it was a stronghold of AFL progressives—or at least those eager to see unskilled workers organized. With precious little help from the federation, old-time socialists led the formation of AFL-chartered "federal" bodies, accompanied by public marches, dinners, and other social events to cement solidarity. Even the occasional Catholic "labor priest" supported this effort, as factory bosses determinedly resisted unionization with violence as well as propaganda. A victorious strike at Columbia Chemical in April 1934 encouraged others to similar actions. National AFL leaders' sellout of a rubber workers' strike prompted Barberton unionists to be among the first to join the new United Rubber Workers union. Repeated incidents of company violence mainly reinforced the sense of determination. Despite setbacks and no doubt because of them, the AFL-affiliated Central Labor Union continued ardent support for industrial unionists in Barberton.[13]

Even larger defeats had their message of solidarity in these exciting times. The textile strike which swept across parts of the South and New England in July 1934 was heir to textile organizing that socialists and other egalitarians had conducted for a century. In Rhode Island, where Socialists in the 1890s and Communists in the early 1930s headquartered their left-wing textile unions, one generation of industrial union effort after another had failed against overwhelming resistance. Suddenly, strikes and riots suddenly threw the state into an uproar, prompting a feigned "even-handed" approach of the Democratic governor (he ordered the dozen or so Communist Party members in the state arrested, meanwhile denying employers the usual support of police) and bringing about indirect legitimation of the mainstream industrial unions soon to come. No such happy ending lay in store for southern textile workers, in large part because the AFL's United Textile Workers overruled local initiatives and foolishly relied upon federal assistance to spur acceptance of union contracts. The opportunity to rally the main body of southern industrial workers passed, this time for generations.[14]

Within a few years after the initial 1934 strikes, workers of many kinds in an array of industries also took fate into their own hands, often staging sit-downs strikes (that is, refusing either to work or to leave the workplace)—just as the IWW had urged during its golden age. The famed 1937 sit-down strike of autoworkers in Flint, Michigan, ably assisted by Communists and Socialists had been preceded by a wave of dramatic moves proceding from south to north, and encompassing the oddest possible assortment of dimestore and department store workers, government relief workers, grave-diggers, housewives (against their husbands) and prisoners (against ill treatment). Ethnic working-class communities supplied one key factor to victory. Immigrants and their descendents had backed the industrial union drives of the 1910s, kept union sentiment alive within seemingly insular cultural and fraternal societies (often linked to the Socialist or Communist movements) through the interim, and now, a generation later, rallied the necessary community support for the unionization of basic industries.[15]

The new unions that formed, and the old unions that grew to meet the challenges, were often autocratic at the upper layers and limited to industrial workers, thus automatically excluding nearly all non-whites and most women employees of those days. In the rules of the game, the Democratic Party (and even local Republican politicians on occasion) would support such a limited unionism, circumscribed by a fairly strict differentiation of proper unionists from the poor, nonwhite, and underemployed. But at the lower levels of activity, millions of working people nevertheless expressed their urgency and their courage in one of the most democratic moments of the twentieth century.[16] Most remarkable, in many ways, were the struggles entirely outside the domains that Gompers, Meany, or even most of the earlier Marxists had considered radical labor's proper domain. Repeatedly during the early Depression, Mexican-American farmworkers with Wobbly traditions and Communist assistance struck the growers of California, enduring brass knuckles, clubs, tear gas, and guns.[17] In Alabama and Arkansas, black and white sharecroppers staged a mixture of rural uprisings and peaceful protests demanding better conditions in the fields and recognition of their special plight, protests which were ruthlessly crushed, while the black steelworkers of Birmingham, led by Communists, mounted the first small strikes leading to the unionization of southern steel.[18]

The atmosphere of strikes and industrial victories in the 1934 epic conflicts obliged the Roosevelt administration to reconsider its own basic political strategies. Industrial unionism of some kind was coming despite repression, and without controls and modest Democratic political assistance, it might well be the radical kind of unionism that the Industrial Workers of the World had once represented. In that spirit, solidarity would surely have meant an outreach to just those communities of color that stood furthest outside the AFL and, in practice, were most vulnerable to manipulation as strike replacements. No such all-embracing radical unionism was to come into existence, despite the hopes of Communist "insiders" and the aspiration of many industrial unionists. Too quickly, indeed from the beginning, emerging leaders chose stability and government assistance over inclusion and radical democracy. The passage of the Wagner Act in 1935 (following the abolition of the NIRA by the Supreme Court) affirmed the right to collective bargaining but also created a National Labor Relations Board to mediate disputes, thus regulating the wider union formation process. Unions could indeed be formed more easily, but without the board's approval, they would have little chance of defeating a stubborn employer. Meany, in contrast to miners' leader John L. Lewis, easily adapted to the conservative implications of these reforms and to the limited perks of the Democratic Party's triumphant sway under FDR.

Lewis: Autocratic Renegade

At first glance—before the cataclysmic events of the middle 1930s— John L. Lewis might have seemed another model type of AFL leader, perhaps more militant in the rougher conditions of coal mines, but just as autocratic and manipulative. This would have been a superficial view, however. Lewis was more complex by far, and an examination of his trajectory provides both a dramatic contrast to Meany and a hint at the nature of labor's changed leadership from the second half of the 1930s as well as the many curious contradictions of the 1940s.

Born in 1880 to two Welsh immigrants from coal mining families in Iowa (by no coincidence in the state's district where the Knights of Labor had their largest following), Lewis grew up poor but not desperate, worked the mines as a teenager, performed as an amateur actor in traveling theatrical shows, and managed election campaigns as a minor union official. At twenty one, he abandoned his post and family for a five-year sojourn "out West," becoming, according to his own unreliable account, a miner and member of the militant Western Federation of Miners. The year of his return, miners selected him as delegate to the national UMW convention, and like Gompers, he also became a "joiner" (in Lewis's case, the Good Shepherds and Masons, where he gained junior warden status). He married the daughter of a highly respected physician in 1907, and she reputedly drilled him in diction and voice inflection on his way up. After a failure in small business, the couple relocated to the largest UMW district, in the company town of Panama, Illinois. Several of his brothers, who preceded him to Panama, advanced themselves simultaneously in union activity, politics, and business. Ten years later, in the first major scandal of Lewis's career, it was revealed that one and all, including Lewis's own father, were looting the union local treasury with two sets of books, forged checks, and similar maneuvers. As John took over the union local, his relatives took over the town.

From the beginning of his career, John L. was fearless about using radicals even while remaining immune from radicalism himself. His first major ally, John H. Walker, was a Scottish socialist who would go on to become a major backer of labor party politics. Lewis simultaneously supported union conservatives (including future AFL president William Green), with the same personal demand for patronage. He served as lobbyist in Springfield for stronger mine safety laws with the same energy that he spoke up at his first AFL convention, in 1911, defending Gompers against a black delegate's charges of racism and defending the seating of Green despite well-documented complaints of voting irregularities.[19]

Lewis soon took Gompers's offer of a job organizing the New Mexico miners, from which he continued on the road, relentlessly organizing until the entry of the United States into the First World War. He achieved his best success in settling jurisdictional disputes (much like Meany) but his failures were more outstanding: he could not bring the mass production workers between Pittsburgh, Wheeling, and Cleveland into the AFL. He did, however, break into politics, serving Gompers as a major labor supporter of Woodrow Wilson in 1912 (against Eugene Debs as well as Progressive Party candidate Teddy Roosevelt and Republican William Howard Taft). As chairman of the UMW convention in 1917, he also won a narrow victory as an international officer. He made his way by backstabbing his old ally John Walker in favor of the reigning president of the UMW, John White. Named by White as official statistician of the union, then business manager of the *United Mine Workers Journal*, Lewis was poised for further rise. Rise he did. As White gained a wartime appointment in the Wilson administration, Lewis moved up to vice-presidential running mate of White's alcoholic successor Frank Hayes. In 1920, when Hayes resigned, Lewis took over—and never let go of the UMW again. He also acquired a personal brain trust, with the liberal economist W. Jett Lauck as his intellectual lieutenant. Unlike Meany, famous for leaving his work at the office, Lewis was all business.

Lewis established himself during the 1920s as a leader of nightmarish qualities, thanks to the twin crises in coal and in AFL leadership. As peace terms guaranteed the continuation of world power politics in Europe,

American coal miners watched prices rising and their wages frozen by wartime agreements. Demands for internal union democracy likewise rocked the 1919 UMW convention, and Lewis showed his mastery of divide-and-conquer, along with other manipulations. Neither Gompers nor Meany would ever have had the wiles to resist the direct election of regional organizers and auditors by insisting that immigrants and non-whites would thereby be deprived of potential leadership (a charge that was only part true, since while the union's left wing was deeply Protestant and white, districts heavy in minorities could have elected their own candidates), giving Lewis backing from minority caucuses. He also ruled against radical upstart locals across the Midwest, and against the Canadian miners who sought a dual affiliation with the Wobbly-inspired One Big Union movement.[20]

Yet, showing his audacity, Lewis soon guided miners into a strike—in effect, a strike against the government—that the radical faction demanded, refusing even Gompers's effort at intercession. Not for the last time, Lewis described the conservative union leaders as lickspittles for the politicians, and complained that the force of the state (in this case, a wiretap at the hands of the brand-new Bureau of Investigation led by J. Edgar Hoover) was being used against him. Unlike the Gompers of 1894, who gladly saw Debs go off to jail for the Pullman strike, the Gompers of 1919 at first pledged support for the miners—and then predictably reneged. Lewis squeezed a compromise out of an ailing Wilson just as the Justice Department threatened mass intervention. Radical miners' leaders later pointed to this moment when, at the UMW's peak of strength and militancy, Lewis and the union might have won heavily and carried organized labor into the 1920s with a stirring victory. As it was, he outmaneuvered his opponents within the union with a compromise success that primarily benefited the machine that he had organized.

Lewis continued to feint both right and left, sometimes simultaneously, in his rise to power. Elected UMW president in 1921, Lewis became a consummate labor politician of that stripe which amazes European unionists: the ardent Republican. Serving on assorted federal boards, he showed a warmth for Herbert Hoover first as Secretary of Commerce, then as a rising force within the GOP. On the other hand, leading a union that had up to a point bucked the decline of other AFL bodies, he audaciously challenged the aging and weakened Gompers, playing for the moment the vigorous radical against the doddering conservative. Most improbably supporting nationalization of the coal mines and railroads, federal pensions, and unemployment insurance, Lewis seemed a strong candidate. But in his bid to wrest control of the federation, he could not attract the support of the ILGWU, which was under the secure control of its own highhanded bureaucratic right wing, and he faced defections from the UMW's own ranks. Taking only a third of the votes, he came no closer than the perennial Socialist Party slate had against Gompers in its best days after 1895.

Perhaps, it has been suggested, Lewis had hoped for the presidency of the AFL precisely because he anticipated the sharp decline of the coal industry and, therefore, the UMW. Not long after the war, fierce, often violent conflicts over management determination to lower wages to pre-war levels brought federal troops and ended UMW hopes in considerable parts of the South. Lewis responded to an imminent national coal miners strike in 1922 by proposing an alliance of miners, railroad workers, and longshoremen (as in Britain), apparently seeking to bluff government and business officials into concessions. Bending to the determination of the miners themselves, he then led or at least supported the largest coal miners' strike in American history until that time. Through the spring and summer, Lewis visiting the miners living in union-constructed tent cities, urging them to hold on and playing mine owners against each other. But he failed to bring large districts under union control, foreshadowing defeat. He then turned savagely against those who continued to strike against assorted grievances including the prerogatives of powerful owners to run non-union as well as union mines. When railroad unionists went out a few months later against the worst of federal anti-strike injunctions, Lewis also turned a cold shoulder. He could talk solidarity with the best of them, but he had no intention of supporting solidarity when it did not benefit his own interests.

Excluding those striking miners of non-union mines from the union and the contract proved, as his critics often pointed out, to be the very Achilles' heel of the strike settlement. As coal production sank and owners shifted the remaining work, the UMW slid rapidly downward. Yesterday's champion of nationalization, Lewis now quashed further talk in the union about nationalizing mines as a conspiracy of "reds" and "parlor pinks." Reinstating himself as labor's foremost Republican, he shored up his national influence by backing the reliably conservative William Green as Gompers's successor to the AFL presidency. In doing so, he assured himself of pervasive if indirect influence, without the resistance of other AFL chiefs, and he also removed Green, his only major bureaucratic rival, from the UMW.

As UMW membership and morale sagged, Lewis devoted himself to isolating progressives of all kinds, including his past and future ally John Brophy. But he kept his main focus on Communists. In 1927 he barred them from UMW membership outright, and he purged the old socialistic phrase from the constitution that workers were "entitled to the full social value of their product." Meanwhile, he appealed, in patriotic terms that foreshadowed New Deal arrangements, for the government to rescue the union from its plight. No luck. Strikes which he had backed (with little choice) to the hilt fell victim to large coal inventories and stubborn management. By 1928, the UMW had lost most of its membership; from a half-million bituminous members alone in the early 1920s it collapsed to fifty thousand. Now it became a union saved from demise only thanks to the Illinois district of his old left-wing opponents. Through all this, much as any labor leader in the United States, he lived the fat life as a stock market investor, the head of his Indianapolis bank, and intimate friend to business leaders.

Socialists, Communists, and other insurgents not so easily designated, trying to avert the mine workers' retreat, formed a Reorganized United Mine Workers of America (RUMWA) based in the Illinois coalfields in 1927, eventually to become the Progressive Miners of America (PMA) under socialist and then conservative leadership. Lewis had the alternative union and its supporters slandered and driven from communities supporting Lewis, even beaten and threatened with death. Luckily for Lewis, non-communist insurgents defected rather than supporting factions of the Communists or the supporters of Brookwood College labor educator A. J. Muste; Lewis then easily crushed the Communist-led National Miners Union after it formed in response to party leaders' call for independent, radical labor bodies.

Despite and in part because of all this history, including support for Herbert Hoover's re-election in 1932, Lewis took the effects of the Depression in measured stride. Years before the New Deal had been set into place, he had told an AFL convention wedded to classic volunteerism that unemployment insurance was inevitable; he had testified to a congressional committee that prices and production would need to be controlled in the name of national interest, and even that workers should have a hand in the management of their companies. He had sagely prepared himself, in other words, for the 1930s political campaigns that would bring demand for federal relief into alliance with industrial unionism.

The revitalization of the UMW rapidly followed the passage of the National Recovery Act's Section 7(a) in 1933. As Lewis knew well, the law served the interests of larger and more effectively unionized northern mines, equalizing wage rates and rationalizing an industry notorious for its chaos. Lewis became an important member of Roosevelt's Labor Advisory Board, and he won from FDR the first code that gave both significant concessions to labor and the power to implement them (unlike the rest of heavy industry, where management alone supervised the codes). Granting the eight-hour day and the five-day week, and abolishing scrip payments and company housing, it included most tellingly the dues checkoff from the payroll. Rank-and-file miners' willingness to strike, as always, played a key role in enforcing the demands, but Lewis's manipulations could not be gainsaid—even if they bolstered the capacity of union leadership to ignore members' restlessness on other occasions, assured of the mandatory flow of dues. Failure to overcome management stubbornness in the crucial "captive mines" (mines owned by steel companies for their own uses), even with the support of Roosevelt, helped persuade Lewis to take the next step. Lewis quietly began reopening channels to the various branches of the left that he had crushed, and he started to encourage others agitating within the AFL for steps toward massive industrial unionism, culminating in the formation of the Committee for Industrial Organization.

Lewis did not have to prime the pump for the wave of idealism that brought millions into the Congress of Industrial Organizations (as the CIO was renamed after the 1936 expulsion of the committee's member unions from the AFL), the most inclusive union federation since the IWW, and a hundred times larger. Although the CIO was not as democratic as the IWW, it did breach the racial barrier. Among most CIO unions, integration remained in the early years more promise than rule, but sometimes the promise seemed on the verge of realization. Such was the case of the Packinghouse Workers of Chicago, whose very symbol was black and white hands clasped together. A quarter of the packinghouse workforce, African Americans mixed better than anyone had imagined in the Packing House Workers Organizing Committee social events; through solidarity they managed to overcome suspicion on both sides, even as ethnic whites returning to neighborhoods from work faced vastly different conditions than black workers, sustaining inequality at every moment off the job.[21]

Nor did Lewis, in his more conservative moods, need to stoke the right. By 1938 the newly-formed House Committee on Un-American Activities, led by Texas Democratic Martin Dies and stocked with unembarrassed Dixiecrat racists, began to hold hearings on the role of labor, especially the UAW in the famed Flint, Michigan, sit-down strikes. Republicans in the fall elections registered their first comeback since the stockmarket crash, a telling blow to the Roosevelt administration's left-liberal leanings.

Meany's Politics

Older craft labor leaders alarmed by developments and the rambunctious behavior of someone like Lewis increasingly appreciated the cut of Meany's jib. He could be trusted to be like them. One of those most impressed by Meany was John Sullivan, president of the New York State Federation of Labor. In 1932, Meany—no stranger to bureaucratic maneuver—won a position on the state executive board with Sullivan's sponsorship. He retained his standing in New York City, adding a post on the executive committee of the central organization of delegates from a wide range of city unions. This last position automatically expanded Meany's personal associations well beyond the construction trades. The state executive board further widened his access both to union leaders outside the city organization and—especially important to his future behavior and outlook—to state politicians. Hitherto never much more than a competent, loyal union functionary, George Meany found his métier on the job of drafting a state unemployment insurance plan. Working with the state commissioner of labor, he formulated a state-controlled fund based on contributions from employers and employees. Approved by Governor Herbert Lehman, it failed to pass the Republican-controlled state legislature in 1934. But it effectively enhanced the prestige of the upwardly mobile Meany.

This move had special importance in New York, where the large bloc of socialistic voters had long since convinced politicians, especially Democrats, of the need to make deals useful to all sides. Certain advances in protective laws, factory inspections, and such owed their origins to labor's voting power in the Progressive Era. During the 1920s, as Communists and Socialists fought employers and each other to a standstill in the needle trades, the once-powerful International Ladies Garment Workers Union lay in a shambles, further threatened by a "dual" union formed at the end of the 1920s by Communist supporters. A few years later, the ILGWU would revive to become one of the largest and most vigorous affiliates of the AFL—and one of Meany's key sources of support in the decades ahead. But the ILGWU had gotten through its worst days (and vanquished its Communist rival in the process) mainly because its leaders found ready support among certain state politicians and financial figures. In 1929, then-Lieutenant Governor Lehman joined three prominent bankers in lending the union $100,000, and with then-Governor Franklin Roosevelt's assistance, impelled garment manufacturers' associations eager for stability within the industry to sign working contracts with the ILGWU.[23]

The garment union had indeed been saved—but at a price. Its independence had been compromised by cosiness with employers, who would be owed favors into the indefinite future. Critics complained, with good reason, that an alliance with mobsters had also underwritten the compact, crime lords receiving in return a freer hand to do business in New York labor circles. Nevertheless, it was a victory of sorts and a clear signal for a certain type of labor leader, scarcely more democratic than Lewis, to move ahead with political projects. Emboldened by events around him, Meany set his sights on wider personal influence.

Fortuitously for Meany, the end of Prohibition opened new political space around labor. Governor Lehman appointed state AFL President John Sullivan to the newly formed State Alcoholic Beverages Commission at the end of 1933, and Sullivan resigned his union post for the lucrative advancement. The executive board of the state federation, mandated to choose an interim president, was perfectly placed for Meany's next advance. He was narrowly defeated by Bartender and Hotel Employees union leader Emanuel Kovelesky, an influential upstate Republican with twenty-four years seniority on the executive committee. Undaunted, Meany prepared for the August 1934 Buffalo convention, using all the political skills that he had acquired. His methods were questioned by some—at considerable expense he bused in his supporters, known as pretty tough customers, from Greater New York—but he had the votes, defeating Kovelesky 235 to 183.[24]

Meany remained head of the New York state AFL for over five years, running four times for re-election, always unopposed, and very much taking part in the day-to-day horse-trading, chicanery, and conservatism that characterized business unionism. Compared to the surging CIO, New York's AFL under his leadership remained throughout the 1930s a bastion of craft privilege and petty fiefdoms. But compared to the average run of AFL leaders, particularly in the building trades, Meany demonstrated a certain independence and vigor. With the exception of a proposed state minimum wage law which he determinedly opposed in 1937, he lent his energies to shaping and pushing through the state version of New Deal social welfare legislation.[25]

Meany's grand accomplishment, a state unemployment insurance program, passed the New York state legislature in 1935. Governor Lehman reciprocated Meany's good will, and the two collaborated on a wide range of issues. Meany might have sooner become the major player in Democratic politics he would later be, but for the peculiarities of New York. A victorious and popular La Guardia irresistibly drew opportunity-seekers like Meany away from their basic loyalties to the Tammany camp. In a 1937 Works Progress Administration radio tribute to LaGuardia, Meany even provided the labor "voice," an odd specimen of working-class leadership but an authentic symbol of bedfellows around the New Deal coalition.[26]

Meany never became a blind loyalist to Roosevelt. The same Works Progress Administration, established in 1935 to administer public works programs, placed large numbers of the unemployed onto the dole. Because its objective was to remove as many as possible from welfare rolls at the lowest possible cost, the question of pay rates strained the relations between the Roosevelt administration and the construction unions. When what was called the "security wage" was divided by the minimum number of work hours required, the result proved to be an hourly pay scale that amounted to less than half the "prevailing wage rate" in contracts covering unionized construction workers in private industry. Meany insisted that if government resources were not adequate for paying the union rate for ninety hours per month, the pay scale should be maintained by reducing the number of hours to be worked. General Hugh Johnson, former head of the National Recovery Administration and then WPA administrator for New York City, made some concessions, but not enough to satisfy the unions. In 1935, the New York City Central Trades and Labor Council struck the WPA, calling upon all its members on WPA projects to walk off their jobs. Joseph Ryan headed the city-wide union council, but the strike committee was led by Meany. The apparent anomaly that the only strike Meany personally led in his entire history was against the U.S. government might reflect an old-fashioned, "no politics" AFL outlook, except that Meany otherwise spent much of his time lobbying for and against legislation or government procedures. This strike, at any rate, was roundly denounced by FDR and the press. Yet enough unionists responded to cripple some of the projects dependent on skilled craftsmen. Two months later, the government settled the strike on union terms.[27]

Yet, in a day when even many conservative AFL leaders talked about the need for a labor or labor-farmer party, Meany did not break with the Roosevelt administration.[30] He had supported Roosevelt in 1932, and though in 1936 he abandoned, at least formally, his strong opposition to any third parties and endorsed the American Labor Party (ALP), Meany had not lost faith in the two-party system or in Gompers's maxim to reward friends and punish enemies within that system. The ALP, a New York state party, was conceived as an electoral device (though it subsequently proved far more than that) to strengthen FDR's chances for winning a second term. Meany was persuaded, like Roosevelt himself, that Norman Thomas, the Socialist presidential candidate, might receive enough votes from leftward-moving Democrats to throw New York State's electoral total into the Republican column and even, possibly, cost the national election. The ALP, organized by unionists with Roosevelt's name at the top of its "independent" ticket, would siphon off those who sought a non-machine, liberal outlet before they would vote for Roosevelt. The ALP did manage to get three hundred thousand votes for Roosevelt, although his margin in New York was so huge, in the end, that the new party's importance lay elsewhere. With Roosevelt's return to office, Meany's third-party detour was quickly forgotten, even though the American Labor Party continued.[29]

Labor had lost twice over in the process. Independent political action, which had rested with the Socialist Party through most of the first two decades of the twentieth century and then shifted partly to the short-lived experiments with national farmer-labor parties in the 1920s, had only survived through regional movements of the upper Midwest. The Depression prompted the election of a handful of socialists, and once again spawned wide third party enthusiasm, this time centered in AFL central labor councils of the East and Midwest. A heated debate at the 1935 AFL convention found labor party advocates continually stifled by parliamentary maneuvers and other steamroller tactics of the leadership. Nevertheless, a labor party resolution barely failed, with a majority of the delegates from state and local federations favoring the move. Mass rallies, alliances with unemployed movements, and local third-party organizations already in motion promised an emergent independent labor politics—that is, until the rising CIO leadership, along with the AFL's conservative wing, pulled organized labor back into line. A national Gallup Poll as late as 1937 revealed that nearly twenty percent of those asked said they would support a labor party. Many unionists believed it inevitable in the future, after Roosevelt left office.[30] Still, enthusiasm for Roosevelt after the passage of the Wagner Act was unquestionably widespread among labor voters. The package of social programs in the "Second New Deal" of 1935-36, including Social Security, brought millions of European-born workers into electoral activity for the first time, energized millions of other apathetic (or even Republican) native-born working class voters, and made Roosevelt a virtual saint in large parts of the Jewish community. But even FDR's greatest labor booster, Sidney Hillman, noted with surprise that third party enthusiasm remained high after the 1936 election sweep. In New York state, ALP voters wanted something more than a shield for Roosevelt, and ILGWU members in particular voted for labor party resolutions over David Dubinsky's vociferous objections. So did the congressional representatives of third parties, especially Minnesota's celebrated father of Social Security legislation, Farmer-Labor Party Representative Ernest Lundeen, and the Progressives who still ruled the statehouse in next-door Wisconsin.[31]

The political situation was complicated by labor's internal division over industrial unionism. As late as 1934, Lewis had no intention of splitting the AFL; he wanted to dominate from within instead. Disappointed in his initial moves toward that end, he upset the AFL old guard by welcoming into the UMW steel worker militants who had been expelled from their archaic craft union for the crime of being Communists. As late as March 1935, Lewis stated the case for industrial comprehensiveness over craft jurisdiction to the AFL's executive council, and was flatly voted down. The passage of the Wagner Act in June set Lewis in motion. At the 1935 AFL convention, Lewis put his opponents on the grill, and as much as called upon delegates to revolt against their masters. Defeated in a vote and insulted, Lewis made his point by punching out "Bill" Hutcheson, the gangsterish leader of the carpenters, in what became known, after a common saying about the American Revolution's onset, as the "blow heard 'round the world." More drama than anything else (Lewis later resumed close friendship with his old poker buddy Hutcheson), the gesture consolidated the Committee for Industrial Organization within the AFL. Lewis meanwhile moved workers like chess pieces on a board, utilizing his influence upon rubber workers to encourage their strikes, but devoting his main attention to steel workers. These maneuvers compelled Green to respond. In July 1935, the executive council expelled all CIO affiliates on the grounds of "dual unionism," an unpopular move among even rank-and-file craft workers, thus giving Lewis the means and legitimacy he required to form an independent organization. In this radicalizing circumstance, the ex-socialist union boss Max Zaritsky of the capmakers and his more powerful counterpart David Dubinsky furiously sought to prevent an industrial union body from forming, pleading instead for a compromise that would keep all labor within AFL hegemony. CIO board members made one last bid for amity and then, spurned by the AFL leaders, they moved ahead.[32]

But they moved ahead to the New Deal as much as toward industrial unionism. Ironically, labor party support among AFL local bodies was actually undercut by the CIO, removing radicals from deliberations and resetting local Communists' intentions. The defection of former labor party local backers toward a New Deal-supporting CIO bloc called Labor's Non-Partisan League (LNPL) during and following Roosevelt's triumph nearly finished off the labor party idea in most places.[33]

Meany, born to be part of a political machine and happiest as part of a larger one, proved himself alert to the need for the occasional threat of a labor party and then relieved when it failed to develop into anything more.

Ties to the New Deal administration were nevertheless strained repeatedly. Once again, the "prevailing rate" issue loomed large. During 1939, hard-pressed by conservatives, Roosevelt signed a bill that increased the number of hours to 130 per month for WPA workers without a commensurate pay increase, thus deeply undercutting the "prevailing rate" of wages in private industry. Strikes ensued. Roosevelt once more rebuked the strikers, and Meany once more championed their cause. But the will to resist the administration had now been softened by changed economic circum-stances. By 1939, unemployment was sharply reduced from 1935 levels, with far fewer skilled union workers dependent on the WPA. That factor diminished the practical threat of lower government rates undermining wage scales in private industry. The strike petered out in several weeks. Meany retaliated by blocking a resolution endorsing Roosevelt for a third term at the 1939 state convention of the AFL, around the same time that mineworkers' leader Lewis again voiced threats of forming a labor party. These gestures were not serious, however, and the wounds healed quickly enough. The next year, Meany rallied New York labor behind Roosevelt and the Democrats in the presidential campaign. The vast majority of AFL and CIO workers went along, while the erratic John L. Lewis actually endorsed the liberal Republican candidate, Wendell Wilkie.

Meany's own star had risen considerably higher by this time. A 1935 *Who's Who in American Labor* failed to mention him among hundreds of union leaders given biographical treatments. After several years as a state federation president, all that had changed. From 1934 to 1939, Meany addressed hundreds of meetings. The 1935 and 1939 WPA strikes placed his name on the front pages of the press. He testified regularly before state legislative committees. His aid and advice were sought increasingly by Mayor LaGuardia and Governor Lehman. Even FDR invited him for a friendly chat. In the AFL, he rose to first-name terms with members of the executive council. His reputation was boosted by a huge labor event that he initiated on the opening day of the August 1939 national AFL conven-tion. At least one hundred thousand unionists marched, and politicians were delighted to be invited guests, making it an event perfect for the era when Democrats at all levels counted heavily upon the "labor vote." The glitter-ing prestige for leaders, without the bother of real contact with ordinary working people, offered a glimpse at the future labor statesman of a media-made world.[34]

Unlike Gompers, who forged the trade union bureaucracy, Meany merely earned the right to move into the established national chain of command. The secretary-treasurer of the AFL in 1939 was long-ago socialist Frank Morrison, age 79, who had held the second spot since 1897, during the early days of Gompers's return to power. The executive board, determined that the old man go, approached Meany to take the job. The pay was no greater ($10,000 and perks) and the shift from Albany to Washington was a trial for a family with three young daughters. But Meany glimpsed his destiny. In November 1939, following a nominating speech by John Coefield of the Plumbers International and addresses by the Teamsters' Dan Tobin, and Joseph Ryan—altogether, three of labor's least appetizing figures—Meany assumed the new post.

Meanwhile, the stodgy federation enjoyed its own geological shift in the middle 1930s. The AFL, which had entered the Roosevelt era as an emaciated federation of primarily craft and frequently corrupt affiliates, had gained weight, thanks in part to the Wagner Act, but had changed its character little, if any. In fact, the institutional security for labor that government made possible also supported the AFL's own bureaucratic growth in ways previously unimaginable. The new dispensation reinforced the inclination of leaders to put business ahead of union members. Newer AFL members, mostly recruited through negotiation with employers rather than won over by persuasion or personal involvement, came to be seen only as clients by union leaders—and often bothersome, ungrateful clients at that. "Sweetheart" contracts arranged by employers to forestall CIO organizing drives were part of an anti-radical strategy that also included cooperation with the Dies Committee, with AFL officials giving investigators "names" of alleged Communists to be interrogated.

Meany's sponsors discerned that this "young man" (as Coefield described Meany, at 45 a generation or more junior to his fellow AFL leaders) could run the office effectively and bring credit to the changing AFL, with no threat to their internal machinations or fundamental conservatism. The most impressive thing about Meany thus far, including his avid lobbying, had been precisely his silence on the questions that concerned the AFL chiefs most: the labor movement's internal power struggle. His tenure as state president coincided with the birth of industrial unionism within the womb of the AFL and then outside. But in all the passionate debates at AFL conventions, Meany conspicuously held his tongue. In subsequent interviews with biographers, Meany rationalized that as a representative of a state federation, he had only one vote at national conventions. It was not a convincing explanation of why the leader of a state affiliate with one-quarter of the total AFL membership should remain silent on critical questions. In fact, he scarcely saw fit to take the floor on any subject at a national AFL convention during this period. His maiden speech was not until 1938, when he was prevailed upon to attack Lewis, the CIO, and the American Labor Party. Just two years after his own temporary endorsement of the ALP, he assailed it as a "class party" and avowed that "there is no place in America for a party founded on class or caste lines," conspicuously absenting those Democratic and Republican machines that operated precisely on the basis of race, ethnicity, and economic privilege.

Gaining the office of AFL secretary-treasurer, Meany assumed that his proven skills in lobbying for the state federation in Albany would be rewarded by comparable assignments on the Congressional level. That was not at all what Gompers's successor as AFL president, the mediocre and insecure William Green, had in mind. Green was not prepared to run the risk of being eclipsed by a hard-working and aggressive collaborator—and he faced new danger in an attempted palace coup launched by Hutcheson and Lewis, who had taken the UMW out of the CIO in 1940 after a fight with fellow industrial unionists over supporting Roosevelt. According to secret plans, if Lewis's union returned to the AFL, Green would be dumped and Meany advanced to his place. When the plot was exposed, Meany denied any complicity. But the vindictive Green made sure to keep his rival out of sight. During the twelve years that Meany remained secretary—until Green's death in 1952—he was called upon only once to testify before a congressional committee.[35]

Meany and the CIO

Meany so despised the CIO and those who had built it that he hardly grasped its importance as a social force—or the subtle changes that brought it from a dynamic birth to a bureaucratic adolescence in a few short years. He had often suggested before 1940 that the CIO was not even a genuine labor movement but merely a vehicle for Lewis and Roosevelt to satisfy the former's ego and the latter's need for a popular political base. This curious view about the larger of the nation's two labor federations, an opinion not unique to Meany within AFL circles, reflected a deep prejudice toward unskilled workers at large, and people of color and women in particular, as being unsuited to form or sustain "real," meaning craft, unions. The social and human impulses that drove the actions of hundreds of thousands of workers, quite apart from the CIO leaders' machinations, were invisible to him, or perhaps simply alien to his notion of what unions should be.

Meany's mental division of "us"—white male workers—and "them" (everyone else) had served him well in the eras of uncontested craft privilege. At the 1934 AFL convention, an overwhelmingly black Brotherhood of Sleeping Car Porters, led by A. Philip Randolph, gained only the support of the UMW and the ILGWU in a call for the AFL to expel any affiliated union that refused to eliminate the whites-only clause from its constitution. (The AFL, piling insult upon injury, ordered the Sleeping Car Porters to dissolve so that the all-white and newly-chartered Order of Sleeping Car Conductors could replace them.) The same attitude would appear again during the purge of Communist sympathizers during the Cold War years, when Meany could count on avowedly racist support, and still later during Meany's assault upon the peace and justice movements of the 1960s and 1970s, when the rhetoric had to be adjusted but the familiar right-wing allies appeared. Stubborn adherence to this division within labor was one element of Meany's strategic straightjacket. In contrast even to the heavily bureaucratized labor federations of Europe, which could nevertheless rally a huge and idealistic social movement, lifting up its leaders to ever greater heights during the political moment of the 1930s-1940s, labor leaders like Meany would intuitively seek personal perks and occasional good publicity rather than power backed by mobilization of lower layers of the evolving society. Nor could Meany comprehend how readily developments in labor would accomodate his own dominance.[36]

Ironically, given the rise of the competitor CIO and its early opposition to Roosevelt's New Deal, the AFL enjoyed a real resurgence toward the end of the 1930s, entirely apart from its will to accomodate. The International Association of Machinists, for instance, with its own historically strong left-wing tendencies, proved able to compete well for aircraft workers rapidly increasing in number with the coming of world war. Teamsters, electrical workers, and others saw similar resurgences especially where (as so often) the CIO organizing drives were created from the outside, without either the old contacts of AFL central federations or the vaunted new industrial democracy of the more flexible CIO unions to give them the advantage. Indeed, in the case of the Teamsters, aggressive encouragement to workers in related industries created in a few places a cross-industrial union more like the old Knights of Labor than the regular AFL or CIO. By 1938, the AFL had more members all-told, if far fewer industrial members, than the CIO.[37]

International politics, meanwhile, reinforced the tendency of Democratic Party victories to absorb the militance in labor's new industrial ranks. The Communist Party's declaration of a Popular Front against fascism subordinated the impulses of yesterday's committed militants and provided rising labor leaders both the rationalizations and the mechanisms necessary to clamp down on restiveness in the ranks. From the Communist point of view—which counted heavily in the large new industrial unions—potential American alliance with the Soviet Union on international issues, however problematic, was paramount. Opposing radical groups and many working people held views closer to a familiar anti-capitalism, but their influence was slight.[38]

Paradoxically and simultaneously, industrial unionism—though born of the radicalism of Toledo, Minneapolis, and San Francisco—became a new mode of enforcing the contract. Attempts to seize back the initiative from foremen and time-study experts were met, now, with directives from industrial union leaders to stay in line until a grievance could be properly negotiated. Soon, union dues would be deducted automatically from wages, so that officials no longer needed to bother making personal contact and monthly appeals to the loyalty of members.[39]

Meany, treating industrial unionists at large as enemies, could not for many years grasp that events were bringing the CIO's elected officials closer to him. He was steeped in a craft tradition to which the very idea of workers united into a single, roughly egalitarian body hinted at revolutionary transformation. But many less conservative sectors were equally surprised by the course of the more democratic CIO unions toward the end of the 1930s. A triangle of government, business, and labor leadership brought about a compact that served mutual interest in stability, though often not the interests of the workers left out of this power arrangement.

Not until 1937 did business unionism confirm its institutional form, when the Supreme Court upheld the Wagner Act. Now, a legitimate union (that is to say, a union legitimated by the National Labor Relations Board) with more than 50 percent of the vote in a union election became the sole bargaining agent for all. Unions stood on the brink of a membership gold-rush. The left-led Farm Equipment union could that same year, for instance, win a tremendous victory of five thousand workers at International Harvester in Chicago without a strike, thanks to the NLRB-sanctioned vote.[40] But union leaders also prepared to reciprocate the assistance with a crackdown against membership indiscipline. The United Auto Workers, a case in point, arose out of Wobbly traditions mixed with a 1920s Communist-led Auto Workers Union and an amalgam of radicals' efforts to work within early CIO formations. The fate of the industry, which fought back furiously against unionization, was set by the famed 1937 sit-down strikes centered in Flint, which seemed for a moment to bring the region close to class and civil war. Only the personal intercession of Michigan's liberal Governor Murphy, it was widely believed, had prevented a bloodbath of employers' armed goons retaking the basic means of production and setting off something like a class war. Therein lay a contradiction which the likes of George Meany could appreciate without being able to comprehend fully. The notorious willingness of UAW members to halt production until their grievances were met did not end because the union had employed the good offices of the governor (and the appeals of Franklin Roosevelt) to bring union recognition. On the one hand, a vast social movement of the unemployed grew up around the auto workers' strongholds in Michigan, generating a sustained classwide movement of employed and unemployed, lasting until wartime brought near full employment. On the other hand, union leaders, including UAW leaders, swiftly traded off benefits for discipline in an uneven process complicated by strategic and often-changing conflicts within the political left.[41]

The continuing struggle for more complete democratic participation was often restricted to the local or the particularistic, and thanks to a long-standing tradition of autonomy, sometimes to insular circles of AFL veterans. For instance, in heavily French-Canadian Woonsocket, Rhode

Island, a vibrant Independent Textile Union had sprung up out of a history of severe repression and the riotous 1934 general textile strike. The ITU remained outside the CIO and set about organizing workers in many industries across Woonsocket; then, after a conservatizing wartime phase, it died slowly with the postwar shutdown of the mills. To take another example, the All Workers Union of Austin, Minnesota—an IWW-like entity which would reappear in spirit during the 1980s as rebellious Local P-9 of the United Food and Commercial Workers—held out for several years in the 1930s against merger. A model par excellence of "horizontal" unionism with wide democratic participation and public support, the AWU (urged by Communist regulars and Trotskyists alike) willingly yielded its autonomy, and in so doing also its internal democracy, to the overwhelming influence of the CIO. In yet another case, the Progressive Miners of America, which grew out of a grassroots rebellion against John L. Lewis's autocratic rule, attempted to place itself in the AFL that Lewis abandoned, on the basis of rank-and-file democracy with a strong dose of anti-foreign and sometimes anti-Semitic rhetoric. Or again: the AFL Seaman's Union of the Pacific, reacting ferociously to Communist efforts to discipline the sea lanes, stirred syndicalist energies and like the PMA simultaneously drew upon a racist exclusionary streak far more typical of the AFL than the CIO.[42]

These and many less dramatic experiments died or collapsed into the mainstream by wartime. But for industrial unionism at large, the damage had already been done to the possibilities of resisting creeping bureaucratization. Indeed, only where union delegates themselves decreed safety measures of decentralization, as in the UAW in 1939 (against the advice of Communists and their rivals), did conventions emerge guaranteeing participation from below, to some significant degree.[43]

The Regulatory Compact of the Second World War

Meany found his calling in the emerging world of labor regulation viewed positively by AFL and CIO leaders alike. American entry into the Second World War created an unprecedented need for the coordination of production. Unions could not be denied a role in agencies designed to mediate and arbitrate industrial disputes and to assure the flow of defense-related goods, creating an atmosphere of relative class peace after a decade of severe conflict. Even before U.S. entry, a National Labor Relations Board strengthened by Supreme Court decisions had begun to certify CIO unions over AFL company unions; where the two federations ran head to head, the CIO won seventy-five percent of the time. AFL leaders naturally turned to southern Democrats and Republicans in Congress to tame the democratic excess; although that legislative initiative failed, Roosevelt appointed two more conservative members to the NLRB. Here were Gompers's First World War hopes, realized at last. The United Auto Workers alone doubled its size, to more than a million. With war, in thousands of workplaces including major industry outside the south where unions had been forcefully excluded, unions were formally recognized—though usually from the top down, and in their most bureaucratic forms. Meany was perfectly suited for this chain-of-command style of deliberation.[44]

The United States had not yet entered the conflict in 1941, when the first such agency, the National Defense Mediation Board, was created. It had serious tasks at hand. More than two million workers, largely in basic industries, went on strike in a burst of militancy as war production and the shortage of labor gave them new confidence in their demands. The NDMB held four representatives each of the unions, government, and the public, labor's share being two CIO leaders, and Meany and Green for the AFL. The board barely operated long enough to flex its muscles, but Meany did have the opportunity to express his extreme conservatism. Lewis's UMW struck the steel corporations' own "captive mines" in 1941. The strike went into temporary abatement, however, after all parties agreed to present their case to the NDMB. The vote there went against the miners' union, Green and Meany predictably voting with public and employer representatives against the closed union shop. The CIO delegates, who cast the only votes favorable to the union, withdrew from the board in disgust—effectively killing the NDMB. Lewis almost as predictably led out the miners, anyway, and on December 7, 1941, the day Japan bombed Pearl Harbor, the closed shop was won in the steel companies' mines, no thanks to Green or Meany.[45] Lewis would quickly become, for Communists and Meany alike, the union leader they most loved to hate. As Meany, always questing for respectability, put it, "The whole labor movement got a bad reputation only because of Lewis."[46] Of course, 1941 had been a banner year for strikes generally, but Meany predictably overlooked this detail.

In 1942, with the country formally at war, Meany joined two other newly formed boards, the Combined Labor Board and the National War Labor Board. The first was a sort of consultative labor cabinet consisting exclusively of union representatives that met regularly with Roosevelt. The second and more significant body began as a wartime continuation of the NDMB with similar representation from the unions, the public, and employers. It lasted for the duration of the war, evolving into a major instrument for containing grievances, with growing jurisdiction over wages. Enfeebled AFL President Green's frequent absences put Meany in the catbird seat. Once more, as in the WPA controversies (but perhaps now for the last time), Meany gave voice in WLB meetings to the legitimate grievances of unionized workers. Profits, along with consumer prices, soared while wage increases were paltry by comparison. Meany took the offensive when the board voted in favor of limiting wage increases to 15 precent, the famous Little Steel formula, grossly inadequate to contemporary living standards. But his pleas and arguments, backed with facts and figures, did not often impress obdurate negotiators. Millions of workers did gain advances during wartime, but only by threatening and using a weapon that George Meany abhorred and condemned: the strike.[47]

Even before the United States engaged militarily, Meany was in the forefront of those labor leaders who pledged to business and the government no strikes for the duration of the war. Industry leaders, for their part, never offered to hold profits at the same levels, or to abandon union-busting when convenient. As Meany reflected in 1944 at the national AFL convention: "I know that we have to sacrifice and no matter how this decision goes against us . . . we will go along, we will not rock the boat. . . ." Ironically, these words paraphrased what American Communist union leaders said from the day Russia was attacked by Germany in June 1941 until the end of the war. Neither Meany nor the CPUSA gave heed to the speed-ups that left some fifty-three thousand workers dead in workplace accidents in 1941-1944, and three hundred thousand permanently disabled. The six-day and seven-day weeks became common once more, inflation was horrendous, and residential overcrowding reached new heights. Restlessness inevitably broke out among workers, and in most instances unions moved quickly to stifle it.

Again, it was the mine workers who brought out the deepest meaning of Meany. Striking in 1943 for a pay increase that went far beyond the limits acceptable to the War Labor Board, they virtually compelled the government to enter the negotiations. Meany took the extreme anti-strike position—virtually the same as that taken by Communists—by arguing that the administration had no right to bargain with a wrongfully striking union. When the mine workers finally won a contract that provided a much-improved wage and benefit package, Meany berated the administration for ever having submitted to an illegal strike.[48] Meany turned his criticism of Roosevelt into arguments for conservatism. In the 1944 presidential election year, when virtually all union leaders placed themselves securely and familiarly in the FDR camp, Meany opted for Republican Thomas E. Dewey. Not that Meany believed the Republicans, hungry to wipe out labor victories, would be friends of the AFL. But Meany perceived the former district attorney to be tougher on the Soviet Union. As Gompers had drawn temporary strength and prestige from his enthusiastic support for the government in the First World War, Meany anticipated the Cold War and set his course accordingly—an irony, given that his own wartime labor policy so closely matched the Communist Party's.

Anticommunist Consolidation

Franklin Delano Roosevelt's death in 1945, like his political career, proved a landmark for federal labor policies and unionists' responses. During his White House years, FDR sought at once to cultivate and to curb the labor movement. By the war, he leaned strongly toward the latter. Even then, Roosevelt's policy was to contain unions and utilize their growing resources, not crush them. In that spirit, he doubtless did help to blunt the ferocious anti-union attack mounted by conservatives during 1940-1941. His "Dr. Win the War," while ending the program of structural reforms begun in the 1930s, also restrained the anti-labor efforts of industry and the Republicans in Congress (who nearly retook the House in 1942, after twelve years out of power). Limited protection from FDR plus the vast growth of the productive forces and a late surge of militancy permitted unions to grow from less than 9 to more than 15 million members, more or less evenly divided between the two federations. Unionists of almost every kind bemoaned FDR's death in 1945. The ascension of Harry Truman was, however, the answer to a conservative unionist's prayers.

Yet the postwar labor movement began unpleasantly for Meany. Strike waves unprecedented even by the 1936-1937 scale, if more narrowly focused for the most part on wages and working conditions, inevitably spilled over into radicals' hopes and conservatives' rage. It was, in retrospect, the last great upsurge before the long night ahead. Local AFLers, not tied to the CIO's enforcement of the wartime "no strike" pledge, several times actually led the way against a threatened return to Depression-era wages in city "general strikes," from Oakland, California, to Terre Haute, Indiana. Walter Reuther, atop a very militant UAW, set upon outmaneuvering the Communists by demonstrating his own militancy, offering (as he would often in the era from the 1940s to the 1960s) the leading contrast to Meany's personality and political symbolism.[50]

In November 1945, a General Motors strike of 113 days launched the charge, and the membership responded enthusiastically. Even the UAW's slogan—"We fight today for a better tomorrow"—was indicative of a determination not to concede to the 1919-style postwar red scare that would persecute radicals and derail labor. Cleverly, Reuther called for wage increases not to result in price increases, but to come out of big wartime profits. For what would be the last time in a long, long time—with Reuther himself greeted as a virtual savior in the *New Republic*—the UAW seemed to be speaking credibly for the public at large, for the right of workers to higher wages in order to participate in the national prosperity. A National Citizens Committee on the strike and a National Committee to Aid the Strikers enshrined notables from the widowed Eleanor Roosevelt to theologian Reinhold Niebuhr in Reuther's defense. *Time* ran Reuther's picture on its cover, and *Fortune* described him as a coming representative of the consumer in a triumvirate of national leadership with capital and government. He was, within the narrow sphere of the acceptable labor leader, Meany's liberal arch-rival.[51]

Reuther's prestige was badly damaged as other CIO leaders readily settled with non-auto industrialists who wanted (and got) permission to take the lid off price controls while holding labor to minimal gains. Simultaneously, Reuther himself agreed to new restraints upon shop floor activity, something which, however reduced from the union's earliest days, had remained the very mark of the UAW's distinction within organized labor at large. Reuther weakly claimed a moral victory at the end of the strike; but within a few months, the explosion of prices eradicated the wage gains, while the new discipline of the membership remained forever fixed—except by occasional wildcat revolts against the union-enforced contract.

The turn of events during the next few years considerably damaged organized labor's influence and prestige, while offering much advantage for Meany's personal positioning within the labor bureaucracy. The press, aroused by the strike wave, rapidly moved to blame "the Communists"— though the CP had been all too eager to maintain wartime unity, usually at labor's expense, into the postwar period, until Cold War tensions ended their hope. Reuther and his counterparts in an assortment of CIO unions made a sophisticated case for anti-communist witch-hunters that was beyond the ken of reactionary politicians, assailing Communists as the "outside influence" interrupting labor unity, an unwanted presence that could only be eliminated by bureaucratic mechanisms or government intervention.

The unpopularity of Harry Truman, bringing Republicans back to power in Congress for the first time since 1930, meanwhile gave labor's conservatives just the encouragement that they needed. The Association of Catholic Trade Unionists (ACTU), earlier engaged in what they considered democratic struggles against minority Communist leaderships of union headquarters and locals, turned swiftly to the right after the war. Demanding the expulsion of Communists and the dismemberment of unions which could not be brought into line, their local members joined local businessmen and the tabloid press, placing labor leftists of all kinds within their crosshairs, working with local FBI branches and the tabloid press on what might be called counter-insurgency campaigns of dirty tricks and libel. The anti-union bloc in Congress meanwhile proved powerful enough, a year later, to override President Truman's veto of the Taft-Hartley bill, a catastrophic legislative defeat for labor.[52]

Meany and his CIO counterparts could now appeal for business unionism and a modest continuation of New Deal social programs against both Republican efforts to roll back benefits and the popular working-class sentiment for more labor leverage within the vast expansion of postwar capitalism. The bourgeois vision of "free labor" and "free capital" bargaining together in good faith was, moreover, one that a suddenly more cautious Reuther now made his own. As the CIO executive body prepared the measures for the expulsion of Communists, liberal union leaders met Meany more than half-way.[53]

Within the AFL, the struggle against Taft-Hartley was led by Meany in one of the very rare courageous or militant moments of his life. Full of provisions generally circumscribing unions' political efforts—especially prohibiting sympathy strikes—Taft-Hartley also required as a condition for NLRB recognition that union officials certify they were neither members of nor sympathetic to Communist organizations. Based upon his record, it would seem that Meany (and most other union officials, save Communists themselves) would have found this measure unobjectionable. And yet, at least for a moment, Meany was enough of a trade unionist to perceive the non-Communist affidavit as a measure to weaken, disorient, and humble the entire trade union movement.

Meany also briefly sought a repeal of Taft-Hartley, but as a practical labor politician, he quickly acquiesced to its enforcement. At the 1947 AFL convention, Lewis, who brought his mine workers union back into the AFL that year, wanted to "boycott" the provisions by refusing to sign the loyalty oath. (So did the proud International Typographers Union, the eldest continuous labor institution in the nation.) Lewis employed all his oratorical skills. The task of answering Lewis fell to Meany. His speech, although no match for Lewis's in style or content, was apparently relished by the delegates, particularly when he charged Lewis with the dreadful sin of having been "a comrade to the comrades." Meany stressed that Taft-Hartley had been democratically enacted and that he, personally, was more than ready to sign the anti-Communist affidavit. He observed later that as far as he was concerned, Taft-Hartley had not been so bad after all and "we sort of over-reacted."[54]

The CIO opposition melted, though Phil Murray briefly took a stand against Taft-Hartley, refusing to sign an affadavit and advising each international to decide for itself. Refusal by an officer or member meant loss of protections under the law, and the CIO center, eager to find reasons to purge its enemies, rushed to comply. Walter Reuther immediately directed UAW organizers to raid anti-communist locals of all kinds affiliated with Communist-led internationals. These raids prompted the United Electrical Workers and Farm Equipment Workers—correctly anticipating the effort to finish them off—to withdraw from the CIO, which responded by chartering a "dual" International Union of Electrical, Radio, and Machine Workers. In 1950, the CIO expelled nine more unions: Mine, Mill, and Smelter; Fur and Leather Workers; Food, Tobacco, and Allied Workers; Marine Cooks and Stewards' Association, Fishermen's Union; the International Longshoremen's and Warehousemen's Union; United Office and Professional Workers; the American Communications Association; National Furniture Workers; and the United Public Workers of America.

These were fascinating cases, and not only because defiant left-wing leaderships were supported by the members. The United Electrical Workers had pioneered the wage offensive for greater parity of women's wages to men's, an idea unthinkable in the AFL and most of the CIO. At its peak, it had reached a membership of almost a half-million. Food, Tobacco and Mine, Mill were the most aggressive and egalitarian unions organizing among African Americans in the South, and, in the case of Mine, Mill, Chicanos in the Southwest. The Longshoremen had distinguished themselves by successfully organizing large numbers of native Hawaiians and Japanese workers on the islands as well as Filipinos in fishpacking factories of Alaska and the mainland; and Marine Cooks and Stewards, allied with the Longshoremen, had a certain notoriety as the gayest union in the nation. None of them, except the Fur and Leather Workers, represented the familiar New York and Jewish left (even the furriers were also heavily Hungarian and Greek); the expelled unions actually represented a fair sampling of the racially variegated American industrial working class that the AFL and CIO had, on the whole, failed to reach. The UOPWA, never supported adequately by the CIO mainstream or the left, was the foremost mobilizer of white-collar women workers, from book editors and dance instructors to direct-mail clericals, and the United Public Workers was the original government employees' union.[55]

Thus, the purged CIO had lost more than the organizational numbers alone could suggest. Tens of thousands of activists from the 1930s-1940s, from the former editor of the *CIO News*, Len DeCaux, to the purely ordinary idealists of the rank and file, were sidelined, often permanently. The task of broadening union ranks to include the vast numbers of workers outside of major manufacturing sectors and the old trades also fell to the side. The long-anticipated and much-discussed "Operation Dixie" of the CIO to organize the largely unorganized South, black and white, at first showed promise; the Food and Tobacco Workers had actually won eighteen elections during 1946-1947 by stressing integrated locals and black organizers and by promoting local black leaders. But as the Cold War accelerated and the most insistently interracial unions were driven from the CIO, the campaign for southern membership was practically reduced to textile workers and steelworkers. By 1951, organized labor had given up the fight, and it would not be renewed until the 1970s. The grand dream of reorganizing American politics in labor's favor by organizing the South had faded away.[56] Likewise, organization of the rapidly expanding "pink collar" trades of office work, heavily female, garnered virtually no concern. Telephone workers organized in the Communications Workers of America, also clerks organized by the Retail, Wholesale, and Department Store Union (CIO) and their rival, the Retail Clerks International Association (AFL), did manage to hold on, without generating much assistance or recognition that they represented labor's future. Even the organization of public sector workers, well underway among the hundred thousand United Public Workers, went into abeyance or simply collapsed with the destruction of politically proscribed unions.[57] Such a revival awaited another day, the late 1950s to late 1960s. The notion that one day unions would desperately need female and non-white workers in order to survive would not have occurred to the likes of Meany, in particular; the AFL had largely gotten along quite well in its way, after all, precisely through the mechanisms of excluding those groups from the best-paid, highest-benefit positions.

In the showdown with Lewis, Meany established himself as the man most likely to succeed the fading Green, particularly because the miners' leader had sent Green his famous "we disaffiliate" memo after the 1947 convention, taking his mine workers out of the AFL again, this time into the wilderness. By defending the purge of the labor movement, Meany had placed himself at the forefront of a bureaucracy eager to benefit from the pork barrel of military Keynesianism, and ready to denounce as disloyal anyone who disputed the need for the military build-up to further hasten the economy's acceleration. This was the kind of labor leader that businessmen could accept, as their predecessors had—especially in moments of general anxiety about the left or industrial workers—accepted Gompers before him.

Not that Meany was incapable of left rhetoric when it suited him. On national radio in 1947, he had inveighed against the "paid spokesmen of big business," presumably Republican rather than Democratic, and asked whether capitalism had in effect ordered that the "class struggle is about to shift from the economic to the political field." Third party talk flourished momentarily as Truman's public opinion ratings sank, and Meany announced the creation of Labor's League for Political Education at the 1947 AFL convention.[58] For some overly optimistic radicals, this appeared an embryonic labor party. Such a belief was bolstered by a stirring of socialists, former New Dealers, and others inspired to establish state organizations along the lines of the Michigan Commonwealth Federation. The independent movement died as the accelerating Cold War pushed Communists and their supporters toward a Henry Wallace candidacy in 1948, and as leading AFL and CIO circles decided to overlook their criticisms of Truman and the Democrats in return for promised pieces of the pie. Like the CIO's Political Action Committee, the LLPE stayed predictably and doggedly loyal to the Democrats, a Gompers-style instrument for punishing enemies and rewarding friends.[59]

Among the friends supported were, inevitably, Truman himself, despite his many anti-labor sentiments. The Missouri backroom politician with a marked dislike of New Dealer braintrust intellectuals had a penchant for paying off old partners with business contracts and bullying opponents. Nor was he all bluff and quiet payoffs: Truman threatened to draft railway strikers, and he implemented the Taft-Hartley provision for banning strikes more often than any subsequent president, despite his symbolic veto of the measure. Like the following Democratic candidate, Adlai Stevenson, Truman had nothing approaching FDR's ability to establish and maintain rapport with organized labor. When the militancy had disappeared after 1950, with Meany in charge of the AFL and the CIO fatally weakened by expulsions, the Democrats could simply take the labor vote for granted.[60]

Bureaucratic Unity: The AFL-CIO

Perfunctory efforts to reunite the AFL and CIO had begun shortly after the split in 1937. That prospect quickly evaporated, and the rivalry was sometimes bitter. Some AFL leaders, most prominently Meany's future intelligence partner Jay Lovestone, had memorably conspired to replace the United Auto Workers with a classic AFL-style, avowedly lily-white organization led by UAW factional loser Homer Martin. But the rivalry was increasingly bureaucratic-competitive rather than substantial. The two federations increasingly functioned similarly, as Communist enforcement of wartime no-strike provisions strengthened the hand of the CIO leader-ship to limit the independence of local unionists. By the end of the 1940s, the twin wings of the labor movement shared political submissiveness and bureaucratic centralization. There was no *principled* reason why the twain could not meet. Just as important, the division had lost its historic structural rationale. The CIO had emerged in the 1930s as a response to the growth of a numerically huge, permanent class of industrial proletarians, ripe for organization since the 1910s. The AFL had refused to organize these workers and the CIO could not, except as an independent organization, undertake the task. During the 1940s, the AFL had defensively and oppor-tunistically moved in upon the field of the industrial workforce. While the proportional weight of industrial workers remained far greater in the CIO, the larger AFL had by the end of the decade as many industrial members as its rival.[61]

Unity sentiment was fostered because a divided movement inevitably gave rise to large-scale, fruitless jurisdictional battles which drained the contenders of energy and resources. Literally millions of dollars were spent by unions raiding each other in battles which produced no more than a barely perceptive shift of membership. Total union membership had, mean-while, begun to decline for the first time in more than a decade. A divided house of labor in a deteriorating climate left each federation, AFL and CIO, vulnerable to attack by hostile corporate and political powers.

Meany, committed to genuine unity, was pretty much in charge of the AFL by this time, but Green was still its president, and lukewarm at best

toward the CIO. A handful of old-time executive council members demanded that the CIO crawl back, penitent. Some insisted upon absorbing
the purged and weaker CIO salami-style, picking off unions a slice at a
time, and worked furiously at the effort, especially among the locals of the
expelled "red" unions. Lewis's independent Local 50, like the Teamsters
and assorted other unions later on, itself meanwhile sought to swallow
anything unaffiliated—and sometimes succeeded.

In 1950, an important if tentative step toward organic unity was finally
taken, with the creation of a United Labor Policy committee. The committee, with representation from both the CIO and AFL as well as delegates
from independent railway unions and the International Association of
Machinists (at the time outside the AFL), was designed to resist encroach-
ments made on workers' living standards, particularly by the Wage Stabilization Board. It also demanded a greater role in various agencies during
the Korean War. The committee met with a modicum of success, but it was
unilaterally dissolved in the fall of 1951 by the withdrawal of the AFL at
Meany's insistence. This move, seemingly inconsistent with Meany's
pro-unity position, remains difficult to fathom almost fifty years later.
Perhaps it was motivated by the fear that ULPC might become a substitution for true organizational fusion. A more likely explanation, offered by a
Meany biographer, is that Meany scuttled the committee in retaliation for
what he described as "the double-crossing tactics of the CIO delegation"
at a meeting of the International Confederation of Free Trade Unions in
far-off Milan, Italy. Ordinarily, that would be a far-fetched explanation. But
it is made plausible by the extraordinary importance Meany attached to his
international commitments, or, to put it another way, the evident depth of
his loyalty to and involvement with intelligence agencies. The purged CIO
was still not ferociously anti-communist enough for him.[62]

By 1952, in any case, Meany was back on a unity course, with the pace
accelerated by biological coincidence. CIO President Philip Murray, who
had temporized on unity, died on November 9, 1952, and was replaced by
Walter Reuther, firmly committed to organic unity. Twelve days later,
William Green, a further impediment to unity, succumbed to a heart attack;
the AFL Executive Council met a few days later and, in a deceptively
unanimous vote, elected George Meany the interim president. (Teamster
conservative Dan Tobin, who also coveted the office, fell one vote short in

an informal canvas of Council members, and declined to challenge Meany in what would surely be a losing battle.)

The AFL convention of 1953 practiced the organization's usual degree of democratic debate and deliberation: Meany was approved by acclamation. In the course of subsequent unity negotiations, Meany's character was put to the test in a new way by William Hutcheson, the carpenters' president and industrial unionism's old antagonist. Hutcheson threatened to resign from the council if the AFL endorsed Meany's "no-raiding" proposal to the CIO. This was a threat that might well have shaken William Green from a course, but not Meany. He remained steadfast before the prospect of possibly losing more than a half million members, with their substantial dues. Caught short by Meany's toughness, Hutcheson made good on his threat. Meany announced that everyone below Hutcheson on the seniority ladder be moved up a notch, and that a vacancy had opened. A month later, humiliated by a drop of support in his own union, Hutcheson brought the carpenters back into the AFL. He did not get his seat back (he died later in 1953), but Meany graciously perpetuated the kind of inheritance labor leaders had come to expect: Hutcheson's untalented son Maurice was granted a place on the council, which had no doubt about who labor's real boss was.

Unity, meanwhile, proceeded jerkily. A no-raiding pact had been worked out and approved in June 1953. By the middle of June 1954, almost all CIO affiliates had accepted the pact, although only 65 of 111 AFL affiliates had. (It did not apply, of course, to the expelled CIO unions, still considered proper targets for cutthroat competitive enterprise.) Under pressure from Meany, the joint committee nevertheless pressed ahead, unanimously agreeing "to create a single trade union center in America through the process of merger [which] will preserve the integrity of each affiliated national and international union." Transit Workers leader Mike Quill described the merger as CIO capitulation to the Three Rs: racism, racketeering, and raiding. Walter Reuther, seeking a positive note, urged unity as "a matter of believing . . . [with] no time for doubt."[63]

A succession of committee and subcommittee meetings followed. By February 1955, top leaders of both organizations had worked out an agreement of principle. Trade unionism, all agreed, had to be protected alike from corruption and Communism, and unity had to preserve the integrity of affiliated unions, while resolving internal differences through merger or other means. More practical merger arrangements followed. The two top posts were slated for George Meany, as president, and to William Schnitzler, who had been elected secretary-treasurer of the AFL in 1953 and would hold that post in the united organization. Walter Reuther, often regarded as the most dynamic of younger union leaders, would head the Industrial Union Department. A potential bridge to the mass of unorganized workers, the IUD would accept into its ranks, along with former CIO unions, only those AFL affiliates of industrial character. A new executive board would consist of executive council members—seventeen from the AFL and ten from the CIO—and the leaders of the international union affiliates. The organization's clumsy title, the American Federation of Labor-Congress of Industrial Organizations (AFL-CIO), hinted at the uncertain marriage vows.

Both organizations convened, independently, in New York during the first week of December 1955 to ratify the agreement. Some dissension marked the CIO session, with Transit Workers president Michael Quill and a few others acutely predicting that the AFL would drag a combined body down to its level. By contrast, the vote in the AFL was unanimous. On December 5, delegates joined together at New York's 71st Regiment Armory under the banner of the AFL-CIO. The joint convention went strictly according to plan. No public manifestations surfaced of the personal rivalries and conflicting conceptions that had divided the union movement for twenty years and could not, with the best will the world, be settled by a unity resolution or handclasp. The steelworkers' David McDonald bombastically hailed "the magnificent opportunity through unity to build to new heights our democratic, responsible, united labor movement." One of the least democratic union leaders, destined to be turned out of office for his incompetence and bureaucratic contempt for the membership, McDonald concluded, "Our AFL-CIO is based upon a full recognition of acceptance of the inherent dignity of the human personality." The usual tide of well-wishers ranged from Eleanor Roosevelt to perennial presidential hopeful (and liberal friend of business) Adlai Stevenson. The American Legion's National Commander J. Addington Wagner voiced the common sentiments of more fanatical delegates from the building trades to the ILGWU that despite the rapidly accelerating arms race and domestic

McCarthyism, President Eisenhower's administration was "soft on communism." Presumably, a Truman Democrat would do better.[64] For his part, Eisenhower, in a telephoned speech, declared that "the class struggle doctrine of Marx was the invention of a lonely refugee scribbling in a dark recess of the British Museum." What Marx had failed to foresee was "the mutual interest of employer and employee ... characteristic of the American economy where barriers of class do not exist." As if in a show of solidarity with the President, Meany obliged by arranging to eliminate the AFL's traditional class struggle preamble—a vestige of the movement's increasingly distant socialist origins—from the new AFL-CIO constitution.[65]

Walter Reuther's special assignment was to place Meany's name in nomination for the presidency of the organization, exalting "that great American, that great trade unionist, a man I consider a great and wonderful personal friend, George Meany." The vote was, naturally, unanimous. President-elect Meany in his acceptance speech warned against the dangers of international or jurisdictional conflicts by appealing to "organize the unorganized ... [and] not waste our time and our efforts trying to reorganize those who are already organized." He called for labor to mount a united campaign against the anti-union legislative trend of the past eight years, and also for federal aid to education, better housing, medical care, and enhanced social security—formally ending the old AFL tradition of resisting government programs in favor of "volunteerism." In a move unprecedented for himself (but probably considered necessary by his advisors for an incoming head of labor), he paused to damn the politicians who, in the interests of white supremacy, defied the recent *Brown v Board of Education* Supreme Court ruling against "separate but equal" public education.

Of course, Meany had taken no steps in the direction of ordering the acceptance of racial minorities into all-white unions under his direction, and never would. Nor did he threaten to announce the political independence of labor from the major parties who directed the Jim Crow policies that he now claimed to abhor. Against the undercurrent of labor party talk that never quite went away, he insisted, as if to reassure Eisenhower or the probable Democratic candidate, Stevenson, that he saw no sentiment for a labor party or for labor to take over the Democrats or Republicans. He had gotten a long, long way personally by rewarding friends and punishing enemies. He was at the highest possible position within the labor movement, leader of a united—if also thoroughly purged and terribly weakened—house of labor.[66]

By this time, still reportedly eager to see the Taft-Hartley Act somehow amended and made harmless, Meany had nevertheless vigorously supported all measures to apply the Act's political litmus test within labor's ranks. Under his leadership the executive council adopted in 1957 an extraordinary resolution on "Racketeers, Crooks, Communists, and Fascists" which stated that non-membership in a Communist or fascist organization was not in itself sufficient proof of loyalty; support or participation (deemed, obviously, by labor officials) was sufficient to deny that person a "position of leadership." Ex-Communists, a large and significant group by this time, were denied the right to hold office if they had not been out of the Party for at least five years. The Landrum-Griffin Act, with a similar statute, was declared unconstitutional by the Supreme Court in 1965, but the AFL-CIO got around to removing this particular phrasing only in 1974, and the remainder of its anticommunist codes only in 1997.

Cold War: Money, Espionage, and Dirty Tricks

That 1957 resolution was, in a large sense, the essence of Meany's legacy in the decades to come. Anti-radicalism was far less important for its direct effect upon Communist Party members or ex-members (whose numbers and weight steadily decreased, by way of attrition, after the McCarthy era ended), than upon the political character of organized labor at large. Meany, his associates, and his heirs held the warning club over the head of all potential and active rebels and dissidents, applied red scare rhetoric freely toward reform campaigns with no Communist involvement and used the public fear of Communist actions abroad to keep labor solidly behind the global corporate agenda. The unanimity of labor leadership in 1955 was unquestionably underpinned by mutual intelligence arrangements. Both AFL and CIO had their own special relations with domestic and international agencies. These came together smoothly, despite some demurrers on both sides, because in conservative triumph the elimination not only of Communist but also of non-Communist dissidents of any but the mildest kind had become a shared goal of the postwar period. One of the greatest curiosities of the next phase was the subversive political pasts of the especially conspiratorial figures now at the center, and the ways in which they retooled to put their hard-earned talents to work for the new establishment.

Any effort to account for the unanimity of labor's leaders on foreign policy and its importance for their overall views must first take into account the Gompers tradition. His immediate successors, contrary to the myths crafted by their apologists, had no special contribution beyond a reflexive anticommunism. Their own activities almost invariably amounted to a defense of American corporate holdings and political prerogatives everywhere in the world.[67] But this was not a uniform CIO policy. Perhaps no incident was so revealing for the future as labor's response to the Mexican government's nationalist-minded attempts in 1938 to repatriate oil profits from American conglomerates. The new CIO leadership, headed by John L. Lewis and inclined to view labor as entitled to more of the fruit of its own returns, urged a hands-off policy. AFL leaders, on the contrary, attempted to establish their own imperial affiliate in Mexico loyally bound to U.S. corporate plans. Roosevelt's Latin America policies, protective of American corporate profits, had been cautious, more given to economic and diplomatic pressures than sending in the Marines. With world war on the horizon, he wisely settled on the CIO side, correctly counting on the eventual recuperation of U.S. control over the resources of a weak neighbor.[68] But by the later 1930s, the rising figures of the AFL, the ILGWU's David Dubinsky in particular, began to look to a different possible future: an independent, hyper-aggressive foreign policy in concert with labor conservatives against all those (including some sections of capital as well as labor) who sought either economic cooperation with the Soviet Union or a hands off politics toward large parts of the globe. Within less than a decade, the Second World War and the ideological campaign against Russia and Communism gave hard-liners the excuse for global extension that they otherwise lacked.[69]

Meany only gradually began to make his own contribution to the planetary war for hearts and minds, including great opportunities for advancement of labor leadership into a global power in its own right. He inherited a key conspiratorial assistant: Jay Lovestone. A Communist leader during the 1920s blessed with a particular talent for faction-building through seductive promises and assorted manipulations of potential allies, Lovestone had personally implored Stalin in 1929 to abandon the sudden shift of the Comintern toward class warfare. Refusing to relinquish leadership of the American Communist apparatus willingly, as the Russian leader demanded, Lovestone was excommunicated. With his several hundred followers Lovestone regathered within ILGWU Local 22, New York, itself caught in a internecine battle against Communist regulars. Publishing one of the more literate left weeklies of the time, *Workers Age,* Lovestone's small expelled group held out almost a decade for reconciliation, believing the world Communist movement would yet vindicate them and return them to leadership. Grasping finally the impossibility of return, Lovestone set upon another plan seen by scholars, even now, only through a glass darkly. According to recently opened documents, Lovestone served as a spy or courier for the Soviet Union during the 1930s even while denouncing the Russian leadership in public.[70] The effects of the third Moscow trial, the Nazi-Soviet pact, and the inevitability of world war completed, in any case, the Lovestone group's political trajectory as such, for the leader announced its official dissolution in 1940. Adjusting his practices within the shifting cloak-and-dagger scene, he and a handful of his leading supporters (including his chief intelligence operative Irving Brown, future conservative writer Bertram D. Wolfe and theologian Will Herberg) joined the anti-Soviet crusade full time. There, some found a lifetime of highly remunerative work within the intelligence apparatus of the AFL and the AFL-CIO, while others collected an assortment of funding sources climaxing with tenure at the Hoover Institution, workshop of the "Reagan Revolution."[71]

ILGWU President David Dubinsky, who had personally introduced Lovestone to Meany, had not only been Lovestone's boss at the ILGWU but was himself a major player in the same game.[72] Enraged at his rival garment leader Sidney Hillman—a great favorite of FDR and a leader of the CIO—Dubinsky had engaged in a series of conspiracies since the later 1930s via Lovestone's operatives. The ILGWU leader not only funded and personally helped guide efforts to overturn specific CIO regimes, in hopes of destroying or fatally wounding the new federation, but he also moved to get a leg up on postwar liberal politics through heavy funding of the new Liberal Party against the now Communist-led American Labor Party and against its unique Congressional champion, Vito Marcantonio, in New York state. Dubinsky, a past master at gerrymandering and vote-buying within his own union, thrived on threats and sneaky maneuvers. Lovestone and

Meany were his natural partners not only in ideology but in character traits. Dubinsky, along with Lovestone and Brown, found themselves warmly received at the center of an AFL plan to rule all labor rather than merely its more backward sections. Only a portion of their intelligence-related activities has so far surfaced from the CIA's rich historical backlog of secrets, but the general direction and importance of these can be traced rather easily. Meany, as nominal head of the Labor League for Human Rights, made Lovestone the operating head, and Lovestone carefully began doling out some $25 million where it would do the most political good for refugees certain to support US policies. In 1944, the AFL convention authorized the formation of a successor, the Free Trade Union Committee under the guidance of Meany, Dubinsky, and Green. Lovestone was formally elected to be the FTUC secretary. The committee was to be the main instrumentality for carrying out the foreign policy of the AFL—and of the State Department.[73]

With the end of the war, Meany and Lovestone had their work cut out. The virtual collapse of capitalism in Western Europe and the triumphant march of the Red Army (over democrats, socialists, and independent-minded communists, as well as the defeated fascists) left gloomy prospects for the reconstruction of capitalism. To counter the influence of Communists and, no less, of aggressive socialists who sought a democratic confiscation of capitalist holdings, Irving Brown was appointed head of a European mission. The ruthless Brown, who had his start spying for Lovestone on the 1930s Socialist Party youth (from within their "Revolutionary Policy Committee"), proved to be an ideal choice for the job.[74] The European Recovery Plan (known popularly as the Marshall Plan), allotting $13 billion dollars to Western European nations between 1948 and 1951, drafted to exclude Eastern Europe and to demonstrate the difference between the two systems, made the labor mission feasible.

Lovestone and Brown set up shop vigorously, doling out to thousands of influential individuals bribes equivalent to several months of a European worker's salary in return for support of assorted activities both open and secret. They drew in part upon what Brown biographer Rathbun calls "unspecific dispensations," amounting to five percent of the total Marshall Plan funds, or $800 million. If Dubinsky and Brown earlier had to rely upon funding from individual corporations and the State Department, now they were flush beyond previous imagination.[75] By 1950, the Central Intelligence Agency had begun directing tens of millions and perhaps far more to the labor spy operation.[76]

In some places, Communist-led strikes would be broken by criminal elements directly in AFL employ or allowed to practice their trades unhindered as quid pro quo; alternatively, where Communist or non-Communist radicals perceived as anti-American had been elected to labor officialdom or public office, strikes would be "arranged" for maximum chaos. Pushing their own candidates for union elections and general elections, the conspirators quickly filled a vacuum of resources in hungry Europe. Most often choosing reliable Catholic conservatives, Lovestone's partners in a pinch were best remembered as the erstwhile supporters of fascist regimes whose officials were now being quietly protected as CIA assets, including some well-known heroin traffickers. Brown, the future winner of Ronald Reagan's Medal of Freedom, used CIA funds (in the words of *Time*) "to pay off strong arm squads in Mediterranean ports so that American supplies could be unloaded against the opposition of Communist dock workers." Generalized violence, including beatings and assassination, proved successful measures against Communist union members. No questions were asked about the other related activities of the hoodlums, or what else they got in return for their generous assistance.[77]

Despite these vigorous early efforts, the AFL's international operatives experienced only limited success, barely holding the line. The split-off union federation they formed in France, the *Force Ouvriere,* was a flop except for its large slush fund. More than a few staunch European anticommunists, like Hubert Gee of Britain's Labour Ministry and UN Foreign Office labor specialist, considered Brown's methods downright sleazy, and his plan for splitting European labor into Communist-led and U.S.-funded factions improper. "In the field of international trade union diplomacy," Gee said, "I regard the AFL in general and Mr. Irving Brown in particular as a model of how not to set about things."[79] Knowing that any direct control of social-democratic strategies would provoke wide resentment, Brown manipulated (and probably funded) the Belgian leadership to take the initiative in a large-scale pullout rather than struggle democratically from within the World Federation of Trade Unions.

Ironically, electrical unionist and determined anti-communist James Carey presented the case for the WFTU to take part in the Marshall Plan, knowing that Communist unionists could not approve participation in a plan that the Soviet leaders (correctly anticipating Russia's exclusion from NATO) flatly opposed.[80] It was a wiser strategy, from the viewpoint of labor independence from either of the Cold War camps, but not a plan that Meany or Lovestone could endorse. The temporary new lease on life for the WFTU found Brown in a tizzy. Lovestone pronounced, "European labor no longer possessed the dynamism, force or self-confidence necessary to fight communism. The mantle of leadership was rapidly passing to the American labor movement, which was now the sole force that could lead the fight."[81] The stodgy British TUC as well as the conflicted CIO, however, deeply resented the AFL's methods and manipulations. Only the implementation of the Marshall Plan, along with the Czech coup and the Berlin Blockade set into place the founding of a specifically American-dominated and probusiness labor international. As R. H. Tawney wrote at the time, "If the leaders of the AFL have a specialism, it consists in power politics, which they employ as readily against their fellow trade unionists as against employers."[82] In 1951, averring that the AFL had operated abroad during the 1940s "totally independent of any government control or influence," Meany was lying through his teeth.[83]

Some of the most important national labor movements and the loyalties of many ordinary union members remained with the WFTU, even as the combination of Stalin's misdeeds and the flat-out purchase of European union leaders had a restraining influence upon both popular resistance to NATO (symbol of U.S. domination) and the return to capitalism-as-usual during the halting economic recovery. It did not quash the dominant influence of Communists in the national labor federations of France and Italy, as Lovestone and Meany had hoped, or the continuing role of Communists within the British unions, but it contributed to the corruption of those Communist leaders on the American labor model, as decades of relative stability sustained ordinary bureaucratic practices.

Brown's biggest successes were preventing the Greek labor movement from taking a democratic vote that would almost certainly have produced a Communist victory within the unions, notwithstanding the well-known history of Nazi collaboration by some of the CIA's prize Greek union leaders; and in preventing unity of the German labor movement, a unity sought from below and not imposed by the powers-that-be in the Soviet zone. The West German union demand for "co-determination," a share of workers' power in business and government, was looked upon with particular horror from AFL headquarters. The United States thus heavily funded a break within the German union federation, unionists buckling to U.S. demands for conservative policies, while British union representatives in Germany surrendered to the fait accompli of U.S. control. Breaking a city-wide general strike in Berlin offered a climax to Brown's own personal claim to labor glory.

The AFL's creation of a new world labor federation, the International Confederation of Free Trade Unions (ICFTU), with the CIO and its British counterpart as charter members, sealed the deal.[84] These accomplishments even extended to the cultural world. The creation of labor's contingent to the CIA's intellectual front of the 1950s, the Congress for Cultural Freedom, was counted as yet another jewel in the AFL crown. Brown considered himself, along with novelist Arthur Koestler, to be chief wire-puller. Meanwhile, the ultimate comeback of capitalism thanks to the Marshall Plan, and the gradual retreat of the European social democrats (including the British Labour government) from early promises of social transformation, practically ended the widely held dreams of democratic socialism in an independent Europe.[85]

Lovestone and Meany were understandably proud of their roles even if they could not take credit for the massive money-shuffling or pride in unsavory allies. Later, after revelations appeared in 1967 about the CIA's key role in all this, Meany still felt compelled to deny any CIA involvement. Without prevarication, Meany (as Brown's biographer notes) would otherwise "have been regarded as an absolute scoundrel by his closest European allies, the Social Democratic unions," whose leaders had presumably allowed themselves to be utterly deceived for twenty years. But thanks to his "formidable persona" (here quoting CIA chief Thomas Braden), Meany could carry off a lie with success.[86] Others might call this persistent lying pathological—but not the CIA, where such denials were standard practice and the assassination of critics' reputations (in the third world, the critics themselves) far from unknown. The AFL, of course, had been vigorously anticommunist from the first day of the October Revolution and involved in quiet schemes against U.S. supporters of revolutionary activity since at least the 1890s. But in the bureaucratic morass after Gompers's passing, fighting Communists was largely left to others, rhetoric apart. As George Meany rose in the ranks of labor, so did the commitment of trade unions to make the fight against Communism into an integrated element of foreign policy, no matter what administration reigned in Washington.

Nothing showed this more clearly than the enhanced role of the AFL in Latin America after Meany took over from Green. Two years after its formation in 1949, the ICFTU created the Inter-American Regional Labor Organization (ORIT), which operated for nine years as the AFL's and then AFL-CIO's political arm in Latin America. Meany and Lovestone selected Serafino Romualdi, an old-time Italian antifascist and anti-communist, to run ORIT, with headquarters in Mexico City. There, personified in Romualdi, hangs the tale of labor democrats-turned-agents in the Cold War years.

Forced to flee Mussolini, and sponsored by Dubinsky with the support of kindred spirits Lovestone and Meany, Romualdi found sanctuary in the AFL. He also received the welcoming embrace of the CIA. According to ex-CIA agent Philip Agee (who spent most of his twelve CIA years as a Latin American field officer), Romualdi was indeed "the principal CIA agent for labor operations in Latin America." Romualdi's links to the CIA began, however, even before he was selected for the ORIT position. Meany surely knew this to be the case, and regarded it as a decisive qualification. Agee's diary offers detailed evidence of interlocking ORIT-CIA activities in Latin America.[87]

The role of the Meany policy in Latin America can be measured most effectively in one crucial instance: the rescue of the backward masses (and more to the point, the United Fruit Company) from the supposed Communist threat of an elected Guatemalan government. In 1950, Jacobo Arbenz ran successfully on an agrarian program in Guatemala against the candidates of the handful of ultra-wealthy families and their principal supporters, U.S. agricultural interests. That electoral victory in itself was considered a blow to U.S. interests. Once in office, Arbenz showed an unacceptable partiality toward individual Communists, a number of whom were placed in administrative government positions. No Communist himself, he favored those who supported him, throwing his weight behind the growing left in the Guatemalan trade unions. In March 1953, he began a series of land expropriations that deprived the United Fruit Company of the vast bulk of its land holdings. Now he had definitely gone too far for United Fruit, the CIA's chief Allen Dulles, and their joint ally, George Meany.

Meany, along with the social-democratic U.S. magazine *The New Leader*, led the publicity counter-attack (or smoke-screen). In February 1954, Meany sent a letter to President Arbenz in the name of the AFL executive council that began on a complimentary note for the "constructive democratic social changes" that had taken place in Guatemala. The letter then veered in an ominous direction. Arbenz was accused of showing favor to Communists in unions and generally moving Guatemala toward the world Communist orbit—a development which Meany viewed with "apprehension." Meany attached an RSVP to the letter, and Arbenz understandably enough did not answer. Journalistic reports in the *New York Times* and elsewhere meanwhile advanced wild and utterly false claims about the "communist threat" within the little jungle nation.[88]

Meanwhile, Meany's friends at the CIA were busy organizing a coup. They found one Carlos Castillo Armas to head a so-called liberation army. The entire operation was CIA-financed, and Meany's man in Latin America, Romualdi, forced out of the country by Arbenz for plotting, offered his services and those of his followers to Colonel Armas. Arbenz was shortly toppled, and Meany rejoiced along with the *New York Times* and the *New Leader*, which had issued a special number attacking the regime (and soon, a paperback by the *New Leader*'s proud editor). "The downfall of the Communist controlled regime in Guatemala," Meany exulted in July 1954, "will be hailed by the free world."[90]

While Meany and the *Times* rejoiced, Colonel Armas was consolidating a right-wing dictatorship which murdered thousands of workers and peasants—their mass graves offering mute testimony to the success of the operation. By September, even Romualdi was a bit disquieted. He suddenly feared that Armas's sweeping suppression of Communist-led unions might prove wide enough "to sweep away the labor movement" generally. As unionists went off to prison or worse, he nevertheless insisted that "all the evidence so far indicates that President Castillo Armas himself favors the development of free trade unionism." As late as June 1956, when the number of victims of right-wing terror numbered well in the thousands, Romualdi nevertheless found that "the President himself meant well and was at heart, favoring the rebirth of a healthy, free and independent trade union movement" and that "freedom of press and speech has been restored."[91] This optimistic observation, like the reportage in the *Times* and *New Leader*, had carefully overlooked evidence in the other direction. The slaughter rapidly assumed the shape that it would take for decades, with hundreds of thousands of government-sanctioned murders directed mainly at Indian populations.[92] The unions that might conceivably have formed safe, sound affiliates of the AFL's Inter-American network had also themselves been destroyed, as even Meany and his friends were eventually forced to conceded.[93]

Nonetheless, the history of this spectacular Meany-CIA collaboration was repeated time and time again, never as farce, only as tragedy. Its bloody consequences were invariably denied, from Chile to El Salvador, from Mexico to Haiti, from Africa to Asia. According to a former leader of Social Democrats, USA, Max Green, the AFL and AFL-CIO deceived themselves about their own influence "promoting democracy" across Latin America and the Caribbean; U.S. support of military forces had the central role, with the role of U.S.-friendly trade unionists a public relations one at best.[94]

Again and again, the fusion of corporate, CIA, State Department, AFL, and then AFL-CIO enterprises, along with satellites like International Rescue Committee and (much later) Freedom House, vigorously supported and hailed numerous terror regimes—with occasional reservations, to be sure—especially those best known for nominal "show elections" between waves of bloody repression. The health of trade unions abroad, whose stability and vigor Meany may well have wished, were perennial afterthoughts, valued only when unions supported the regime against left-wing unions or when they joined with the American embassy and investors in suppressing political opponents. For Meany, nevertheless, intrigue and payoffs was worth trying again and again. His more sophisticated advisors, usually ex-socialist careerists, had been well experienced in extensive, heavily funded covert operations by the time Meany left office. This factor, rising above any other, was to set the tone for Meany's AFL-CIO regime and that of his successor.

3. MEANYISM: APEX AND DECLINE

George Meany and his surrounding circle devoted, in retrospect, amazingly large quantities of time and concern during the 1950s and early 1960s to self-congratulation (above all, praise of Meany himself) for the state of the labor movement and of American democracy. With the exit of John L. Lewis from the federation scene and the expulsion of the Communists, rivals to institutional leadership and threats to the respectability of the movement had been wiped out for the foreseeable future. The Taft-Hartley and Landrum-Griffin Acts, despite early fears, proved to be acceptable and in some ways even helpful legislation for disposing of opposition and for governing restless memberships. Communism abroad and the Chamber of Commerce at home gave Meany and his cohorts something to tilt at, an angle from which to gather their own like-minded allies, from the diplomatic corps to business. Everything considered, big labor had "arrived," as the intimacy of the AFL-CIO leaders and the Kennedy administration demonstrated. All was well in the house of labor— or so it seemed, anyway—until the troubles of the middle 1960s.

The affinity of labor lawyer and intelligence veteran Arthur Goldberg for the Kennedy circle and acceptance of Goldberg by Meany symptomized what the AFL-CIO president called a shift toward assembling proper "guidelines for just and harmonious labor-management relations."[1] The combination of liberalism at home and stealthy anticommunist (others would call it neo-imperial) commitment abroad seemed almost ideal, the goal toward which Meany had always striven. White-collar unionists, notwithstanding Meany's skepticism, had meanwhile begun to shore up the federation's membership, only beginning to weaken because of decertifications, factory closings, and a palpable failure to organize in the industrializing South or among office workers. The AFL-CIO, to its publicists, was on the doorstep of a golden future.

This was, of course, a grand illusion. Meanyism contained the seeds of its own destruction. The narrowminded, vindictive approach toward all critics on the left, and above all the hypocritical posturing as the most democratic social force of the nation (while being deeply undemocratic, segregated, and exclusionary in numerous other ways within), ill-prepared the AFL-CIO for challenge or Meany's reputation from the public savaging which it sustained from the middle 1960s onward. Widely caricatured and often ridiculed as a bloated anachronism in the mainstream press, Meany became (many would say) his true self as the 1960s closed. A sort of political aneurism exploded in Meany's brain at that point, and he never regained his self-confident pose. Despite a gruff front, he spent the rest of his life a bitter man grumbling at his defeats and taking satisfaction only in the worse fates of too-liberal Democrats, "extreme" environmentalists, peaceniks, feminists, and gay liberationists.

Corruptions of State: CIA and AIFLD

An upper-echelon veteran of the left-gone-right in the AFL-CIO leadership later recalled that the ideological combination of anti-Stalinism and anti-capitalism during the 1940s was replaced among the climbers by a very different conception during the 1950s-1960s. The possibility of reapportioning the world's wealth or even holding steady the current extreme imbalance had been moved off the agenda. The main struggle in the world was now between democracy (meaning Western capitalism, or capitalism in other places with elections) and a force described as "totalitarianism" either on the right or (overwhelmingly, in this group's view) on the left.[2] Michael Harrington, writing a decade later about the main movers of this tendency, put it a little differently: "My friends had turned themselves into a fanatically anti-Communist clique of people with staff jobs in unions and related institutions," a process by which "morality became a sophisticated adaptation to tactical necessity" of holding power while the old vision of social transformation had been reduced to the political programs of the AFL-CIO leadership.[3]

In the place of opposition to exploitation, racism, and class bias across the capitalist world, the constant task of the labor's upper echelons and its friends became persuading the press and public that George Meany and his cohort were not at all the narrowminded racists and conservatives so often caricatured as labor's fat cats, but rather an admirable, liberal-minded regime with a great world vision. The emerging operators found their reliable enemy in Stalinism, at home and abroad, though their tactics and their political claims to combat supposed subversion rang strongly of Gompers's bureaucratic measures and anti-socialist rhetoric during the First World War, *before* the Russian Revolution. Although the measures were supposedly protective of democracy, moreover, the AFL (and the emerging conservatives of the CIO) declined to embrace the anti-colonial movements of assorted peoples seeking their own destinies unless those movements had pledged loyalty in advance to the United States and to their own propertied classes. "What's good for capitalists in Latin America," as field officer Philip Agee would testify in his diary, "is good for capitalists in the USA."[4] And the same went for any other part of the third world. A socialism of unmediated workers' power, appealing for a dismantling of the world empires in all their forms, would surely have found AFL-CIO leaders and their ideologues as brutally eager for business recuperation as the worst of Communist bureaucrats determined to cling to state power.

The Cold War did entail something new: a qualitatively different level of collaboration with the federal government. Many old-time local AFL local officials, jealously clinging to their autonomy, would just as surely have resented the regular presence of Federal Bureau of Investigation operatives in their offices, as many had rejected the AFL's own internal witch-hunt of the late 1910s and early 1920s. In the all-out battle against Communist-led unions, however, the Bureau and sections of the Catholic hierarchy became unquestioned heavy players. During the process, some CIO unions even more than their AFL counterparts became virtual adjuncts of national security agencies.

Consider the relationship of the FBI with former United Electrical Workers leader and new International Union of Electrical Workers (IUE) President James Carey. The FOIA release of documents in recent years reveals that as early as 1943, Carey had begun exchanging information with the FBI, a relationship growing into a pattern of selective collaboration that included local Catholic leaders and the House Committee on Un-American Activities, which conveniently held hearings before or during local strikes to pinpoint union rival "reds." Owing his victories to such forces and his public reputation to flattery by ardently anticommunist liberal intellectuals, Carey actually ruled the new union with an embarrassing degree of incompetence, bringing about his own downfall. Of course, to admit Carey's compromised position or lack of leadership ability would have been considered bad judgment by liberals and the press. Much like the contemporary intellectuals of the American Committee for Cultural Freedom adamantly denying CIA participation, Carey feigned ignorance or adopted denial as the last best response when queried about agency support of activities and similarly covert maneuvers to keep his membership in line.[5]

Carey's regime was by no means unusual in its degree of collaboration with the FBI or CIA. An embarrassed Walter Reuther later admitted taking $50,000 in fifty dollar bills from the CIA for international bribes, and chalked it off to naiveté.[6] Such practices, and the attitudes they fostered, helped usher in a new era of coordination with intelligence agencies focused on the international front. David Dubinsky and the FTUC had been, properly speaking, allies of the CIA during the later 1940s and 1950s. The union leaders had an agenda which coincided with that of U.S. foreign policy except when they sought more extreme measures, whether against purported Communist threats or in support of Israel. This system apparently operated at relatively low levels, with dramatic infusions of funding for bribes during elections or contests over political and labor leadership in many nations. Matters shifted dramatically, however, with the election of John F. Kennedy as American president in 1960.

Younger social-democratic intellectuals such as future Congressman Allard Lowenstein, earlier involved with intelligence operations on campus, had thrown themselves into the Kennedy camp during the nomination process. Arthur Goldberg, an official of the CIA's predecessor OSS and one of the drafters of legislation to create the CIA, had a strong record as attorney of the labor leadership and as architect, in some technical ways, of the merger. By 1960, Walter Reuther and David Dubinsky were his biggest boosters. He was introduced by the new administration as labor secretary in a flourish that few recognized at the time as decisive to the new era of union intelligence operations. Dubinsky later took credit for maneuvering Meany's support, curiously by citing the contributions that revered lawyer-socialists Morris Hillquit and Meyer London had made to labor earlier.[7] More comfortable with fellow WASPs and Republicans, embracing their own élan of highly secret (and highly paid) international activists, CIA staff officers had been up to now rather uncomfortable mates for most of the self-avowed liberal-political wing of labor officialdom. But the world had changed.[8]

In retrospect, the acceleration of third world revolts and revolutions had already begun to give U.S. foreign policy a sharper focus beyond the global arms race and European "captive nations." If the aims of the ICFTU and the State Department had often been to support a "safe" form of national independence which did not challenge either U.S. investments or local allies, then the steady eclipse of European colonialism placed the United States increasingly in the driver's seat with hardly anyone on the conservative-colonialist side to oppose. Indeed, military coups were deemed more and more necessary (and quietly supported) against elected governments overly influenced by populist economic demands. Only a few years after the Sino-Soviet split had ended the monolithic Communist threat and drove the former Communist partners toward supporting rival movements, candidate John F. Kennedy heated up the lagging Cold War by warning of an imaginary "missile gap" and promising a New Frontier of American greatness worldwide. The latter phrase was no mere slip of the speechwriter's pen. As long as economic expansion continued, society was deemed safe from ideological subversion. According to the gospel of growth, anything that threatened the process had to be isolated and finally eradicated. The re-emergence of buoyant liberalism after the McCarthy era and the dull later days of Eisenhower changed this thesis not at all. The Kennedy camp had made the necessary adjustments to the standard American view, but left the essentials unaltered.[9]

The events in Guatemala had already reflected the rise of Cold War liberalism in and around the labor movement. By the later 1950s, as even important figures within the Catholic Church began to speak up against the monumental poverty accelerated through the spread of U.S.-guided monocrop production-for-export, the future began to look uncertain. Suddenly, the Cuban Revolution seemed to speak to the deepest fears of subversion from within "our" hemisphere and within the Caribbean, long known to labor leaders as well as businessmen and politicians as the "American lake." The Kennedy administration swiftly established a special counter-guerilla strike force, the Green Berets. Kennedy himself was said to have designed the Berets' logo. As part of this initiative, Labor Secretary Goldberg led the move to establish the American Institute for Free Labor Development (AIFLD). Its stated mission was to offer training, assistance, and money to unionists across Latin America and the Caribbean, in short to fulfill Gompers's dream with full government support for a global neo-colonial operation. Its offshoots, within a few years, included two additional regional bodies: the African-American Labor Center (AALC), and the Asian-American Free Labor Institute (AAFLI). All were to be funded partly out of AFL-CIO budget but also from government agencies ranging from the Agency for International Development to the CIA. Later, they increasingly acquired "outside" sources of wealthy corporate executives and foundations, neatly previewing the "privatization" of aggressively militarized foreign policy during the 1980s.

Former agent Philip Agee's *CIA Diary* offers a candid snapshot of AIFLD's early intentions and operations. The ineffectiveness of ORIT had prompted "Washington's answer to the limitation of current labour programmes undertaken through AID as well as through ORT and CIA stations," that is, previous CIA-sponsored unions' "direct dependence on the U.S. government." The sensitivity of the issues involved—the determination to best and finally supplant left-led unions with better-funded pro-American and pro-business unions—determined that "training institutes" and social programs would serve as fronts for funding CIA-loyal labor leaders. The supposed training institutes would indeed be "nominally and administratively" guided by AIFLD, but actually "headed by CIA agents with operational control exercised by the [CIA field] stations." Advanced training courses for leaders brought to the AFL-CIO's Washington headquarters would follow "spotting and assessment of potential agents for labour operations." At first operated at the Communication Workers' encampment at Front Royal, Virginia, AIFLD/CIA training eventually passed on to the new George Meany Center in Silver Spring, thus combining modestly funded legitimate research, and scholarly and social events with vastly funded "spook work" halted only in 1995. It was a neat "labor spy" operation, whose financial sources and ultimate control were, of course, flatly denied by the AFL-CIO for decades.[10]

According to independent observers, official budget figures drastically understated the actual amounts dispensed to such labor agencies—very likely by up to 90 percent. On perhaps $100 million per year, at a conservative estimate, a great deal of activities could be undertaken and a large number of quietly generous payoffs made to those foreign labor leaders who could be persuaded to share AFL-CIO views. After early problems with the regional AIFLD officials who were not actually CIA agents, the administrative apparatus was smoothed out.[11] The diplomatic corps' own labor attachés, whether occupying a career position or a plum for loyal labor bureaucrats, quickly became known as liaisons between the intelligence agencies, national officials of the U.S. labor movement, and a mostly invented middle level of "friendly" native unionists.[12]

AIFLD emerged full-blown in 1962, building upon counter-insurgency strategy documents filed by General Richard Stilwell and Colonel Edward Lansdale (one of the counter-insurgency masterminds of intelligence activities and killing fields across the Pacific, climaxing in Vietnam) and circulated with the imprimatur of the Council for Foreign Relations. AIFLD's board of directors featured, alongside top leaders of the AFL-CIO, a group never known for eagerness to assist labor: business leaders with heavy U.S. investments in the Caribbean, Central America, and South America. These businessmen included David Rockefeller, representing the substantial Rockefeller family interests in Latin American minerals; executives of the United Fruit Company and its chair J. Peter Grace, noted conservative Catholic supporter of American rightwing causes, as well as president of the CIA-thick Knights of Malta; and the fascinating figure of Eric Johnston, who as a young man was part of the U.S. expeditionary force against the new Soviet Union in 1919 and later served as president of the Motion Picture Association, enforcing the Hollywood blacklist. George Cabot Lodge, like his father Henry Cabot Lodge said to be deeply involved in covert activities, was the assistant secretary of labor under Arthur Goldberg as the AIFLD took shape.

The first major AIFLD operations came shortly after its formation. In 1963, the AIFLD sponsored and funded a strike in the little country of British Guiana, successfully pitting black workers against the predominantly East Indian supporters of elected president Cheddi Jagan. It offered reputedly well over a million dollars to provide strikers better than normal daily pay and thus keep Jagan out of power. The same year, when the U.S. government feared the legally elected Juan Bosch taking power in the Dominican Republic, AIFLD bodies supplied heaving funding, strategic assistance, and publicity for U.S. favorites. Two years later, as the Marines actually moved in to halt Bosch and his followers, the AIFLD ardently supported the invasion.[13]

Brazil, with the largest and most important economy in Latin America, was another matter altogether. President Joao Goulart, not unlike Guatemalan President Jacobo Arbenz in the early 1950s, had announced neutrality in the Cold War and proposed to begin nationalizing oil as a repatriation of the nation's own natural resources. A Brazilian Institute for Democratic Action, heavily funded by the CIA and run by businessmen intimate to U.S. interests, sprang into existence with a CIA-trained AIFLD operative, Richard Martinez (according to the agent's own later account). Serafino Romualdi met quietly with proposed military coup leaders, meanwhile graduating future "labor leaders" under Histradrut auspices in Israel. In 1964, the CIA staged the demonstrations of the native middle class against the regime, and General Vernon Walters (accompanied by an American aircraft carrier, offshore) was fortuitously on hand to welcome the military uprising. The pro-Goulart labor federation CGT, the sole functioning national union, immediately fell under repression, its leaders replaced by AIFLD "graduates" and collaborators. The era of torture, death squads, and "disappearances" began. In these innocent, early years of their activity, eager to demonstrate their significance, AIFLD officials bragged about the role that they had played in the overthrow.[14]

Edwin Doherty, Jr., named director of AIFLD in 1965 following the retirement of Romualdi, was the son of a reputed CIA ally within labor and sometime ambassador to Jamaica. Almost miraculously attaining the presidency of the American Federation of Government Employees only a year out of college and after a brief career as an administrator of the Marshall Plan, Doherty was, like future AFL-CIO President Lane Kirkland, a child of Cold War times: the labor leader with no appreciable working-class background and no rank-and-file following whatsoever. Doherty embraced the new era warmly, making statements on behalf of AIFLD as bold as, "The cooperation between ourselves and the business community is getting warmer day by day." (Philip Agee's *CIA Diary* described the sentiment a bit more accurately, naming Doherty, Jr. "one of our more effective labour agents.")[15] Real social reform such as unionization of national workforces evidently had value as well, in beating out the competition for workers' loyalty, but was regularly subordinated to more immediate needs of supporting allies among the business and military elites.

So intense were AIFLD efforts by the middle 1960s, as Philip Agee reported, that in tiny Uraguay alone the CIA invested $8 million in housing projects (half of it "loaned" by the AFL-CIO) to literally build loyalty against the dominant union federation. The "most effective" programs gave unionists of the impoverished country a generous nine-months' salary in return for merely attending classes; meanwhile, the field office sought to identify still more prospective collaborators for sponsorship. In another small country, Ecuador, the AIFLD had "trained" some twenty thousand workers in the first half-dozen years of the program, obviously at enormous expense. But the expense of dealing with militant (or even truly independent and democratic) trade unions would surely be higher.[16]

So overriding were the political priorities of AIFLD unionists that their own staff, U.S. citizens stationed abroad, often occupied the key offices of affiliated national unions, presumably on the assumption that nationals could not be trusted to carry out orders. Further up the food chain, Jay Lovestone himself had to take orders. According to the *Washington Post* revelations in 1967, "Lovestone, sometimes called Meany's minister of foreign affairs . . . takes orders from Cord Meyer of the CIA. No CIA money for labor is spent [however] without Lovestone's approval, and few labor attachés are appointed to American embassies without his OK."[17]

Lovestone carried out his mandate in later decades with the assistance of two key, if de facto, political partners with their own equally remarkable left-wing personal histories: Max Shachtman and Bayard Rustin. An American Bolshevik of the 1920s, Shachtman, unlike Lovestone, never shifted his loyalties toward the bureaucratic upper echelons of labor during the 1930s-1940s. On the contrary, along with former Wobbly James P. Cannon and a circle of a thousand or so militants, Shachtman had remained true to the Bolshevik legacy upheld by Leon Trotsky's Left Opposition to both Stalinism and social democracy. Shachtman and his supporters broke in turn with Trotsky only in 1940, refusing to accept Trotsky's sanguine designation of Russia as a merely deformed "workers state" and therefore to be defended "unconditionally" in the event of war. In their "Third Camp" perspective, every class system deserved overthrow.

The small Workers Party, never numbering more than a thousand, distinguished itself through the war years in fighting the no-strike pledge, criticizing the Roosevelt administration for its undemocratic war conduct, including the Jim Crow army, its treatment of Japanese-Americans, and its callous indifference to European anti-Semitism. As an activist organization, the Workers Party engaged in factory struggles far and wide, distributing a lively labor weekly completely opposed to the bureaucratic drift of world politics.

After the war failed to end in a world revolution (as Trotsky had, with so many others on the left, mistakenly predicted), Shachtman's growing doubts gradually turned into inklings of reorientation. The GI Bill, the economic upswing fed by military spending, and the easing of anti-Semitic hiring practices all allowed an unprecedentedly swift upward mobility of educated youngsters into the middle class and away from Marxist commitments. Not surprisingly, a handful of precocious, career-minded but heretofore radical intellectuals including Saul Bellow, Gertrude Himmelfarb, and Irving Howe, moved away from the group into promising personal advancement as they proceeded with a continuing political shift that would take them to the rightward edge of liberalism and (with the exception of Howe) far beyond, into neoconservatism and ferocious racial positions.

Shachtman, holding for a time to visions of an impending radical breakthrough, simultaneously made a fateful move toward the more liberal sections of the labor leadership which profited from the expulsion of Communists. Walter Reuther's United Auto Workers, cracking down severely on local union autonomy, nevertheless offered many non-communist veterans of labor some hope for a bloc within the Democratic Party. Ideally, that party would at some point purged itself of its Dixiecrat wing (which had actually exited during the 1948 election season, only to return afterward) and would become a sort of American version of the British Labour Party. Over the course of the 1950s, most of the remnants of Shachtman's group entered a Socialist Party badly faded but still led by "Mr. Socialism," Norman Thomas, and blessed with wide contacts in New York's Liberal Party and the Americans for Democratic Action (ADA). For these entrants, the notion of the Third Camp had been replaced by lesser evilism as a guiding political and organizational principle. The firm embrace of "democratic capitalism" as the lesser evil brought further rightward shifts at breathtaking speed. Situated in his new milieu, Shachtman soon supplied both hawkish speechwriters and safely "moderate" civil rights executives to Meany's office, while building a powerful machine for political operations within the leadership of the United Federation of Teachers, and downplaying at each opportunity the struggle against the bureaucracy of unions.[18]

Bayard Rustin, another to travel from the political left to the Cold War labor bureaucracy, joined the UFT operation at the close of the courageous phase of his life. The son of West Indian immigrants, Rustin joined the Young Communist League during the 1930s, leaving it to support A. Philip Randolph's March on Washington movement, which targeted racism at home during the Second World War years. As an adamant pacifist on the staff of the Fellowship of Reconciliation, he resisted the draft, learned folk singing in prison, organized the Journey of Reconciliation (the first "freedom ride" through the South) and played an important role in American circles supportive of African anticolonialism. After moving to the War Resisters League, he joined Martin Luther King, Jr.'s staff until forced out by threatened revelation of his homosexuality. In 1963, Rustin finessed administration support of the labor-linked March on Washington for Jobs and Freedom, a definite shift toward his next position within the Meany-approved A. Philip Randolph Institute. From there, he attacked King's later campaigns, bitterly opposed Black Power, and shifted steadily to the right, even opposing the 1983 King Memorial March on Washington. Supporting the war in Vietnam and Israeli actions in the West Bank and Lebanon while attacking "no growth" environmentalists, he increasingly abandoned his progressive roots, condemning third world movements for their violence while insisting upon the propriety of U.S. foreign policy. By the 1970s-1980s, he played a quiet but important role of AFL-CIO point man in Africa, shuttling to shore up U.S. clients and supporters, including State Department "constructive engagement" in South Africa and the labor federation's favorite alternatives to Nelson Mandela and the African National Congress.[19]

During the early and middle 1960s, it was just these milieux whose leaders had rallied most energetically to the favorite causes of the AIFLD, such as a proposed second and all-out Marine invasion of Castro's Cuba, the invasion of the Dominican Republic, and the war in Vietnam. Not surprisingly, their subordinates received important appointments and funding from Democratic-run government agencies.

One other foreign policy feature bears open discussion. If never determinant for labor functionaries leaning more and more heavily upon American imperial ties, a peculiar history of sympathy for Israel proved increasingly important, both ideologically and personally. With memories of the New Deal and class conflict growing ever more distant, nationalism (or rather, twin nationalisms for the United States and Israel) supplied ideological glue to increasingly fractured claims of social justice. According to Israeli historians Yossi Melman and Dan Raviv, an early moment of truth arrived when in 1956 the Israelis suddenly seized the Sinai Peninsula, including the Suez Canal, and Prime Minister David Ben-Gurion announced that the biblical Jewish kingdom would be re-established upon the conquered territory. The Eisenhower administration promptly cut off all aid to Israel. Leaders of the newly combined AFL-CIO lobbied furiously to end the sanctions. Israel nevertheless yielded in two weeks.[20]

Sections of U.S. labor leadership were from this moment on drawn deeply into Middle Eastern politics. Heretofore, except in assorted branches of the labor left (and the needles trade), Jewish issues had never been considered central to union leaders. The Holocaust—viewed for some years after the war as an embarrassment to America's new strategic ally, Germany—and the birth of Israel barely made them so. But by the middle 1950s, labor leaders increasingly dwelt in public speeches, and in private or public meetings with recognized Jewish leaders as well as numerous trips to the Jewish state, on questions which hardly concerned the great majority of their members and would have been less important to their own members than the far less discussed situations of Ireland or Italy, to say nothing Puerto Rico, Greece, or assorted sites in Africa. As American liberalism redefined itself within a Cold War garrison mentality, Israel became an operative affection as well as a perfect symbol of the garrison itself for many a career-conscious union functionary.[21]

This move had an extremely important byproduct, broadening the AFL-CIO options for intelligence-related activities within Africa. Israeli intelligence officials had been encouraged and funded by Washington to penetrate governments, labor unions, and civic organizations in the newly independent states of the continent. As Israeli experts in many fields, including construction, agriculture, and military training showed African leaders how to create the bureaucracies to run their nation-states, Israeli commandos typically formed a Praetorian armed guard around the person of new leaders friendly to the West. The CIA thus quietly underwrote hundreds of projects and tens or hundreds of millions of dollars in annual spending, building infrastructural dependence upon the United States, including a myriad of labor-related connections filtered through the AFL-CIO. In this way, U.S. tax monies and AFL-CIO dues together began to fund sharply rising levels of furtive collaboration. For that matter, Israel's gradual conversion from a bureaucratic but also intensely populist Labor-Zionist project into an ambitious regional economic and military elite helped to reinforce a parallel shift from social-democratic to military-intelligence politics within American labor leadership. Years later, after the occupation of the West Bank and in the face of third world criticism of Israel within the United Nations, Bayard Rustin announced himself the leader of an American trade union bloc for Israel. He was paying his dues for his new status.

Eisenhower, always somewhat uncomfortable with what he labelled the "military-industrial complex," had made himself more and more unwanted to America's labor leaders (as well as unforgiving Israeli supporters) by the end of his administration. Kennedy was correctly viewed as a more cooperative figure on Middle Eastern as well as labor issues.[22] Into the later 1960s, the same labor leaders who remained verbally supportive of the Civil Rights Act and the War on Poverty spoke and acted vigorously on Middle Eastern issues to cover both the retreat from the socialism of their youth and the increasing anti-affirmative action inclinations during their older years. Perhaps, in sentimental moments, they still nurtured the hope of a two-party "realignment" in which the Democratic Party might be transformed into a social-democratic party with themselves as kingmakers. Even as they grudgingly adjusted to the newer liberal acceptance of an individualistic and class-based consumer society as the highest form of attainable democracy, Kennedy fulfilled their image of a dashing, sexy, and accessible transition figure to some potential New Jerusalem.

Corruptions of the Underworld: The Mob

President Meany, already positioned as the successor to the ailing William Green in 1951, had placed unity with the CIO high on his agenda.[23] As the CIO expelled Communist-led unions, he felt the need for a parallel gesture against mob unions. Even before his presidency was rubber-stamped by the convention, Meany made a leap toward consummating the courtship by moving against the hopelessly corrupt, mobbed-up International Longshoremen's Association. In no small measure of historic irony, the ILA was now headed by Meany's former chief sponsor in New York labor matters, Joseph Ryan. Never strong on personal loyalties or AFL traditions when career chances opened, Meany adroitly bypassed the AFL's traditional teachings on union autonomy. Charges against the ILA were presented to the Executive Council which, under pressure from Meany, agreed to suspend the union. The ILA was expelled from the federation by the 1953 convention.

Observers and critics have mused to what extent Meany's campaign against the ILA was motivated by ethical standards and to what extent by more practical considerations. The evidence of abundant unpunished corruption in assorted AFL unions suggests the latter. The move against the ILA came on the heels of a widely publicized investigation by the New York State Crime Commission, which proved that the ILA was less a union affiliate than a branch of organized crime. The commission's compelling revelations of extortion and assassination naturally discredited all organized labor. Legislators, then, made an implicit threat to the AFL: remove the ILA or suffer the penalty of restrictive legislation. What role did this threat play in the new AFL president's move?[24]

The ILA had a long and publicly exposed history as a crooked organization going back to before the days of Meany's stint as business agent of Local 463. As a Manhattan labor functionary, president of the New York State federation, and second in command at the AFL, Meany knew intimately about the misdeeds on the New York City docks. Yet it has never been claimed, even by his ardent biographers, that he urged suspension or expulsion for this corrupt International or discipline for any of the mob-tainted unions (including numerous building-trades locals under his jurisdiction) around him—until, that is, the crime commission's shocking public revelations.

Indeed, some of Meany's strongest supporters came from the same construction trades, or from those (like the ILGWU's president, David Dubinsky) who echoed Meany's fulminations about the moral corruption of America's enemies, but had generally turned a blind eye toward mob activity in and around their own locals. Six years after the expulsion, Meany invited the ILA—with a better-crafted public image—back into the fold. In fact, it remained an organization which hardly conformed to the requirements for affiliation established by the official code of ethics adopted by the AFL and CIO at the 1955 unity convention. But neither, of course, did many of the less notorious internationals, from those representing hotel and restaurant workers to those representing carpenters, painters, and musicians, among others.

Unity inevitably brought rising expectations for labor, not all of them welcome. Radicals and labor idealists of various kinds who somehow survived the purges or who now looked at the labor movement longingly from the outside, optimistically forecast a new era of militancy and even political independence. A more powerful union movement would, they believed, be inevitably emboldened to organize politically and in its own interest. Unions had special reasons to do so, as labor leaders recognized: continuing a slide downward from the influence and prestige of the 1930s-1940s, they now faced a Rubicon. Organized labor would go forward toward the unorganized and toward transformation of the American political system, building upon its still considerable strengths, or it would surely go backward toward marginal importance.

Other national labor leaders had their own enthusiasms, but of a more limited character. Walter Reuther envisioned additional millions enrolled, with union membership tripling in a decade or so. This was a pleasant prospect for more routine labor bureaucrats who, on the whole, were more concerned with numbers and cash flow than anything else. By contrast, Meany was skeptical if not downright hostile. He recalled later, looking back to the days of the unity convention, that Reuther's imagined organizing drive never materialized because the AFL-CIO could not and should not endorse a powerful "national trade union center" whose existence and activities threatened the internationals' "autonomy."[25]

Meany did promise, on the convention floor, to "use every legal means at the command of American citizens to organize the unorganized" and "to bring the benefits of the trade union movement" to the wider working class.[26] But without the concerted effort that Reuther foresaw and Meany rejected, this was empty rhetoric. As it turned out, few other means, whether industrial or political, were used to any such end. The Committee on Political Education (COPE), organized as the AFL-CIO's political arm just after merger, was limited to preforming yeoman services for the Democratic Party, often for centrist candidates whose nearest approach to labor was voting for gigantic defense appropriations as job-creation for their districts. "Operation Dixie," regarded as a dead issue even as textile plants and others continued moving south to escape unions, gained no new support. Not surprisingly, membership hit a numerical plateau in the early merger years and then proceeded to slip downward as a percentage of the workforce at large, a slide that has continued across forty years.

AFL-CIO membership, at the time of the merger, stood at 12,305,000. Ten years later, thanks largely to the spurt of public employment unions, it was slightly higher: 12,982,000. This 5 percent growth did not come close to the 15 percent increase of jobholders, and (more to the point) missed the boat almost entirely in the most rapidly expanding sectors of the non-governmental workforce. During the same period, the presumably dynamic UAW actually declined from 1,260,00 to 1,150,000. AFL-CIO allocations for organizing never came close to the mostly secret funds expended on international adventures. Sporadically, various unions announced organizing campaigns, nearly all of which fell flat. They suffered not even so much from bureaucratic penny-pinching or administrative incompetence as from labor's steadily worsening public image.[27]

Union leaders had themselves substantially to blame. Walter Reuther convinced himself, in the early years, that the large AFL purses would sooner or later open to fund fresh organizing drives. Rather than reaching out to the unorganized and contrary to promises, most internationals continued to devote their membership drives mainly to capturing members of other unions. It took six contentious years before the 1961 AFL-CIO convention finally adopted an internal disputes plan, and that did not prevent assorted bodies like the Teamsters from continuing old raiding practices when opportunity knocked again.

Meanwhile, Congress hammered away at union corruption and racketeering. Persistent criminal activity, especially in current and former AFL affiliates, offered an inviting target for publicity-hungry politicians (unsurprisingly, rampant price-fixing in big business failed to elicit similar levels of concern). A conservative but heartily bipartisan House and Senate drafted legislation, partly corrective and partly punitive, for the labor movement as a whole. The legislation took its particular shape from a committee run by Arkansas Senator John L. McClellan with young Robert Kennedy as chief counsel. Offered a wide choice of potential union targets, it zeroed in on the Teamsters headed by the imperial Dave Beck.[28]

Subpoenaed by the committee and exposed to television cameras, Beck took the Fifth Amendment repeatedly, a distinct embarrassment to Meany and the AFL-CIO. Under Meany's prodding, the executive council had recently passed a motion instructing union officials to testify openly and completely to committees investigating union corruption. The AFL-CIO ethical practices committee (known, of course, for its extremely selective targets) also grilled Beck about his demeanor and about whether the IBT was "substantially dominated or controlled by corrupt influences." The findings offered foregone conclusions. Indicted by Congress, Beck was also suspended from the Executive Council. He resigned as president of the IBT. The council ordered the Teamsters to clean up their union within thirty days or face disciplinary action. The Teamsters, at their September 1957 convention, replaced Beck with James R. Hoffa, who was possibly even more of a crook, and certainly rougher and more independent-minded (above all notorious for his threats to ally the IBT in an all-transportation workers bloc with the expelled left-led body, the west coast International Longshoremen's and Warehousemen's Union). Hoffa, therefore, presented a further affront to Meany. The council suspended the Teamsters, who were then formally expelled from the AFL-CIO at its December 1957 convention by a vote of 10,450 to 2,225 bloc votes (598 actual delegates to 497: in truth, a fairly close democratic vote). Likewise expelled, by a wider margin, were two other targets of the McClellan committee, the Bakery and Confectionery Workers Union and the Laundry Workers Union.[29]

Meany's campaign against Beck, Hoffa, and the Teamsters was not all clear sailing, either in the council or at the convention. Those who voted against expulsion included delegates from the crime-ridden building and construction trades, along with Patrick Gorman, a maverick and sometimes militant leader of the Meatcutters and Butcher Workmen's Union. Even

after expulsion, the Teamsters had powerful allies pressing for early reaffiliation, including NMU boss Joseph Curran, Michael Quill, and David
McDonald. A. Philip Randolph, by now the eminence grise of a limited
core of African-American unionists, noted sharply that the Teamsters were
far better on race than many unions in good standing and concluded that
expulsion, on those critical grounds alone, constituted excessive punishment. A final effort was made in 1961 to bring the IBT back into the fold.
It took all of Meany's persuasive powers, along with the manipulations of
Arthur Goldberg and a personal appeal by Robert Kennedy, to turn back
the move by a minority of council members for IBT reinstatement.

Exorcising the corrupt Teamsters, like Meany's move against the ILA
in 1953, was inevitably portrayed by the press, liberal intellectuals, and
union leaders themselves as proof positive of Meany's personally high
ethical standards. In truth, Meany responded to the stimulus of legislative
invasion which threatened public condemnation and further restrictive
laws. He also responded one-sidedly, ignoring unexposed corruption that
he knew existed. The mess uncovered by the McClellan Committee, for
example, might not have been known to Meany and the AFL-CIO council
in detail, but enough was known that a crusading president could have
moved decisively against Beck and his corrupt union long before, without
waiting for his hand to be forced by a legislative committee.

Meany's role in fighting corruption proved, in any case, ambivalent at
best. Under pressure from the McClellan Committee, he announced that he
felt very strongly that "racketeering and trade unionism cannot mix" and
promised the AFL-CIO's "full cooperation in the current Senate invasion."
At the same time, he underplayed the gravity of the problem, insisting that
corruption involved only "very, very small portions of the trade union
movement." At an absolute minimum, he must have included the 13 pecent
of organized labor expelled by the end of the year for its unions' corrupt
practices. More than the tip of an iceberg, this portion was far from the
entire corrupt floating mass.

Meany thus showed himself once more ambivalent and contradictory
about AFL-CIO policy toward corruption. His enthusiasm, moreover,
varied remarkably with time, place, and circumstance. In 1956, for instance, he had warned a local of the Distillery Workers Union that they had
been under Senate investigation since 1954 and that union autonomy could

not be used as a cloak for corruption. He repeated the same message to the Teamsters in 1957 but refused to intervene directly, on the grounds of autonomy. The purge of the Teamsters was in any case the last major purification undertaken by Meany, as the ethical practices committee demonstrated only timidity in its own investigation of a scandal in the International Union of Operating Engineers in 1958. By 1959, Meany's war on corruption moved into reverse with the official readmission of the ILA and Meany's moves to protect his ardent supporters. Carpenters' President Maurice Hutcheson, a true successor to his late father, was found guilty of contempt of Congress after being questioned in 1963 about dipping into the union treasury. He received a six-month jail term, a judgment which Meany vigorously and successfully protested. The hapless scion got two years probation, and, later, a pardon from President Lyndon Johnson. Meany's preference was clearly for labor peace, and for the avoidance of *appearances* of impropriety, rather than for any consistent and firm policy to uproot corruption.

The McClellan investigation meanwhile culminated in legislative action, the Landrum-Griffin Act (officially known as the Labor Management Reporting and Disclosure Act). Passed by a House and Senate controlled by Democrats after their 1958 electoral sweep (a victory assisted notably by AFL-CIO mobilization), it was signed into law by President Eisenhower in September 1959. The act had its genesis in a Kennedy-Ervin bill which Meany reluctantly supported, but underwent a number of changes credited to Congressmen Landrum and Griffin. One section of the new act actually tightened the restrictions of Taft-Hartley, outlawing the closed shop and secondary boycotts, and restricting picketing rights and other measures of solidarity. But a section known as the Bill of Rights appeared to offer democratic guarantees to the rank and file, though other provisions made it difficult for dissidents ever to reach the courts and claim such rights. Despite these limitations and the now-permanent danger of government involvement in union internal life, the Bill of Rights abstractly provided ordinary union members a minimal opportunity to protect themselves and their unions from the depredations of labor bureaucracies. It was up to members and their supporters to claim their rights.[30]

This was not the way Meany looked at it, however. He lashed out at the Bill of Rights provisions with more than usual vigor. He viewed them as a direct assault on the kind of trade unionism that had nurtured him and which he proudly represented. He could not deny that violations of membership rights did regularly occur. But it was, he insisted, the responsibility of labor to clean its own house. His arguments against government control had a certain militant ring, but they were actually the effort of an autocratic leader to maintain the chain of command, of a bureaucracy to defend its interests.

The assassination of a prominent dissident brought this issue home. In 1969, Jock Yablonski, the leader of a democratic reform movement in the United Mine Workers who sought to challenge incumbent Tony Boyle for the union presidency, was murdered along with his wife and his daughter. Not a single official representative of any trade union organization could be found at their funeral. Mike Trbovich, who had managed Yablonski's campaign, sent a telegram to George Meany asking that Miners for Democracy (organized by Yablonski's supporters immediately after his murder) be allowed to plead their case to the AFL-CIO executive council so that labor might "clean its own house without Senate or Administration inference." Meany would have none of it, responding flatly to a reporter's questions, "The AFL-CIO traditionally has refrained from intervening in the internal affairs of its own affiliates, let alone outside organizations." Thus, Meany clearly disapproved of labor and government assistance in cleansing a union of corrupt officials, even those who hired hit-men; that assistance, in his estimation, constituted a violation of a union's "democratic structure." It had been Meany's widely known view, in any case, that Yablonski the insurgent was merely "one of the boys from the kitchen trying to move into the living room." With the reds gone, nothing but the personal contest for power mattered, and with the exception of a rival or two, Meany naturally favored those already in power.[31]

The Troubled View of Race

The early AFL-CIO, troubled with an image problem arising from mob corruption, was even more troubled by race. For public relations reasons, and no doubt with a degree of sincerity, labor leaders anticipated a long climb of non-white Americans toward racial equality, and a social equalization of the races so smooth and perhaps so gradual that white workers (and presumably the white middle class as well) would be won over without pain. Meanwhile, the loyalty of a rising class of non-whites would be assured, especially in the voting booth, and any dangerously polarizing restlessness on their part would be held in check by their leaders. So long as African Americans remained largely in the South, in a terrorized condition, that last premise logically held. But labor leaders should have recognized, at least for the sake of their own futures, that the radically increased migration to the North for war work in the 1940s had brought the first great waves of a new and permanent struggle to the factories of the industrial heartland.[32]

The postwar red scare certainly slowed down the pace of that struggle, by making it hard for people of color to take positions or join associations without fear of retribution. The FBI and the AFL and CIO unions themselves had engaged in widespread personal harassment and the calculated destruction of several deeply interracial Communist-led unions, as well as pressure on non-Communist radicals who raised racial issues of power distribution within organized labor. Even Arthur Goldberg, apologizing for the AFL-CIO in its early days, admitted "that neither federation has a perfect record [!] on racial discrimination . . . [and] the new federation will [not] be perfect from the start." But, he insisted, "ultimately every vestige of discrimination anywhere in the trade union movement in the country can be eliminated." When was "ultimately" and when would its leaders ("sincere and principled men," to Goldberg) move determinedly toward that goal?[33]

Momentum picked up again with the Montgomery, Alabama, bus boycott in 1956 (creating a new enemy for J. Edgar Hoover, who ordered his field officers, referring to Martin Luther King, Jr., to "Get the Burrhead!").[34] African Americans, it became clear, were not waiting for "ultimately" but were reshaping American society around *themselves,* relying on their own resources, in no small part because the labor movement and leading liberals at the time offered them scarcely more than rhetorical support, seasoned with stiff warnings.[35]

The labor intelligentsia around Meany worked overtime to give the AFL leader credence in a world where the gross and overt marks of bigotry (like segregated locals or the time-tested AFL convention delegates' favorite "darky jokes") had rather suddenly become an unacceptable embarrassment. Black workers in the prime employment years between twenty-four and forty-four experienced unemployment levels three times greater than their white counterparts in the mid-1950s, with more likely layoffs and injuries at work. By a combination of negative factors (especially shorter life spans and the regressive character of taxation), they actually put more into Social Security than they received—effectively subsidizing whites.

Samuel Gompers, as we have seen, not only shared the prejudices of his members, but gave those prejudices the crucial enforcement of job control. His successors, for many decades, did not even claim to do better. The Social Security Act of 1935 specifically exempted from coverage those job categories most likely to gather nonwhite applicants—farm workers and domestics. As the Wagner Act went to Congress, and the NAACP very properly demanded that it should contain an anti-discriminatory clause, the AFL executive retorted that it could not support any such legislation with that provision. Better to forego legal protections for labor than to lose the power to discriminate—a view consistently held by George Meany. After extended discussions, the Roosevelt administration accepted the AFL rule, giving unions simultaneously both legal standing and the right to enforceable discrimination.[36]

The stark circumstances had not presented themselves so clearly or continuously earlier, because people of color had been so relatively few in the North or so isolated that "competition" had seemed abstract. By wartime, the racial conflict over work and home life became more intense and violent in many cases as neighborhoods changed occupants and the new spirit of demand inevitably reached the most protected sections of labor, like the building trades, where "skill" had less than ever before to do with job opportunities. Thus the raw prejudices of Gompers's generation took different shapes in succeeding eras, but lived on, from the boiler room to the classroom. Seeking assurance of their own proper place and upward mobility for their children within a firmly racist culture, many white working people behaved in racist ways as they succumbed to the manipulations of employers and demagogues and to the assurances of their political representatives; in the process, they were made both victims and victimizers through a process that George Lipsitz acutely labels the "possessive investment in whiteness."[37]

It was not union failure but outright accomodation by labor officials to the racial status quo that was to blame, though in the context of a rising civil rights movement, Meany and his speechwriters labored long and hard to demonstrate that AFL-CIO executives were "leading" the apparently stubborn white union members toward a more liberal attitude. To be sure, the CIO had its civil rights committee, headed by International Union of Electrical Workers President James Carey (best remembered by this time for quipping that while the last war had been fought in alliance with Communists against Fascists, the next war would likely be fought in alliance with Fascists against Communists). The committee made public statements and established local committees on civil rights, with predictable feel-good results. But when, at the AFL-CIO merger meetings, Transport Workers President Michael Quill pushed for the abolition of outright segregated (i.e., AFL) locals and for binding language prohibiting all discrimination, Reuther, eager to soft-pedal the issue, rebutted Quill for speaking out of turn, and Quill's efforts were unsuccessful.[38]

Characteristically, in a February 1955, speech at the Trade Union Conference on Civil Rights sponsored by the Jewish Labor Committee, Meany had insisted that "for seventy-five years, we have constantly turned our energies in the direction of that which is right on the question of racial and religious discrimination." In one swoop, he had abolished all past sins. True, he admitted, discriminatory practices might yet continue in labor but "there are very, very few small and minute spots that have to be cleaned up." The audience of social-democratic functionaries, who knew better from their own experience (some of them in the South during Operation Dixie) and that of their predecessors in fighting against the immigration restriction policies of the AFL, rushed to congratulate the self-congratulator. He was their man.

If the problem seemed that small for Meany, the matter of public image remained troubling, which partially explains why during the merger convention and subsequent meetings of the AFL-CIO executive council an anti-discriminatory constitution and ethical codes and statutes were adopted. But they were so weakly formulated as to remain merely the *intention* of good deeds. The constitution spoke only about the "objective" of overcoming discriminatory practices. When A. Philip Randolph protested that provisions must be made for immediate and complete implementation of the anti-discriminatory statute, Meany held his ground. He preferred "to do it in the shortest possible time," which was to say, voluntarily and in no hurry. Even today, that time has still not come in many unions—especially not in those building trades whose leaders have unfailingly supported Meanyism at home and abroad.

Meany argued on many subsequent occasions that the imposition of racial equality on unions was in any case prohibited by the federationist structure of the AFL-CIO. Not even in a noble cause could the executive council deny affiliates the internationals' autonomy. Gompers could have struck that pose more credibly seventy-five years earlier (but also conveniently ignore it when finding reasons to remove the charters of rebellious local central labor councils, to collude with authorities against assorted radicals, or otherwise to beat back challenges). By the time of the merger the AFL had steadily been shifting in a yet more centralized direction; witness the expulsion of the ILA and the Teamsters. If organized crime and Communist affiliations provided proper cause for discipline and even expulsion, why not the organized acts of institutional racism or personal affiliations with assorted right-wing societies bent on keeping white prerogatives? (White Citizens Councils in the South were openly endorsed in many cases by craft union locals.) Discriminatory practices were so widespread in the new AFL-CIO that to present affiliates with the ultimatum to reform or suffer penalties would have brought Meany into major confrontations, most especially with his beloved building trades. The merger constitution had authorized Meany to appoint a civil rights committee that would "assist the executive council" in implementing the principle of non-discrimination "at the earliest possible date." How serious this effort was can be gauged by the choice for president of the new civil rights committee: George Harrison, head of the Brotherhood of Railway Clerks. Like some other committee members, Harrison personally represented one of the deepest corners of discriminatory practices.[39]

Not surprisingly, anger among African American union members over Meany's ineffectiveness and insincerity on these issues mounted. After many promises, progress remained nil. Black unionists increasingly turned to organizations like the NAACP and the courts, rather than the workplace, for redress. At the 1959 AFL-CIO convention Randolph reminded the president of the organization's unwillingness to fulfill its promises. Meany shot back: "Who the hell appointed you as guardian of all the Negroes in America?"

But Meany could no longer keep a lid on the situation. One response to AFL-CIO inaction was the formation of the Negro American Labor Council (NALC) headed by Randolph himself. The name and stated purpose immediately brought to mind a sanitized version of the vanquished National Negro Labor Council (NNLC), a left-led body which during the early 1950s had set up local Negro Labor Councils and pressed for fair employment practices in union contracts.[40] The NALC's demands, following those of the vanished NNLC, centered around a model fair employment practices clause in every union contract. These were still too advanced for Meany's cohorts. This time around, direct action from below moved past institutional efforts. Locally organized, nonviolent protests against discrimination in publicly financed construction projects from Newark and New York to Philadelphia and St. Louis, demanded that unions abandon the circuitous means (like "grandfather clauses" awarding extra points to the descendents of earlier generations of construction workers—who had, of course, been white) used to retain exclusive access to jobs like plumbing, roofing, sheet metal, and electrical work.[41]

The status of Mexican-American labor was hardly better. Following the collapse of the CIO agricultural workers' union, the United Cannery, Agricultural, Packing, and Allied Workers of America (UCAPAWA), former Southern Tenant Farmers Union head H. L. Mitchell gamely pressed Meany for support of the National Farm Labor Union, in reality more a movement than union (and sometimes hardly more than the "littlest lobby in Washington," run in person by Mitchell). Meany's sympathy, however, was nominal, and the AFL's financial support almost non-existent. A certain embarrassment continued toward the execrable conditions of farm workers in the Southwest, but growers successfully pleaded their case for more bracero (temporary migrant) workers and illegal immigrants, over the heads of powerless union officials who, ironically, insisted upon stricter enforcement of immigration laws. In 1959, the AFL-CIO's executive committee chartered the Agricultural Workers Organizing Committee (AWOC), assigning a white former steel mill foreman and UAW veteran to direct it. AWOC prided itself on "professionalism," in contrast to the social movement-style NFLU, but had no better luck. As agribusiness takeovers proceeded and the stirrings of a Chicano movement arose from community campaigns, the United Agricultural Workers Union of Delano successfully negotiated a contract with DiGorgio, which might, with the energetic support of the labor movement, have been the beginning of a new era. Thanks again in considerable part to the obstacles presented by the existing labor movement, it wasn't.[42]

The AFL-CIO failures among black workers remained better publicized and therefore more painful. The much-touted liberal Negro-labor alliance, an indispensable element of Democratic electoral victories, was coming apart just as liberals congratulated themselves upon the pronouncements and appointments of the Kennedy administration. The NAACP issued its own report detailing charges of widespread labor discrimination, not only in the usual building trades and railway unions but in the United Steelworkers, International Chemical Workers, and other prominent AFL-CIO affiliates. Meany denied everything.[43]

But a price had to be paid. When A. Philip Randolph complained about the Virginia AFL-CIO's unaltered plans for a strictly segregated state convention in 1960 and when he further called for AFL-CIO state and local councils to end *all* segregation practices within six months, the director of the AFL-CIO's civil rights department delivered Meany's response: the AFL-CIO was doing just fine in the South, and deserved to be complimented rather than criticized. Meany cleverly proposed turning over a whole day of the next AFL-CIO convention to civil rights leaders—then, on the eve of the convention, issued an attack on Randolph (written in part by yet another old socialist gone rightward, Jacob Potofsky of the Amalgamated Clothing Workers) reaffirming the complete propriety of AFL-CIO behavior. Meany himself moved to censure Randolph formally, for merely denouncing union segregation, for being "divisive." As if on command, not one single member of the council supported the black leader. The next day a beaten and further humiliated Randolph described AFL-CIO positions as the "best ever." The censure motion was withdrawn.[44]

Luckily for Meany, Randolph did not renew his moral advantage during the next, crucial phase. Indeed, Randolph resigned after a few years in the leadership of the NALC, and it crumbled. NALC, in retrospect, was the aging socialist's last independent-minded act. Like his ally Bayard Rustin, Randolph had become personally convinced that Democratic administrations supported by labor would faithfully carry through the civil rights revolution begun on the streets. Supporting the Democrats in turn meant loyal support of the Cold War (including the endless arms race, with its union jobs dividend), and a strictly voluntary encouragement of the construction trades among other historically exclusionary unions toward achieving real integration. The generational differences that divided Randolph and Rustin from young Black Power advocates would be crucial in this regard, because younger people, white or non-white, understandably had no faith in a more-than-nominal integration of such unions, irrespective of "jobs training" programs launched by the AFL-CIO and frequently praised by in-house black spokesmen.

It was easier to bully the AFL-CIO dissidents than to convince the public. Meany, hungry for public relations triumphs, occasionally promised to demand the inclusion of black applicants as members of a handful of locals. He rarely found the results satisfying. One cause célèbre ironically involved his literal home turf, New York Plumbers Local 2 (formerly Local 463), and a major municipal project, the Bronx Terminal Market. Four plumbers—three Hispanic and one black—sought employment on the city-financed project, applied for membership in Local 2, and were predictably refused. The city hired them, anyway. When they showed up for work, Local 2 walked off the job, calling non-white plumbers "scabs" just as the AFL had always treated the employment of those barred from unions. And as always, it was a classic Catch-22 situation: the qualified minority worker denied membership in a racist union was then bitterly denounced for not being a union man. Predictably, Meany did not see it that way. "As far as I'm concerned," he pontificated, the men who walked off the job "are going to stay off. This union won't work with non-union men." If they did, "I'd resign from the union and join some other union." It was a remarkably bold defense of race privilege by Meany, in 1966—very late in the game.[45]

All this came to a head in the historic March on Washington in 1963. In that year of anti-segregration demonstrations and civil unrest, with President Kennedy calling for a civil rights act in Congress, A. Philip Randolph appealed for a national march, proposing that Bayard Rustin outline a memo for the project. In a twist that his later career would make ironic, Rustin was thrust aside as too dangerously radical, thanks to his past as anti-war activist and his status as homosexual. The Kennedy administration moved in quickly to take control of the event, while the media responded with general hostility. Meany, notes Manning Marable, opposed the march from the first mention of it to him. The executive council, embarrassed into backing the march, put up very limited support. The mobilization of some forty thousand union members for the march nevertheless marked the largest labor demonstration ever in Washington. Young black activist John Lewis (no relation to the mineworkers' leader), speaking for the Student Nonviolent Coordinating Committee, was successfully urged to tone down his message, but an important element of black radicalism remained. Over Meany's opposition, progressive sections of labor had joined the battle.[46]

In a determined effort to get criticisms out of sight, Meany did lobby for the 1965 Civil Rights Bill in Congress. Most remarkably given his own record, he insisted upon the inclusion of Title VII, relating to equal employment opportunities. This is one of history's little ironies, since it was this section of the act that became the basis for much of the litigation against discriminatory practices in unions. Offering Congressional testimony, Meany said he supported Title VII because "we need a Federal law to help us do what we want to do—mop up those areas of discrimination which still persist in our own ranks."

Nothing but personal reluctance had, of course, had prevented Meany himself from doing so earlier. And Meany evidently did not anticipate the wide use of Title VII in unions themselves. The hundreds of cases subsequently utilizing the provision involving local unions of steel, machinist, electrical, paper, maritime, garment, railroad, and above all construction workers gained no active sympathy from him. On the contrary, the AFL-CIO leadership soon engaged in the first phases of a losing legal battle to neutralize the use of Title VII within its own bailiwick. Meany's allies managed to hold back meaningful integration longer than civil rights advocates of the 1950s might have anticipated. The Equal Employment Opportunity Commission, even if its officers had been determined to right the wrongs of discrimination, lacked the power to redress grievances. The Department of Labor's Bureau of Apprenticeship Training was worse, simply because its staff was filled by the veteran union functionaries with no intention of taking stronger action than "warning" unions—which needed only to promise to comply in future. Numerous craft union locals meanwhile developed new "tests" and "education" requirements to get around any possible enforcement. To this appalling situation, Meany and his staff showed none of the determined response they had applied, for instance, to labor's Communist suspects.

Among the labor movement's intellectuals, meanwhile, a flurry of discussion surrounded the controversial issues. Herbert Hill of the NAACP tore into the ILGWU in Congressional testimony in August 1962 for restricting the lowest, worst-paid jobs of the needles trades to people of color, blocking blacks and Puerto Ricans from advancing into the leadership of a union dominated by an aging generation of Jewish functionaries. Hill's charges were so stingingly true, so rooted in procedures that eliminated younger (and therefore darker-skinned) contenders for high union positions, that the aging Dubinsky dispatched former socialist leader (and current ILGWU Educational Director) Gus Tyler on a tirade of denial. Inasmuch as the union was, Tyler insisted, completely "color blind," all charges of discrimination must perforce be false. Besides, the ILGWU was known widely for its rhetorical denunciations of racial discrimination. As more cynical observers noted, Meany would presumably have been, even at this late date, more blunt and unembarrassed in his acceptance of exclusion's heritage as one of labor's prerogatives; Dubinsky, Tyler, and the ILGWU offered exclusionism of the sophisticated style, with hypocrisy laid on thick. Hill acidly responded to Tyler as he could have to Meany: ILGWU leaders, like so many of the older unionists with social-democratic backgrounds in particular, were not conscious racists at all. They were simply determined to keep control of their ranks, by hook or by crook, in the same fashion that they had purchased and gerrymandered votes against the Communist opposition during the 1920s and 1930s. The most liberal of them dispatched marchers to join one civil rights leader or another, or sent an occasional modest check from the union treasury—amounts rarely rising to the expense of a year's banquets toasting their own notables. By such gestures, they considered themselves sacrosanct from criticism, despite their firm alliance with Meany and continuing practices on internal union matters distinctly similar to his.[47]

After automation was introduced in the middle 1950s, it became clear to far-sighted observers that the millions of well-paying industrial jobs due to disappear would never be held by non-whites. Provisions of Title VII presumably intended to protect workers' seniority actually protected the benefits of racial discrimination occurring before 1964. During the recession of 1973-1974, layoffs fell on minorities by a vast disproportion; most of the gains made since the 1950s in manufacturing, across large regions, were wiped out in one blow. Only affirmative action could cause further barriers to fall, and if the courts along with the politicians shifted away from such solutions, a racial status quo would have been preserved—at what expense to labor's claim of supporting human rights, can only be imagined.

Labor's reputed liberals were no better, rhetoric aside—sometimes, rhetoric included. The aging and increasingly cranky David Dubinsky himself adamantly denied, in Congressional testimony, that "his" ILGWU had *any* obligation to upgrade the conditions of non-white members. Formal equal opportunity (here the union leader foreshadowed the later neoconservative arguments of the 1970s and 1980s taken up by erstwhile liberal intellectuals long friendly to the ILGWU) was all that any institution in America had the duty to offer. Besides—and this was his real point—the existing leaders had won the right to govern their unions just as they chose. Newer members had no right to upset the established apple cart. Never mind that the ILGWU had begun slipping badly in membership and influence thanks to the developing world market, and even further in credibility with younger, dark-skinned members for whom the triumphs of decades past were unknown (and the distant glories of the Jewish state unevocative), while the sweat-shop conditions of the present were a palpable reality. Walter Reuther, seemingly determined to make himself a champion of civil rights, was well-placed to rebut these thin rationalizations on behalf of a progressive labor bloc, elements of which could be found here and there. But to do that would unsettle his intimate supporters within the UAW. Reuther therefore sharply defended the ILGWU, further strengthening their camp and the logic of Meany.[49]

Walter Reuther's Curious Opposition

When new social movements began to emerge a generation later, the internal opposition to Meanyism within the AFL-CIO's upper circles had nevertheless only one official name: Reuther. The dynamic president of the powerful United Auto Workers and the darling of liberal commentators, Reuther had accompanied his outmaneuvering the Communist bloc in his union during the 1940s—and his ruthless crushing of all internal opposition, Communist or otherwise, during the McCarthy era—with declarations of liberal idealism. The rise of the civil rights movement, evoking the sentimental socialist memories of Reuther's milieu, coincided, however, with most unpleasant developments in the UAW's home territory. The union's fair practices department generally failed to support black workers' grievances in auto plants where local white leaders had loyally supported the Reuther machine against Communists.[50] The problems would, Reuther's lieutenants believed, largely solve themselves given enough time.

In the meantime, they kept the lid on. The founding of the National Negro Labor Council in 1951 alarmed Reuther because local Negro Labor Councils were most substantial in communities with automobile plants. The petition drive for a citywide Detroit referendum on a municipal fair employment practices organization, sponsored by the city council, was stridently—one might say meglomaniacally—opposed by Reuther. The notion that, as founding NNLC conventioneers put it, "the day has ended when white trade union leaders . . . may presume to tell Negroes on what basis they shall come together to fight for their rights" could only be viewed as intolerable heresy and a personal slight to Reuther on his home ground. To inform African Americans of the proper basis for activity and to proscribe improper (i.e., Communist-tainted) ones was precisely what FBI regional offices and local red squads demanded of the liberal-labor establishment's favorite outlets.

The fact that a charismatic Detroit attorney and future mayor, Coleman Young, was a leading figure in the proscribed National Negro Labor Council, as well as a personal counsel for Communists, only rubbed salt into Reuther's wounds. So did the NNLC presidency of William Hood, best known for criticizing the UAW's failure to support the upgrading of trained black auto workers. By 1956, the NNLC had been driven out of existence, unable to pay legal fees to defend itself from attack by congressional investigating bodies. It had brought real if limited successes to the struggle against job discrimination in a half-dozen cities, but that potentially constructive influence was all but erased except to serve as precedent for future efforts at affirmative action within the labor movement.[51]

Big changes, meanwhile, were transpiring within the automobile factories. As a recent careful sociological study indicates, automobile workers had largely won, by the end of the 1940s, a "quota system" in the place of management's detailed and arbitrary command-authority as the working standard of daily factory life. Soon, however, rising competition of corporate giants against each other and a sense that the combative era of labor had ended (as, indeed, Reuther himself often suggested) prompted a sharp turn toward a new rationalization of production, including intensification of every job for time and process efficiencies. Rebellions followed (sixty wildcat strikes in 1956 and eighty in 1958 marked all-time highs), but this time the UAW firmly joined management in ending the actions. "Outsourcing," a word that would become notorious during the 1970s-1990s for management shifting work to nonunion plans in the United States or abroad, actually began during the later 1950s in response to these struggles.[52]

Race and work-classification played strongly into the issues and Reuther's solutions. Deskilled and demeaning jobs awaited African Americans entering the industry during the 1950s. Conceding in advance the prerogatives of management to reorganize work, the UAW focused its attention upon cooling down conflict and winning comfortable pensions. Intermittently avowing to win or win back the black and militant members' loyalty, staffers talked often during the later 1950s about a dramatic march on Washington for jobs—while actually doing little, if anything, to bring it about. *Fortune* magazine savant Daniel Bell characteristically congratulated Reuther on his bold statesmanship for negotiating with top Democrats rather than marching; Reuther had thus successfully put behind him and unionism the antiquated unrest and potentially explosive class sentiment of the 1930s-1940s behind him (Bell reflected kindly that the union president's "dogmatic edges" had "been dulled" by reality).[53] Bell omitted that the old dogmatism included the power of the rank and file to push leadership, through some faction, away from the ruling bloc. By the early 1950s, union democracy became more convincing to the intellectuals at the Americans for Democratic Action than on the shop floor. Reuther himself regularly won elections with 98 percent of the vote, akin to Communist regimes in the East, based upon systematically rooting out potential opposition. Increasingly feeling their isolation from young workers, especially black ones, Reuther's supporters counted on an aging and deeply racist bloc of near-retirees to outvote insurgents. By the end of the decade, Reuther's faithful bused in retirees for their votes and resorted to a variety of practices very much like Chicago's notorious machine politician Mayor Richard J. Daley—himself originally put into office with the zealous support of the Chicago Federation of Labor.[54]

But the restlessness caused by deteriorating shopfloor conditions and frustrated expectations could not be suppressed. A statistician comments that "the main challenge to the system . . . came from the protests of the rank and file," the UAW's "pattern of accommodation with the industry survived largely unchanged and the issues on which the pressure was focused left unresolved."[55] The "institutionalized system" established by Reuther successfully survived every onslaught from below, but Reuther had grown much more similar to the Meany method than he imagined himself to be. Surely UAW leaders wanted to pass beyond the prevailing 1950s liberal-conservative consensus around business interests. They not only verbally welcomed Martin Luther King, Jr.'s activities, but modestly funded civil rights groups of the later 1950s and actively lobbied Democrats to stake out stronger positions. But time and again, they gave in, predictably, to political opposition. As Texas Senator Lyndon Johnson built a congressional consensus against a strong civil rights bill, he convinced the AFL-CIO leadership (never very hard to convince on these points) that openly and aggressively treating race issues would damage the bipartisan coalition around Social Security improvements. Reuther, as so often, wavered and demurred.[56]

The Kennedy administration offered many new domestic possibilities for the Meany-Reuther combination. Naively, the Reuther bloc had hoped for a program of sweeping social reform. They had worked furiously for a Democratic victory after Kennedy flattered Reuther personally and endorsed the auto leader's old notion of a Peace Corps. Reuther did gain wide access to the White House under the new regime—the kind of attention that annoyed Meany, who paid him back by vetoing (through contacts with Kennedy's advisors) Reuther's nomination to the United Nations delegation.

But despite sweet words in public and a long nostalgic remembrance afterward, the administration disappointed even Meany. Kennedy first shelved the AFL-CIO's appeal for rapid building of low-cost housing. Reuther himself urged comprehensive economic planning—the kind of social-democratic rhetoric unheard since the 1940s. But Kennedy's heart, especially after a national economic dip, belonged to Wall Street. Trickle-down tax cuts for corporations (justified as investment credits for factory modernization) predictably swelled the bankbooks of the rich without similar compensations at the other end of the social scale. Liberals feared that opposing Kennedy's give-away would undermine the principal of economic planning, and Meany vetoed even a planned meeting of AFL-CIO economist Stanley Ruttenberg with the president's advisors to attempt to persuade Kennedy to take a different approach. On such issues, it was no use. Labor would get the jobs created by massive new military spending, and the Kennedy administration proved genuinely helpful in facilitating the unionization of federal jobs. That was the limit, approved by Labor Secretary Goldberg and Meany, despite reservations.

Reuther and Meany meanwhile continued to spar with each other from the acceptable edges of labor's left and right, with the ILGWU's aging David Dubinsky typically weighing in heavily on Meany's side while rhetorically insisting on his union's commitment to "social justice." Reuther, ever more nostalgic for his past public acclaim among working people rather than intellectuals, repeatedly complained that the crusading spirit of labor had been lost somewhere along the way; Meany, not nostalgic at all, unembarrassedly derided the days of "anemic union payrolls." Reuther nearly got his lieutenant Jack Conway an appointment as under-secretary of labor, and once again Meany blocked a Reutherite move into high government circles. Reuther similarly tried to get the relatively progressive Ralph Helstein of the Packinghouse Workers onto the AFL-CIO executive committee to replace a retiring president of the Rubber Workers (another former CIO union) and was stopped yet again by Meany. Reuther's slight revenge, to name Conway to the head of the industrial union department, had little real effect; the IUD, sabotaged by Meany, had been a dead letter office for years.[57]

The prestige and influence of the AFL-CIO continued to be sapped by this running battle between Meany and Reuther, the latter increasingly aware that time was running out on his hopes of leading a great labor movement. Heeding the pleas of Democrats to maintain unity through the 1964 elections, Reuther soon advised "Dear Sir and Brother" George Meany that "the UAW formally disaffiliates from the AFL-CIO." With that stroke, by early 1965, the federation had lost over a million members and its most dynamic unit. Meany partisans naturally and not altogether inaccurately blamed Reuther's personal ambitions for the fracture. He had set his sights on Meany's job, and when that moved out of range, he moved his union onto the fringes of the AFL-CIO and beyond. Reutherites, though, saw it differently. The UAW, in their sanguine vision, was still the innovative, socially conscious, and democratic organization led by a president of parallel personal qualities.[58]

The revolt came too late. In the well-chosen words of *New York Times* journalist William Serrin, Reuther's union had become "a right-of-center union with a left-of-center reputation." Less strident than Meany in his repudiation of socialist ideals and also of his proclamation of capitalism's virtues, Reuther was scarcely less sincere. On the explosive issue of the day, the Vietnam War, the differences of the two were largely symbolic, at least until public opinion shifted at the end of the 1960s and Reuther followed in the wake. Even here, where he might conceivably have led a grand peace campaign to rouse working-class political loyalties against the all-powerful labor hawks, the auto leader's departures counted mostly for public appearance.[59]

Labor Officials against the Movement

The political conflicts within labor unquestionably opened wider at the 1964 Democratic Party convention. The AFL-CIO staked its political capital on a second consecutive national victory, but the challenge they had long hoped to see to the powerholders of the Dixiecrat South now came back as a nightmare in real life. After the first stirrings of a floor-fight, the delegates of the integrated Mississippi Freedom Democratic Party, veterans of threats and beatings at the hands of lawful authority, flatly refused the demeaning offer of token representation within an otherwise lily-white and ferociously racist official delegation. Labor leaders grumbled audibly at the ingratitude of the MFDP turning down a deal worked out by the social-democratic *Wunderkind* Allard Lowenstein, among others. Subsequently, historians tended to view this moment as the decisive break between African Americans moving toward the radical demand for black power and the AFL-CIO moving toward a narrowed vision of liberalism.[60]

Yet a spirit of hope unquestionably prevailed through the Selma, Alabama, march of the following year, including the activity of a multitude of ordinary unionists in various marches of kindred spirit for full civil rights, in Washington, D.C., New York, Chicago, San Francisco, and many smaller cities. It was, retrospectively, one of the last moments of officially sanctioned and encouraged labor heroism of any kind nationally, for decades to come. Union members, polled across the country, reported strong support for the Selma marchers and—contrary to popular belief—more enthusiasm for integration than white-collar respondents. The successful push for the Voting Rights Act of 1965, the last significant measure on behalf of minorities strongly pushed by the AFL-CIO leadership, was unquestionably a product of cooperation between the young radicals, liberals, and labor. For that reason, not even the growing differences over the Vietnam War can be accurately seen as the single, overriding cause for the decisive breakup of the liberal coalition.[61]

Class divisions on all sides, as well as divisions within the working class, grew more evident as the 1960s wore on. Within the civil rights movement, differences had surfaced as early as the March on Washington and became ever more obvious as the prospects for institutional desegregation appeared within sight. In part because the labor movement had done so badly in the past at incorporating the needs or articulating the grievances of the underemployed, the older generation of top black leaders (and Martin Luther King, Jr., himself) had little sense of what the underclass wanted or how explosive its temper could be when denied decent jobs and real social equality. The AFL-CIO expressed mock disillusionment in the black movement's rising militancy while calculatedly exaggerating its own contributions to racial equality. The AFL-CIO's civil rights department, guided by former socialists who had become hardened cold warriors, made itself into a new kind of internal warning system and press release operation against labor peaceniks and black radicals alike. Meany himself arranged a large portion of a budget—rising eventually to more than half a million dollars per year—for its sister operation, the instinctually conservative A. Philip Randolph Institute.[62]

This was another revealing facet of AFL-CIO policy. In the conflicts which had begun to break out between black working people and the black propertied class over a score of issues, the Meany office positioned itself firmly with the latter. As in foreign policy matters, the interests of "labor" were placed properly with businessmen and property rights rather than with the poor and underemployed. Analogously, the loud self-congratulations of labor leaders like Walter Reuther for their own contributions to the cause of civil rights were likely to be a celebration of institutional victories with less value for the black working class than professionals, and still less for the jobless class produced by the onslaught of automation. Actual black unionists, who demanded better jobs and higher union offices, proved less attractive to Meany and Reuther alike than did distant causes involving dignified black ministers and other prominent leaders.

The Vietnam War rendered this breech, within just a few years, into a political and perceptual canyon. Popular opposition to the war had enraged Meany. That the United States was being defeated by a Communist-led coalition in a small jungle nation was bad enough; that his military enthusiasm was not shared by America's youth, the African-American community in general, and increasing numbers of working people was almost too much to bear. The resulting stresses exposed the raw edge of visceral sentiment that his advisors had long struggled to conceal. While Tom Kahn, a gay speechwriter best known for fingering left-wing dissidents, emerged as a top-ranking Meany loyalist and the quietly gay Bayard Rustin supplanted the aging Randolph as the most important African-American labor spokesman, the chief himself openly raved at Democratic peacenik delegates from New York as "fags," suggesting how embarrassingly difficult the situation had become.

The AFL-CIO milieu had a significant pre-history of relations with Southeast Asia even before U.S. entry and dramatic expansion of the war. The American Friends of Vietnam (AFVN), a CIA-linked agency established and run by Cold War liberals close to the labor leadership, played a critical role selling the impending conflict to Congress and especially to liberal intellectuals during the 1950s and early 1960s. AFVN was the child of the International Rescue Committee (IRC), one of the most interesting Cold War operations to extend through the 1980s "low-intensity" wars in Africa and Latin America.[63]

Founded mainly to assist European refugees, the IRC carried on useful work after the Second World War but evolved by the middle 1950s into a Cold War propaganda mechanism not so dissimilar from the CIA's pet intellectual operation, the Congress for Cultural Freedom. The young Daniel Patrick Moynihan, working as the IRC's public relations officer en route to his career in Congress as a special favorite of Meany and Lane Kirkland, proudly described the IRC as the "ideal instrument of Psychological Warfare." The key "psy-war" over Vietnam was actually conducted by leading IRC figure Joseph Buttinger who even fooled aging Norman Thomas into making flattering public statements about the viciously repressive Diem regime of Vietnam, a government facing far more pressure from its own beleaguered citizens than from the feared North Vietnamese. *Dissent* magazine, with Buttinger's wife (a future benefactor of assorted later Cold War campaigns) as its key financial supporter, devoted most of a 1959 issue to Buttinger's apologias for the brutal South Vietnamese dictatorship. The labor leadership's favorite socialists thus guaranteed the moral standing of the hardline positions.[64]

By the time the bombs began to fall in huge numbers on Vietnamese villages and tons of Agent Orange had poisoned Vietnam's rainforests, Buttinger had haughtily withdrawn from the AFVN. But the work of the propagandists had been well done. The American public, its politicians, and its journalists had been amply prepared for outright lies about the Gulf of Tonkin incident. Labor's key converts to "counter-insurgency," like the rising teacher's leader Albert Shanker, stayed converted. They were convinced, like Meany, that the United States should never, *never* have left Vietnam to the Communists. Like the Civil War for the American South, Vietnam thus remained the great lost cause. It was the source for binding emotional ties between the AFL-CIO executive and cold warriors otherwise adamantly hostile toward labor and its presumed social concerns. Meany himself insisted as late as 1975 that only two reasons could be adduced for the U.S. defeat in Vietnam: a "loss of will on the part of the South Vietnamese; and the complete and final refusal by the U.S. Congress to provide them with the material resources needed to defend their country from Communist aggression." This despite the fact that the United States supplied immeasurable quantities of materials, dropped more bombs in a smaller area than in all of Europe during the Second World War, and contributed sixty thousand American lives along with the several million Southeast Asian civilians killed or maimed in the useless, decades-long, and ecologically devastating conflict.

Increasing popular opposition to the war had predictably heightened Meany's ire. Trade union leaders sharply reminded the ranks and also middle-level leaders—including many of the same civil rights marchers who now turned to Vietnam protests—that the leadership was not able to tolerate elected labor representatives willing to countenance peace short of victory. By 1967, the *AFL-CIO News* began a seemingly endless series of Meanyite attacks on labor peaceniks and their sympathizers.[65]

Meanwhile, Meany's attitude toward the civil rights movement turned increasingly upon private resentments toward King, the veritable symbol of non-violent resistance. Labor leaders viewed with a sense of particular betrayal King's avowed opposition to the war and his rhetorical description of the United States as the "most violent society in the world." Once viewed as a savior and a safe alternative to black radicals, he suddenly became in their eyes a monumental ingrate and a disrupter of the historic Negro-Jewish-labor alliance.[66] According to later investigative journalism, the Anti-Defamation League, interlocked with social-democratic circles and close to AFL-CIO leading lights, even sent spies into King's inner circle in a conspiracy to provide material on King's left-wing advisors to the civil rights movement's unequivocal enemy, J. Edgar Hoover.[67]

Only King's assassination in 1968 endowed him with a sainthood that Meany's office definitely did not feel toward the great leader in the last years of his life. Crocodile tears from the AFL-CIO executive suites after King's death were unconvincing. Complaints about Hoover (whose Southern regional offices notoriously celebrated the assassination) and the many abuses of FBI power would have been more convincing, but Meany naturally remained Hoover's admirer unto the chief's death and beyond, even after public exposure of Hoover's involvement in civil rights violations and (surely even more embarrassing for Meany) his cross-dressing. After all, the Meany generation still owed the FBI for generous assistance during the early Cold War decades.

Early in 1968, as a despondent President Johnson announced that he could not run for re-election in the existing atmosphere, Meany laid the blame on the "phonies," the "eggheads," the "liberals." When antiwar demonstrators were attacked by Mayor Richard J. Daley's police outside the Democratic Party convention, Meany applauded the skull-cracking. He told an audience of machinists shortly after the convention that the demonstrators were "invaders," not real citizens deserving ordinary civil liberties. Stumbling for words, he denied that the police had "overreacted or whatever that means," and added, "I know what you would do with this dirty-necked and dirty-mouthed group of kooks." This was just the kind of zeal for police misconduct—whether directed at young people or residents of minority communities—that so many of Meany's devotees relished.[68]

Mayor Daley's own favorite candidate, Hubert Humphrey, who bizarrely argued against critics of the war that Vietnamese resistance to U.S. presence was all a red Chinese plot, naturally had Meany's full support in the following election campaign.[69] Perhaps the guns-and-butter Minnesota politician could not have reinvented himself as a peace candidate without losing the labor leader's staunch support. At any rate, his last-minute effort to convince voters that he intended a bombing halt and possessed a credible peace program (but one that he could not reveal) came too late to save his campaign from a more convincing, consistent Richard Nixon.

With that came a geological shift in labor politics and American politics at large. During the Republicans' 1968 campaign and Nixon's post-campaign effort, determination to widen his coalition through adding a considerable section of blue-collar, deeply racist Democratic voters, Nixon shrewdly played the Meany card. It was, as Republican pollsters later observed, a logical and historically blessed alliance coming of age. Old-fashioned Republicans had almost always run against labor, although blue-collar workers turned in fair numbers to Eisenhower mainly because he was an estimable military man who had a real peace plan to end the Korean War—and because they mistrusted his two-time Democratic opponent, Adlai Stevenson. By the late 1960s, something more important was happening.

Gradually, the infrastructure created by military spending and its spin-offs, especially in the Southwest and West, had helped create a new class of working people who identified their way of life with the fruits of the arms race, and their suburban neighborhoods with the middle-class escape from an assortment of urban problems connected with race. Not only in the West and not only under the umbrella of military spending, of course: the East Coast's Levittowns, assembly-line model of blue-collar suburbia, had sprung up with explicit prohibition of anyone but Caucasians, a rule that many inhabitants found natural as well as attractive. As the postwar decades wore on, working people could be and were increasingly wooed by tele-vangelists and other programmatic right-wing agitators. In many ways the shift in white working-class opinon, from liberal to conservative Democrat and then to Republican, represented, in its focus on property (with minimum taxes) and racial insulation, the logical trajectory of Harry Truman's assorted programs. Interracialism was never really intended to reach beyond the armed services to the workplace and neighborhood, certainly not on an egalitarian race-mixing basis, and many of Truman's coalition supporters had never seriously believed that it would.

The massive expense to promote the welfare and upward mobility of the 1930s-1950s white working class (even more, its children) had performed its task and continued to do so. Democratic constituents still quested after entitlements like Medicare and Social Security. But any newer version of the dramatic social programs that had worked for them or their parents twenty or thirty years earlier appeared to be unnecessary and obnoxious giveaways to the undeserving, especially when directed at poverty of the inner cities, which their families had left behind for the crabgrass pastorale.

Nixon himself, a shrewd California politician, embraced a steadily increasing military budget as the best sort of jobs program. An instinctive law-and-order man, he also naturally pleased middle-aged and middle-income workers feeling threatened by black militancy and seeking revenge against radical youngsters. Most of all, Nixon was hell-bent on winning the war even after a large bloc of liberals close to labor had changed their minds and now thought it would be best to write off Vietnam as an embarrassment best left behind. In office, Nixon sagely depended on Meany's thirst for victory on the international front and hatred of domestic dissenters to count for more than distaste for the administration's patently anti-labor legislation and the punishing wage controls imposed to limit wartime inflation. Up to a point, the wily Republican was right.

Not that he held all the cards. When Nixon dramatically escalated the war in April 1970, saturating Cambodia with bombs and toxic chemicals, he anticipated a big response but nothing so dramatic or politically damaging as the massive campus uprisings, the fatal Kent State and Jackson State incidents. Nixon's coterie nevertheless responded gamely, with inviting labor symbolism. In New York, where students planned to march down Broadway toward Wall Street, Nixon's strategists prepared a response that

few earlier Republicans would have attempted, orchestrating "labor" violence against youth dissent. It was one of the most brilliant uses of political
imagery of the day, accomplished thanks to the New York building trades.
Protesters were brutally assaulted by construction workers, the very section
of the building trades that nurtured Meany. Reversing the old Wobbly vision
of proletarians taking on Wall Street capitalists, photo-ops showed hard-hat
workers defending Wall Street against capitalism's enemies. Construction
trades leader Peter Brennan—widely known as Meany's personal
protégé—was praised and quickly honored in White House ceremonies.
Two years later, as a reward for his bravery in domestic action and for
having headed a Labor Leaders' Committee for the Re-Election of Nixon,
Brennan became secretary of labor for Nixon's second and ill-fated administration.

Whatever his ties to Brennan and other Cold War operators like Max
Kampelman who had switched from Democrat to Republican, Meany faced
resistance in the AFL-CIO to an endorsement of Nixon's re-election in
1972. Fewer than usual international unions chose to endorse anyone, and
those that did loyally endorsed Democratic candidate George McGovern.
Not Meany, however. McGovern had a generally strong pro-labor voting
record in the Senate, but to Meany he had stolen away the Democratic Party
and given it over to the radical left. Although Meany never urged a vote for
Nixon, he did make it plain that he would never vote for a man who
"advocates surrender." The message was clear. By 1973 and the Watergate
scandal, Meany was sorrowfully admitting that the nation "has sounded the
trumpet of retreat and withdrawal—retreat from decency at home and
withdrawal from principle everywhere else," an allusion to Southeast Asia,
a retreat that he blamed by now upon Nixon as well as the peaceniks. In
public statements, Meany enjoyed flattering "my friend Henry" Kissinger
and he continued attacking Senator Fulbright, "the well-known intellectual
from Arkansas" who had led the charge against the Vietnam War in
Congress. But Meany was clearly out of sorts. Détente with Russia,
ping-pong diplomacy with China, and above all the withdrawal from
Vietnam left him both bitter and impotent.[70]

Those labor leaders who were still widely considered left-of-center,
meanwhile, looked upon all this with a growing sense of dread. Time and
events had passed them by, and they had missed their chance to lead the

day at the climax of their careers. Bureaucratically speaking, they had outfoxed themselves. According to insiders, Walter Reuther genuinely wanted to break with the Meany hard line (his brother Victor had taken a prominent role in the exposure of long-time AFL-CIO collaboration with the CIA) on the war and other social issues. But he lacked the courage to do so. In youth he had ferociously braved the clubs of scabs, but in middle age the UAW president found no road back to the radical ways.

Such bureaucratic timidity played, in any case, very badly with the real American victims of the unpopular war. Vietnam vets, whether white, black or brown, often returned to working-class life full of rage (often drugs as well), bitter toward a society eager to send them away to fight and now equally eager to profit from their sweated labor. It was this generational factor, within a relative vacuum of other organized forces, which led to a politics of race, culture, and protest, more than factors of economics as such or even structural changes in unions. Older left-wingers could readily point out the limitations of a dope-smoking, anti-work ("youth culture") attitude, but they had long since lost their own following and had no credible strategic alternatives to offer.

Rebellious movements of the past had been coopted as well as crushed; this time, cooptation was hardly even attempted. A major radical challenge to the UAW, the League of Revolutionary Black Workers, centered in Detroit with a following in various industrial cities around the country (Mahwah, New Jersey, Cleveland, and Los Angeles, among others) collapsed under the weight of union discipline and disappearing jobs. The UAW leadership, still consistently white and chosen from within a small circle of loyalists, had no room for militant outsiders, not even (or especially not) those with wide support from younger workers.[71]

Other unions hardly did better. Outside of the embattled farmworkers union vigorously and often violently opposed by Teamsters, the assorted Asian, Chicano, Latino, and African-American movements mobilizing around labor issues and unions produced only a thin stream of labor officials, their futures in positions of prominence often delayed for decades. Even the beloved Cesar Chavez, determined to make peace with AFL-CIO leaders, willingly sacrificed his most radical and most talented cadre, with the predictable dire results part of the downward spiral of his United Farm Workers. More and more on the losing side of contemporary bargaining with management, labor leaders sought to make up in patriotism and bluster against students what they otherwise lacked in vigor and public standing.[72]

And no wonder. During the 1960s and early 1970s, a series of court decisions imposed numerical quotas and time schedules on discriminatory unions to improve the lot of black workers victimized by unions or employers. Ironically, Meany's followers complained that these were a device by Nixon's administration (which in other racial matters they so loyally supported) to divide the working class. Meany ally Patrick Moynihan described an affirmative action plan for New York City's schoolteachers as similar to "the sorting out of human beings for the death camps of Hitler's Germany" (teachers' union leader Albert Shanker, always alert to political analogies using the Holocaust to advantage, gleefully reprinted parts of Moynihan's speech in his *New York Times* paid political column).

Such presumably unlikely allies as the Anti-Defamation League, the American Jewish Congress, the American Jewish Committee, the Ukrainian Congress Committee, and the Polish American Affairs Council, along with veteran Cold Warrior Sidney Hook and neoconservative Nathan Glazer joined Meany in the counter-attack against affirmative action. Actually, of course, preferential treatment like congressional gerrymandering was as American as apple pie and vote-fixing. All these groups had lobbied for it on behalf of their own constituents. Crucial preferences had been applied to Second World War veterans so as to give them advantages on civil service examinations as well as generous scholarships to higher education, housing loans at low rates, and so on.

For Meany, as for the emerging brand of neoconservatives with whom he shared so many assumptions and enemies, the old racial rules against non-whites were doubtless now seen to be crass, but strenuous efforts to compensate for past injustices were simply unendurable. For society to take any responsibility for the consequences of such past discrimination (as his own home construction unions had practiced so long and so effectively) simply had to be, as Meany himself put it, plainly "nuts . . . to say that we've got to sacrifice our kids and our rights to take care of people who merely say that we've got to be employed because our skin is black, that is discrimination in reverse and we don't buy it."[73] Quickly facing the "glass ceiling," women and non-whites in many unions pushed, sometimes successfully, for affirmative action in particular cases. Local union offices occasionally sought to assist, although vigorously holding the line against shifts that might bring labor staffs in line with the changing demography of the membership. At the top, any and all formal AFL-CIO support of affirmative action remained a face-saving operation.

Beyond Alliance: The AFT and Labor Decline

During Johnson's later years in power, when the clashes over the Vietnam War became more dramatic, a seismic shift in labor politics became increasingly noticeable. Just as third world movements abroad—suspiciously anti-capitalist, at least in their rhetoric—came under the rubric of threats to U.S. interests, their domestic equivalent seemed, likewise, to spin out of the control of liberal leadership. During the second half of the 1960s, many labor officials who had been supporters of the civil rights movement became increasingly fearful that African Americans as a group might become disloyal to the Cold War. In the view from Meany headquarters, African Americans stubbornly refused to appreciate how well they had been treated by labor and now childishly demanded an immediate end to racism's effects rather than patiently awaiting America's good graces. In reaction against the rising left, labor's emerging bureaucrats moved swiftly rightward on a wide swath of issues. Among the prominent newer figures of a rightward-leaning union power, none was quite as strident or influential as Albert Shanker, leader of New York's United Federation of Teachers (UFT) and soon to become president of the American Federation of Teachers (AFT). At the same time, the conflicts between the African-American community and Jewish professionals—mirroring larger conflicts of urban society shifting demographics as whites raced to the suburbs—came to a head.

The role of the teachers, symptomatic of white-collar unions, was critical to labor by any standard. The labor movement successfully slowed its loss of members—which is to say, postponed catastrophic decline for twenty years—through recruiting a government workforce at all levels of federal, state, and local agencies. In the Cold War context, this advance came at a heavy price. The history of teachers' unions stretches back to the movements of high school instructors in the golden days of Debsian Socialism. The AFT's true if unacknowledged precursor, however, was the Teachers Union, originally an AFL body led largely by Communist regulars and their factional rivals in New York, Philadelphia, Boston, Chicago, and elsewhere, encompassing college instructors and public school teachers. During the explosive late 1930s, the TU was disproportionately New Yorkish and Jewish, especially influential among substitute teachers. With the union split on a handful of issues (including philosopher John Dewey's bold defense of Leon Trotsky against Stalin's charges of treason to the Soviets), the anti-Communist faction first seceded, and then successfully arranged the expulsion of the TU from the AFL in 1941. Reformed as Local 2 of the American Federation of Teachers, Dewey's faction eventually received the respectability that the isolated TU lacked, and might have had the field to itself when the latter gave up the ghost in 1964 but for a competitor organization, the more professionalist National Educational Association.

The AFT, picking up TU members as much as possible and conditioned by a certain social-democratic bearing, sought to maneuver teacher unionism around the challenge of the civil rights movement. Whatever its other traits (mainly a weakness for things Russian), the TU had consistently urged an anti-racist curricula and fought for the rights of African American teachers, few as they were. By contrast, the AFT faithfully filed friend-of-the-court briefs for school desegregation while ferociously resisting organized efforts to integrate student bodies and teacher staffs. This calculated ambivalence demonstrated that the AFT leaders (and no doubt many members) wanted it both ways: liberal credentials with unchallenged racial prerogatives.[74]

Internal changes strengthening the hands of the AFT bureaucracy played a counterpart role to this political double-dealing. Establishing the "Unity Caucus" within the UFT and the "Progressive Caucus" (hilariously mistitled) within the AFT, Shanker assured a discipline that the pre-1917 Bolsheviks could only have wished for. No member of either caucus would vote contrarily or even disagree in a public forum. To vote or speak against the leadership risked exclusion from the caucus and (approximately a thousand times more important) loss of a staff position. Even while Robert's Rules were formally upheld, conventions showed no exception to public unanimity of caucus members (at the prospect of such a vote, issues were customarily and quickly referred to the executive council). It was a remarkable achievement within an organization whose liberal members were often horrified by Shanker's craving for victory in Vietnam, his endorsement of feminist-baiting politicians, and his alliances on the out-spokenly right-wing, seamy side of union life. Meany, recognizing a leader of his own calibre and style, passed over AFT President David Selden in 1972 to add fellow hawk Shanker to the AFL-CIO executive council.[75]

The status of public unions had intensified the ambivalence all along. The experience of lobbying state legislatures for permission to organize and for larger benefits on the one hand, and the ongoing relationship to an urban public on the other, lent itself both to strenuous efforts at coalition and to closed-door deals with centrist and conservative politicians. Rather than generalizing issues of public resources, most public union labor leaders narrowed the terms of negotiation to members' welfare and their own prestige. Effectively cutting themselves off from potential community allies and making fiscal counter-attacks inevitable, they nevertheless re-sponded to their own changing sense of class and to those whom they now perceived as business allies. Like so much of the newer middle classes, many teachers and public servants increasingly enjoyed (or consoled themselves in) their insular suburban life-styles, rationalizing that minori-ties had "ruined" city life. Faced with classroom problems accelerated by shortages of all kinds (except, of course, of students), they romanticized their own past roles in the early civil rights era, complained early and often at the ingratitude of minority students, looked forward to retirement pack-ages, and put aside moral qualms about the internal operation of the union.

Seen in broader terms, teachers' leaders concluded that the AFT/UFT's lobbying model was itself the logical and inevitable successor to labor's historic mass mobilization and the logical outcome to the CIO experience. According to this widely held liberal version of labor history, the expulsion of Communists and the suppression of internal dissent were no doubt painful measures, but a necessary price to free union leaders' hands and to provide needed assurances for the assistance from responsible politicians to permit white-collar unionism. The state and business community rewarded order, just as they punished the movements from below which they inevitably characterized as encouraging disorder and disloyalty. It seemed the era of true class conflict had ended, for once and for all, with the old dream of socialism not only archaic but transcended by meritocracy. Now a modern, democratic civil society (a "complete civil society, perhaps the only one in political history," as rightward-turning Daniel Bell put it) faced uncivil masses, and had every right to protect itself from illiberal outsiders.[76]

Such a perspective, heir to liberals' insistence upon a polity of "American exceptionalism" of consensually shared goals, had always presumed racial empire, with common assumptions of propriety among all (white) respectable classes, from capitalist to craft worker.[77] The heirs now deigned to include not only the children of eastern and southern European immigrants, but also the non-whites who would willingly join the meritocratic rat race for privilege and influence. Apart from racial considerations, they mistook the wheeling-dealing of leaders for the sacrifices of thousands of union activists who urgently wanted to be both good teachers and good citizens, in the inner cities quite as much as the suburbs and surviving villages. Often the children of blue-collar unionists or others crushed during the Depression years, such teachers lived their lives without embracing either the military Keynesianism which Shanker so admired in politicians or the meanness toward disadvantaged students that his leadership epitomized.

All of this played out very strangely in the later 1960s. The very victories of teacher unionism placed unionists in the paradoxical position of having won a crucial base within the cities just as the cities themselves drastically changed. Self-proclaimed supporters of racial equality rapidly adopted the pseudosociology of Daniel Patrick Moynihan, in which a "culture of poverty" rooted in a matriarchal black community was the real hindrance to African-American advance, rather than the repressive social conditions of the rural South or the increasing joblessness and suburbanization of the North. The newer cultural determinists prided themselves upon banishing genetic theories of inferiority, but by assuming youth could be remolded without broad changes in the property relations of society at large they created an equally race-linked hypothesis. Moreover, they insisted that this version of "justice" was the true spirit of organized labor.[78]

Tensions between blacks and Jews meanwhile flared, and not only in New York or among teachers, students, and parents, but among the populations at large. Power-seeking nationalists seized the moment on both sides—notwithstanding the media spin that portrayed one side of the polemic as civilized discourse and the other as barbaric noise.[79] Albert Shanker's chief historic role was to pour gasoline on the spreading fire.

New York's black community leaders in 1968 demanded their own version of the decentralization that Shanker repeatedly insisted he would have favored, under other conditions, for the good of teachers and students alike. Even then the impending disaster might have been avoided through careful negotiation. But Shanker, like Johnson plunging deeper and deeper into Vietnam, called "his" teachers out on strike. After months of increasing bitterness on all sides, he declared victory in a war against community control that destroyed what was left of the Jewish-Black alliance.

The New York teacher's strike was small potatoes compared to labor's past battles for industrial unionism, or to events of the same year like war protests, the assassination of Robert Kennedy, or the presidential election. Few non-teacher unionists west of the Hudson and off the UFT rolls were likely, before or after the conflict, even to know Shanker's name. But if he had earned high points in Meany's office, he brought another image to the AFL-CIO's status measured in its emerging man of power. In 1968, New York columnist Jimmy Breslin described the then-UFT leader as being "only an accent away" from race-baiting segregationist George Wallace. RWDSDU District 65's David Livingston sagely predicted that Shanker had set back by twenty years the long-envisioned Jewish-black alliance with labor.[80] Shankerism, hammered out against a background of political Machiavellianism, middle-class yearnings, and ghetto rage, became the oddest possible test of American-style "democratic socialism" in labor's history, demonstrably neither democratic nor socialist. It was a catastrophic misunderstanding which, in a microcosm, set the accelerating downward path of labor to follow.

On the heels of the 1972 elections, the debacle of Watergate and the reorganization of American politics robbed the AFL-CIO of its remaining advantages. Senator Henry Jackson, never a serious presidential candidate, became the symbol of a weary and nostalgic empire for a Meany leadership perennially pining for Truman substitutes.[81] Known first to last as a lobbyist for Boeing and the military-industrial sector of his own native Washington, Jackson succeeded only in attacking a field of moderate presidential Democratic candidates in 1968, 1972, and 1976. His 1972 flop impelled a collection of oldfashioned Cold War labor (now right of center) intellectual allies, from Sidney Hook to Max Kampelman, to shift directly into the Nixon camp. By 1973, Senator Jackson had become the voice at the

AFL-CIO convention attacking "far out" environmentalists' warnings about the Alaska oil pipeline and insisting only a rightward turn from McGovernism would put the Democrats on the winning road again.[82] Jackson and the neoconservatives prepared the way, in both personal and political terms, for the AFL-CIO leaders' future working relationship with Ronald Reagan. Jackson's most ardent supporters, concentrated in Social Democrats USA, plumped continually for the recapture of the Democrats from the recklessly anti-war, feminist, and environmental "New Politics" crowd.

The steady decline of the industrial workforce and the emergence of "rust bowls" during the 1970s deprived the AFL-CIO leadership of resources even before the severity of the oil crisis had struck home fully. Less able to deliver votes to Democratic candidates, labor found itself ever more dependent upon backrooms allies and arrangements. Labor politics now increasingly represented, at its leaders' most passionate and candid moments, the rage and resentment of older union members against younger ones, the privileging of pension packages over internal reform, playing working-class whites against underemployed non-whites. Meanwhile, the AFL-CIO continued the international policies of aggressive Cold War action against the non-interventionist proclivity encouraged by Watergate and the new liberal Democratic Congress. For Meany and his circle, the "Vietnam syndrome" now prominently on display was monstrous. To see it destroyed was their obsession.

The Meany Legacy

The departure of Reuther and the UAW from the AFL-CIO in 1964 not only meant no charismatic personality was left to combat Meany but also no bloc of aggressive unionists to offer significant, concerted resistance to rightward-drifting union leadership and social policies. The executive committee functioned as a glorified rubber-stamping agency rather than a representative body. Seen in retrospect, centralization of power was the inner logic of the subsequent institutional consolidation. Neither William Green nor Walter Reuther nor even Samuel Gompers, an expert autocratic manipulator in his day, wielded as much personal control as did Meany and his entourage. One traditional labor historian, admiring the advance of the bureaucracy, put it most politely: labor evidently no longer had any great need for services beyond the negotiation and enforcement of existing contracts. Everything else could more safely and efficiently be handled better from above.[83] In December 1977, at the last national convention where Meany played an active role, the only names offered in nomination for president and secretary were Meany and Lane Kirkland. Neither was resistance offered to any of the nominees for the thirty-three vice presidencies. A lone dissident of sorts who did manage to get onto the council, the socialistic machinists' president, William Winpisinger, was widely regarded as window-dressing for the steady rightward drift. Carefully directing his political views toward the public sphere, Winpisinger restrained his personal criticisms of Meany, much as some socialist craft unionists of the 1910s insisted that Gompers was a symptom and not the cause of labor conservatism, better endured than combatted. Meany responded by savaging Winpisinger's favorite views without mentioning Winpisinger himself.

By the 1970s, Meany grew more candid—or perhaps merely more arrogant. He held his ground proudly against his internal enemies and gleefully watched the mass social movements of the 1960s fade away. Admittedly, he also saw power within the Democratic Party slip further from his potential grasp and the AFL-CIO fall precipitously by any measurement of size and influence. Asked in 1972 why AFL-CIO membership was sinking as a percentage of the work force, he responded, "I don't know, I don't care." When a reporter pressed the issue, "Would you prefer to have a larger proportion?" Meany snapped, "Not necessarily. We've done quite well without it. Why should we worry about organizing groups of people who do not appear to want to be organized? If they prefer to have others speak for them and make the decisions which affect their lives . . . that is their right." Asked whether he expected labor's influence to be reduced, he responded, "I used to worry about the . . . size of the membership. . . . I stopped worrying because to me it doesn't make any difference. . . . The organized fellow is the fellow that counts. This is just human nature." Unorganized and lower-paid workers were less-than-irrelevant to Meany; they were unwanted.

Never particularly supportive of strikes except those protecting jurisdictions, Meany became steadily more hostile to walkouts as time went on. (He made one key exception, urging political strikes by maritime workers against, of all things, wheat being loaded onto Russian ships.) In 1970, he observed, "Where you have a well-established industry and a well-established union, you are getting more and more to the point where a strike doesn't make sense." Rather than strikes and organizing, Meany put his eggs into the basket of electoral campaigns, legislative activity, and involvement in a panoply of government-management-labor commissions and agencies in the Nixon, Ford, and Carter administrations. In some circles, these activities actually reinforced the myth of the powerful Meany, labor statesman and public figure. They did demonstrably little for labor. And no amount of them could quite dispel the image of the narrow-minded, unabashedly feminist-baiting and gay-baiting labor boss eating at four-star restaurants and puffing a high-priced class of cigars once restricted to capitalists and mobsters.

The AFL-CIO politicked actively for Jimmy Carter in 1976, after its leaders had expressed their real preference for "Scoop" Jackson. Ironically, the Georgia Democrat's narrow margin of victory actually made the support of labor, the African-American community, and feminists, among others, the crucial margin between defeat and victory. Once more, given a different approach, it might have been a moment for the labor movement to flex very real muscles and work for legislative assistance in breaking down barriers to organizing the unorganized, just as the women's movement reached an early apex and as assorted movements among people of color looked to advances within the mainstream. For that kind of enterprise, however, Meany had no stomach whatever.

Once in office, Carter offered symbols instead of substance: a modest assortment of anti-poverty pilot programs amid a generalized retreat from the Great Society promises. Secretary of Labor Ray Marshall would be remembered not for his speeches saluting labor but because he was the last labor secretary who apparently believed that unions were necessary for working people. As so often, labor had rewarded its friends, gaining little in return. Meany soon let it be known that he was giving Carter a "C–" as president. Did he wish to see anyone else in the race for 1980? "Yes," he shot back, "Harry Truman. I wish he were here." To be fair, the old strikebreaking "Give 'Em Hell Harry" could not likely have accelerated the growth of American weaponry any faster than Carter did after the Russian invasion of Afghanistan in 1979. He might have bombed Iran into oblivion, and he surely would have *sounded* tougher. That kind of rhetoric, joined perhaps with robust new liberal-led red-scare against peaceniks, feminists, and radicals at large, would surely have had more appeal to the frustrated, aging bully that Meany had become.

The AFL-CIO of the later 1970s was especially keen to win a $3 per hour minimum wage with a formula for annual increases. The best that Carter would support was $2.50, well below the established national poverty level. Another of Meany's major legislative goals involved over-coming legal restrictions against unionists picketing more than one en-trance to a construction site. This had more than symbolic importance to Meany's home constituency, as non-union construction began to take larger shares of the market, especially but not only in the Sun Belt states. After an enormous investment of time and money, the campaign for a labor reform law—described exaggeratedly as allowing labor to regain the legal territory lost since the enactment of Taft-Hartley—also went down to defeat. More than a few Democrats joined with Republicans to ensure its final demise.[84]

Worse than losing out with Carter and Congress, the organized labor movement was losing out with the public—a fact of which Carter and congressmen were acutely aware and which encouraged them to turn a deaf ear to pleas for a set of institutions no longer able to deliver the vote. A 1977 Harris poll, for instance, found that 64 period of those questioned believed that union leaders were connected to criminal elements. Only 13 percent rejected this notion, revealing a perception, all too accurate in many cases, of labor leaders as being only slightly less unsavory than automobile salesmen and shyster lawyers. A considerable portion of voters shifting rightward—or becoming politically active for the first time, as in the case of many evangelical conservatives—considered unions to be obstacles to free enterprise and supported a new wave of state right-to-work laws. The more openminded younger people, enraged at corporate depredations like profiteering during the oil crisis, or themselves influenced by the women's movement, the gay movement, or other rising causes of the decade, frequently sympathized with the poor and with working people generally. But they found very little to admire in the expressions of organized labor and even less in the behavior and public personae of its leaders. Even the Progressive Alliance, launched in 1979 by Reuther's successor as UAW head, Doug Fraser, along with seventy-one other labor, consumer, and environmentalist organizations, was dead in the water. Labor had given up its ability to lead on public issues.

For just a moment, around 1978, as the waves of Watergate continued to ripple through Congress and buoy up younger reformers, a section of the Democratic Party had seemed to be moving toward a more environmentalist and New Deal-style pro-labor stance. But the deepening recession was no Great Depression, and the Democrats had no taste for mobilizing such a class constituency—now very much a race constituency as well—equivalent to that ethnic shift behind the New Deal triumph. Instead, the reorganization of society from the top down accelerated. "Economic reform," the magic phrase of the 1980s-1990s signifying not modest controls on capital and modest increases in assorted benefits for the poor (as in the 1930s) but a drastic shift in reverse, had begun in earnest. Massive plant shutdowns disrupted or virtually dismembered communities stable for generations; prospects for upward mobility across generations suffered enormously as unemployment, crime, and violence proliferated. Investments in plant and equipment declined sharply, as thirty-eight million Americans lost their jobs during the 1970s. The industrial working class had by this time definitively lost its numerical preponderance in the workforce. Automation, outsourcing, the growth of multinationals, and general shift of investment from basic and mass production industries to high-tech all cut drastically the numbers of union members involved in the old centers of industry. Lucrative tax cuts and other bribes delivered by corporations to cities and states had little effect or actually permitted companies to gather the capital needed for a total reorientation. Corporations massively accelerated their relocation to the South and West and to the suburbs if not abroad, in no small part to escape unions as well as restive minority workers.

Some unions scrambled to make up for the losses with the organization of white- and pink-collar workers in service sectors and government. The drastic increase of sales and service jobs at considerably lower wage rates than the industrial work they replaced should have put unionization on the agenda—all the more so as housing costs effectively doubled and the costs of other basic necessities raced ahead. Here and there, as among teachers and selected groups of state employees, the changes appeared drastic. But by the end of the 1970s, only 12 percent of service workers and 20 percent of government workers had been successfully organized, and even there, despite some promising moments, the figures soon flattened out. George Meany himself had no great confidence and very little real interest in the successful organization of the office workforce, and he had scarce awareness of the need for a solution to the ever-greater pools of union-free workplaces like the fast-food chains. Not surprisingly, by 1980 less than 10 percent of the retail and wholesale trades were organized, somewhat less than 50 percent of industrial production, and in all, less than 15 percent of the organizable workforce.

The labor movement had neither credible answers nor organizing capacity as the country in recession and unemployment reaching double digits with inflation (now called "stagflation") running rampant alongside previously unthinkable interest rates. The political right, stoked by unprecedented outpourings of funds and the think-tanks sprouting up aplenty (boosted by some noted intellectuals who were both former Cold War liberal favorites of unions and future intimates of the Reagan White House), meanwhile shifted into high gear. Catholic leaders, seizing the issue of abortion to combat feminism and to build fresh constituencies amidst aging ethnic flocks, eagerly joined the swift march toward the right. Even public television became, thanks to "Firing Line" and other corporate-funded features, a favorite site of Reagan-style propaganda. Not surprisingly, far more young unionists were likely by now to be followers of Jerry Falwell or even Jesse Helms than of Michael Harrington.

Renouncing traditional Christian anti-Semitism (although not the superiority and inevitable triumph of Christianity over Judaism), the new right avidly proclaimed its faith in the state of Israel against the presumed Arab and Soviet enemies. The same new right did not proclaim an end to its traditional hatred of organized labor and, especially in the South and Southwest, frequently pointed to local teachers' unions as proof of an evil state intervention (*permitting* public unions at all) within local community life. Nevertheless, over the course of the 1970s, conservatives found themselves avid partners to hawkish labor in a wide variety of international and national issues. As George Meany entered his final decline, their public admiration for his anticommunism, his resistance to affirmative action, and his eagerness for new weapons programs offered the stumbling leader a last measure of credibility. Protégé Lane Kirkland, with one foot firmly planted in these same locations, edged toward becoming something beyond a mere successor. Not properly even a leader in the traditional sense, Kirkland entered office as a power-broker of political factions positioned to shape a most uniquely depressing and defeatist era of American labor history. Not that the labor bureaucracy understood its fate. When incoming AFL-CIO President Kirkland told the assembled functionaries in 1979 that "words cannot match in eloquence the record of George Meany's . . . contributions to the enhancement of human life" and that his life's work "would do honor to a dozen men, if divided among their histories," the familiar rhetoric had become ludicrous.[85]

By the end of Meany's career, as little as labor leaders would be likely to admit it, organized labor had already seen its best days. For decades to come, it would retreat further and further. Once more, as in the case of Gompers' gloomy loss of First World War optimism, but more dramatically this time, one can stop to wonder how this had all come to pass.

Was it corruption, poor leadership, conservatism, or something more subtle that brought the workforce percentages and unions' moral authority both down so far? Robert Zieger, the most sophisticated of the traditionalist historians defending the postwar turn of the CIO away from organizing and toward collaboration with authorities, reiterates his earlier view that having taken advantage of federal support earlier, the labor movement was compelled to continue its participation under very different conditions and to take its lumps, not excluding the witch-hunt and the transfer of leadership to labor's least enlightened sectors in issues of race, gender, and so on.[86] This has been, since the 1950s, a persuasive argument for those who wish to be persuaded. But the presumed benefits have eroded so badly (or turned monstrous, like modest suburbanization become endless sprawl) that the crux of the argument has collapsed, most especially for younger generations—workers and scholars alike. A longer and more demanding view toward labor's liberals as well as its outspoken conservatives, its confirmed racists, and its ever-present mobsters, would find that the 1930s-1940s vision of a social contract had deteriorated from within, long before dissolving into a mere business contract. By the time the CIO had reached a set of policies on "reds" and war contracts that Samuel Gompers could have claimed as his own, the possibilities of organizing the unorganized had been precluded.

Some employers had, of course, resisted even conservative unionism during the wartime boom. Others, more wisely, submitted to government pressure to negotiate with the sole elected bargaining agent of the workers. Many came to see the wisdom of legislation consciously designed to maintain social peace, curb militancy, and dissuade unionists from moving in radical directions. It had worked well, if not perfectly, bringing a degree of stability to industries that only yesterday had been torn by strife. Most obstinate employers arrived sooner or later at the realization that collective bargaining was based on respect for the right of the owners and stockholders to profit from the corporation's ownership of needed capital and to be mostly free from union interference in the day-to-day management of the workplace. Sometime later, as sage stockholders envisioned, the limited gains could be reversed.

On the union side, the legion of specialists needed to prepare, negotiate, and supervise a contract covering provisions for wages, vacations, pensions, medical coverage, and so forth, had quickly and inevitably assumed a quasi-independent role, much as Robert Michels had described socialist officials in turn-of-the-century Germany. Well-paid professionals, responsible to themselves and the labor leadership which paid them, they represented a crucial layer of the bureaucratic apparatus unaccountable to those below. Even had the AFL-CIO been led by progressive, idealistic men and women, it is hard to see how a labor movement committed to the dogmas of business unionism could have avoided the impasse. And there were precious few such enlightened leaders; notwithstanding the "socially concerned" rhetoric of speechwriters, the George Meanys practically covered the field. The innate bureaucratic impulses of business unionism had few if any restraints under Meany.

Perhaps the most striking element of a labor leadership whose rhetoric constantly referred to "democracy" at home and abroad was its own personal and familial longevity. Nowhere else, not even the military (whose officers' chain of command most nearly reflected labor leadership's principles of internal organization and quiet moral corruption), did leaders remain until overcome by sickness and death—often to be replaced quite literally by a favorite son. No corporate takeover or shift in corporate profits, no war lost or won gloriously, virtually no degree of scandal either moral or financial, nothing could unseat the mighty. The rare exceptions, due usually to a push or putsch from above, only served to demonstrate the overall power of the rule. At the executive heights of the AFL (with the exception of 1894-1895 when reformers temporarily removed Samuel Gompers from office), and then the AFL-CIO, the presidential suite had only known four inhabitants in 115 years of organizational ups and downs. No world government, however dictatorial, and virtually no corporation of any size and significance could match this bureaucratic record.

Not many generations earlier, organized labor was successful (to the degree it succeeded, despite all the combined hostility of employers, legal authorities, and the commercial press) because of public support. It could and did call upon the talent and devotions of many thousands of self-sacrificing activists. Even its craft unions based in ethnic enclaves, as we have seen among German immigrants and others, were frequently leavened with far-sighted idealists. In time, and with increasing assistance of government sanctions for a leadership distanced from the rank and file, that reservoir of idealism had drained almost dry. The generations of the 1930s-1940s that built the CIO (and some of the better AFL unions or locals, as well) represented the tail end of an era, and the middle-aged or older activists of later days could by the 1970s be seen as the dwindling cadre of survivors.

A similar, if smaller, cohort of idealistic youngsters in the 1960s-1980s answered the call of a failing labor movement whose leaders did not seek or even want "outside" assistance, however generously offered. Meanwhile, corporate leaders and their favorite politicians, rightly confident of labor's inner weaknesses, prepared to choose their moment for an anti-labor offensive matched only by the open shop (or "American plan") drives sixty years earlier. It was the dawn of the era of crackdowns marked by the breaking of the air controllers' strike by President Reagan, of accelerated givebacks, strikebreaking, and outright union-busting. That story is a significant part of the saga of the disastrous Kirkland phase that followed Meany's era—and of how it ended.

4. THE KIRKLAND YEARS

The tottering of business unionism's hierarchy in 1995 was one of the most remarkable developments in all of U.S. labor history. It reversed, at least symbolically, the triumphal return of the Gompers machine from its temporary defeat just over a century earlier. The AFL-CIO's most single-minded Cold War hawk, American Federation of Teachers President Albert Shanker, winced visibly at the 1995 convention while handing the gavel over to the newly-elected federation president, John Sweeney. Shanker's faction, discredited by its failures to maintain labor's position or prestige, had been publicly trounced.

The historical and institutional background to this development is no secret. Business unionism had its own inherent laws of centralization and power. But less cynical labor leaders, too, including Communists and Socialists, had more than willingly consented during the 1940s in the creation of more bureaucratic structures which, in the second half of the century, steadily insulated the star chamber around George Meany and Lane Kirkland. Union-imposed discipline removed the need for union delegates to appeal regularly to workers' loyalty, and labor leaders had, of their own accord, wiped out the vestiges of shop steward systems that might have given ordinary workers means of redress against union leaderships. It had taken not much more willingness for the majority of them (including quite a number of former Communists) to agree to the extraordinary security measures surrounding expulsion of the left-led unions, a mirror of international operations styles within different wings of the intelligence community.

Two generations later, as what one prominent labor historian called the "breakdown of labor's social contract" neared completion, labor's internal "security state" imploded.[1] Employers no longer accepted the inevitability or even existence of unions, and the iron-clad loyalty of labor leaders to U.S. foreign policy gained them less and less credit on the domestic front. The day of the AFL-CIO members enjoying steadily rising wages and benefits, shorter hours and increasingly affordable home-ownership had passed. To the great surprise of most observers, middle-of-the-road business unionists facing the near-collapse of their dues-paying constituency suddenly escorted a new type of leadership, including some reputed radicals, back in the house of labor—through the front door. Service Employees International Union (SEIU) President John Sweeney, known for efficiency in organizing although not for any unusual commitment to democratic union procedure, arrived in office with a slate that included activists respected for their participation in militant struggles and eagerness to draw people of color, women, and gays into the movement.

The reversal of 1995 lacked one decisive element. The new leaders did not stand at the head of—or invite—anything like 1940s-style antibureaucratic unrest or Wobbly manners back into their ranks. It remained to be seen, therefore, how leadership could rebuild the labor movement without tapping vast unreleased energies and hidden talents from below. It likewise remained to be seen what kind of new social movements that new organizing initiatives, not to speak of proposed alliances with assorted reform and radical groups, might encourage around labor. Any such major shift would inevitably find deep roots in the reform tendencies of the 1960s to the early 1990s, impulses characteristically beginning with high hopes and frequently (if not always) ending in defeat, suppression, or cooptation. It would also reflect upon the ultimate meaning of the AFL-CIO's leadership style on display in those years. Labor's most intellectually retrograde era and its modern organizational nadir had a name: Lane Kirkland.

Enter Lane Kirkland

Kirkland was, far more than any institutional leader in American labor history, a child not of labor experiences but of inside-the-Beltway policy maneuvers. Unlike Gompers, Meany, and all his other predecessors, Kirkland had no actual, personal history of unionism—with one brief but conspicuous exception. Son of a southern businessman and descendent of a Confederate Senator, he attended Newberry College and the Merchant Marine Academy, spending most of the Second World War as a deck officer on non-combat vessels. He joined the labor movement indirectly; as a member of the International Organization of Masters, Mates, and Pilots, he also became a member of a small craft union, the International Seafarers, destined to remain obscure save for widely rumored intelligence connections. After less than a year as an active unionist, Kirkland left the sea behind. He earned a B.S. at Georgetown University's School of Foreign Service in 1948 with the apparent intention of his classmates: a diplomatic career.[2]

Here the optic begins to grow dark. Georgetown, during the intense Cold War years especially, was a hotbed of intelligence recruitment, and indeed a number of those future officials with whom Kirkland later had intimate dealings probably attended some of the same classes. Why did Kirkland himself choose neither diplomacy nor intelligence as a career? He had, first of all, certain political aspirations inconsistent with the quiet career paths of the government services. Going to work for the AFL as a staff researcher, he was loaned to the Truman campaign as speechwriter—just as Truman stepped up the Cold War with rhetoric and plans for an unprecedented peacetime military expansion. Although assigned to brighten up the rhetoric of Truman's mediocre running mate, southern Senator Alben W. Barkley, Kirkland had proven his loyalties. From there, the Georgetown graduate made a more fateful decision.

According to his own testimony, Kirkland was fascinated by union work and union people, by which he evidently meant those functionaries whom one would meet in Washington. Nowhere does he claim to have known many ordinary unionists, even to bribe and bully them as Meany had done with his construction industry brothers during the latter's slow rise to glory. Later admirers would confirm that labor leadership had been Kirkland's lifelong constituency. Writing a pamphlet on pension bargaining for the recondite research department of the AFL, Kirkland joined the AFL staff just in time for the ascension of Meany to the federation's leadership in 1952. Meany, when later fumbling to build up his successor Kirkland after twenty-seven years as a protégé, insisted that the younger man "got out this brochure [on pensions] which was distributed all over the country . . . a very, very valuable service to the trade union movement." It was not much of a claim for the impending chief of American unions.[3]

In spells broken only by speechwriting for Adlai Stevenson in 1952 and 1956, Kirkland toiled obscurely in the new AFL-CIO's social security department. If this seems an unlikely course for an ambitious young man and improbable for one of potential leadership character, bear in mind that fate had robbed him (like other Truman faithfuls) of the appointed political office that he would presumably have gained under a Democratic administration. Instead, he found himself quietly maneuvering for allies and biding his time, working in the shadows.

His appointment in 1960 to the post of special assistant to George Meany brought him suddenly into public view. Having just spent two years as director of research and education of the International Union of Operating Engineers (one of those bodies cited in Congress for rampant corruption and threatened with discipline from the AFL-CIO), Kirkland evidently owed bureaucratic recognition and drastic elevation to something more than unusual technical competence. In one of the small hints of information offered to reporters, Kirkland recalled that he met his future (and second) wife, Irena Neumann—an Israeli citizen of Czech social-democratic background—in Paris during 1956, the year of the Hungarian uprising and much eager AFL-CIO anticipation of a bright future in a post-Communist Eastern Europe.[4] Young Cold Warrior Kirkland may have been on a standard union junket or even a private vacation, but he also would have had very good reasons to be on hand at European regional headquarters with intelligence operatives Jay Lovestone and Irving Brown to plan the takeover of post-Communist institutions that Kirkland himself unsuccessfully spearheaded decades later.

After 1960, Kirkland made himself indispensable to Meany in any number of ways. Active in seeking accommodations between unions and employers, as well as among fractious labor bodies engaged in jurisdictional disputes, he increasingly turned his specialities into something more personally promising: the path to power that he had presumably left behind at Georgetown and in the Democratic presidential campaigns. Rubbing shoulders with congressmen and senators, he presented position papers, gave testimony, and offered himself as model labor leader come of age not in the factories but in Washington politics.

He never wavered from the Trumanism that he had learned when young. A. H. Raskin, the veteran *New York Times* reporter now best remembered by scholars for collaborating on a highly varnished autobiography of David Dubinsky, amiably described his friend as a "superhawk," and Kirkland confirmed in 1969 that as he saw things, the "pell-mell withdrawal [from Vietnam] . . . would start us down the long road at the end of which lies total isolation . . . a universal loss of faith in America's world and will."[5] This was as Kissingeresque a view as anyone could hold in American public life. Columnist George Will, later a close friend of the Kirklands and one of the key contacts to a circle of neoconservative notables and foundations, described Kirkland's position on the class and political spectrum as "middle and middle," certainly an odd status for an up-and-coming leader of American workers. His friend's deepest aspiration was, however, Will opined, to serve in a future Democratic cabinet—not as Labor Secretary *but as Secretary of State.*[6] Once there, Kirkland's particular labor interests would presumably fade into the background, while his more compelling international views could finally be put directly into practice.

Although a future frequent ally to Jesse Helms and similar distant right-wing figures on a host of international issues, Kirkland could never be described accurately as a domestic conservative. He was, instead, a compromiser between rightward-drifting mainstream politics and the old Truman programs of guns plus butter. He took the job, in the middle 1960s, of finessing the exceptionally timid AFL-CIO legislative program to elimi-nate racial discrimination in housing, voting, health care, education, and employment practices. Adamantly loyal to Meany, Kirkland made no efforts to get unions themselves to abandon their own discriminatory practices. Instead, he lobbied actively for inclusion of employment provi-sions within the 1964 civil rights bill, trusting legislation to do the job, gradually and without pain, that labor would not be asked to do for itself. In low moments, he mourned the passing of an old time liberalism which had combined aggressive global policies with the successful domestic legislation (civil rights, minimum wage, Medicaid and education) whose "net effect has been a bloodless social and economic revolution." The "bug-out liberals, anti-labor liberals, anti-Semitic liberals, and elite liber-als," all sinners real or imagined in the peacenik wing of the Democrats, had soiled the cause, although not beyond redemption.[7]

The shift to the center of a small handful of former civil rights functionaries such as Bayard Rustin during the later 1960s helped provide Kirkland with a new status. Their embrace of Cold War rhetoric, intelligence-related internationalism, and charitable or voluntary domestic projects (i.e., in place of major redistributive social programs), gave Kirkland's supportive milieu the opportunity to celebrate such figures as the *proper* African-American leadership. The A. Philip Randolph Institute, best known for its opposition to black militancy, in turn finessed his entrée into the philanthropic world as Kirkland raised private funds for showpiece ghetto renewal programs. Within a few years, the institute and its sister organization, the neoconservative Freedom House, would become Lane Kirkland's close allies.[8]

In 1969, acting through the AFL-CIO executive council, Meany personally tapped Kirkland to succeed William F. Schnitzler in the secretary-treasurer spot, compelling a forced retirement on Schnitzler's part. This decision, made against the late-1960s background of industrial and political rebellion in labor's ranks, offered undisguised evidence that the badly aging, ill-spirited chief—by this time known best for lashing out at peace demonstrators—had already chosen his successor. In the years ahead, Kirkland was heard to joke painfully about being "the oldest, established, permanent, floating heir apparent in history," a clever way of acknowledging that the chain of command was absolute but also slow-moving.[9] It is safe to say that he never imagined himself, the future leader, being forced out of office by pressures from below. Kirkland waited patiently because he, too, expected to be federation president for life.

Not that Kirkland was inactive while he bided his time. Apart from collecting art and spending heavy social time with some of the powerbrokers of the future Reagan camp, he served as a lobbyist and increasingly a policymaker in executive council circles. Thus situated, Kirkland met the Vietnam crisis by seeking to insist upon the kind of wage advances known to be the price for labor's warm support of Harry Truman a generation earlier. Nixon responded by appointing Kirkland to a blue-ribbon defense panel, the commission on financial structure, and the productivity commission. He had thus entered, with influential right-leaning Democrats like Sen. Daniel P. Moynihan, the higher circles of bipartisan influence.[10]

For all his efforts during the 1970s, Kirkland did not achieve anything like the kind of patronage status his circles would enjoy from White House officials during the Reagan years. For starters, Kirkland considered Nixon's wage and price controls plainly unfair to union members. He also almost certainly considered Nixon more and more an unreliable, even dovish, figure on foreign policy, weak enough to back off from use of all the force required in Vietnam and the Cold War. As the revelations of deception, the accounts of war crimes, and the public disillusionment all grew, Kirkland's boss Meany publicly resolved that if Nixon could not stand firm, he should stand aside.[11]

Like Meany's favorite Democrat, superhawk Senator Henry Jackson, Kirkland thus almost certainly considered Nixon's China tilt yet another sign of Republican diplomatic weakness. Kirkland could hardly have disapproved of the AIFLD's role in the overthrow of Salvador Allende's democratically elected Chilean government in 1973, although without the further release of security documents, it is impossible to say to what degree the AFL-CIO leadership took direct part.[12] But like AIFLD leaders and Meany, Kirkland was certainly distressed by Augusto Pinochet's severe restrictions on U.S.-affiliated unions, evidence that Nixonian foreign policy had failed once more in keeping the world safe for business unionism. Perhaps, however, because of the anomalous status of hawk Democrats, perhaps also because some of the aging Truman Democrats actually organized against the president on China and other issues, and perhaps because of his warm connections with the Israel lobby, Kirkland improbably joined the "enemies list" of an increasingly paranoid Nixon White House. This, undoubtedly, was the most "subversive" moment of his career.

Kirkland stood with Meany in refusing to endorse Democratic candidate George McGovern in 1972, and was an enthusiastic backer of the post-election Coalition for a Democratic Majority, the Democratic Party's anti-McGovernite caucus which stood against defense cuts and the ongoing retreat from Vietnam. These hardline strategists were undone, for the time being, by the impossibility of actually purging the idealists and younger people who had been brought into the Democratic constituency work by the "New Politics" wave of the late 1960s and early 1970s. Support for labor's economic programs at the grassroots depended upon a certain degree of rapprochement, and the bad odor of the hardliners as well as Democratic leaders' efforts at amity with fresh and energetic constituents prompted the AFL-CIO in 1974 to withdraw its financial backing of the CDM, which promptly folded.[13]

It could not have been an easy moment for Kirkland. From the later view of fellow social democrats destined to become embittered neoconservatives, the post-Watergate Democratic Party had begun making a fateful turn leftward on a variety of issues, including limits on presidential prerogatives to act on the world scene, unhindered by Congress.[14] Moving with the tide on domestic issues at least, Kirkland took a leading part in a coalition of various groups opposing the austerity of budgets of the Carter administration punishing the poor. The less hawkish figures at AFL-CIO headquarters held particular hopes for Edward Kennedy, who but for his personal disgrace might even have pulled off a coalition to bring the fractured Democrats together a while longer around the Kennedy charisma, the ERA, and a national health-care program. That, at least, was big labor's best chance for the electable liberal in something like the New Deal tradition.[15]

But Kirkland, seeking to establish himself and his position with as many allies as possible, always had another agenda. Harkening back to Gompers, he urged protective legislation to limit particular imports but also endorsed the general goal of a freer international market as the truest key to a free society. Accepting a Eugene V. Debs Award with the same degree of unconscious irony as Meany, he waxed eloquent in 1976 about "the restoration of the United States' initiative in the world," that is to say the abandonment of the dangerous and defeatist logic of détente; he demanded instead the consolidation of the West around America, with "such a force, in market power, in industrial power, in technical power" as to be irresistable.[16] Kirkland therefore urged a Truman-style package of federal funding for education and health along with increased Pentagon budgets. He thereby placed himself squarely against a mini-trend within the Democratic Party and sections of labor for a transfer of further military appropriations into sustainable jobs within a cleaner environment. Echoing Meany's Eugene V. Debs Award sentiments that "many of the [socialist] movement's old dogmas have been rightly discarded by Debs' modern descendents," a clear reference to the labor movement's uncomfortable past links with socialist ideas and socialism, Kirkland carefully described the AFL-CIO's aims as revealing "no visionary world, no utopia, that we're working toward" but rather the "building blocks" for a society where "everybody has his chance."[17]

Kirkland's own upward climb was, meanwhile, fatefully affected by a key shift in his personal life. In 1973, he remarried. Whatever its romantic significance, this move was especially important as the Cold War heated up one last time. His new wife, Irena Neumann, was an intimate friend of Nancy Kissinger and a personal guide to the world of diplomatic high-rollers.[18] Lane Kirkland had moved, personally and politically, into the upper government circles where plum appointments and public reputations are made. He quickly received the first of his major rewards. In 1976, amid a Congressionally mandated reassessment of the intelligence community's competence and widely reported overreach, President Gerald Ford appointed Kirkland to the presidential commission on CIA activities within the United States. A board predictably stacked with veterans of the very same shadowy activities, it was a good spot for a relative newcomer to demonstrate his loyalties. If such a commission had *not* arrived at a whitewash of magnum proportions, all concerned would have been dumbfounded. Patently guilty of civil liberties violations against U.S. citizens (not to speak of its antidemocratic role in the world), the CIA escaped morally tarnished in the post-Watergate cynicism but institutionally and financially intact.[19]

In that bicentennial year, along with a handful of his new neoconservative cohorts, Kirkland also cofounded the most important bipartisan right-wing initiative of the times: the Committee on the Present Danger. Its major figures (several of them long known for dual connections to labor and the intelligence agencies) demanded accelerated armament and an aggressive posture against both the economically staggering Soviet Union and the sometimes vigorous international disarmament movement. Retrospectively, they were lobbying hard for the future Reagan program of renewed military build-up.

There, in the revanchist section of American liberalism (merging with a section of conservatives, producing both neoliberalism and neoconservatism), Kirkland found both the intellectual-political milieu for the remainder of his career and the source for binding emotional ties between the

Christian new right, the cerebral neoconservatives, and the AFL-CIO executive. Hawks of all sizes and shapes flocked to these circles: Sidney Hook, Norman Podhoretz, Daniel Patrick Moynihan, Jeane Kirkpatrick, and Kirkland himself, appearing at conferences sponsored by the numerically small but extremely well-connected Social Democrats USA. Indeed, SDUSA and its milieu might be described as the chief breeding ground for future aspiring heavy hitters on the right: Podhoretz, his wife Midge Decter (SDUSA's most prominent female figure and its leading polemicist against "women's lib"), Joshua Muravchik, Carl Gershman, and Penn Kemble.

In another time, the younger figures probably would have inherited the mantle of union intelligentsia. With labor weakening, that time had passed. As the supporting milieu of elderly social democrats faded, youngsters moved on, mostly to the pages of Commentary magazine, to think tanks and to the National Endowment for Democracy. In those circles, they came back in touch with the eldest institution striving for recovery from the Vietnam loss, the International Rescue Committee, which set the course of assorted international operations, some of them genuinely humanitarian, but invariably with the intent of advancing U.S. interests. Most characteristic for the IRC's strategic engagements was the work of the body's Central America teams. As during the U.S. saturation bombing in Southeast Asia, the IRC followed behind U.S.-trained and U.S.-funded military forces decimating large districts of El Salvador, driving peasants out of their homes and into makeshift camps. There, surrounded by the misery that American foreign policy had created, the IRC offered sufficient logistical support to make a favorable (i.e., pro-American) impression on the survivors. Those refugees of the attacks who had not already died or were not scheduled to be dragged away for torture and "disappearance" could presumably rejoice in the charitable side of counterinsurgency.[21]

IRC's chair for almost four decades was veteran operative Leo Cherne. An all-out supporter of the Vietnam War bitterly opposed to George McGovern's peacenik campaign of 1972, Cherne served as vice-chair of Democrats for Nixon. By the later 1970s, he warned repeatedly that public feelings of "guilt" for past ill deeds by Americans threatened paralysis of global actions.[22] Like the AFL-CIO leadership, the IRC under Cherne's increasingly powerful influence found in the Reagan administration nearly all its leaders could hope for in foreign policy, including a former Cherne protégé, late Cold War spymaster William Casey.[23]

President of IRC in 1970-1971 and a major player in the organization's Asian affairs, Casey joined Reagan as campaign director in 1980. Casey's circle of intimates found a close ally in Kirkland's office, with such multiple arrangements as AFL-CIO participation in the CIA-fathered U.S. Youth Council and the Labor Institute for Transatlantic Understanding (its leading members included several former Reagan White House officials, also Sol "Chic" Chaikin of the ILGWU and Kirkland) which in turn launched the Labor Committee for Pacific Affairs, intended to persuade New Zealand's unionists to reject the denuclearization of the zone urged by the current New Zealand labor government and to accept, instead, U.S. hegemony over the region. Exposed by the *New Zealand Times* as a CIA front, the Labor Committee denied the claims—and proved its credentials by establishing a series of Washington seminars bringing conservative foundation and business executives together with carefully chosen labor representatives.[24]

Casey, as CIA chief and IRC loyalist, also guided the Iran-contra operators' deceptions of Congress. He faithfully carried the secrets of assorted illegal and flagrantly unconstitutional activities to the grave. His IRC cohort and Kirkland intimate, erstwhile idealist Bayard Rustin, remained unto death a vice president of IRC, as Albert Shanker was steadfast upon its board, both of them in lock step with the contra wars and "low intensity" (but extremely high civilian casualty) episodes in southern Africa and Latin America. During happier Cold War days, at least for the credulous, this story would read like a spy novel or film, a sort of *Hunt for Red October* carried out among peasants, peaceniks, environmentalists, and rebellious trade unionists.[25]

But hard times lay on the horizon for Meany's heir apparent. He was not troubled, as a friendly but unusually candid journalist put it, by his limited relationship to actual union members, because "Kirkland does not view the rank and file as his primary constituency, he sees the international union presidents . . . as his real constituency. As for them, they say he's doing fine."[26] This illusion could not be permanently maintained. With fewer dues-paying members, labor's social democrats dying off or defecting, and the only available crusades on the right, the labor movement steadily lost both its grip on the Democratic Party and its badly faded reputation for idealism.

Much as Stalin's seizure of Eastern Europe had given Truman the hand he had urgently wanted to play, so in a smaller measure the last waves of Russian military activity provided Kirkland his opportunity. In the wake of the Soviet invasion of Afghanistan, Carter's defense budget broke all previous peacetime records, opening the bipartisan road to the further huge increases by the Reagan administration. Labor's Cold War stalwarts had bitterly resisted the impulse among Democrats to reduce defense costs after the unprecedented spending of the Vietnam War, and unsurprisingly, Kirkland took the opportunity in 1979 to testify to Congress on the renewed importance of an ardent national defense, albeit not one "purchased at the price of social programs."[27] It was hard to take the second half of the proposition as more than rhetoric, given the massive cutbacks of social programs carried out under both parties since the Johnson years and the logic of 1970s-style "shared austerity." In the traditional guns-and-butter fashion, Kirkland probably did want additional butter, but he wanted expensive guns a great deal more.

The bulk of the 1970s had proved depressingly uneventful for the AFL-CIO chiefs, but further prepared their shift toward bipartisanism and big ticket Republican payoffs. President Jimmy Carter, initially greeted by labor leaders as a return to the hawk section's hegemony over the party, enraged erstwhile supporters by suggesting that an "overextended society," in Carter's words, would need to reconsider its mass consumption behavior. Then, too, the near melt-down of a nuclear power plant at Three Mile Island, Pennsylvania, rocked those (including labor's top leaders) who had looked upon nuclear power, like nuclear weapons, as benevolent so long as they remained in firm U.S. control. In another and deeper generational sense, the Democratic Party itself lost its brief momentum of revival and sagged at the grass roots; the AFL-CIO leadership's long-term prospects sagged with it. Struggling to find something recent to say about the protégé about to become successor, Meany credited Kirkland in 1979 with personally finessing an accord between the Carter administration and the AFL-CIO, even if the Carter years had been anything but satisfying to labor.[28]

Democratic Decline

Not only did Carter, a southern Democratic president, lack the old-time enthusiasm for organized labor, but the Democratic Party was badly weakened by this time. How had it come to this state?

George Meany had viewed the CIO as an invention of Franklin D. Roosevelt's to buoy up his electoral support. Although a wild exaggeration and a misunderstanding of the labor movement's own dynamics, this allegation contained a grain of truth. The Roosevelt-led Democrats, especially in the then more proportionately populous east and midwest, thoroughly depended upon the labor movement's efforts. The CIO and even AFL cadre, along with the personal charisma of FDR, restored faith in a Democratic Party soiled by public disillusionment in the First World War and in government programs. But the boost was more temporary and limited than Democratic pols hoped.

Shortly after Truman's ascension into the White House, CIO-PAC lost much of its earlier idealism, its army of volunteer footworkers, its progressive big-name entertainer-fundraisers, and even many of its most talented speechwriters. How many of these energetic and talented boosters had belonged to labor's purged left wing could only be appreciated after they had gone. Democrats held up relatively well by warning that Republicans would take away all or most of the New Deal social programs, also by adding new social programs and by perfecting the process of job-creation district by district via military-related spending as vital pump-priming for consumerism. Notwithstanding the liberal enthusiasms of Americans for Democratic Action and the high prestige of politicians like Adlai Stevenson and Hubert Humphrey, Democratic election campaigns tended more and more to become as depressingly bureaucratic as the unions themselves. For the same reasons the Democrats had become firmly attached to the promise of upward mobility and outward mobility, away from historic working-class neighborhoods. Implicitly, through the promise of education and upward mobility for the worthy, the labor-Democratic message pointed away from the working class itself.

The faithful cadre thus aged, as did the associated liberal Democratic volunteers. The eclipse of the street meeting and urban street life by television and the ongoing media transformation accelerated the process, but it was well underway by the middle 1950s for more basic reasons. John

F. Kennedy's presidential campaign brought excitement and a somewhat newer generation of functionaries, but otherwise altered little, except for the minority of Catholic Democrats of various social classes who felt symbolically empowered, respected, and at last truly "Americanized." Now, fading but doggedly proud versions of social class somehow disappeared, and (although Democratic candidates didn't say so openly) reappeared along the color line, as a marker of victimization if not shame. Ironically, just as the black vote had become more important to the Democratic Party than ever before, so did the presence of the need to escape the presumed humiliation of a lower-class past into a suburban future where anyone white and holding a steady job was "middle class," a mythical member of the same meritocratic league. Yesterday's blue-collar Truman fan was often tomorrow's Reagan Democrat, an evolution that became a great deal clearer in retrospect.

Repeatedly, from the middle 1960s to the later 1970s, "children's crusades" or youth infusions nevertheless brought further new life to the local and state Democratic machines. They had little marked effect until 1972 upon Democratic inner power structures or sustained grassroots contacts. Nor did these infusions notably involve labor, whose leaders distanced themselves, for a variety of reasons, ever further from left-leaning parts of their earlier political base. Democratic kingmakers like Chicago's Mayor Daley despised the idealistic youngsters, while the Kennedy camp sought to encompass the available energies of the time. Hardly anyone at the top envisioned a real turnover of Democratic leadership beyond a generational elite being replaced by another generational elite.

Labor leadership was no small part of this problem. The mere handful of youngsters attracted to the AFL-CIO's political wing and (more to the point) its staff positions were vastly out of tune with the idealists of their generation. They were doggedly pro-war as the campuses rose up against the Vietnam misadventure.[30] The riotous 1968 Chicago Democratic convention and the election confirmed that Cold War liberalism had suffered greatly, losing its constituencies to the left and right. As the post-New Deal drift toward political disintegration of its constituencies continued, Democratic prospects, destined to be temporarily buoyed up by an assortment of hopeful developments including the Republican debacle around the Watergate scandal, had entered a long-term overall decline.

A sharper-edged liberal politics, always influenced in one way or the other by unions—by now, most often by the self-interest of the public employee unions—paradoxically enjoyed a modest resurgence. Black Democrats at various levels, mostly local, took office on the crest of liberal-left coalitions, defining themselves best against the often grotesquely racial politics of their opponents. Their own modicum of interracial egalitarianism remained in practice, as might be expected, administered by and for the rule of elites. But in city after city it possessed at least a different rhetoric, gave hope and rallied voters. As lobbies of environmentalists and gay and lesbian organizations worked with public figures (and often union members) of non-white communities, the 1930s-1940s image of Democrats as an army of activist volunteers briefly came back into view. In Oakland, Gary, or Chicago, but more completely in exceptional communities like Madison, Wisconsin, Santa Cruz, California, or Burlington, Vermont, radicals of every generation could be found shoulder to shoulder with unionists in what seemed a rainbow of reformism often influenced by third-party or non-partisan leftism, but always somehow connected to the Democrats.

There was always a basic flaw to sunny expectations for this kind of liberal revival. Only in scattered cases did the regular Democrats make way for such activists to take over large sections of party operations or to shift the working ideology in directions of structural economic, foreign policy, or environmental reform.[31] Disillusionment therefore regularly followed hope. In the end, save for those limited if important circumstances where progressive liberals like Ron Dellums, John Conyers, or, later, Paul Wellstone could actually gain office through independently organized armies of volunteers and infusions of cash, the enthusiasts tended to drift away. During the next election cycle or the one following, some of these idealists or others would drift back in, and then out again. They had scant hope of influencing the Democratic Party beyond the local, or at best, the state level; the decisions that counted were made at the top by big money lawyers whose clients' list included far more corporations than unions. AFL-CIO leaders surely wanted virulently anti-labor Republicans defeated—but never at the price of diluting their influence over party mechanisms. The political renewal envisioned and continually discussed negated, under these circumstances, the possibility of a liberal crusade even when Republican humiliation seemed to hand the baton to Democrats.

The local Democratic reformers with strong labor links tended to burn out for other reasons as well. In office, progressive liberals with genuine alliances on the left learned that they had little control and scarce influence on corporate life-or-death decisions over community jobs. They feared more and more to use the discretionary power that they could exert over the building permits, highway construction, and traffic-control patterns which steadily redesigned the daily life of communities around the automobile.

The AFL-CIO issued dire warnings before and after the crucial 1980 election. Union activists worked, although with less enthusiasm than anxiety, for Carter's re-election. The aftermath of Reagan's triumph (by a relatively small margin, it should be remembered, and due to the Iran crisis and the economy rather than any great public fondness for the former California governor) quickly justified the forebodings. As the new president broke the air controllers' strike and sent a message to the labor movement, both Reagan's rhetoric and policies proved brutal. The Republican administration's appointees to the National Labor Relations Board, notoriously slanted against unions, moved quickly to remove restraints upon opposition to unionization and to all but encourage fresh efforts at decertification. Especially for people of color, disproportionately poor and barely-working class, the prospect of factory shutdowns and worsening healthcare with few resources was aggravated by their being depicted as the ungrateful recipients of various undue privileges and taxpayer largesse. Union membership fell for an assortment of other reasons as well, but heightened employer resistance stood near the head of the pack.[32] And yet, if labor leaders distrusted or even despised Reagan's allies, many experienced an unanticipated degree of self-realization in hating Reagan's enemies, those feminists, peaceniks, and assorted left-liberals destined to become radio host Rush Limbaugh's favorite targets.

Besides, labor did have an elusive, thoroughly institutional fallback on the national political stage. In 1981, in the wake of Reagan's victory, a hard-pressed Democratic National Committee granted the AFL-CIO twenty-five at-large seats, and four out of thirty-five seats on its executive body. Within a diminished party suffering an early bout of Reaganism (and whose congressional delegation would indeed vote for so many of Reagan's programs), the AFL-CIO became in return the largest single Democratic financial donor, supplying the DNC with more than a third of its annual budget. The defeat of a modest labor reform bill in Congress in 1978 showed that the conservative counter-offensive had begun in earnest with simultaneous Democratic president and Congress for the last time in at least a generation. Wall Street analysts warned that a new era of militant labor leadership might emerge out of political defeat.

Instead, defeat bred timidity and an eagerness to shift far enough rightward to recuperate the "Reagan Democrats." Along with an increasingly unrealistic hope for a major change of labor laws, the specter of protectionism—which labor's top leaders did not themselves particularly desire—offered the only popular fight-back issue imaginable. In the absence of a real internationalist program of protecting working people across borders, the new protectionism mainly added a meanspiritedness to organized labor's perennial self-concern. The downward spiral of labor's claim to special protection within the liberal coalition thereby led further and further to its isolation.[33]

President Kirkland was a true-blue Walter Mondale Democrat in 1984, so much so that he endorsed the hapless Minnesota Senator even before the Democratic convention and reportedly suggested to him the pokerfaced loser's carnivorous slogan of the hour, "Where's the Beef?" (borrowed, naturally, from a television commercial).[34] It was Kirkland's boldest domestic political move ever, and a disaster. Mondale, who so often claimed to be labor's representative, had little to offer but the tired rhetoric of Trumanism-warmed-over, this time promising American workers less rather than more. Compared to the exalting images of a glorious Marlboro Country America that Reagan speech writers offered the public, a Humphrey clone was no improvement on Humphrey himself. Whole state Democratic parties, fearing Reagan's coattails, quietly deserted the Democratic contender entirely.[35]

The election-year consolidation of the new right around massive fundraising and the charisma of Reagan practically finished off the hopes of Democrats. The overwhelming election victory also finalized the status of the full-time partner, the union leader, in the final Cold War crusade. But the old reciprocal magic of the Cold War bilateralism had become now almost irrelevant, save for its publicity advantages. The Reagan administration happily used the AFL-CIO leadership for its purposes, but hardly needed them. Unlike Meany's or Gompers's regimes, the AFL-CIO of the 1980s represented too little on the political map to bring about the kinds of domestic compromise packages that had been extracted from Woodrow Wilson, Harry Truman, or even Dwight Eisenhower. Powerbroker was by now the leaders' only trade, and the Republicans owned the only game in town. Labor leaders could only deliver themselves and maneuver to silence opposition, notably including that of the most vigorous younger idealists of the movement. The dilemma of the escalating U.S.-backed war in Central America and the accompanying Iran-contra scandal was that events served to dramatize the divisions within labor and expose subterranean intelligence activity, frustrating the public and private gestures that AFL-CIO chiefs made to the White House.

Oppositionists set an accelerating political pace as the 1980s progressed. Rich Trumka of the mineworkers was the most important labor leader to show a fondness for Jesse Jackson and his run for the 1988 Democratic nomination. But Kenneth Blaylock, president of the American Federation of Government Employees, endorsed Jackson, as did many union locals. Financially thin, the Rainbow campaign of that year was politically rich with a leftish mix of black, white, and Asian-American radicals. Whatever his personal weaknesses, due largely to the headline-grabbing impulse so familiar to Reuther-watchers, Jesse Jackson walked picket lines and voiced militant slogans that top union officials now shunned. Briefly winning the largest number of pre-convention delegates, Jackson faced off against Albert Gore in a fractious New York campaign memorable for black, liberal, and radical unity on the one side and an all-out offensive by centrist Democrats and right-leaning Jewish agency officials on the other. Massive anti-Jackson spending and widely publicized attacks by Al Shanker and Ed Koch, among others, did not defeat Jackson at New York's polls or stop David Dinkins from winning the mayoralty on Jackson's coattails. But they successfully poisoned the well for unity of those fighting Reaganism.

Exit polls showed that more than a third of union households in the "Super Tuesday" primaries had backed Jackson, making him at all odds American labor's favorite popular figure since Martin Luther King, Jr., John L. Lewis, or Gene Debs. AFL-CIO top officials, considering Jackson a spawn of the 1960s and an enemy of Israel to boot, quietly bided their time.[36] Down the presidential home-stretch, Massachusetts Governor Michael Dukakis, a budget trimmer with bankers increasingly calling his tune, amplified the neoliberal intimations of the Mondale campaign. No one explained why unionists, among others, would appreciate this kind of candor, and Dukakis—no labor candidate in the first place—went down to defeat by the unpopular and decidedly anti-labor Republican candidate, George Bush.

On the campaign trail that year, Jesse Jackson had often observed that the accelerating business offensive against unions remained the great undiscussed political issue. He might have added that the labor movement was by this time hoisted on its own petard. Employer agendas were most successful with white, male workers (and least among female and non-white workers), coinciding precisely with voting patterns of Reagan Democrats busily discarding their old loyalties. The AFL-CIO could no longer reach the workers they wanted, and had little wish either economically or politically for the workers that they could most easily reach along class lines. In a long-term sense, the feeble response of the Democratic machine and its labor reps to right-wing challenges—so often blamed on their constituents as an effect of the media-saturated postmodern condition—was also a clear consequence of what their predecessors had accomplished. Life had indeed become more privatistic, for the working class as well as middle classes, when the regulated atmosphere of the shopping malls replaced the inclusive chaos of city streets and when the accelerated push to make a living (or raise money for future college education for the kids) amid spiraling expenses of all sides, found adults exhausted and impatient. A world which once seemed so open, beyond the ghettos and the neighborhoods of blue-collar Democratic voters, had now closed in. All that remained was the fervent wish for security, something liberals promised (more properly, warned that the Republicans would take away) but could not actually deliver. Millions of middle-class, working-class, and poor Democrats could still be counted upon to vote against cuts in social security or health care. But ever fewer felt strongly enough to be involved in the political process. By 1990, political analyst William Greider estimated, Democratic Party "regulars" (members and activists in off-election years) dwindled to perhaps one hundred thousand, many of advanced age. Time and disillusionment had taken their toll on the rest.[37]

Foreign Policy as Substitution for Domestic Failure

Kirkland's accession to power in 1979, endorsed unanimously by the executive council, was an obvious outcome for Meany's candidate and therefore inevitable successor. Nevertheless, one dimension of it remained unique, almost staggeringly so. In the history of the labor movement, never had someone so completely unknown to union members themselves become their master. After more than a decade of publicity, Kirkland had successfully raised his "name recognition," according to polling sources, to around 3 percent of the AFL-CIO membership. It never rose above that figure.[38]

The intimate circles around Kirkland met the reality of Reaganism, after the initial shock wave, with curiously mixed signals, often registered at first in private. Al Barkan, longtime director of COPE, resigned with bitter complaints about the growing influence of "black ingrates," "pansies," and "women yelling about equal rights in Lafayette Park."[39] Barkan's friend Max Green, long a top AFT staffer (and SDUSA official), defected to Reagan's retrograde U.S. Commission on Civil Rights and thence to White House liaison, joined by Linda Chavez, who stepped directly from the AFT staff into the world of neocon think-tankers. These were, strictly speaking, lateral career moves, with little political change of heart from most of the rest of Shanker's staff. Like some of the other youngish professionals formerly gathered around Meany's circle, they had given up on their own careers in the labor movement and sometimes on the labor movement entirely. A decade or so later, some of the same former AFT functionaries would pronounce school vouchers a marvelous educational reform, and public education a virtual lost cause; they and their families had already gotten their benefits out of the system.

Portions of labor meanwhile took their own independent anti-Reagan course, and for a very few years the efforts were impressive. Reagan's success at breaking the PATCO strike prompted White House crowing that the AFL-CIO (and Kirkland in particular) no longer represented anyone, a blow to prestige so severe that Kirkland accepted the proposal of a Western New York state leader (originated among a handful of longtime left-wingers) for a nationwide march.[40] The resulting Solidarity March on Washington brought out a quarter-million participants from every corner of union life, with an especially memorable response from interracial unions. But the march's success at stirring the rank and file, quickly creating more anxiety than enthusiasm in Kirkland's office, received no follow-up beyond the customary urging to vote Democratic. The massive Martin Luther King, Jr., memorial March for Jobs, Peace, and Freedom which marked 1983 received enthusiastic if selective union support (most especially from health care workers' unions), but gained an even more tepid response from above, where "peace" was still an enemy slogan. These events and the organized impulses behind them faded quickly. Later marches against U.S. policy in Central America were more than shunned by Kirkland's office, which sent out repeated warnings against participation. Those few union leaders who supported anti-war activities were treated with intense hostility. Even if the former Screen Actors Guild president had once saddled Hollywood actors with the worst contract in their history and continued to act predictably toward labor throughout his career, Reagan was offered more political breathing space by official labor than any Republican since the New Deal.[41]

Continuing to insist that a more favorable climate would one day make revival, including a membership renewal, virtually inevitable, top union leaders set themselves instead on what might be described as a crypto-political path. In their peculiar internationalist perspective, the inheritors of vast bureaucratic machinery literally found new worlds to conquer. Their strategies for the end of the century and beyond had been generations in the making but took definitive shape around Jeane Kirkpatrick's United Nations office. By the new calculation, the "realignment" of the Democratic Party was not to be realized in any near future, if at all; the old vision that liberals, civil rights activists, and labor might grasp the leadership of the nation now seemed absolutely anachronistic. Labor's top echelons envisioned a very modest compact of social programs combined with grand imperial adventure.

Thus the AFL-CIO continued to posture against Reaganism on issues ranging from welfare to the Equal Rights Amendment, hoping somehow to reverse the Republican sweep. Meanwhile, according to the worldview of Kirkland, as with Meany, the fate of humanity rested upon the predominance of the West, meaning Western Europe and the United States, within the world scheme. Predominance in turn depended upon permanent mobilization on a near-war footing. The Cold War's military spin-offs had long since become a necessary part of the corporatist arrangement, with the retention of ever-fewer but still well-paying jobs linked to congressional powerbrokers simultaneously collecting industry's political contributions and labor's votes.

Popular social movements, political parties, and armed revolts against U.S.-backed regimes in Africa, Asia, and Latin America during the 1980s would have been viewed with adamant hostility irrespective of the various self-definitions offered. The aim of AFL-CIO international programs had always been to promote a loyal labor component to the junior partners of U.S. foreign policy and business arrangements. A cautious and highly selective anti-authoritarianism, applied to various struggles against the military regimes of tiny but all-powerful ruling classes, had been intended to restore the legitimacy of American influence. Any threats to repatriate U.S. corporate holdings or to jump ship of the U.S. clients list signaled, as it had in earlier anti-colonial days, an unendurable interference in "free trade unionism," setting in motion intelligence operations and usually including AFL-CIO affiliates or operatives.

In the war of words, Kirkland's staff dwelt endlessly upon the absence of labor rights in Communist regimes. This was sheer hypocrisy given the fact that the international department indirectly supported U.S.-financed authoritarian regimes guilty of egregious violations of labor and human rights in dozens of cases, with contemporary deaths from starvation, malnutrition, and assassinations far greater than in the deservedly collapsing Communist regimes. The standard rhetoric was nonetheless good for appropriations, especially for and from the new National Endowment for Democracy, providing openly and legally a certain portion of what the intelligence agencies had previously provided under cover. But only the naive confused the AFL-CIO sentiments for real support of democratic anti-corporate movements in non-Communist societies; there, the AFL-CIO wanted effective social controls, not dramatic social change from below in either property or politics.[42]

The AFL-CIO's one stirring victory, or believed victory, came in Poland, with the uprising of the Gdansk steelworkers in 1980. An authentically grassroots movement seeking workers' control over society at large, the heroic Solidarity movement's leadership was soon enough wheedled into becoming a wedge for the return of old-style capitalism. The AFL-CIO provided funds for Solidarity, while encouraging the eclipse of its ultra-democratic or syndicalist phase. But according to insiders, the AFL-CIO also consistently exaggerated its own importance. Other trade unionists with more credibility, including even the French (and nominally Communist) CGT, gave generously to Solidarity in its time of need. Within the United States, ordinary unionists from left to right with but few exceptions on either side greeted the Polish movement with interest and pleased amazement.[43]

From 1980 onward, international spending by the AFL-CIO exceeded its domestic budget, and not because of Eastern Europe: rather, the third world. Earlier efforts outside Latin America, according to inside accounts, had been almost without exception failures to establish U.S.-style unions, but they had not been unsuccessful in providing favorite regimes supported by the State Department some useful cover, and it was in this guise that the labor chiefs excelled during the last days of Russian-style Communism.

Most important in this maneuver was the "privatization" of foreign policy under Reagan. When post-Vietnam congressional prohibitions of aid to contras and such parallel movements as Jonas Savimbi's terrorist force in Angola prompted a strategic shift, the AFL-CIO apparatus leaped into the breach, often in partnership with the intelligence agencies of Israel's conservative Begin government. Indeed, the *Free Trade Union News* devoted an entire issue to rehabilitating Savimbi, by now well known for the worst war crimes record in southern Africa. Irving Brown praised him, very remarkably, as a "great fighter for freedom whose concept of democracy comes as close as anyone in Africa to our image of what is a free and democratic society," asserting he had known the African ex-Maoist intimately for twenty years. Actually, AFL-CIO agencies had been quietly funding Savimbi since at least 1978, sharing that duty with his geographically proximate allies, the South African apartheid regime. Savimbi's "dirty war" tactics such as the destruction of crops, hospitals and clinics and schools might have caused a little embarrassment, but if so, Brown and Kirkland showed no sign of it. During the 1980s, Kirkland's office had been compelled by internal opposition to transfer a reception for the visiting

Savimbi from its own Washington suites to those of the uncontested neoconservatives of Freedom House. By the later 1990s, even former allies admitted that the AFL-CIO's favorite African son had always been a vicious scoundrel.[45]

The fuller African story has now begun to be known. Brown had worked especially hard at setting up an AFL-CIO operation in Kenya, through the Kenya Federation of Labor. Brown's notable protégé Tom Mboya, who made his way among African unionists with his signature Mercedes, designer clothes, and unshakable pro-capitalist leanings, was being prepared for Kenya's presidency—until publicly embarrassed by charges of CIA manipulation and assassinated. Because business unionism in Africa floundered again and again when it could not create credible figures, it fell back squarely upon clients of the South African government and their political counterparts elsewhere.

Operations within South Africa, in tune with Reagan's aggressive international style, therefore intensified. Directing intelligence operation from Paris until 1985, Brown also established the African American Labor Center in New York, a publicity agency of AFL-CIO-style business unionism intended to offset the influence of the militantly anti-apartheid left and its Christian liberal allies. Above all, an alternative needed to be created to the Communist-linked African National Congress and to the jailed Nelson Mandela. Brown's major effort went into the wooing of Chief Mangosuthu G. Buthelezi, the apartheid government's appointed ruler of the Zulu "homeland," KwaZulu. Known as South Africa's most prestigious black opponent of sanctions—a tactic favored by almost all black and labor organizations in South Africa—the chief was widely mocked and had to be rebuilt with AFL-CIO help. Brown (reputedly with the help of the ILGWU) had built up Buthelezi's pet conservative union, the Workers Union of South Africa, which scarcely existed except to disrupt the ANC-related Congress of South African Trade Unions (COSATU) and to collect funds from the supportive South African government and its business partners. While setting up the Council of Unions of South Africa and funding the Pan African Congress, best known for its violent attacks on COSATU, Brown's job became steadily harder. The ANC, coming up from the underground, openly embraced the South African Communist Party as ally. AFL-CIO reps fumed and presumably plotted furiously.[47] The effort to displace Mandela with Buthelezi failed miserably. But the sorry chief received a consolation prize, the George Meany International Human Rights Award, in 1982, not long after disclosures of widespread Inkhata brutality. It was a match for the Meany Award given posthumously to Brown in 1989, with the CIA's labor cortege on hand, which provided an opportunity for the stumbling Kirkland to proclaim, without irony, that "wherever working people are rising from the knees and walking erect, they are choosing the path of Irving Brown."[48]

In the Philippines, meanwhile, AIFLD's regional labor clients, the Asian American Free Labor Institute, had naturally sought to rally regional support for the war in Vietnam and for the brutal dictatorship of Ferdinand Marcos as long as it managed to survive. Bitterly opposed to the independent-minded Kilusang Mayo Union (KMU) which fought heroically to topple Marcos, the Trade Union Congress of the Philippines (TUC) was founded in 1975 under martial law conditions, urged support for Marcos, and praised the waves of arrests directed at KMU activists. Recipients of millions of dollars before and after the fall of Marcos in 1989—mostly from NED via the AAFLI—the TUC called for deregulation of business and denounced demands for the repatriation of corporate profits to Filipinos. Especially impressive bribes were reportedly given to those Filipino labor leaders willing to support the extension of U.S. naval occupation of the island. As support activists keenly noted, TUC leaders avidly supported Polish Solidarity's political strikes against an authoritarian state yet somehow opposed political agitation by local unionists who demanded an end to widespread Filipino government human rights abuses and an end to U.S. occupation.

Across Asia and the Pacific, similar stories could be told. The South Korean government-sponsored union and AFL-CIO partner, FKTU, was funded heavily to counter the appearance of a genuinely independent and militant union federation. Similarly substantial contributions (one million dollars, according to figures released under the Freedom of Information Act) went into a Fiji Trade Unions Congress which pledged to counter the Fiji islands' budding antinuclear movement.[50]

The same rules held for Central America. Named by Reagan to the President's Commission on El Salvador headed by his friend Kissinger, Kirkland played what the *Wall Street Journal* described as a central role.

Urging a hard line with few if any concessions to human rights activists, Kirkland "had the respect" (as the *Journal* put it) of conservatives and liberals alike "because of his influence in the Democratic Party," meaning his control of labor election funds and use of them for ardently hawkish Democrats. Under the commission's direction, Congress abandoned its insistence upon semi-annual certification of human rights improvements.[51] A cocky Kirkland might better have been alluding to international operations than to domestic policies when he said, on taking office, "everything that we [the AFL-CIO] have done and every program that we have undertaken, I think, has mine among the fingerprints on it."[52] In return for this assistance, AFL-CIO leaders received a great deal more than conservative good will. Via intermediaries within Jeane Kirkpatrick's United Nations office, the intelligence services, and the NED, labor's foreign policy apparatus garnered financial subsidies as a rising proportion of total AFL-CIO income.[53]

By the mid-1980s, as opposition-minded local labor solidarity groups grew up around an array of issues, the Kirkland leadership concluded that it faced aliens and heretics akin to the Communists of old: political subversives, environmentalist "tree huggers," gay and feminist activists. But the "red" label applied poorly this time around. The AFL-CIO chiefs took their lumps more than their predecessors had since at least the 1940s, and were forced to back down some and accept more moderate positions even if quietly pursuing the familiar goals. Exposure of flagrant engagements of AFL-CIO bodies with human rights abusers like Savimbi and ongoing complaints by leading national figures like Jack Scheinkman of the Amalgamated Clothing and Textile Workers (ACTWU) prompted further secrecy but no policy changes. Even a limited democratization of labor policies was, moreover, never without a cost: in public and in private, national labor officials warned that sanctions would be taken against unions and individuals too far out of step.[54]

Kirkland and his subordinates regretted labor's declining social weight, surely, although bursts of uncontrolled enthusiasm from below would have been even less welcome. Wherever Communism could be rolled back abroad, however, a more inviting vacuum of power would perforce exist in the labor field. With the necessary funds and support or neutrality from the new barons of privatized economies, the AFL-CIO would be positioned to take its share of the spoils. Admittedly, this scheme had only limited success in Africa, Asia, and Latin America, where the AFL-CIO's pet organizations were usually little more than fronts for U.S. diplomacy, supporting the aims of American corporations far more energetically than their own members' needs. But it might work yet among Europeans—given a massive collapse of Communist regimes at large, and an equally massive injection of funds.

AFL-CIO strategists therefore regarded the transformation of Polish Solidarity from a workers' movement to a pro-business political organization as a definitive case in point, although their own apparatus had been unable to take hold. Their favored political figures, now in positions of power, were unable to restrain a severe decline in the standard of living for ordinary Poles; even the Gdansk shipworks that spawned the workers' control formation were closed by the new government in one of the many measures described as "economic reform." The radical aspirations of the early demonstrators were quickly put aside by the new rulers. Shanker, in later years, bragged that he had personally helped fill the infrastructural gap by bringing investors to buy denationalized industry—at a tiny fraction of its actual value, he might have bothered to add.[55]

The subsequent changeover throughout Eastern Europe offered great occasions for public declarations, but few opportunities to make real advances on the envisioned globe-girdling business unionism. From nation to nation, intellectuals, students, and citizens—especially environmentalists—took the lead, while AFL-style union sympathizers had only a minimal role to play, far less even than in Poland. Nevertheless, from 1989 to 1995, the strategy of takeover became, writ large, the AFL-CIO's foreign policy raison d'etre and almost the entirety of its domestic policy as well.

Here Kirkland took cheer from the counterattack against the lingering effects of Vatican II. As Pope John Paul II's advisors singled out the supporters of liberation theology in Latin America for replacement by trustworthy conservatives, they installed a new echelon of American bishops and cardinals after the spirit of New York's former Vietnam War propagandist, Cardinal O'Connor. Aiming to recuperate church influence through the anti-abortion campaigns and "discipline" of more liberal bishops, such clerical figures looked warmly toward neo-traditionalist leaders in the building trades (and especially the bricklayers) who could be counted upon to assail feminists and even Bill Clinton in the Catholic press. The labor and Catholic establishments also shared the desire to tap the new Latino population for members and congregants, although neither the AFL-CIO nor the Church proved willing to allocate to those constituencies the kinds of resources eagerly devoted to picketing abortion centers and to lobbying Congress against women's reproductive choices. The Pope and the labor chief now shared an agenda as they had not since the Cold War years, even if one increasingly further from the female workforce and the practical secularism—on issues like birth control—of even late twentieth-century American Catholics.

Some of Kirkland's bitterest internal critics from within the apparatus, meanwhile, complained about his mounting absenteeism from his Washington suites and the halls of Congress. He spent much of his time during the early 1990s traveling in Europe, seeking to create the style of union institutions in Russia and Eastern Europe at large that would prove loyal to the "American system." Defeated at home, the AFL-CIO would thereby have gained the awesome influence of major powerbrokers in the future world economy. Judged realistically, this was a mad scheme. As the Alliance for Progress during the Kennedy administration had the fantastic premise of creating a vast Latin American middle class able to live like U.S. consumers amid economies choked with suffering masses, so this plan was first of all based upon the false vision of a world able to produce and profit without regard to ecological limits. The plan further presumed that the eradication of Communism would prompt business to welcome or at least tolerate unions in the familiar Euro-American tradition. The previous twenty years, however, had pointed relentlessly toward downsizing and union-busting in the United States, and foreign employers were in no mood to reward gratitude of Kirkland's favors with better wages and conditions for the world's working class. Finally, the assumptions of the Kirkland office demanded a level of stability in Eastern Europe, especially the former Soviet Union, nowhere in prospect for populations simultaneously deprived of social services and raked by a new class of "vampire capitalists." As the popular joke went in the former Soviet Union: everything the Communists told us about socialism was a lie, but everything they told us about capitalism was the truth.

Ironically, it had been Lane Kirkland's political confidence in riding out the storm of Reaganism—or rather, his faith in surfing the waves of global capital expansion—that proved his doom. He had faithfully followed the American corporate lead in the international arena, and with the collapse of Communism he actually expected to be rewarded. With AFL-CIO membership sinking, and defeated so often in his choice of political candidates, he staked the future of the labor movement on the 1994 election. If only the Democrats could win back Congress, he believed, labor's time (by which he meant really, Kirkland's time) would come at last. The sweeping Republican victory led by the extremely conservative Newt Gingrich ended the illusion. Lane's time had finally run out.

Bureaucratic Collapse/Democratic Revival

The AFL-CIO leaders' globalism, combined with a pallid and increasingly nominal domestic liberalism, always had its challengers. Indeed, efforts of labor reformers from the early 1970s onward, covering a wide spectrum of issues, carried both rank-and-file and middle-level disgruntlement into policy debates and often unsettled old-time leaders. In the long run, such efforts facilitated the unpredicted downfall of Kirkland's team.

During the 1970s and even the 1980s, labor leaders repeatedly insisted that the AFL-CIO represented the historic basis of social reform. But the limits of their style of reforms had long since become evident. A good example can be found in the environmental agenda of Andrew Biemiller, an amiable figure who emerged as a chief legislative aide to Meany and labor liaison to Congress. Along with a handful of UAW officials, Biemiller urged clean water and air protection, the extension of national parks, and the preservation of forest lands gravely threatened by unfettered development. The parks and green space, Biemiller argued with good logic, offered the vacation spots that working people could best afford. This was the strongest, and in many ways the final environmental agenda of the labor mainstream. Hidden behind such evidently good intentions, however, was the assumption that any type of preservation had to prove its economic value and serve the function of greater automobile use, with more and more autos traveling from the giant freeways to the new roadways cut through formerly virgin or regrown forests. What else could the UAW possibly favor? The worker, and especially the retired worker to whom the UAW officials increasingly looked for loyal votes, was to share the privatized pleasures of advanced capitalism without limits.[56]

Notwithstanding the face-saving resolutions offered at AFL-CIO conventions against environmental destruction and potential job loss alike, the great majority of labor officials would have been ecstatic to have legions of dues-paying members build unsafe nuclear facilities, or prisons for whole cities of juveniles (especially non-whites), so long as union scale were included in the tax base. As well-intentioned politicians learned when speaking with these leaders, the demand for "lower taxes" rarely applied to public-funded construction projects, however unneeded, whether the underwriting of suburban sprawl or the creation of high-end shopping malls in renovated downtowns. Even more rarely would labor officials endorse "slow growth"—even when many of their local members urgently wanted to preserve the services and small-town atmosphere of familiar surroundings. So long as developers called the shots and the economy experienced no major crisis, environmental reformers found themselves labelled "New Politics" disrupters of labor's historic coalitions, fighting on alien turf in union halls every bit as much as in the Chambers of Commerce.[57]

AFL-CIO officials' response to such characterizations, understandable in a certain vein, was that they had consistently supported the Clean Air and Clean Water Acts. Leaving the problems of the first aside (here, too, labor leaders stressed the need to compromise on all-important issues touching U.S. coal extraction and steel and automobile production), the Clean Water Act of 1977 depended upon certain "win-win" high-tech solutions for the treatment and possible reuse of excreta. Rather than being converted locally, with a point-of-production halt to toxic chemicals used in various parts of industrial production and commerce, the AFL-CIO eagerly backed the laying of millions of miles of new sewer lines and costly construction of treatment plants. The wishes of industry for convenient dumping were thereby served, at public cost, with huge side benefits for engineering and construction firms (and good wages for their blue-collar employees). Apart from initial expense, however, the "sludge" problem remained. Often dumped out at sea (until ocean dumping was banned in 1988) or burned (this, too, discovered to be a toxic hazard), sludge was most often placed in landfills, predictably poisoning the groundwater. In the 1990s version of supposed environment-friendly decisions, it could be made into "natural" and "organic" pellets, actually so full of heavy metals as to endanger agricultural workers and the consumers of products grown in it. Labor leaders did not originate the faulty thinking behind the treatment of sewage. But any other solution would have seemed "anti-growth" to them, a restraint upon the social measures that treated pollution only at the end of the pipe, and added jobs in the process.[58]

Nor did the AFL-CIO ever seek in any sustained way to involve ordinary union members in backing preservationist measures. The AFL-CIO officially supported the creation of the Environmental Protection Agency and, unenthusiastically, the Species Preservation Act—but from the top down, in the conventional lobbying manner. As late as 1975, the official resolution of the federation attacked the "no-growth advocates who want to clear up every form of pollution except the human pollution of unemployment," and savaged state bottle deposit laws as the worst sort of disruption of economic progress.[59] Assorted resolutions of the metal trades were, if anything, still worse. In later years, convention resolutions moved slowly and painfully toward toxic use reduction and even the Endangered Species Act reauthorization—the last supported, with measures "minimizing economic dislocation and job losses," as the convention recorded in 1991, seeking middle ground between the unrestrained clearcutting of old-growth forest and minimal plans for species preservation.[60]

In the real world of campaign politics, corporate anti-environmental campaigns actually accelerated to mobilize local or regional union leaders of fur workers against restrictions on commercial use of skins, fishery workers against protections for dwindling species, and so on. By the 1980s, loggers and paperworkers in particular were vigorously pursued to the grass roots, through campaigns guided by corporation-friendly pressure groups.[61]

The same political momentum largely coincided, as Republican commentators acutely discerned, with the sharpening division of the nation along race lines. The erosion of the old predominantly urban and eastern New Deal constituencies for an expansive south and southwest created no new mass enthusiasts for the labor movement.[62] As late as the end of the 1960s, labor journalist Gus Tyler confidently predicted the south would one day come into line, reviving labor.[63] But as Stanley Aronowitz observed, because union organizing had been given up there almost before it started, and because subsequent efforts so rarely adopted the "community" kind of campaign that went beyond the haphazard, here-today-and-out-tomorrow style of signing up cards, the situation never grew better.[64]

History operated against the familiar modes of business unionism, because even where they tapped natural sympathies, mostly in the south-west rather than the deep south, the AFL-CIO with few exceptions had looked only to a white working class which gained appreciably from the racial stratification and felt little impulse toward solidarity with the mass of (non-white) working people. As in so many other cases, the unions had adopted a blind and no-win strategy. Famed novelist Barbara Kingsolver, in her skillful reportage of the Phelps-Dodge strike in Morenci, Arizona, of the middle 1980s, thus observed that the AFL-CIO not only failed to recognize the strength in the women (that is, family members) who essen-tially took over the strike support, but disdained the cross-border and international solidarity which made so much sense to Mexican-American employees and their relatives.[65]

Neither was the attraction of the white, male worker to the right as inevitable as the historical narrative makes it sound. Even the defection of blue-collar whites in increasing numbers from mainstream Protestant churches to evangelical sects with conservative theologies and aggressive political leaders contained a host of ambiguities. Union members and working people at large still tended to favor funding for education and social programs over military spending, as well as progressive taxation of corporations and the rich. Even working class members of the ultra-right Assemblies of God could sometimes be seen pitching in to help the families of local strikers. The person-to-person interaction of races in many cities and some suburbs after the demise of segregation might have provided a basis for interracial democracy, if only organized labor had found a unify-ing, progressive social agenda while it still held the loyalties of large sections of the working class and institutions (like union halls) in commu-nities to put the message across. The opportunity was squandered.

Much of this particular possibility depended upon memories fading in the sunrise of the suburban sprawl and the re-emerging racial divides. The older left or progressive sector—in some places ex-Communists or ex-So-cialists hanging on as liberal Democrats—might yet have supplied that kind of labor politics. But labor officials in general had no fondness toward manifestations of excess liberalism, and not infrequently denied their own members access to union facilities for unwanted campaigns, whether environmental, feminist, or race-based.

In union strength as in electoral politics, the AFL-CIO thus effectively wiped out its own secondary line of defense. But it had not successfully eradicated the class struggle—especially the one directed by employers against workers to lower labor costs. Routine bureaucratic responses were especially unequal to the challenges by foreign competition against American manufacturers' control of key markets. The United Steel Workers, never a particularly democratic union, responded to the crisis of a once highly privileged sector by bargaining away the accrued privileges a few at a time, so as to cling to the diminishing pool of jobs. The 1977 challenge to USW President Lloyd McBride by reformer Ed Sadlowski never reached much beyond Big Steel, in large part because the insurgents had no real program to meet the threat of factory shutdowns.[66] Defense of working conditions, the old standard for militancy, quickly went by the board, and collective defense of job security and defense against job reclassification were undercut in turn by the fearful individualism of union members.

Kirkland's regime had, indeed, emerged under this shadow. The wave of rank-and-file labor militancy from 1966 to 1974 posed a rejection of corporate take-backs that the UAW, for instance, could not adopt as its own without destabilizing the historic compromise with automakers. The same was true in many other industrial sectors. By 1977, organized resurgence had practically ended, a victim of recession, lowered expectations, and sheer bureaucratic sabotage. Desperate strikes, like the nation's longest walkout of the era during 1981-1982, at North Kingstown, Rhode Island, by proud machinists against the Brown and Sharpe Company, long famous for precision tools, ended in stalemate. Older independent companies and historic unions alike practically exhausted each other in these struggles.[67]

Not everyone caved in. The Teamsters for a Democratic Union within the IBT was the one major rank-and-file caucus that outlived the wildcat insurgency. It managed to do so for assorted practical reasons, because the trucking industry practically forced workers to choose between gangsterism and militancy, and in part because the economically decentralized structure of the business helped preserve a degree of democratic autonomy. But the TDU also held on and grew because younger radicals (mostly connected with the International Socialists, a group descended from the

"Third Camp" politics that Max Shachtman had abandoned) made it their aim and dedication to stay with the struggles. After two decades of work, TDU's network of activists provided the launching pad for Ron Carey's successful run for Teamsters president in 1993. Not even the scandal hurling Carey from office or the victory of business-unionist lawyer James Hoffa, Jr., as Carey's successor could end the base-building in defiant Teamster locals.[68]

Thousands of largely unaffiliated idealists from the later 1960s, encouraged and occasionally led by older activists, also kept the faith in similar ways. The women's group Union WAGE (Union Women's Alliance to Gain Equality), for instance, arose among mostly white working-class women in the San Francisco Bay Area, led by erstwile Trotskyist Anne Draper and other veterans of 1940s movements. Founded in 1971 and never growing beyond an extended circle of perhaps a few hundred, it raised a multiplicity of issues of women's work and union limitations, trying to infuse class issues into the women's movement and women's issues into the labor movement. Indirectly, WAGE and similar grassroots impulses spawned the Coalition of Labor Union Women in 1974, sponsored by the UAW and supported formally, at least, by the AFL-CIO leadership. As an "insiders' organization," CLUW was best at publicizing women's issues that organized labor could support (if often half-heartedly or less). Union WAGE and CLUW also encouraged the activity of "9 to 5," a courageous if notably underfunded group aiming at unionization of office workers.[69]

The limits of the hoped-for women's impact upon labor may be measured in the tales of woe from some of those who actually took middle-level AFL-CIO staff jobs from the early 1980s onward. In the best case, the rather reform-minded Service Employees International Union whose leader John Sweeney would one day take the AFL-CIO presidency, staffer Susan Eaton later recalled the deeply gendered mistrust by fellow staffers, the off-work union culture of strip clubs, the inevitable sexual harassment and jokes, and perhaps most of all the inability of union leaders to differentiate women staffers from the clerical workers, women's "natural" assigned work.[70] In some respects, or at least in some unions, things got better. In other respects, however, things hardly got better at all. Former union staffer Kim Feller reflected about women like herself:

> For those who can limit their vision to the small daily tasks, survival in the labor movement is possible, even rewarding: You can manage to do good organizing, if you don't concern yourself with issues of foreign policy; you can rise in the union hierarchy, if you don't defend your clerical staff; you can edit the union paper, if you don't encourage debate. Some make the compromise, for others the cost is too high. When the divide between the principles and the practice becomes too wide, people, both inside and outside the institution, lose faith.[71]

That could happen even when reformers struggled hard among hardened male union veterans to keep the faith. In Ohio, for instance, steel mill retirees facing the collapse of company pension funds organized themselves with the activist-lawyer Staughton Lynd into "Solidarity USA." At a contract meeting in 1987 over LTV Steel offers, they were placed behind a rope (as non-voting USW members), and saw their activity denounced by union leaders as unnecessary and divisive. Workers Against Toxic Chemical Hazards (WATCH) likewise held their own citizens' meetings and forced local union leaders to cease ignoring company indifference to industrial health risks. Most distinctively, Ohioans formed Workers Solidarity with a variety of members from various unions, picketing with strikers, organizing rallies, and generally promoting a spirit of common purpose which had all but disappeared since the 1940s. In virtually every case, they ran up against stone walls of bureaucratic resistance.[72]

The 1984 strike of Hormel meatpackers in Austin, Minnesota, which continued in the face of bitter opposition from the parent union, eventually evolved into a war against higher-ups as well. In the most spectacular grassroots labor struggle of the day, the small community united behind workers while outreach beyond the community gained support from some three thousand union locals nationwide, drawing tens of thousands of union members to the industrial town outside Minneapolis-St. Paul. Demonstrating courage and also hope through moments of picnics, parades, and dances (and an astounding mural, painted by unionists and dedicated to Nelson Mandela), Local P-9 showed for a moment what was possible. The United Food and Commercial Workers, a reliable ally of the Kirkland administration, in the end succesfully beat the strikers down, as might be expected. But they showed the latent potential for unionism to return to decentralized militancy against employers and independence from the labor chiefs.[73]

That aspiration proved impossible, except in limited and local conditions, under Kirkland. Labor initiative and worker self-mobilization nevertheless could and did inject enormous energy into particular struggles. The strike of more than a thousand frozen-food workers in Watsonville, California, during the middle 1980s offered another case in point. Mostly women of Latin American backgrounds, they found themselves much as their predecessors had, the racial outcasts of a minority white government and business community. Working closely with TDU (and gaining support from a nearby progressive community, Santa Cruz, in which the left actually held a majority city government), the strikers organized a series of parades and demonstrations, elected new leaders, and created a sense of labor solidarity in California rare since the grape strikers' days of Cesar Chavez. In April 1997, an AFL-CIO rally held in Watsonville for strawberry workers, with John Sweeney and his staff personally on hand, was an echo of a struggle that Kirkland in the 1980s considered both uninteresting and left-tainted. The impetus of union support had come too late, and offered too little for the long-delayed victory against the growers—in this case, further limited by the near-collapse of the frozen foods sector. But any victory looked impressive when set against the threadbare reality of claims to labor leadership at the national level.[74]

The Last Days

In the face of all contrary evidence, a *New York Times* reporter insisted in 1987, Kirkland had effectively demonstrated "the sort of quirky, independent spirit that made Meany such a formidable leader" in years past. The occasion for this warm endorsement was the reaffiliation with the AFL-CIO of the Teamsters, running for cover from Department of Justice investigations for corruption. Labor consultant Victor Kamber described the merger as the "major jewel in [Kirkland's] crown," and indeed it should be credited as his major accomplishment, with far-reaching consequences that he did not anticipate. Meany had expelled the Teamsters more than three decades earlier for the same purported corruption. But now, Kirkland insisted, Meany's ghost was fully in support: the vision of unity had been the old man's gift to his successor.[75]

William Serrin, a somewhat disillusioned former labor correspondent of the *New York Times*, saw things differently. In a biting commentary on the 1986 AFL-CIO convention in the *Village Voice*, Serrin opened up on the dishonesty and hypocrisy at large on the scene. In the face of massive defeats and the reduction of large parts of the workforce to part-time jobs without health coverage, unions could find lots of nasty and powerful opponents but had themselves more to blame than anyone else: "faceless, passionless, uncreative institutions," in the reporter's estimation. Labor's leaders, Serrin noted, identified with, dressed like, and acted like the corporate executives whose personae they most nearly replicated—except that they would never reach that level of power and influence. Business unionism had become a palpable failure. The issues they cared most passionately about could be measured by an exchange in the hallway between Albert Shanker and Edwin Doherty, Jr., the executive director of the AIFLD. "How do we look this afternoon?" asked a fretful Shanker about the upcoming debate with those who opposed aid to the Nicaraguan contras. "All set," replied Doherty, either unsuspecting of or uncaring about reporter Serrin's presence, "There may be some hotheads...but the mikes will be covered."[76]

Labor officialdom had, however, only suppressed the symptoms of revolt. A few years earlier, the rise of United Mine Workers' leader Rich Trumka had been ferociously resisted by the old right of business unionism and social-democratic leaders alike. Successful challenger against Sam Church, whose regime was suspiciously connected with the assassination of previous challenger Jock Yablonsky, Trumka was a former miner who had earned his law degree in his off-hours, and portrayed himself as militantly within the tradition of John L. Lewis. He also aligned himself with the remnants of the non-Communist left tenaciously surviving among the descendents of Croatian and Slovene miners who returned to coal from white-collar layoffs and kept up their membership in old-time socialistic fraternal associations.[77] During a 1982 campaign full of redbaiting, veteran Cold War labor columnist Victor Riesel—one of Meany's special favorites—accused Trumka, quite absurdly, of being an agent of the Communist conspiracy. Like the claim of Building Trades Council leader Robert Georgine that Ralph Nader was "infiltrating" labor, this was the ridiculous sort of charge given credence in the days of McCarthyism, but now dismissed out of hand. Trumka won by a commanding 68 percent of the vote. Sometimes quite cautious economically, the new miners' leader soon proved himself politically bold, a leader in the struggle against South African apartheid and the Nicaraguan contras, and for a new labor politics—perhaps or eventually, he sometimes hinted, a third party. He emerged from a fierce struggle of miners in Pittston, Virginia, during 1989-1990 against a union-busting coal company, and a monumental campaign of outside support, as someone who did not necessarily carry the flag but who could be counted upon *not* to sabotage the struggle. That alone set him in place as a potential alternative figure in the struggle over AFL-CIO leadership just a few years ahead.[78]

Kirkland's response to all this, right to the end, remained perfectly autocratic, giving no ground to dissidents of any kind, confident that he could ride out both the internal restlessness and the larger labor decline. He was dead wrong. By any standard, organizational membership and prestige were by now sinking at a disastrous pace. Nevertheless, the nineteenth biennial AFL-CIO convention held in Detroit in 1991 unanimously elected Kirkland to a seventh two-year term with a voice vote only, even though this procedure expressly violated Article V, Section 3 of the AFL-CIO constitution, which required a printed ballot.[79]

Two years later, when the pro-labor consulting firm Greer, Margolis, Mitchell, Burns & Associates hired Democratic pollster Peter D. Hart to conduct a survey, at considerable expense, with eleven focus groups, it discovered that the AFL-CIO was less favorably regarded than "unions" as such, that many people (but especially low-income people) regarded unions as "largely undemocratic bureaucracies that impose decisions on their members from the top down." Worst of all, that most focus groups participants considered unions "dinosaurs," has-been institutions with no relevance for modern society.[80] All this had been obvious for Kirkland's entire tenure, despite his frequent attempt to put a positive spin on falling membership. The massive attrition in traditional strongholds inadvertently increased the proportions of women and people of color: supposed proof of "progress" toward inclusiveness.[81]

As the 1994 elections approached, Kirkland signalled to reporters that the sixty-four House and Senate Democrats who voted to support the North American Free Trade Agreement (NAFTA) would nevertheless continue to be endorsed. Indeed, Kirkland denied contrary reports that the executive board had *ever* suggested that politicians who voted for NAFTA would be held accountable. He remained likewise taciturn as Congress prepared to vote for the General Agreement on Tariffs and Trade (GATT), and the AFL-CIO staff opted for no struggle at all but rather for a behind-the-scenes amending of the document—a strategy that fell absolutely flat.[82]

Kirkland as much as admitted that labor law reform of all kinds had also failed. But he adamantly denied that Democrats increasingly took labor votes for granted or had slipped away from their moorings in any significant way. Clinton, a conservative southern Democrat not unlike Kirkland himself, was someone whose record the AFL-CIO president had "no difficulty in defending." Those who dared to hint (at the suggestion of a reporter) that labor "is not working as hard as in the past" were, from Kirkland's point of view, "contemplating their own navels." Labor was still a major political force, on the Gompers model of "reward your friends and punish your enemies." Nothing could change that. Yet reality looked steadily worse despite the AFL-CIO president's demurrers.[83]

Predictably, the last burst of Kirkland energy went to the former Soviet Union, especially Russia itself. In 1990, as the USSR dissolved, a mass convention of trade unionists there had voted with secret ballot to replace the old artificial and controlled government bodies with an independent General Confederation of Trade Unions (FNFR), representing some fifty to sixty million workers. This body established labor colleges, published its own daily paper, supported strikes, and fought to keep benefits and protective legislation that existed under the old regime. The Kirkland regime wanted, however, nothing to do with existing Russian labor organizations. The AFL-CIO intended instead to splinter the FNFR membership and reap the rewards. Funded heavily by the NED and other U.S. agencies, paying salaries huge by Russian standards, the so-called Free Trade Union Institute's client organizations set out to "organize" unionists who already belonged to other labor organizations. Promising vast future improvements based upon privatization of the market, these pet unions constantly deferred strikes and other actions. They made little progress, even where they entered existing labor disputes with promises of investment to employers and quantities of cash to dispense to potential leaders and strikers. Seeking their own strategic ground, they could only set themselves against the popular unrest.[84]

In an atmosphere of severely declining public health and growing poverty, as well as accelerating divisions between the rich (mainly speculators and swindlers) and the poor (especially older citizens), FNFR had increasingly formed the most significant barrier against social disaster. Indeed, sections of the FNFR became the strongest supporters of the anti-Stalinist socialist legislator Boris Kagarlitsky. By opposing Yeltsin's illegal dissolution of the Duma in 1993 and violent attack upon its elected members, the FNFR placed itself outside official patronage, which the American-guided unions rushed in to accept. The "social accord" naturally banned strikes, another proof to observers of the American favorites' real interests against "independent" union prerogatives.[85] Even after Kirkland's unseating, the FTUI unions continued to act faithfully for the State Department, pouring money into Yeltsin's 1996 re-election campaign, financed by assorted U.S. sources with tens of millions of dollars, against election rules. It was, so at least one hopes, the last major instance of massive foreign election-tampering by the old, standard Cold War rules of the AFL and AFL-CIO.

By 1995, nevertheless, the known funding of this operation by the AFL-CIO's Free Trade Union Institute and its intimate allies (AID and NED) had reached approximately thirty million dollars. Experience had shown, critics charged, that client unions had never been intended to be "independent" but simply that—clients. The Russian-American Foundation of Trade Union Research and Education, a classic intelligence front, doggedly published a handful of books and funded a newspaper, *Delo*, with $240,000 from the NED, offering views suspiciously identical to those of Albert Shanker's and vigorously supporting Russia's president even as the vast flow of semi-official corruption was revealed and as Boris Yeltsin's reputation sank with living standards. *Delo*'s peak (or claimed) sixty thousand circulation sank close to zero when funds were cut in 1996: no one had learned to love it.[86]

The AFT leadership, undaunted by the death of Shanker, continued to sink members' dues payments into a so-called Teacher Organizing and Education Resource Center in Moscow. Known best in recent years for an anti-affirmative action agenda at home, AFT specialists sought replacement of the old Russian curricula with a "democracy curriculum" idealizing U.S. global leadership and the American way of life. As a journalist noted wryly, the AFL-CIO, which had repeatedly refused to finance a radio station for American workers (just as it had refused to publish a daily newspaper in labor's own interests), miraculously found, via the AFT, $660,000 for four radio stations in Russia during 1994 alone.[87]

Kirkland could and did continue to make greater claims for the Polish labor movement, and for those in the Eastern European regimes where prosperity so far held off the disintegration of social security systems and assorted other down-sides of privatization. Yet the AFL-CIO made little real progress in establishing the full-blown client union movement that it so deeply desired. Somehow the new capitalists were ungrateful and stubbornly anti-union, and the working people themselves unenthusiastic for Western-style unions. For all the money, effort, and boasting, what might be called the AFL-CIO's Eastern Front had been a bust after all.

Despite such accumulating bad news, Kirkland remained the darling of the hawkish labor brass.[88] As Shanker once quipped to a friendly reporter about Kirkland, "There's just no one else around who comes close in their ability to lead."[89] Not, at least, in the direction that Kirkland and Shanker had in mind. The 1994 Republican election victory was, then, not a wake-up call but a stunning shock. Yet Kirkland insisted—almost literally until the last days in office—upon business as usual. During the months after the election, it was SEIU President John Sweeney who decided that Kirkland had to go. Propelled by the urgency of government employees' leader Gerald McIntee among others, Sweeney and an emboldened set of allies rapidly built up so much pressure that in February 1995, Kirkland, defeated (or quite suddenly modest), announced that his time to retire had come. Under slightly different circumstances, Sweeney himself might have been a possible candidate for designated succession. Instead, Kirkland chose an iron-clad loyalist, Thomas Donahue, who like Kirkland was a colorless functionary (and like Meany, the son of a New York labor official), but with vastly more of a genuinely labor past than the current AFL-CIO president.

Sweeney, a middle-of-the-road union leader with a personal history somewhat muddied by the common (though still misguided) practice of double-dipping salaries for overlapping jobs, had nevertheless managed to distinguish himself in two respects. First, he had encouraged innovation in organizing among home healthcare workers, janitors, and office clericals, encouraging through "Justice for Janitors" the style of public demonstrations and street theater that the AFL-CIO had generally opposed since civil rights days. Second, he had offered the landmark AFL-CIO convention resolutions in 1983 on gay rights and AIDS.[90]

In neither area was his practice up to the promise. Much of the increase of SEIU's membership in his fourteen years of office—from 625,000 to 1.1 million, in contrast to the atrophy in most other AFL-CIO internationals—occurred through mergers of existing locals. Those locals, once merged, were in practice more geographically far-flung and less democratic in terms of ordinary members' participation than they had been before. Even Sweeney's personal support for Justice for Janitors seemed more symbolic and half-hearted than his devotees claimed later. Nor did SEIU do much to act upon its progressive stance supporting gays and people with AIDS within labor.

Nevertheless, Sweeney had been wise enough to take elements of the left in hand. This was something that Kirkland would never have done and that Donahue could not bring himself to do despite his quiet support of expanded organizing and his modest efforts to coordinate a very low-key (some would say throw-in-the-towel) anti-NAFTA campaign. Ironically, Sweeney had months earlier actually wanted Donahue to run against Kirkland, which might have resulted in a far quieter and less meaningful shift of authority. Donahue, known a decade earlier for supporting negotiations in Central America rather than the contra enthusiasm of Kirkland and Shanker, could never have brought himself to buck the machine.[91] That proved decisive in one more respect. Paul Booth, an early leader of Students for a Democratic Society (SDS) and in the years since a force in community organizing through the Saul Alinsky-inspired Midwest Academy as well as the middle levels of AFSCME leadership, worked out the strategy for overturning the Kirkland-Donahue bureaucracy.

The campaign called upon the votes of the UAW, the UMW, and the Steelworkers—all down in numbers since their heroic CIO days—together with those of AFSCME and SEIU. This group of unions constituted altogether the most interracial segment of the labor movement. They would not have been strong enough without the Teamsters, whose change in leadership would not have been possible without the TDU. It was if the old Reuther opposition to the Meany leadership had been reborn, on different terms. The center had collapsed, in the process of moving steadily rightward.

A few months later, Albert Shanker threatened to pull his AFT and presumably his allies in the federation out of the AFL-CIO entirely. But this was an evident bluff, perhaps to slow the erosion of forced "retirements" within the AFL-CIO bureaucratic reaches and especially the international department. It did not work, no doubt because the alleged Communist bogey upon which Shanker and his allies had staked so much of their careers had now vanished.

"New Voices," as the mobilization coalition styled itself, cultivated support in all directions, from a handful of the construction locals that had shrunk and now were more open to progressives, to state feds and local labor councils that had simply been inactive in national labor politics for decades. At last there was something to talk about, and visitors from the international who wanted to do more than congratulate themselves and tell locals to rally votes for particular Democrats waxed enthusiastic. Momentum built quickly. Despite the later indications of a palace revolution, more than twice the usual number of delegates registered to attend the October AFL-CIO convention, a bad sign for a leadership accustomed to purely nominal participation. These were not, in large part, ordinary union members or even chosen by union members, but the larger presence of delegates counted nevertheless.

At the convention itself, Donahue returned to the kind of issues that Gompers, Meany, and Kirkland would have emphasized, warning Sweeney that he had become the voice of those who want "to shout louder and break down the system in the hopes . . . that out of the ashes of the old comes something better." Donahue thus signalled the threat of the left to the bureaucracy's get-along, go-along methods. He distinguished his program from Sweeney's in yet one other important way. If Sweeney promised to transfer money from current intelligence-linked international programs into badly needed domestic organizing, Donahue avowed that all such domestic organizing monies would need to come from elsewhere, and the international program maintained. Under his projected regime, the satraps of the intelligence contacts would be preserved along with the big ticket international programs that generations of Dubinskys, Lovestones, Meanys, and Kirklands had founded or kept in motion.[92]

The conflicting symbols of the two slates continued to run in these ways, despite the sometimes mixed signals of the Sweeney team. The old team had no equivocation in its aspiration for a Cold War after the Cold War. Bricklayers' president John Joyce (by now known jokingly to members as "Air Joyce" because of the constant motion of his Lear jet, reputedly paid for by grateful donors as he turned over the union's political offices to SDUSA operative Joel Friedman), growled audibly at a resolution on the establishment of a new executive vice-president position to be held by Linda Chavez-Thompson, a sort of living symbol of labor leadership's new diversity. As a Steelworker official rose to concur with Joyce, a New Voice leader asked why delegates could not speak to the resolution from the podium instead of the floor. This was a crucial moment. The leaders had, as was well known, generally kept opposition speakers at distant microphones, and not uncommonly turned the mikes off whenever the debate got a little hot and embarrassing. This time the room was filled with a roar of approval. The most notoriously heavy-handed of the bureaucrats had clearly lost control.

Some of the key new leaders were curious, ambiguous, and fascinating in equal doses. Arthur S. Coia had inherited the Laborers International Union of North America (LIUNA) from his father, Arthur E. Coia, an old-fashioned, unpolished functionary whose power had been built (like many labor figures before him, not excluding the needle trades conservatives of old) with the reputed assistance of the underworld. When the younger Coia took over, he tried to clean up LIUNA quietly, while opening a new front in tackling the problem of workplace toxic hazards. No one would say it was a democratic organization, and yet it demonstrably did not belong to the Kirkland machine. Its new leader, said to be further influenced by leftish liberation theology, was naturally viewed as a heretic by the Meany-Shanker team. Donahue's lieutenants offered Coia the very executive vice-president slot that they had bitterly opposed creating for Chavez-Thompson—if only the Laborers' Union president would switch his vote to the Old Guard. Coia replied that he intended to stand by the promise that he had made to the reformers. Unable to enforce the familiar menu of threats against dissenters, the Meany-Kirkland machine was truly and fittingly defeated on a matter of personal integrity.[93]

The 1995 victory over decades of misleadership was neither unalloyed nor especially democratic. A constitutional amendment intended to expand the executive council so as to include all seventy-eight union presidents (and maintain the old guard's hold over the federation) was defeated soundly. But a "Unity" slate, revealed to delegates only moments before open nominations for the executive council, had been hand-picked in secret meetings of negotiators for the Donahue and Sweeney forces. None of the new officials had risen to explain their positions to delegates, or to explain why they should be elected. The very method of balloting further encouraged bloc votes rather than individual choices, by presenting the familiar picture of people who had understandably expected to be re-elected term after term without opposition. And the officials, as in the past, had good reasons for these expectations: of the fifty-one members to the new executive council, forty-four were actually union presidents, representing nearly all of the total convention votes of the 13.3 million AFL-CIO members. Seven women, nine African Americans, two Hispanics and one Asian American had been included to sweeten the deal and to symbolize the forces of change. The subsequent October 1997 convention reaffirmed the new existing arrangements. It remained unclear, of course, what precisely, beyond the symbolism, could be expected of labor's promised reinvigoration.[94]

And yet, for all these limitations, the most inept labor leadership in American history, as well as the most thoroughly corrupted by decades of misdeeds in the third world and the local union hall, had been voted out of power. Shanker and Kirkland in particular had been shamed, their followers now too far from power (in the case of the familiar high-level operatives, mostly too aged) for any early recovery even if the new, reform leaders stumbled. The old truisms that leadership belonged properly to white males exclusively, and to the most ardent supporters of intelligence agencies, weapons programs, military interventions, and economic growth at all ecological costs, had been turned to dust. Whatever happened afterward, the mountain-moving day had come. Revival had become *possible*.

CONCLUSION

In May 1997, AFL-CIO President John Sweeney addressed a meeting of seventy-five unabashedly left-wing labor history scholars, artists, campus activists, and older scholar-intellectuals with a message of hope and determination. Labor was "back from the dead," he proclaimed, making a none-too-subtle comment on macabre qualities of the Kirkland era. Now it would come to its own through an alliance with progressive social movements. Secretary-Treasurer Linda Chavez-Thompson, the first woman and the first Mexican-American ever to serve in such a high capacity, elected in 1995 on Sweeney's New Voices slate over the bitter opposition of labor conservatives, drove home the message. Labor had to be militant, had to be progressive, and had to support feminists and environmentalists, among others, if it expected to be supported in return.[1]

The symbolism of the meeting was difficult to miss. The most distinguished of the scholars on hand, Yale professor David Montgomery, labor history's leading sage, had been fingered by labor right-wingers in the 1950s, blacklisted from his machinist trade before entering graduate school. Also present was National Organization of Women founder Betty Friedan, in that same dark era a columnist for the proscribed *UE News,* and at loggerheads with the bluntly anti-feminist Meany-Kirkland leadership for decades. The main body of labor historians at the meeting, now themselves mostly advanced into middle age, had provided the backbone of scholarly revisionism, displacing the hagiographic school of leadership profiles and giving the Gompers tradition low marks for its historic racism, red-baiting, and otherwise destructive behavior. Devotees of the old guard, the Cold War liberals of the labor history trade and out-of-luck former functionaries, were absent, except for a conspicuous spy or two from Albert Shanker's inner circle.

Conservative columnists and many erstwhile liberals (some of them former boy socialists) expressed continual distress during the following months at the apparent alliance between new labor and "the left." Indeed, the entire Democratic Party seemed, in the view of establishment alarmists, to be tilting away from the safe-and-sound political center of Clinton's bullish-on-business "New Democrats" back toward the dangerously leftish combination of labor, women, minorities, and liberals. This was, of course, a decidedly fanciful interpretation, disregarding the appeals by John Sweeney for a "cooperative" relationship with business (as well as the embarrassing eagerness among leaders of labor, as of African-American and women's organizations to indulge Bill Clinton no matter what the effects of his social programs). It also overlooked the inclination of labor leadership, especially in public unions and the building trades, to continue looking rightward for political coalitions, and to use any means to hold the line against dissenters complaining about deteriorating wages and conditions. The story of New York's District Council 37, AFSCME, offers only a particular vivid example of abuses so widespread as to be commonplace. What DC 37's leadership achieved through stuffed ballots, other union leaders have accomplished and continue to accomplish by other means: iron-tight caucuses, like that in the American Federation of Teachers; indirect federal assistance, like James Hoffa, Jr.'s benefit from zealous prosecution aimed at the reform faction of the Teamsters rather than the old guard; or, as in so many other cases, through simply assuring by juryrigging that union offices are bound to remain in family hands.

Yet a growing nervousness among those who could rightly be called "Giuliani Democrats" makes sense as an advance warning against the political shifts that a serious economic downturn may well bring. Nothing is likely to turn a "cash-box" Democratic Party machine far away from its sources of money, but even a residual rhetoric of populism might play dangerously in the era to come. Opponents of NAFTA and other harmful trade agreements, likewise of destructive practices by the IMF and World Bank, won an important congressional victory over "fast track" in the fall of 1998, humbling the bipartisan support which stretched from Newt Gingrich to Al Gore.[2] Future redefinition of the trade debate, raising crucial questions about the global environment and working conditions, could make life difficult for international corporations but also for the neoliberal politics represented by the Democratic Leadership Council. Opponents might line up with Americans of assorted types against military intervention and against the larger but also familiar pattern of international intrigue, now redirected at newer targets. In some future crisis situation, they might even turn upon the roots of ruthless corporate behavior.

The new AFL-CIO leaders showed little sign of this potential turn during their first few years of office, not even much resistance to the accelerating shift of Clinton-Gore politics away from New Deal-style labor politics as well as environmental and feminist concerns (rhetoric and tokenism entirely aside). To be as fair and sympathetic as possible, daunting challenges faced an AFL-CIO which by this time was barely holding its own, due to plant closedowns, job exports, and unreplaced retirements. Nothing less than a surge of organizing could reverse the tide, and nothing but a tilt of American society away from the contemporary business agenda, along with a new climate of international labor solidarity, could rally the combined social forces to make that possible. AFL-CIO leaders hoped to draw centrist Democrats like Gore leftward, but labor's success rested upon the prospects of a mass social movement that no one less skilled than a Franklin Roosevelt could both encourage and call into line for a future reconstructed economy.

To claim accuracy in predicting such a development would be folly. It is more than possible that Hoffa, Jr., new boss of the Teamsters, will join with the disgruntled conservatives of the building trades and the surviving old guard hawks in a familiar alliance against labor progressives, directing a stealth attack against the Sweeney leadership and leading finally to a suuccessful counter-coup. Hardly anything, even a rumored Teamsters pullout from the AFL-CIO, could be more certain to reduce organized labor to the point of no return. But in a global economy falling (at least in many places) into severe recession, and mass apathy (again, in places) shifting unpredictably against the ultra-wealthy world elite, neither could a happier outcome be excluded. The AFL-CIO was by no means certain to benefit, not only because of its structural weakness but because until very recently its leaders had treated themselves as partners with the elite and constantly fortified their positions in the midst of apathy, sealing themselves off from challenges. Yet in the vacuum of organized forces, the weakened and shamed AFL-CIO might yet serve the purposes that the labor movement, at its best, has always served.

Legacies of Solidarity

Models of solidarity inevitably return to the Knights of Labor and the Industrial Workers of the World, those two historic movements despised and in considerable part destroyed by the machinations of Samuel Gompers's AFL. More social movements than organized institutions in the modern sense, the Knights and Wobblies proclaimed the universality of their emancipatory cause and rebutted the claim of capital and government to set the standards for civilization. By their very existence—whatever their practical weaknesses—these two movements propelled sympathizers toward building a new society within the shell of the old, a society of decentralized self-government and voluntary cooperation. The best of today's labor reformers have only begun to point in the same direction.

At least one living model for AFL-CIO reinvigoration had, however, already started to take hold during the early 1990s. Wisconsin, home alike of Milwaukee "sewer socialists" in city government from the 1910s to the 1950s and of the Progressive Party which commanded the governorship from the 1910s to 1930s, had never quite lost its uniqueness, even during periods of general conservatism. During the 1970s, an early successful Teaching Assistants Association took hold at the University of Wisconsin in Madison after a dramatic strike and a major union-busting effort of staff reduction by the university administration. White-collar workers in Madison, their numbers swelled by expansion of state government, warmly supported the leftish mayor Paul Soglin. Even the Democratic Party often leaned leftward toward labor's progressive edge.[3]

State capital and commercial center, Madison had never historically been a city of major labor activity. But in 1979, a lockout of pressmen at the two daily newspapers (including the prestigious *Capital Times,* one of the few dailies to oppose the Vietnam War) spurred a memorable solidarity struggle. As workers lost the battle to shut down the papers, they tried to win the war through their own strikers' daily, publishing some twenty-seven months despite an economic slump and a business boycott. Community cooperative ownership, always difficult, often contradicted the impulses of collective self-management by the paper's workers, and yet the paper represented in many ways a model labor effort of the day—which predictably earned it the cold disinterest from Kirkland's AFL-CIO leadership. Like virtually all strike papers, the *Press Connection* failed in the end from financial pressures. It might have survived without the successful corporate campaign to elect an anti-labor, mainstream politician in place of the radical Paul Soglin's intended successor, by no coincidence the son-in-law of the same George McGovern scorned by Meany's team a few years earlier.[4]

The progressive mood of Madison and sections of its labor movement prompted a near-walkout of the building trades locals from the Madison Federation of Labor during the 1970s. A reconciliation on narrower practical grounds aided the transformation of the state labor movement at large. The Madison Fed, with former TAA leader David Newby its president, soon published the best and most progressive of America's local labor monthlies (*Union Labor News*), and the Newby team began to propose ways to reinvigorate Wisconsin labor at large. The team found especially willing listeners in the white-collar and service unions which shared the feminist, the gay-friendly, and environmentalist impulses of the new Fed leadership. It also found eager allies in the survivors of the older Wisconsin radicalism, still alive in the militant *Racine Labor,* in the labor veterans of socialist Frank Zeidler's Milwaukee popular mayoralty (1948-1960) as well as the outspoken Zeidler himself, and in the locals and trade councils of various trades eager to find a way forward. The University of Wisconsin's School for Workers, since the early Cold War years a site for AFL-CIO international department scheming and frequent visits of CIA-friendly reps from assorted unions, underwent a change at once remarkable and predictive. The School for Workers returned to real labor education during the 1980s-1990s, back from anticommunist obsessions and international junkets. Its newest leading public figure, Frank Emspak, once a prominent anti-war campaigner on campus and nationally, was none other than son of Julius Emspak, a founder and longtime leader of the United Electrical Workers.

Most of the newly dynamic activity in Wisconsin labor took place at the local level, where a younger generation of activists, rainbow-hued in their diversity, challenged management and the city to do better—in fact, to return to the honesty and semi-egalitarian atmosphere of municipal socialist days. The New Party found a home here, with strong labor support, electing local officials in Madison, Oshkosh, and Green Bay. Left-leaning Democrats, including the first open lesbian to be elected to Congress, learned that AFL-CIO educational efforts made all the difference.[5] By 1990, a natural turnover in state labor leadership opened the doors to Newby himself. As the most progressive president of any state federation by a long stretch, Newby added a major cultural strategy to the agenda of labor support, education, and fresh organizing. Not since the 1930s-1940s had labor choruses blossomed at the state and local levels and labor theatrical shows offered rousing musicales. By no accident, the long banned labor-feminist film of the early 1950s blacklisted Hollywood unionists, *Salt of the Earth,* was chosen in 1997 for restaging as a "labor opera." Labor still had a long, long way to go in Wisconsin, but morally, things had truly begun to come around again.[6]

Another regional sign of the times could be found in the Twin Cities and surrounding districts. Not many decades before, Minneapolis and St. Paul had been not only the milling center of America but also the home to a vibrant left-wing unionism, within both the AFL and CIO. It ended sadly. Hubert Humphrey personally led the purge of left-wingers from the Farmer-Labor Party after it merged (with Communist approval) into the state Democratic Party. Loud on civil rights rhetoric but more solidly behind corporate globalism and political repression, Humphreyism became synonymous with Cold War lib-lab strategies. Pockets of progressive activity had nevertheless survived the red scare years in Minnesota, and these in turn encouraged many small labor reform impulses over the decades. By the 1980s-1990s, Twin Cities labor activists found untapped resources among sympathetic professors, graduate students, and staff at regional colleges and universities, as campus activists found outlets for their idealistic political aspirations. Not only solidarity with Austin's P-9 strikers but also struggles against privatization of bus service and hospitals and working conferences around broader revitalization of unions brought together bus drivers, electricians, teamsters, postal workers, and labor artists.

A true internationalism of the new kind could now be seen in a project like the Resource Center for the Americas, based in Minneapolis. The product of the solidarity movement which peaked during the middle 1980s around anti-interventionist campaigns, the Center and its widely-read quarterly, *Working Together,* increasingly publicized and helped coordinate campaigns by Mexicans, Guatemalans, and others "south of the border" with Americans and Canadians. Thus, too, the Coalition for Justice in the Maquiladoras, founded in 1989 by religious organizations and several unions resolved to improve conditions in factories along the border. With projects in a half-dozen Mexican border cities, supporting several Mexican unions independent of the corrupted official Mexican Congress of Labor, the CJM helped put into place the needed mechanisms for future efforts. NAFTA, backed heavily by the Clinton-Gore team and hardly resisted by Kirkland, had created the sea of misery demanding redress. A wild increase at the number of maquiladoras from the mid-1990s onward, with poverty-level weekly wages at $26-$42 for up to forty-eight work hours, offered the side effect of an unprecedented spew of toxic chemicals along the border. Clinton's officials predictably ignored the mess, and before Sweeney, the AFL-CIO made only rhetorical gestures at solidarity.

Such over-the-border sweatshops and toxic floods, indeed, presented only one major problem to the Meany and Kirkland regimes: the danger of radicals gaining influence. Official Mexican union reps in evidence at the George Meany Center had continued until the end of Kirkland's days to be brought in for "training" in compliant unionism. After 1995, however, the AFL-CIO began making small steps in the other direction. In 1996 Steel-workers President George Becker, who often recalled to sympathetic listeners that he grew up in an Illinois coal-mining town heavy with old socialists, and a delegation of union leaders personally examined a few of the maquiladoras. In self-interest, as well as with a glimmering sense of humanity, American labor officials resolved to take an active role support-ing independent Mexican unions and assorted progressive coalitions. By 1998, John Sweeney began meeting with the independent and more radical Mexican unions. As the NAFTA-exaggerated crisis in Mexican society and the Mexican economy continued—the vaunted "recovery" consisting mainly in a financial bonanza for the wealthy classes—the possibilities for real internationalism loomed. The Minneapolis-based activists also helped bring together Americans with Canadian trade unionists who had never been so shackled with Cold War logic and intelligence agency guidance.

These gestures, along with campus activities across the country, like the struggle against fast track NAFTA expansion helped put the White House (and especially presidential aspirant Al Gore) on the hotseat for the environmental and labor-standard protections. Clinton himself promised to establish a sweatshop task force to monitor labor conditions, albeit with standards set so abysmally low (workers as young as fourteen, with sixty or more hours of work per week, and no better wages than existing norms in the country of production) and enforcement so lax as to offer an insulting symbolism. Yet in a growing number of cases, like the Guatemalan union STEMCAMOSA, cross-border support campaigns with groups like the Chicago-based Guatemala Labor Education Project, and mobilization at U.S. retail outlets from Van Huesen to Walmart, pickets and letters from unionists, church people, and students put corporations on the defensive and evidently began to made a difference. Victory at a Nicaraguan garment factory in 1998 by a Sandinista-federated union, after years of efforts with labor, human rights, and faith-based movements, offered promises of deeper hemispheric solidarity ties in the future. On many campuses, the anti-sweatshop campaigns of undergraduates spawned the most important waves of labor support in decades. Even cross-border mural projects of and by working people showed light in the dark tunnel of post-NAFTA Americas.[7]

Such assorted activities pointed toward one of the great unrealized goals of labor reformers during the 1960s-1980s, networking and communication among workers themselves, within and outside normal union channels, across the state, the country, or the world. Electronic mail, substituting in some ways for the union hall once rooted (in pre-suburban times) within the neighborhood and serving as social meeting center, has opened up space for what labor historian and activist Staughton Lynd calls "horizontal" labor activity. Abandonment of the bureaucratic vertical style, akin to corporate or military models, will not be easy and is not likely to come soon. But the possibilities, at least, lay closer to the vision of the Industrial Workers of the World than anything seen during the decades since.

The struggle against the lockout of agribusiness workers at Staley in Decatur, Illinois, during much of the 1990s offered an illuminating example of horizontal activity or solidarity-from-below. The transformation of a traditional family-owned business intimately linked to a small midwestern industrial town into the outpost of a sweetener giant dramatically worsened working conditions. After many complaints and one death, OSHA investigators turned up eight thousand violations and a fine of $1.6 million, the largest single levy from that agency to date. An enraged company tightened the grip on work life and prepared for a strike to break the union in 1993. Facing desperate conditions, the union local did what few unions have done for decades: it engaged family members deeply in the fight-back effort, and (thanks in part to the proposals of St. Louis-based Jerry Tucker, formerly head of the New Directions caucus challenge to UAW leadership) suggested to workers the old Wobbly strategy of working-to-rule, that is, technically meeting all enforced regulations but slowing production down decisively.

Decentralized and apparently individualized resistance, exercised as the refusal to use any worker initiative or quality control, flourished alongside picnic-like weekly solidarity meetings. Staley production fell dramatically, and the company responded with a lockout. During the later 1970s-1980s, workers facing such a situation had repeatedly called in Ray Rogers, best known for his "corporate campaigns" to pressure management. Rallies, pressure on company stockholders, and constant meetings built up hopes. As in so many of Rogers's campaigns, hope at Staley faded when no early results could be recorded. The very approach also tended to telescope the campaign into an expensive personality contest, *Rogers v Management*. After ten months and $300,000 in fees to Rogers, the discouraged but unbeaten workers determined to take over their own struggles again through face-to-face contacts with unionists elsewhere; solidarity committees branched out from Chicago, St. Louis, and Milwaukee to points distant. Coalitions with local clergy and the black community boosted new demonstrations at the plant gate, with civil resistance pepper-gassed by city police and state troopers. By mid-1994, Milwaukee supporters had successfully pressured Miller beer to dump Staley as supplier, the first major union victory. Meanwhile, a tri-union solidarity committee (with auto workers and rubber workers, involved in their own Decatur plant strikes) went on a forty-mile, two-day march to the capital in Springfield. Chanting the old Wobbly slogan, "We Are All Leaders," they demanded collectively to see Illinois Governor Jim Edgar.[8] By that time, the campaigners were exhausted. A company return to the offer originally refused by over 90 percent of the workers brought acceptance of some jobs in a limited union environment. Most strikers refused to return under these conditions. The Staley settlement was far from victory, but the old democratic impulse, long vanished beneath bureaucratic stolidity, had been renewed by fresh generations. What labor journalist and lawyer Steve Early called "structures of accountability" for union leaderships had only begun to make a real difference, mostly in less dramatic situations. An hour's drive from Decatur stood the Mount Olive Cemetery, where Mother Jones had been put to rest three generations earlier. Now her reputation returned, in a small, significant way, to those for whom she had sacrificed.[9]

The Organizing Institute (OI) at the AFL-CIO headquarters offered a hopeful sign of a different, mainly generational, heavily gendered sort. OI's earliest versions were launched even before the fall of Lane Kirkland: in 1995, half of its $2.5 million budget went to campus recruitment for "Union Summer," a series of student blitzes on unorganized zones. The Peace Corps style unquestionably generated great publicity but also tended to obscure the difficult problems of establishing and building from a local support base among the workers to be unionized.

Whatever its limitations, the AFL-CIO's shift of emphasis was a dramatic and welcome one since the determined rebuff to the summer "work-in" promised by Students for a Democratic Society back in 1969. In those days, Meany's staff sent out sharp warnings to affiliates to watch out for student troublemakers who might be encouraging anti-war sentiment or engaging in union reform campaigns or unwanted organization of the unorganized, mostly in and around campus or in service jobs. Sad to say, the new left work-in, with nothing but energy on its side, had little lasting effect save initial encouragement for campus teaching assistants and some assorted university workers. The later OI program, by contrast, built upon years and in some cases decades of activity, mostly the independent vehicles of younger people such as 9 to 5, United Labor Unions (affiliated with the community organizing group ACORN), or the Rhode Island Workers Association (directed mainly at jewelry workers). By no accident and without much encouragement from the rising figure John Sweeney, all these latter efforts had since merged into SEIU.

Reoriented toward supplying recruits from campuses to various unions, the OI has not yet drawn fully upon the experiences of those locals (notably some Teamsters locals closely affiliated with TDU) that have trained, engaged, and employed over the long haul the idealistic youngsters willing to go the distance. Learning from experience, the OI has nevertheless launched year-round campaigns of various kinds, including an organic connection to the potential campus base for union support. Similarly, the new merged needle trades union UNITE, which draws partly upon the dark element of David Dubinsky's ILGWU bureaucracy along with the much more democratic legacy of the Amalgamated Clothing and Textile Workers, has enshrined programs of volunteer committees and "member organizers" to see early unionizing efforts through to a successful conclusion. Perhaps most impressive, the Communications Workers of America (CWA) moved a decade ago from servicing members to expanding membership through dedication of at least 10 percent of all annual resources to outreach. In extraordinarily difficult times, CWA added seventy-five thousand members by looking to the new workforces employed in telephone companies, and by tapping the regional labor activity of Spanish-speaking workers in Southern California. In October 1995, just as Sweeney's slate unseated Kirkland's chosen successors, a Convoy for Justice stretched thirty miles from the L.A. harbor to city hall, bringing together three thousand workers and their friends demanding better conditions for over-the-road drivers. In 1996, in a rally so large that it was held outside a college stadium (and notably supported by CWA strike benefits), five thousand drivers cut traffic to 10 percent of normal. Not perhaps more than six thousand workers had been added to a CWA local, mainly of telephone workers, in the L.A. area. But the union had joined the entourage of Spanish-speaking drywall workers, hotel workers, agricultural workers, and others who were fast changing the élan and even the shape of regional labor. During 1998, the CWA won another dramatic victory among more than six thousand Connecticut phone workers on a platform of leadership accountability.[10]

Of all the other national examples of renewal that could be cited, Jobs with Justice is without a doubt the most impressive. Bringing together community-labor coalitions of activists—from feminists and environmentalists to consumer groups—it has rallied around the rights of janitors and others through pickets, civil disobedience, rallies, and fundraisers. Strapped in most regions by an absence of resources for full-time staffers, JwJs have turned to volunteerism. Union members sign pledge cards committing every signer to "be there" regularly and to fight "for someone else's fight as well as my own." No better sustained example of the IWW's slogan, "An Injury to One is an Injury to All," could likely be found today.[11]

Politics as Usual—or Not?

Could such long-delayed efforts to organize be isolated from the top-heavy quality of union institutions? Or from the failure of social vision that had long stymied labor? The oddly developed movement for a Labor Party revealed the ambiguities of the attempt to move beyond labor's political patronage of its economic enemies, and toward a concerted campaign for collective self-improvement.

The least "new" element of the new AFL-CIO leadership since October 1995 has been its obeisance to almost anything that the Democrats have to offer. The millions of dollars and hundreds of thousands of staff hours spent on phone banks with get-out-the-vote messages surely made waves with Republicans during the 1996 election cycle. For the first time in several decades, conservative candidates and GOP spot commercials issued dark frequent and loud warnings about "big labor" special interests—as if the politicians of both parties hadn't made catering to business's special interests the central meaning of politics during the same era.

The AFL-CIO unarguably tipped the balance in a few dozen local races, and could have, with more money, better luck, or less sleazy candidates, made the difference in enough of them to diminish the Republican congressional majority to zero. It did still better in 1998, when phone-calling and face-to-face constituency work turned out a large union vote, fully 70 percent of it against the Republicans. It was a moment for John Sweeney to proclaim that labor had become a social force again. But had it?

Three generations after the New Deal, labor was stuck without any engine for social change that would link them to Democrats in ways that served both sides. As Democrats ardently proposed anti-labor free trade legislation, welfare reform, privatization of social security, and other measures that represented a setback for most working people, some activists, for the first time since Truman succeeded Roosevelt, began to seriously explore the prospect of an independent labor politics. Tony Mazzocchi, whose dynamic leadership helped spur the passing of the Occupational Safety and Health Act of 1970, had intermittently been a top officer of the Oil, Chemical, and Atomic Workers and had a reputation as labor's leading radical, along with International Association of Machinists President William Winpisinger. In 1991, a founding convention of Labor Party Advocates was held in Cleveland, supported by OCAW, the Brotherhood of the Maintenance of Way Employees (a railroad union), the International Longshore and Warehouse Union, United Electrical Workers, and—joining at the last minute—the United Mine Workers and American Federation of Government Employees. Longtime labor radicals took heart. Seven years later, the first constitutional convention of the Labor Party, held in Pittsburgh with twelve hundred delegates, six endorsing internationals (and the California Nurses Association), and ten thousand individual members, signalled the potentialities and problems of the independent labor political action.[12]

All along, Mazzocchi proposed a sort of wait-and-see approach by which LPA locals did not endorse candidates but instead agitated for support of the program and recruited membership to take part in the long-term struggle. The campaign for a constitutional amendment for a living wage seemed to be borrowed from the right's recent constitutional campaigns (against abortion and burning of the flag, etc.). In some cities and states, mainly those with histories of sustained and community-based left wing activities, Labor Party Advocates took off. Elsewhere, little was heard from them.

This experiment posed the problem left parties have always had in American politics: running candidates on its own line meant threatening links with union leaders closely connected to Democrats. And then again, even under the best conditions, working-class independent electoral practice might be a miserable failure—the frustration that led to the formation of the anti-electoral Industrial Workers of the World. Mazocchi's supporters held to the waiting game, collecting endorsements and denouncing labor's rubber-stamping of Democrats, without offering any early road out of the Democratic Party. Sweeney himself had made friendly noises toward Labor Party enthusiasts but not around election time, when no effort is spared to elect Democrats and precious few demands are made upon them.

Which Way Forward?

"Unions perform significant functions in capitalist society, and they are not likely to disappear. But their future is not bright." So wrote two former auto workers become acute observers of the labor movement, pessimistic that the drift toward authoritarianism could be reversed, or that the shift from industrial to post-industrial economy could be matched by a transformation of labor organizing.[13] There were ample reasons for such pessimism. No major Western economy, as David Brody argues, has been so deeply affected by such global developments as capital mobility and competitive labor markets.[14] The American working class had indeed changed drastically and irrevocably in structural terms since the high days of the CIO or the earlier era of the AFL's greatest influence. The millions of old industrial jobs lost will not return, and the millions of new jobs in fast foods or similar merchandizing or the white-collar business sector all seem daunting prospects at best for unionization.

But this was not the whole story. Studies regularly finding 25-40 percent of workers who would welcome unionization reveal a potential that grows with the well-recorded rising sense of insecurity and deep resentment of many strata of working people toward their employers.[15] At a historic point that President Clinton describes as the economic apex of modern times, life is certainly worse for working people around the globe and in many ways worse or certain to grow worse for working people at home. The Reagan Revolution, as Michael Meeropol writes, was completed by the Clinton administration during the middle of the 1990s with the virtual abandonment of the social safety net except for the elderly, the principal emphasis of social policy given over to restraining inflation, financing the growing police and prison sector, and maintaining armed might for international purposes.[16] When the bubble of speculation-fed prosperity bursts and the larger effects of environmental ruthlessness become more evident, the punishment can be expected to increase significantly.

A decisive reversal demands a mental leap for Americans used to being the aristocrats of the planet, with their flagrant waste of resources and their suburban lifestyles. For that very reason, it also depends significantly upon organized labor "becoming a social movement," as United Mine Workers President Richard Trumka has phrased it. The theme of social solidarity brings us back immediately to the divisions of labor from women's rights and black rights movements in the Reconstruction era, and to the narrowness that can be attributed to Marx's own First International outlook. It brings us through the subsequent moments when the Industrial Workers of the World promised social redemption through the democratic actions of ordinary people. It brings us up to the New Deal moment and the war years, when sections of labor sought to become that social movement by encouraging motion from below, and breaking (at least in aspiration) from the often icy grip of the Democratic Party. It even takes us to all those seemingly small moments when union activists of various kinds reached out, mainly at the local level, to peace, environmental, feminist and gay and other social movements, effecting alliances that might have grown strong and changed the course of society.

Labor's national leaders, with few if admirable exceptions, have stood in the path of such hopeful developments. From Samuel Gompers through the forgotten William Green to George Meany and the already obscure Lane Kirkland, they cast their fate with what they perceived to be society's winners. With the partial exception of Kirkland, they too won—in purely personal ways. But their members lost, diminished not only by the virtually unchecked rise of a powerful system breaking down the real options for autonomy in daily economic life but also degraded by the narrowing of the movement's purpose from human emancipation to special favors for the connected.

With the onset of the Sweeney era, the distance between the bureaucracy and ordinary union members has not been significantly lessened, nor has the historic dependence upon the Democrats been reconsidered. Ultimately, the problem of labor bureaucracy cannot be isolated from the labor politics of exclusionism and imperial commitments. The near-collapse of the American labor movement in the second half of the twentieth century was the result of the same sorry policies of race and gender pioneered by Gompers, of cynical expectations to win abroad what has been given away at home. The answer to the moral and material corruption of the ensuing Meany and Kirkland eras lies in social commitment and leadership defined in the old Wobbly fashion: ordinary working people acting as their own leaders.

NOTES

Introduction

1. "A Wholesale Sellout," *New York Times,* 28 November 1998; Steven Green-house, "System of Voting Tainted, City Union Leaders Say," ibid.

2. See Mark Leier, *Red Flags and Red Tape: The Making of a Labour Bureauc-racy* (Toronto: University of Toronto Press, 1995), which offers a sweeping overview of the question of bureaucracy.

3. Paul Buhle, *Marxism in the United States: Remapping the American Left,* 2d ed. (London: Verso, 1991), Chapter 4, "Leninism in America."

4. John H. M. Laslett and Seymour Martin Lipset, eds., *Failure of a Dream? Essays in the History of American Socialism* (Anchor Press: Garden City, N.Y, 1974).

5. Several essays in *American Exceptionalism? U.S. Working Class Formation in an International Context* (London: Macmillan, 1997), edited by Rick Halpern and Jonathan Morris, analyze the conceptual flaws of the exception-alist perspective and their source in the imperial standpoint. See especially Rick Halpern and Jonathan Morris, "The Persistence of Exceptionalism: Class Formation and the Comparative Method," 1-13; Michael Zuckerman, "The Dodo and the Phoenix: A Fable of American Exceptionalism," 14-35, and Robert Gregg, "Apropos Exceptionalism: Imperial Location and Comparative Histories of South Africa and the United States," 270-306.

6. Sigmund Diamond, *Compromised Campus: The Collaboration of Univer-sities with the Intelligence Community, 1945-1955* (New York: Oxford University Press, 1992), 133. As Diamond notes, the $192,655 allotted to the project would be equivalent to many times that sum today; the Fund for the Republic was to manage the actual funding.

7. David Roediger, "What If Labor Were Not White and Male? Recentering Working Class History and Reconstruction Debate on the Unions and Race," *International Labor and Working Class History* 51 (spring 1997): 74.

8. Ibid., 76-83.

9. Sadly, the journal *Labor History,* which began publication just at the dawn of

the 1960s and might have made itself the exemplar of the newer scholarship, has remained too often instead the captive of the old institutional history. *International Labor and Working Class History, Radical History Review, Left History,* and the remarkable Canadian journal *Labour/Le Travail* have made larger contributions to sharpening the cutting edge of scholarship. *Radical America* (1967-1996), a journal which I founded and edited for some years, made a signal contribution to a newer labor history during its first decade or so, and then turned to other matters.

10. John Laslett, *Labor and the Left: A Study of Socialist and Radical Influences in the American Labor Movement, 1881-1924* (New York: Basic Books, 1970); Franklin Rosemont and David Roediger, eds, *The Haymarket Scrapbook* (Chicago: Charles H. Kerr Co., 1986).

11. All but the last point are owed to William E. Forbath, *Law and the Shaping of the American Labor Movement* (Cambridge: Harvard University Press, 1991); this treatment stands in stark contrast to the analysis of benevolent state authority in the neo-traditional account of Melvyn Dubofsky, *The State and Labor in Modern America* (Chapel Hill: University of North Carolina, 1994). See also Victoria C. Hattam, *Labor Visions and State Power: The Origins of Business Unionism in the United States* (Princeton: Princeton University Press, 1993); Karen Orren, *Belated Feudalism. Labor, the Law, and Liberal Development in the United States* (Cambridge: Cambridge University Press, 1991); and Christopher L. Tomlins, *The State and the Unions: Labor Relations, Law, and the Organized Labor Movement in America, 1880-1960* (Cambridge: Cambridge University Press, 1985).

12. Steven Fraser and Joshua B. Freeman, eds., *Audacious Democracy: Labor, Intellectuals, and the Social Reconstruction of America* (New York: Houghton-Mifflin, 1997), a largely useful volume with too many apologetics past and present for the AFL-CIO's institutional failings.

13. This is most clearly stated in the conclusion, where Zieger fumbles at explaining away the logical connections between labor's purge and the loss of labor's will to organize: *The CIO, 1935-1955* (Chapel Hill: University of North Carolina, 1995), 372-77.

14. C. Wright Mills, *The New Men of Power: America's Labor Leaders* (New York: Harcourt, Brace, 1948), especially 290-91.

15. C. L. R. James, Raya Dunayevskaya, and Grace Lee, *State Capitalism and World Revolution* (Chicago: Charles H. Kerr Co., 1986).

16. Rorty, "The People's Flag Is Deepest Red," in Fraser and Freeman, eds., *Audacious Democracy,* 61.

1. Samuel Gompers and Business Unionism

1. Stuart B. Kaufman, *Samuel Gompers and the Origins of the American Federation of Labor, 1848-1896* (Westport, Conn.: Greenwood Press, 1973), the key work by the founder of the historical archives at the George Meany Center,

and director of the Center until his sudden death in 1996. Kaufman actually admired what might be called the "right-wing Marxism" or "right-wing syndicalism" in Gompers, insisting upon its remaining socialistic potential (through the 1890s) while recognizing its ultimate conservative character. The Gompers orientation was fortified by Marx disciple Friedrich Sorge's own accounts, from journalism written for the German socialist press since collected into Philip S. Foner and Brewster Chamberlin, eds., *Friedrich A. Sorge's* Labor Movement in the United States: *A History of the American Working Class from Colonial Times to 1890,* tr. Brewster and Anna Chamberlin (Westport, Conn.: Greenwood Press, 1977). See also Hermann Schlüter, *Die Internationale in Amerika: Ein Beitrag zur Geschichte der Arbeiter-Bewegung in der Vereinigten Staaten* (Chicago: Deutsche Sprachgruppe der Socialist Partei der Ver. Staaten, 1918), as well as Dorothee Schneider, *Trade Unions and Community: The German Working Class in New York City, 1870-1900* (Urbana: University of Illinois Press, 1994).

2. See Hartmut Keil, ed., *German Workers' Culture in the United States, 1850 to 1920* (Washington, DC: Smithsonian Institution Press, 1988); Bruce C. Nelson, *Beyond the Martyrs: A Social History of Chicago's Anarchists, 1870-1900* (New Brunswick, N.J.: Rutgers University Press, 1988); Scott Molloy, *Trolley Wars: Streetcar Workers On the Line* (Washington, D.C.: Smithsonian Institution Press, 1996); L. A. O'Donnell, *Irish Voice and Organized Labor in America: a Biographical Study* (Westport, Conn.: Greenwood Press, 1997); and Joshua Freeman, *Irish American Radicalism and the Transport Workers of America* (New York: Oxford University Press, 1989).

3. As Marcus Rediker rightly complains, nearly all accounts of sailors' lives are about the nineteenth century. C. L. R. James's description of Melville's Moby Dick remains classic: *Mariners, Renegades and Castaways* (London: Allison and Busby, 1984). For a larger and earlier history of the transatlantic working class, see Rediker, *Between the Devil and the Deep Blue Sea: Merchant Seamen, Pirates and the Anglo-American Maritime World, 1700-1750* (Cambridge: Cambridge University Press, 1987).

4. See the long-awaited text by Jesse Lemisch, *Jack Tar vs John Bull: The Role of New York's Seamen in Precipitating the Revolution* (New York: Garland, 1997), lamentably an unrevised dissertation from decades earlier. See also Alfred Young, "Revolutionary Mechanics," in Paul Buhle and Alan Dawley, eds., *Working for Democracy: American Workers from the Revolution to the Present* (Urbana: University of Illinois Press, 1985), 1-10.

5. David Montgomery, *Citizen Worker: The Experience of Workers in the United States with Demoracy and the Free Market During the Ninteenth Century* (Cambridge: Cambridge University Press, 1993), 13-51.

6. Alexander Saxton, *The Rise and Fall of the White Republic: Class Politics and Mass Culture in Nineteenth-Century America* (London: Verso, 1990);

Notes   267

David Roediger, *The Wages of Whiteness: Race and the Making of the American Working Class* (London: Verso, 1991).

7. Bruce Laurie, *Working People of Philadelphia, 1800-1850* (Philadelphia: Temple University Press, 1980); and Mary Blewitt, *Men, Women and Work: Class, Gender and Protest in the New England Shoe Industry, 1780-1910* (Urbana: University of Illinois Press, 1990).

8. Lawrence B. Glickman, *A Living Wage: American Workers and the Making of Consumer Society* (Ithaca: Cornell University Press, 1997), 19-22.

9. Eric Foner's classic study analyzes the search for individual freedom behind many of these movements, which makes some of them as pro-capitalist as anti-slavery: Foner, *Free Soil, Free Labor, Free Men: The Ideology of the Republican Party Before the Civil War* (New York: Oxford University Press, 1970).

10. Franklin Rosemont has an incisive treatment of this subject: "Workingmen's Parties," in *Working for Democracy*, 11-20. See also David Montgomery, *Citizen Worker*, especially 137-45.

11. David Roediger, *The Wages of Whiteness*, chap. 2-4.; and Sean Wilentz, *Chants Democratic: New York City and the Rise of the American Working Class, 1788-1850* (New York: Oxford University Press, 1986).

12. Iver Bernstein, *The New York City Draft Riots: Their Significance for American Society and Politics in the Age of the Civil War* (New York: Oxford University Press, 1990).

13. Mari Jo Buhle, "Needlewomen and the Vicissitudes of Modern Life: A Study of Middle Class Construction in the Antebellum Northeast," in Nancy A. Hewitt and Susanne Lebsock, eds., *Visible Women: New Essays on American Activism* (Urbana: University of Illinois Press, 1993), 145-65; Mari Jo Buhle, *Women and American Socialism* (Urbana: University of Illinois Press, 1991), chap. 1.

14. Timothy Messer-Kruse, *The Yankee International: Marxism and the American Reform Tradition, 1848-1876* (Chapel Hill: University of North Carolina Press, 1998), 35-36.

15. Mari Jo Buhle and Paul Buhle, eds., *The Concise History of Woman Suffrage* (Urbana: University of Illinois Press, 1978), 213-88.

16. Montgomery, *Citizen Worker*, 123. Montgomery drew heavily upon the work of his student Peter Rachleff, *Black Labor in Richmond, 1865-1880* (Urbana: University of Illinois Press, 1989), an important study of black and white workers in the immediate postwar South.

17. Eric Foner, "Black Labor Conventions During Reconstruction," Ronald C. Kent, Sara Markham, David R. Roediger and Herbert Shapro, eds., *Culture, Gender, Race and U.S. Labor History* (Westport, Conn.: Greenwood Press, 1993), 91-104, especially 92-93, 100-102.

18. David Montgomery, *Beyond Equality: Labor and the Radical Republicans, 1862-1872* (New York: Knopf, 1967).

19. Freethinkers, it should be noted, constituted the scant forces behind women's

rights in the German-speaking community (which at large feared, with good reason, that woman's rights crusaders intended to banish beer from social life).

20. Alexander Saxton, *The Rise and Fall of the White Republic: Class Politics and Mass Culture in Nineteenth Century America* (London: Verso, 1990); and Roediger, *Wages of Whiteness,* Chap. 7.

21. Ira Steward, "The Power of the Cheaper Over the Dearer," reprinted in John R. Commons, et al., eds., *A Documentary History of American Industrial Society* (Cleveland: Arthur H. Clark Co., 1910), Vol. IX, 326. See also Charles Leinenweber, "Immigration and the Decline of Internationalism in the American Working Class Movement, 1864-1919," unpublished dissertation, University of California, Berkeley, 1969, chap. 2.

22. "National Labor Congress Proceedings," *Workingman's Advocate,* 4 September 1869.

23. "National Labor Congress Proceedings," *Workingman's Advocate,* 7 August 1870.

24. David Roediger notes that only in recent years have historians writing about race and labor in this period put the "records of the unions regarding racism . . . on trial." Roediger describes at some length current controversies and ongoing research in "What if Labor Were Not White and Male? Recentering Working Class History and Reconstructing Debate on the Unions and Race," *International Labor and Working Class History* no. 51 (spring 1997), 87-88.

25. Much of the older literature is summed up in Stan Nadel, "The German Immigrant Left in the United States," in Paul Buhle and Dan Georgakas, eds., *The Immigrant Left in the United States* (Albany: SUNY Press, 1997), 45-77.

26. Marx quoted in Messer-Kruse, *The Yankee International,* 54-55; and in Marx's 1871 letter to Friedrich Bolte, in Saul K. Padover, ed., *Karl Marx On the First International* (New York: McGraw Hill, 1973), 543.

27. Messer-Kruse supplies an able overview of the various "American" sections and their personalities: *Yankee International,* 106-19.

28. David N. Lyon, "The World of P. J. McGuire: A Study of the American Labor Movement, 1870-1890," University of Minnesota, unpublished dissertation, 1972, chap. 2; and Messer-Kruse, *The Yankee International,* chap. 1-3.

29. Mari Jo Buhle, *Women and American Socialism,* and Messer-Kruse, *The Yankee International,* chap. 6, especially 158-83. Newer biographies of Victoria Woodhull contain little of value in regard to her socialism and socialist connections, just like Sorge, Marx, and others who refused to take this crucial phase of her activities seriously.

30. Schlüter, *Die Internationale in Amerika,* 156, 173.

31. Samuel Gompers, *Seventy Years of Life and Labor,* ed. Nick Salvatore (Ithaca, N.Y.: ILR Press, 1984), 20.

32. David N. Lyon, "The World of P. J. McGuire," especially chap. 1-3.

33. Messer-Kruse, *The Yankee International,* chap. 2, especially 48-60.

34. Herbert Gutman, "Trouble on the Railroads in 1873-1874: Prelude to the 1877

Crisis?" in Daniel Leab, ed., *Labor History Reader* (Urbana: University of Illinois Press, 1985), 132-52.

35. David Burbank, *Reign of the Rabble: The St. Louis General Strike of 1877* (New York: Augustus M. Kelley, 1966), and Jeremy Brecher, *Strike!,* 2d ed. (Boston: South End Press, 1997).

36. Report of a public speech in *The People,* 12 December 1887.

37. See Rachleff, *Black Labor in the South,* for a vital treatment of black and white Knights working in concert and against each other; and two valuable, recent essays, Douglas Monroy, "Fence Cutters, Sedicioso, and First Class Citizens: Mexican Radicalism in America," and Robert Lee, "The Hidden World of Asian American Radicalism," in Paul Buhle and Dan Georgakas, eds., *The Immigrant Left in the United States,* 11-44 and 256-288.

38. David Montgomery, *Workers' Control in America: Studies in the History of Work, Technology and Labor Struggles* (Cambridge: Cambridge University Press, 1979), 21.

39. Robert E. Weir, *Beyond Labor's Veil: The Culture of the Knights of Labor* (University Park: University of Pennsylania Press, 1996).

40. For a microcosm of the larger process, see Paul Buhle, "The Knights of Labor in Rhode Island," in Buhle, *From the Knights of Labor to the New World Order* (New York: Garland, 1997), 3-39.

41. For criticism of the Knights, see Gerald Grob, *Workers and Utopia: A Study of Ideological Conflict in the American Labor Movement, 1865-1900* (Chicago: Quadrangle, 1961), and Philip S. Foner, *History of the Labor Movement in the United States,* vol. 2, *From the Founding of the A.F. of L. to the Emergence of American Imperialism* (New York: International Publishers, 1975).

42. Kim Voss, *The Making of American Exceptionalism: The Knights of Labor and Class Formation in the Nineteenth Century* (Ithaca: Cornell University Press, 1993), especially 86, 172-73, 194.

43. Franklin Rosemont and David Roediger, eds., *The Haymarket Scrapbook* (Chicago: Charles H. Kerr Co., 1986).

44. Leon Fink, *Workingmen's Democracy* (Urbana: University of Illinois Press, 1983).

45. Gompers, *Seventy Years of Life and Labor,* 78.

46. Selig Perlman, *Upheaval and Reorganization,* 427. Gompers's own account of the struggle with the Knights is full of evasions, especially on issues of AFL's exclusionary policies and the Knights' vastly more generous intentions, and on Gompers' all-out efforts to destroy the organization. See Gompers, *Seventy Years of Life and Labor,* 77-85.

47. Montgomery, *Workers' Control in America,* 18-23.

48. Foner, *History of the Labor Movement in the United States,* vol. 2, 178-88.

49. Gompers, *Seventy Years of Life and Labor,* 1-7.

50. John H. M. Laslett, "Samuel Gompers and the Rise of Business Unionism,"

in Melvyn Dubofsky and Warren Van Tine, eds., *Labor Leaders in America* (Urbana: University of Illinois Press, 1987), 62-87.

51. William E. Forbath, *Law and the Shaping of the American Labor Movement* (Cambridge, Mass.: Harvard University Press, 1991), 39-41.
52. Quoted in Laslett, "Samuel Gompers," 68.
53. Gompers, *Seventy Years of Life and Labor,* 67.
54. Among the traditional historiography, H. M. Gitelman, "Adolph Strasser and the Origins of Pure and Simple Unionism," reprinted in *Labor History Reader,* 153-65, manages to exclude race questions entirely. Alexander Saxton, *The Indispensable Enemy: Labor and the Anti-Chinese Movement in California* (Berkeley and Los Angeles: University of California, 1971) made an important beginning in the larger subject. Robert G. Lee, "The Hidden World of Asian-American Radicalism," in *The Immigrant Left,* especially 256-64, carefully discusses the subsequent scholarship. See also a key original source: Gompers's notorious racist pamphlet written with Herman Gustadt, *Meat vs Rice: American Manhood Against Asiatic Coolies, Which Shall Survive?* (San Francisco: Asiatic Exclusion League, 1906).
55. Messer-Kruse, *The Yankee International,* 209-12.
56. Nick Salvatore, "Introduction," in Gompers, *Seventy Years of Life and Labor,* xxiii-xxiv.
57. Lawrence Glickman, "Inventing the 'American Standard of Living': Gender, Race and Working Class Identity, 1880-1925," *Labor History Reader,* 221-35.
58. Julie Greene, *Pure and Simple Politics: The American Federation of Labor and Political Activism* (Cambridge: Cambridge University Press, 1998), 39-40.
59. *Proceedings,* AFL Convention, 1894, 12.
60. Gompers, *Seventy Years Life and Labor,* refers in various places to the AFL's energetic expression of anti-immigrant feeling, usually attributing the animus to regional feelings in which Gompers only acquiesced, or to some special emergency, like the outbreak of the First World War, which alerted Californians to the purported dangers of further Japanese-American land holdings in California.
61. Isaac A. Hourwich, *Immigration and Labor: Economic Aspects* (New York: Putnam, 1912).
62. Glickman, *A Living Wage,* 70, 24-29.
63. Ibid., 85-87.
64. Schneider, *Trade Unions and Community,* Chap. 4-7.
65. Clark D. Halker, *For Democracy, Workers, and God: Labor Song Poems and Labor Protest, 1865-95* (Urbana: University of Illinois Press, 1991).
66. Elizabeth Fones-Wolf and Ken Fones-Wolf, "Rank and File Rebellions and AFL Interference in the Affairs of National Unions: The Gompers Era," *Labor History* 35 (spring 1994), 237-59.
67. In ibid., Fones-Wolf and Fones-Wolf offer more evidence along these lines,

but without details on how most of the rebels, German-language in their periodicals and daily discussions, perceived the tightening grip of the AFL leaders. The authors argue, based upon evidence available to them—too limited for the early period—that the AFL leader's authoritarian tendencies grew far worse after the formation of the IWW.

68. Voss, *The Making of American Exceptionalism,* 58-60.
69. Molloy, *Trolley Wars,* 47-49.
70. Voss, *The Making of American Exceptionalism,* 243.
71. See Paul Buhle, *Marxism in the United States,* chap. 1-2.
72. See Paul Buhle, "Themes in American Jewish Radicalism," in Buhle and Georgakas, eds., *The Immigrant Left in the United States,* 77-118.
73. See, e.g., Melech Epstein, *Jewish Labor in the U.S.,* 2 volumes (New York: Trade Union Sponsoring Committee, 1950, 1953) for the orthodox Jewish social-democratic view; and Melvyn Dubofsky's history of the IWW, *We Shall Be All* (Chicago: Quadrangle, 1970) for a spectacular mistreatment of DeLeon in terms of IWW (and more generally, American labor) history.
74. For scattered insights into the 1880s-90s Jewish labor and socialist movement that still remain absent in English-language sources, see N. Goldberg, "Di Yidishe Sotsialistishe Bevegung in di 80er Yorn," N. Goldberg, "Di Yiddishe Sotialistishe Bevegung euf di 80er Yorn," and Dr. Herman Frank, "Di Anheib fun der Trade Union-Bevegung," in A. Tsherikover, ed., *Geshikhte fun der Yidisher Arbeter-Bevegung in di Fareinikhte Shtotn,* Vol. 2 (New York: YIVO, 1945), 276-96, 319-45; 346-94; and Leon Kobrin, *Mayne fufzige yor in Amerika* (New York: YKUF, 1966), section 1, chap. 5-7, the memoir of a leading author ("the Jewish Zola") about the 1890s.
75. Baruch Rivkin, *Di Gruntendentsin fun Yiddishe Literature* (New York: YKUF, 1947).
76. For the AFL's decisive turn to exclusionism from the internationalist traditions of the NLU on immigration questions, see Charles Leinenweber, "Immigration and the Decline of Internationalism," especially chap. 6.
77. William Forbath, *Law and the Shaping,* 90-97.
78. Mari Jo Buhle, "Illinois Women's Alliance," *Encyclopedia of the American Left* (New York: Oxford University Press, 1998), 2d ed., 350; Melvyn Dubofsky, *The State and Labor in Modern America* (Chapel Hill: University of North Carolina Press, 1997), 32-34.
79. David Lyon, "P. J. McGuire," 236-40, 262, 350-51.
80. See especially Montgomery, *Workers' Control in America,* 9-47.
81. Messer-Kruse, *The Yankee International,* 244.
82. Foner, *History of the Labor Movement in the United States,* Vol. II, 290-94.
83. Among the severest, and to my mind least fair critics of the ST&LA has been Philip Foner, who regarded the "dualism" or "dual unionism" of the 1890s as the catastrophic error of the left. See for instance his presentation of the issues in "Socialism and American Trade Unionism—Comment," in John

H. M. Laslett and Seymour Martin Lipset, eds., *Failure of a Dream? Essays in the History of American Socialism* (Garden City, N.Y.: Anchor/Doubleday, 1974), 233-43.

84. The ST&LA has eluded major treatment by labor historians. See, however, John Laslett, *Labor and the Left* (New York: Basic Books, 1970).

85. Regarding an SLP organizer of infant cloakmakers, Theresa Serber, later (as Theresa Malkiel) active in the Socialist Party, see Mari Jo Buhle, *Women and American Socialism,* 176-77.

86. My reading of the Yiddish anarchist newspaper, the *Freie Arbeter Shtimme,* for the years 1900-1920 has been decisive for this interpretation; the *FAS,* which functioned increasingly as a libertarian-minded literary or philosophical publication of note in the Yiddish world, showed however no enthusiasm for the IWW and no inclination under any circumstance to criticize the rightward turn of Sam Gompers.

87. Quoted by Nell Irvin Painter, "Black Workers from Reconstruction to the Depression," in Buhle and Dawley, *Working for Democracy,* 68.

88. See in particular DeLeon's two early speeches which became notable pamphlets, "Reform or Revolution" (1896) and "What Means This Strike?" (1898), reprinted in DeLeon, *Socialist Landmarks* (New York: New York Labor News, 1948).

89. Forbath, *Law and the Shaping,* 46-48, 68.

90. These conclusions emerge from an important dissertation by Matthew F. Jacobson, "Special Sorrows: Irish-, Polish-, and Yiddish-American Nationalism and the Disaporic Imagination," Brown University, 1992, chap. 4-5.

91. Quoted in Dubofsky, *The State and Labor,* 39.

92. Craig Phelan, *Divided Loyalties: the Public and Private Life of Labor Leader John Mitchell* (Albany: SUNY Press, 1994), 92.

93. David Brody, *Workers in Industrial America: Essays on the Twentieth Century Struggle* (New York: Oxford University Press, 1980), 24-25.

94. Julie Greene, *Pure and Simple Politics,* 162-78.

95. Ibid., 178-79.

96. Kenneth L. Kusmer, *A Ghetto Takes Shape: Black Cleveland, 1870-1936* (Urbana: University of Illinois Press, 1976).

97. Greene, *Pure and Simple Politics,* 190.

98. See "The Socialist Reconstruction of Society," in DeLeon, *Socialist Landmarks,* and DeLeon's two-part address of 1902 entitled *Two Pages of Roman History* (New York: New York Labor News, 1960).

99. Joyce Kornbluh, ed., *Rebel Voices* (Chicago: Charles H. Kerr Co., 1998); Archie Green, "Industrial Workers of the World Songs," *Encyclopedia of the American Left,* 2d ed., 362-63.

100. Among many available interpretations, see the still-valuable unpublished dissertation by Donald M. Barnes, "Ideology of the Industrial Workers of the World: 1905-1911," Washington State University, 1962; and Sal Salerno, *Red*

November, Black November: Culture and Community in the IWW (Albany: SUNY Press, 1989). Both sources are hobbled—like virtually all IWW interpretations—by the scant use of non-English language sources.

101. Meredith Tax, *The Rising of the Women* (New York: Monthly Review Press, 1980) best describes and analyzes the shirtwaist strike.

102. Justus Ebert, *The Trial of a New Society* (Cleveland: Solidarity, 1912); see also Paul Buhle, *A Dreamer's Paradise Lost: Louis C. Fraina-Lewis Corey (1892-1953) and The Decline of Radicalism in the United States* (Atlantic Highlands, N.J.: Humanities Press, 1995), chap. 1-2.

103. Mary E. Cygan, "The Polish-American Left," Maria Woroby, "The Ukrainian Immigrant Left in the United States, 1880-1950," Dan Georgakas, "Greek American Radicalism: The Twentieth Century," and an essay dealing with a group which chose to affiliate with the IWW rather than the SP, Michael Miller Topp, "The Italian-American Left: Transnationalism and the Quest for Unity," in *The Immigrant Left,* 119-47, 148-233.

104. "In a Pithy Address Showing Keenest Insight, Comrade Austin Lewis Points out the Necessity for Consistent Revolutionary Tactics," *Oakland World,* 20 January 1909.

105. "Austin Lewis Gives Final Lecture on 'Story of Socialism,'" ibid., 6 February 1909.

106. This account of Fraina (as of Lewis) differs sharply from Brian Lloyd, *Left Out: Pragmatism, Exceptionalism, and the Poverty of American Marxism, 1890-1922* (Baltimore: Johns Hopkins University Press, 1997), which both holds pragmatism to be the legitimate American philosophy and attacks Fraina among others, including Lewis, as insufficiently Marxist, on the basis that only consistent and self-conscious Leninists count; see especially 360-69.

107. William English Walling, *The Larger Aspects of Socialism* (New York: Macmillan, 1913), iii; *Socialism As It Is* (New York: Macmillan, 1912), 352-53; *Progressivism—and After* (New York: Macmillan, 1914), xxxii, 319.

108. Montgomery, *Workers' Control in America,* 73-83; Marc Karson, *American Labor Union and Politics 1900-1918* (Boston: Beacon, 1958), chap. 9.

109. William Preston, *Aliens and Dissenters,* 2d ed. (Urbana: University of Illinois Press, 1994).

110. Louis C. Fraina, *Revolutionary Socialism* (New York: Revolutionary Age, 1918), 197; see also Louis C. Fraina, "The Problem of Nationality," *New Review* 3 (1 December 1915) and Fraina, "The Class and the Nation," *New Review* 4 (15 January 1916).

111. Louis C. Fraina, "Literary Gleanings: The Chasm," *Daily People* (New York), 9 April 1911.

112. Elizabeth McKillen, *Chicago Labor and the Quest for a Democratic Diplomacy, 1914-1924* (Ithaca: Cornell University Press, 1995) details both the Chicago federation's attempt to steer its own course, and Gompers's collaboration in a virtual government conspiracy against the anti-warriors.

274   *Taking Care of Business*

113. Louis C. Fraina, "The Future of Socialism," *New Review* 3 (January 1915), 9.

114. Roy Rosenzweig, *Eight Hours for What We Will* (Cambridge: Cambridge University Press, 1983).

115. Fraina, "Literary Gleanings: The Chasm." At nineteen, Fraina was the key literary contributor to the *Daily People,* organ of the fading SLP.

116. Louis C. Fraina, "The Case for Ragtime," *Modern Dance* 2 (August-September 1917), 7.

117. Dubofsky, *The State and Labor,* 51-57.

118. Green, *Pure and Simple Politics,* 246.

119. Ibid., 247.

120. Ibid., 257-59.

121. Montgomery, *Workers' Control in America,* chap. 4, especially 93-100.

122. Donald Grubbs, *Samuel Gompers and the Great War: Protecting Labor's Standards* (Wake Forest, N.C.: Meridional Publications, 1982), 46-49, an extremely valuable, obscure, and evidently self-published work. See also Brody, *Workers in Industrial America,* 42-43.

123. Cited by McKillen, *Chicago Labor,* 51.

124. Sinclair Snow, "Samuel Gompers and the Pan American Federation of Labor," unpublished Ph.D. dissertation, University of Virginia, 1960, 84.

125. Ibid., 1-2, 41, 49, 50, 63, 84-90.

126. The AALD few but faithful were joined by the most prominent anarchist editor of the day, Saul Yanofsky of the Yiddish-language *Freie Arbeter Shtimme,* accurately spotting a future place for himself in the ILGWU labor bureaucracy. In 1919, he delivered a touching and personally successful tribute to Gompers ("head of the labor movement for these many years because he knows best how to voice the true sentiments, views and aspirations of the workers of America," adding that "only the man who will truly reflect their views and give them voice will be acknowledged as their leader"). Quoted by Philip S. Foner, "Comment," in *Failure of a Dream?,* 237-38. Yanofsky could be counted upon thereafter for unstinting support of the bureaucracy. Regrettably, the main body of Yiddish-speaking anarchists went over to the bureaucracy with him, while holding to their philosophical anarchism.

127. David S. Foglesong, *America's Secret War Against Bolshevism: U.S. Intervention in the Russian Civil War, 1917-1920* (Chapel Hill: University of North Carolina Press, 1995), 35-36.

128. Ibid., 36-43, 258-71.

129. Quoted in Glickman, *A Living Wage,* 90, from Gompers, "East St Louis Riots—Their Causes," *The American Federationist,* August 1917, 621-66.

130. Grubbs, *Samuel Gompers and the Great War,* chap. 3-7, has a good description of this process.

131. Cited by McKillen, *Chicago Labor,* 75.

132. Ibid.

133. Ibid., 123.

134. Gloria Garrett Samson, " 'Education for a New Social Order': The Ideological Struggle over American Workers' Education in the 1920s," in Ronald C. Kent, et al., eds., *Culture, Gender, Race and U.S. Labor History,* 152-64.

135. Snow, "Samuel Gompers and the Pan American Federation of Labor," 159.

136. William English Walling, *American Labor and American Democracy* (New York: Macmillan, 1926), 76-78.

137. This is not to dismiss other, very different efforts of contemporary labor intellectuals, especially in the realm of labor education. A fascinating recent study shows that the Chicago Federation of Labor, so vital in resisting Gompers's entreaties to support the First World War, was also the most successful in shifting media from the press to the air. See Nathan Godfried, *WCFL: Chicago's Voice of Labor, 1926-78* (Urbana: University of Illinois Press, 1997).

140. Lizabeth Cohen, *Making a New Deal: Industrial Workers in Chicago, 1919-1939* (Cambridge: Cambridge University Press), chap. 1-4; Brody, *Workers in Industrial America,* 78.

2. Meany Takes Command

1. David Langley, "The Colonization of the International Trade Union Movement," in Burton Hall, ed., *Autocracy and Insurgency in the Organized Labor* (New Brunswick: Transaction Press, 1972), 299-300; "Social Democrats Honor Meany With Eugene V. Debs Award," *New America*, May 1977.

2. Eugene V. Debs, *Walls and Bars* (Chicago: Socialist Party, 1927), 191.

3. For this and much other background biographical information, the best source remains the badly outdated and almost comically hagiographic "official" biography by Joseph C. Goulden, *Meany* (New York: Athaneum, 1972), 7-14, and its only slightly better successor, based substantially on interviews with an aging Meany, Archie Robinson, *George Meany and His Times* (New York: Simon and Schuster, 1981), 29-45.

4. See Nathan Godfried, *WCFL: Chicago's Voice of Labor, 1926-78* (Urbana: University of Illinois Press, 1997), especially chap.1-4.

5. Goulden, *Meany*, 12-14.

6. Ibid., 15-17; Robinson, *George Meany*, 40-42.

7. On the 1924 campaign see James Weinstein, *Decline of Socialism in America* (New York: Monthly Review Press, 1967), chap. 8.

8. See Thomas Kessner, *Fiorello H. LaGuardia and the Making of Modern New York* (New York: McGraw-Hill, 1989) and Gerald Meyer, *Vito Marcantonio: Radical Politician* (Albany: SUNY Press, 1989).

9. Robert Zieger, *American Workers, American Unions, 1920-1985* (Baltimore: Johns Hopkins Press, 1986), 10-14.

10. Benjamin J. Taylor and Fred Witney, *U.S. Labor Relations Law: Historical Development* (Englewood Cliffs, N.J.: Prentice Hall, 1992), 78-79.

11. Melvyn Dubofsky, *State and Labor in Modern America* (Chapel Hill: University of North Carolina, 1994), 111-12.

12. David F. Selvin, *The 1934 Waterfront and General Strikes in San Francisco* (Detroit: Wayne State University Press, 1996). See also Farrell Dobbs, *Teamster Rebellion* (New York: Pathfinder Press, 1972), and Art Preis, *Labor's Giant Step* (New York: Pathfinder Press, 1965), 19-24.

13. John Borsos, "'We Make You This Appeal in the Name of Every Union Man and Woman in Barberton,' Solidarity Unionism in Barberton, Ohio, 1933-41," in Staughton Lynd, ed., *"We Are all Leaders": The Alternative Unionism of the Early 1930s* (Urbana: University of Illinois Press, 1996), 238-93.

14. Gary Gerstle, *Working Class Americanism: The Politics of Labor in a Textile City, 1914-1960* (Cambridge: Cambridge University Press, 1989), 127-230; Janet Irons, "The Challenge of National Coalition: Southern Textile Workers and the General Textile Strike of 1934," in Lynd, ed., *"We Are All Leaders,"* 72-101.

15. On the sit-down strikes, see, for instance, Jeremy Brecher, *Strike!* (Boston: South End Press, 1997), 224-32. About Polish-American support for unions in Michigan, see Martha Collingwood Nowak, *Two Who Were There* (Detroit: Wayne State University, 1989).

16. A point made strikingly in a neglected volume: Louis Adamic, *My America, 1928-1938* (New York: Harper & Brothers, 1938), and reiterated in Brecher, *Strike!*, chap. 5.

17. See, for instance, Douglas Monroy, "Fence Cutters, *Sedicioso,* and First Class Citizens: Mexican American Radicalism in America," in Paul Buhle and Dan Georgakas, eds., *The Immigrant Left in the United States* (Albany: SUNY Press, 1996), 26-35; and Rosemary Feurer, "The Nutpickers' Union, 1933-34, Crossing the Boundaries of Community and Workplace," in Lynd, ed., *"We Are All Leaders,"* 27-50.

18. Robin D. G. Kelley, *Hammer and Hoe: Alabama Communists During the Depression* (Chapel Hill: University of North Carolina Press, 1990); H. L. Mitchell, *Mean Things Happening in This Land: The Life and Times of H.L. Mitchell* (Montclair, N.J.: Allanheld, Osmun, 1979).

19. Melvyn Dubofsky and Warrent Van Tine, *John L. Lewis: A Biography* (New York: Quadrangle), 3-42.

20. Ibid., 43-111.

21. See Rick Halpern and Roger Horowitz, *Meatpackers: an Oral History of Black Packinghouse Workers and Their Struggle for Racial and Economic Equality* (New York: Monthly Review Press, 1999); and Robert H. Zieger, *The CIO, 1935-1955* (Chapel Hill: University of North Carolina Press, 1995), especially chapters 2-4, before the point where his account is badly tainted by sentiment against the left-led unions.

22. Goulden, *Meany*, 38-43; Robinson, *George Meany*, 61-63.

23. Much thanks to John Holmes for his unpublished paper, "The ILGWU and

the American Communist Party in the 1920s," rethinking the triangular relationship between various Communist party factions, the garment industry, and New York state officials.

24. Neither side was saintly. Kovelesky had on his side the partisans of the mob-infiltrated theatrical union, IATSE, which conducted a company-union style operation in Hollywood and later administered the blacklist against writers, directors, and technicians, the great majority former Communists who had left behind their party affiliations but refused to testify against old friends. See Goulden, *Meany*, 34-36, and the interviews of victims in Patrick McGilligan and Paul Buhle, *Tender Comrades: A Backstory of the Hollywood Blacklist* (New York: St. Martin's Press, 1997).

25. This account here differs markedly from the flattering treatment by Robert H. Zieger, "George Meany," in Melvyn Dubofsky and Warren Van Tine, eds., *Labor Leaders in America* (Urbana: University of Illinois, 1987), 329, in which the heavy-handed bureaucrat becomes the admired champion of labor. It also differs from Melvin Dubofsky's youthful and far more critical assessment of Meany in "George Meany: Pefect Bureaucrat," *New Politics* 10 (Old Series, winter 1973), 30-33.

26. Golden, *Meany*, 60-69; "Tribute to LaGuardia," Radio broadcast, in archives of the Federal Theater, Works Progress Administration, Library of Congress. See Dubofsky, *The State and Labor in Modern America*, 119-67, for an overview of changing federal policy and of labor leaders' activity in and around the New Deal.

27. Goulden, *Meany*, 52-63.

28. See Eric Leif Davin, "The Very Last Hurrah? The Defeat of the Labor Party Idea, 1934-36," in Lynd, ed., *"We Are All Leaders,"* 117-71.

29. Goulden, *Meany*, 61-68.

30. Davin, "The Very Last Hurrah?" 129-32.

31. See Steven Fraser, *Labor Shall Rule: Sidney Hillman and the Rise of American Labor* (New York: Free Press, 1991).

32. Dubofsky and Van Tine, *Lewis: A Biography*, chap. 10-11.

33. Davin, "The Very Last Hurrah?" 139-49.

34. Goulden, *Meany*, 68-69; Robinson, *George Meany,* 101-02.

35. Goulden, *Meany*, 80-82; Robinson, *George Meany,* 107.

36. Goulden, *Meany*, 71-77.

37. Farrell Dobbs, *Teamster Power* (New York: Monad Press, 1973) and *Teamster Politics* (New York: Monad Press, 1977).

38. See the lively controversy over this question in *Against the Current*: Charlie Post, "Rethinking CPUSA History," no. 63 (July-August 1996), 22-33; Ernie Haberkern, "A Reply to Charlie Post: On the CPUSA and the Unions," no. 68 (May-June 1997), 38-40, and Post's reply, ibid., 40-42. For a yet sharper anti-Stalinist view see Phyllis Jacobson, "Americanizing the Communist

Party," *New Politics* 1 (1986), 152-71, and Julius Jacobson, "The Russian Question," *New Politics* 6 (1995).

39. C. L. R. James, *State Capitalism and World Revolution* (Chicago: Charles H. Kerr Co., 1986).

40. Barbara Warne Newell, *Chicago and the Labor Movement: Metropolitan Unionism in the 1930s* (Urbana: University of Illinois Press, 1961), 180-81.

41. Joyce Shaw Peterson, *American Automobile Workers, 1900-1933* (Albany: SUNY Press, 1987); Roger Keeran, *The Communist Party and the Auto Workers Unions* (Bloomington: Indiana University Press, 1980); and Peter Friedlander, *The Emergence of a UAW Local, 1936-1939* (Pittsburgh: University of Pittsburgh Press, 1975), an account of the bureaucratization of well-intended Socialist leaders. See also Bert Cochran, *Labor and Communism: The Conflict that Shaped American Unions* (Princeton: Princeton University Press, 1977), 103-55, by a leader of a UAW Trotskyist faction who became in later years more rigidly anticommunist and more apologetic toward the labor bureaucracy, but retained many shrewd and close observations. I also wish to credit an interviewee of mine, Phil Raymond, former leader of the 1920s Auto Workers Union (and sidelined by the CP afterward), for many insights; Oral History of the American Left archive, Tamiment Library, New York University. See, finally, James J. Lorence, *Organizing the Unemployed: Community and Union Activists in the Industrial Heartland* (Albany: SUNY Press, 1996).

42. Peter Rachleff, "Organizing 'Wall to Wall,' The Independent Union of All Workers, 1933-37," in Lynd, ed., *"We Are All Leaders,"* 41-71; Staughton Lynd, *Solidarity Unionism* (Chicago: Charles H. Kerr Company, 1993); Stephane Booth, "Progressive Miners of America," *Encyclopedia of the American Left,* 2d ed. (New York: Oxford University Press, 1998), 635-36; and Gerstle, *Working Class Americanism*, especially chap. 3-6.

43. Cochran is particularly lucid on this point, although he would not admit to the relatively greater degree of democracy among left-led unions like Mine, Mill or the Furriers, the low salaries, and lack of adulation courted by their leaders. See *Labor and Communism*, 142-43.

44. George Lipsitz, *"A Rainbow at Midnight": Class and Culture in Cold War America* (Urbana: University of Illinois Press, 1994), chap. 1-3.

45. Dubofsky and Van Tine, *John L. Lewis*, chap. 17, especially 395-404.

46. Robinson, *George Meany*, 112.

47. Goulden, *Meany*, 93-107.

48. Robinson, *George Meany*, 115.

49. Goulden, *Meany*, 108-11 covers the territory of the strike without admitting that Meany called for a federal crackdown. A more accurate account is in Dubofsky, "George Meany: Perfect Bureaucrat," 30-33.

50. Lipsitz, *"A Rainbow at Midnight,"* 120-54.

51. Nelson Lichtenstein, *The Most Dangerous Man in Detroit: Walter Reuther and the Fate of American Labor* (Basic Books, 1995), 234-40.

52. Douglas P. Seaton, *Catholics and Radicals: The Association of Catholic Trade Unionists and the American Labor Movement, from Depression to Cold War* (Lewisburg, Penn.: Bucknell University Press, 1981), 222-27. Msgr. Charles Owen Rice, one of the most influential figures of the ACTU in the campaign against the UE, later bravely repented his action, declaring that he and his fellow activists had been pursuing the wrong enemies. See also Steve Rosswurm, "The Catholic Church and the Left-Led Unions: Labor Priests, Labor Schools, and the ACTU," in Rosswurm, ed., *The CIO's Left-Led Unions* (New Brunswick: Rutgers University Press, 1992), 119-37.
53. Lichtenstein, *The Most Dangerous Man in Detroit*, 254-61.
54. Robinson, *George Meany*, 146, 151. On the ACTU's collaboration with the FBI, see Steven Rosswurm, "Federal Bureau of Investigation," *Encyclopedia of the American Left*, 218-21.
55. See the assorted entries on left unions in the *Encyclopedia of the American Left*, especially Toni Gilpin, "United Farm Equipment and Metal Workers," 854-55; Sharon Strom, "United Office and Professional Workers of America," 856-57; Bob Korstad, "Food, Tobacco Agricultural, and Allied Workers," 254-55; David Paskin, "District 65, UAW," 192-93; Bob Greene, "Western Federation of Miners/Mine, Mill and Smelter Workers," 869-70. See also the most poignant labor novel about the local effects of the purge and blacklist, Katya Gilden, *Between the Hills and the Sea* (Ithaca, N.Y.: ILR Press, 1989), and an interview with Gilden about the writing of the novel (with her husband, a blacklisted unionist), Oral History of the American Left, Tamiment Library, New York University.
56. Stanley Aronowitz has shown that this failure was decisive to the subsequent history of organized labor: *From the Ashes of the Old: American Labor and America's Future* (New York: Houghton-Mifflin, 1998), chap. 3.
57. Aronowitz, *From the Ashes of the Old*, 143-48. See the *Encyclopedia* items noted above, Mark Maier, *City Unions: Managing Discontent in New York City* (New Brunswick, N.J.: Rutgers University Press, 1987), and Rosswurm, ed., *The CIO's Left-Led Unions.*
58. Goulden, *Meany*, 157-59.
59. Swallowed up by the Communist-led Progressive Citizens of America and Progressive Party, the postwar third-party movement has been forgotten. For many veteran activists like Lewis Corey, it was their last campaign; Paul Buhle, *A Dreamer's Paradise Lost: Louis C. Fraina/Lewis Corey, 1892-1953* (Atlantic Highlands, N.J.: Humanities Press, 1995), chap. 6.
60. Robinson, *George Meany*, 152.
61. Zieger, *American Workers,* 108-36. Quoted in John Mack Faragher, et al., *Out of Many: A History of the American People* (Englewood Cliffs, N.J.: Prentice Hall, 1994), 834.
62. Goulden, *Meany*, 170-76. A sidelight on this activity was Meany's support for the Emergency Detention Act proposed by Hubert Humphrey, by which

internment camps would be established to place dangerous subversives without the trouble of *habeas corpus*. Humphrey, who in 1954 proposed the Communist Control Act to make even membership in the Communist Party a crime, thereby established his bona fides with the Meany wing of the labor movement, swinging a bit further than standard ADA liberals like Schlesinger and Reuther, who had both energetically supported the EDA. See William W. Keller, *The Liberals and J. Edgar Hoover: Rise and Fall of a Democratic Intelligence State* (Princeton, N.J.: Princeton University Press, 1989), 46-48, 66-67.

63. Quoted by Lichtenstein in *The Most Dangerous Man in Detroit*, 323. Goulden, *Meany*, 365; see 353-70 for a more general picture of Meany's war zeal.
64. Ibid., 199-206.
65. "Telephone Broadcast to the AFL-CIO Merger Meeting in New York, Dec. 9, 1955," in the *Published Papers of the Presidents of the United States, Dwight D. Eisenhower* (Washington: Government Printing Office, 1959), 852-53. Thanks to Scott McLemee for this citation.
66. Goulden, *Meany*, 177-78.
67. William Green made a classic statement of this position in a 1928 speech, "The AFL and the Middle Way," in Jerald Auerbach, ed., *American Labor In the Twentieth Century* (Indianapolis: Bobbs-Merrill, 1969), 192-96.
68. See Dubofsky and Van Tine, *John L. Lewis*, 332-33; Walter LaFeber, *The American Age: United States Foreign Policy at Home and Abroad from 1750 to the Present* (New York: W. W. Norton, 1989).
69. An absurdly flattering and idealistic perspective on Dubinsky's aims in this regard is contained in David Dubinsky and A. H. Raskin, *David Dubinsky: A Life With Labor* (New York: Simon and Schuster, 1977), especially 239-61.
70. According to recent reports, the Comintern archive reveals Lovestone, his ideological lieutenant Bertram D. Wolfe, and Wolfe's wife Ella were actually conducting Comintern business; Harvey Klehr, John Earl Haynes, and Freidrikh Igorevich Firsov, *The Secret World of American Communism* (New Haven: Yale University Press, 1995), 131-32. There are ample reasons to be skeptical about the conclusions of this volume, but its chief limitation is an unwillingness to draw conclusions about corresponding intelligence ("spy") activity on the other side of the Cold War. By the time Lovestone had given "friendly" testimony to the House Committee on Un-American Activities he was certainly embroiled in such activity within the labor movement. See the fascinating if hagiographic volume by Ben Rathbun, *The Point Man: Irving Brown and the Deadly Post-1945 Struggle for Europe and Africa* (Montreux: Minerva Press, 1996).
71. See Paul Buhle, "Lovestonites," and "Secret Work," in Mari Jo Buhle, Paul Buhle, and Dan Georgakas, eds., *Encyclopedia of the American Left*, 462-64 and 735-37; also Paul Buhle, *A Dreamer's Paradise Lost*, chap. 3. A curiously ignored subject, the Lovestone group may in the future enjoy new scholarly attention—if the release of CIA documents allows more insight into the

practices of international subversion. See also the hagiographic volume by Ted Morgan, *A Covert Life: Jay Lovestone, Communist, Anti-Communist, and Spymaster* (New York: Random House, 1999).

72. Robinson, *George Meany*, 128-29, offers a predictably upbeat treatment of how Meany underwent (in Lovestone's words) "an interesting evolution" in foreign affairs.

73. Ibid., 131, offers a description delivered in elegiac terms of humanitarian caring never known to be anywhere in Meany's character.

74. Sidney Lens, "Labor Lieutenants and the Cold War," *New Politics* 7 (summer 1968), 47-57; David Langley, "The Colonization of the International Trade Union Movement," in Hall, ed., *Autocracy and Insurgency*, 296-309; Ronald L. Filipelli, "Luigi Antonini, The Italian-American Labor Council, and Cold War Politics in Italy, 1943-1949," *Labor History* 33 (winter 1992): 102-25.

75. Another scholar puts it differently: "In the years following the war, the AFL expended large sums of money and much energy playing a substantial role in the eventual division of the French Italian, German and Greek trade union movements. Irving Brown thus boasted in late 1947 that 'our trade union programs and relationships have penetrated every country of Europe. We have become . . . an army . . . a world force in conflict with a world organization in every field affecting international labor as well as American labor.'" Peter Weiler, *British Labour and the Cold War* (Stanford, Calif.: Stanford University Press, 1988), 91. Weiler further notes that the political sentiment in many unions led in the direction of world labor unity, compelling the AFL to conspire with these leaders against their own union memberships—a familiar maneuver for Dubinsky and his lieutenants; ibid., 94.

76. See Rathbun, *The Point Man*, 210, 220, 222. Rathbun is especially emphatic on the "politicking" required to evade Italian laws forbidding the purchasing of Italian elections by foreign powers. "Diplomatic pouches" filled by ILGWU officials with large quantities of cash did the job.

77. Ibid., 117. The most eloquent tribute to local struggles, as seen in popular memory, and description of the turn of Communists toward accommodation to post-war capitalism and its consumption economy, is in the classic oral history essay by Alessandro Portelli, "The Death of Luigi Trastulli," in *The Death of Luigi Trastulli and Other Stories: Form and Meaning in Oral History* (Albany: SUNY Press, 1991), 1-28.

78. Weiler, *British Labour*, 113-14.

79. Ibid., 115-16.

80. Quoted in ibid., 120.

81. Quoted in ibid., 124.

82. Quoted in Robinson, *Meany,* 137.

83. On Greece, see Weiler, *British Labor*, 152-59, and on Germany, ibid., 165-85. As Weiler notes, virtually every labor movement in the world except the AFL condemned the collaborationist-linked postwar Greek government which held

power for a small group of rich and corrupt figures, and launched a brutal wave of repression and executions during the Civil War. "The arrival of the American Mission," read the British labor report, "was the signal for . . . profit-taking on the part of trade union leaders. . . . ." Ibid., 164. Meany struggled to gain admission of conservative Christian unions to the anticommunist federation, but as he lamented, the "old prejudices" of social democratic unionists prevailed. Robinson, *Meany,* 138.

84. Rathbun, *The Point Man,* 239, 245.

85. Ibid., 121.

86. Philip Agee, *Inside the Company: CIA Diary* (Hammondsworth: Penguin Books, 1975), 302.

87. Later the *Times* would admit that it had consented in banning reporter Gruson from Guatelemala at a crucial moment of the counterrevolution. As if to show history repeating itself, during the 1980s Gruson's son Lindsay also became a *Times'* reporter from the region and quickly gained a reputation as a particular enthusiast of the contra forces in Nicaragua. See "Role of C.I.A. in Guatemala Told in Files of Publisher," *New York Times,* 7 June 1998; and Walter LaFeber, *Inevitable Revolutions: The United States in Central America* (New York: Norton, 1983), 120.

89. Quoted in Julius Jacobson, unpublished manuscript, "George Meany."

90. Quoted in ibid.

91. LaFeber, *Inevitable Revolutions,* 126.

92. Goulden, *Meany,* 223-25, remarkably finds Meany in the wrong, then moves rapidly onward to describe more of Meany's otherwise virtuous activities; so does Zieger in *American Workers, American Unions,* 172-74.

93. This is not to say that Green's own views on international issues were anything but predictably conservative, but that his criticism of the AFL-CIO's continual assertion of self-importance, as of its rectitude, was on the mark; Max Green, *Epitaph for American Labor: How Union Leaders Lost Touch With America* (Washington: American Enterprise Institute, 1996), 61-64.

3. Meanyism: Apex and Decline

1. Archie Robinson, *George Meany and His Times* (New York: Simon and Schuster, 1981), 222.

2. Interview with Donald Slaiman, 16 December 1994 (Tamiment Library, New York University). Slaiman was Meany's man running the AFL-CIO civil rights department and a follower of Max Shachtman, moving from the socialist left into the labor movement's operational center.

3. Michael Harrington, *Fragments of a Century* (New York: Saturday Review Press/Dutton, 1973), 224. Only in 1972 did Harrington break with those he criticized, which raises other questions.

4. Philip Agee, *Inside the Company: CIA Diary* (Hammondsworth: Penguin Books, 1975), 566.

5. See Steven Rosswurm, "Federal Bureau of Investigation," in Mari Jo Buhle, et al., eds, *Encyclopedia of the American Left* 2d ed. (New York: Oxford University Press, 1998), 218-21. See also Ron Schatz, *The Electrical Workers:A History of Labor at General Electric and Westinghouse, 1923-60* (Urbana: University of Illinois, 1983), especially chap. 8; and Ronald L. Filipelli and Mark McColloch, *Cold War In the Working Class: The Rise and Decline of the United Electrical Workers* (Albany: SUNY Press, 1995), 168, and much of chap. 6, with especially ample material on Carey's maneuvers in the 1950s after an early career as a militant leader, sometimes in alliance with Communists, sometimes against. The Senate hearings led by Hubert Humphrey concommitant to HCUA to "investigate" supposed Communist influence in defense plants (i.e., UE locals holding contracts) were only two more dimensions of the Cold War liberals' and the government's campaign for Carey. Carey himself left office in 1965 when the Labor Department ruled that he was guilty of massive vote-stealing; Filipelli and McColloch, 169.

6. Fred Halstead, *Out Now! A Participant's Account of the American Movement Against the Vietnam War* (New York: Monad Press, 1978), 363fn.

7. David Dubinsky and A. H. Raskin, *David Dubinsky: A Life With Labor* (New York: Simon and Schuster, 1977), 297-300.

8. See the uncritical biography by David L. Stebenne, *Arthur J. Goldberg: New Deal Liberal* (New York: Oxford University Press, 1996), which admits no wrongdoing on the part of its protagonist but describes briefly his influence upon "government support" of the AFL-CIO's international program, adding that Goldberg's highly colored Cold War rhetoric, intended to win conservative support, was outdated by the Vietnam conflict soon to follow. Too bad Goldberg was not as acute as his biographer. See 314-15. Amazingly, "Israel" does not even appear in the index. Goldberg's own brief treatment of labor history, in *AFL-CIO: Labor United* (New York: McGraw-Hill, 1956), contains little on foreign policy and no mention of the intelligence agencies' role in it. *Spearheads of Democracy: Labor in the Developing Countries* (New York: Harper and Row, 1962), by Goldberg's assistant in the Kennedy adminstration, George Cabot Lodge, neatly laid out the role for world unions as the "first line of defense against communism," and labor attachés as possessing "credentials that will open many doors closed to others."

9. Paul Buhle and Edward Rice Maximin, *The Tragedy of Empire: William Appleman Williams* (New York: Routledge, 1995); William Appleman Williams, *Empire As a Way of Life* (New York: Oxford University Press, 1980).

10. Agee, *Inside the Company*, 243-45, 488.

11. Ibid., 306-07: "Sooner or later all the AIFLD programmes will be run closely by the stations. . . ."

12. See Sidney Lens, "Labor Lieutenants and the Cold War," in *Autocracy and Insurgency in the Labor Movement* (New Brunswick, N.J.: Transaction Books, 1972), 310-23.

13. Ibid., 320-21.
14. Fred Hirsch and Virginia Muir, "A Plumber Gets Curious About Exporting McCarthyism," in Ann Fagan Ginger and David Christiano, eds., *The Cold War Against Labor,* vol. 2 (Berkeley, Calif.: Meiklejohn Civil Liberties Institute, 1987), 746-50.
15. Quoted by Beth Sims, *Workers of the World Undermined* (Boston: South End Press, 1991), 52.
16. Agee, *Inside the Company,* 473, 588.
17. Quoted in David Langley, "The Colonization of the International Trade Union Movement," in Hall, ed., *Autocracy and Insurgency in the Labor Movement,* 307-8.
18. Harrington, *Fragments of the Century,* 224. In Harrington's sympathetic (and self-serving) account, his political mentor Shachtman had worked himself into a corner through a mistaken approach to the Vietnam War, but was right to remain mum as the escalation continued during the mid-1960s and socialists tried to sell Lyndon Johnson on a more vigorous war on poverty. (Harrington himself practiced the same tactic.) Harrington does confess with regret, however, that Shachtman's lieutenants, as editors of *New America,* dismissed the assassination of rebel miners' leader Jock Yablonsky; see ibid., 204, 224.
19. Jervis Anderson, *Bayard Rustin: The Troubles I've Seen* (New York: Harper-Collins, 1997), contains extraordinarily little on Rustin's later career, especially his missions to Africa. The file of *New America* for the 1970s contains rich information about Rustin's increasingly hardline views and his intelligence-connected comrades. Michael Harrington proposed a more typical rationalization: that Rustin decided to support the Vietnam War in order "to subordinate his anti-war convictions to what he became convinced were the imperatives of domestic coalition politics." See Harrington, *Fragments of the Century,* 206. This would hardly explain Rustin's permanent change of mind in favor of hardline international policies or support of the Reagan collaborators within the AFL-CIO.
20. Yossi Melman and Dan Raviv, *Friends In Deed: Inside the U.S.-Israel Alliance* (New York: Hyperion, 1994), chap. 5. This book contains valuable information about Israeli intelligence and the clout of American friends, told in a boasting fashion.
21. As late as 1998, John Sweeney was hosted in Washington at "A Gala National Tribute" for Israel Bonds (*Forward* advertisement, 1 May 1998), "in recognition of five decades of friendship and solidarity between the State of Israel and the American Labor Movement," although all but the last two years had been devoted, from the side of Israel's staunchest labor friends, to supporting the bureaucratic conservative side of U.S. labor. Indeed, observers noted that the labor leaders most firmly behind Lane Kirkland and his would-be successor Tom Donohue during the 1996 convention could be easily ascertained by checking their names against the Advisory Board of the Jewish Labor

Committee. Almost certainly, the awarders of 1998 would have been happier to see the Sweeney team dumped in order to award the hawks' candidate for president, Sandra Feldman, as the *Forward* repeatedly reminded readers. According to insiders, Feldman renounced such internal jockeying for power.

22. This background, like the U.S. backing for Israeli military victory in the Six Day War of 1967 as the United States was floundering in Vietnam, helps explain some key AFL-CIO leaders' determined sympathy for an increasingly unpopular Lyndon Johnson. As the Americans for Democratic Action threatened to fragment over proposals to "dump Johnson," ILGWU ideologue and ex-socialist Gus Tyler—struggling against the overwhelming anti-war Jewish American liberal community—reportedly commanded the forces back into line, at least for the moment.

Goldberg, by now United Nations ambassador, proposed Resolution 242 urging the Israeli withdrawal from occupied lands, making sure, however, not to specify the conquered territories from which the Israelis would need to withdraw. It was a clever ruse, much like the administration's "peace offensive" in Vietnam, setting the terms for refusal in advance and providing the rationale for further military action. AFL-CIO chiefs positioned themselves to resist opposition to long-term and (as insiders already knew) permanent occupation and eventual absorption of formerly Palestinian territories. See Melman and Raviv, *Friends In Deed*, 132-64. After Kennedy's assassination, Lyndon Johnson had hiked Israeli aid to previously unthinkable levels, from $40 million to $71 million and then $130 million within just three years. All this might have been foreseen from plans laid and alliances established during the 1950s. See Melman and Raviv, *Friends In Deed,* 129-31 and chap. 7.

23. See Robinson, *George Meany,* 162-84, for the rosiest possible treatment of Meany's maneuvering toward unity.

24. Goulden, *Meany,* 184-92.

25. Robinson, *George Meany,* 181.

26. Ibid., 182.

27. Goulden, *Meany,* 286.

28. On the McClellan Committee, see Burton Hall, "Law, Democracy and the Unions," in Hall, ed., *Autocracy and Insurgency in Organized Labor,* 111-14.

29. Statement at AFL-CIO Industrial Relations Conference, June 1957. Meany's action on behalf a crime-tainted set of officials at the Painters District Council in New York is also instructive. Embarrassed when local leader Martin Rarback was indicted for accepting more than $800,000 in bribes from employers, painters' officials placed the District Council in trusteeship, the trustee reappointing all the officials but Rarback himself. As the case worked its way through the courts and the rank-and-file stirred, Meany rushed in to declare to the press that the trusteeship had cleared up all the difficulties, and

that the reappointed trustees were noble characters. Burton Hall, "The Painters' Union: A Partial Victory," in Hall, ed., *Autocracy and Insurgency,* 41-43.

30. See the discussion of the Bill of Rights in Hall, "Law, Democracy and the Unions," in ibid., 109-35.

31. Fred Barnes, "The UWMA Dictatorship on the Defensive," in ibid., 21-29.

32. See Sumner Rosen, "The CIO Era, 1935-55," in Julius Jacobson, ed., *The Negro and the American Labor Movement* (Garden City, N.Y.: Doubleday, 1968), 201-2.

33. Goldberg, *AFL-CIO: Labor United,* 202.

34. Ward Churchill and Jim Vander Wall, *The COINTELPRO Papers: Documents from the FBI's Secret Wars Against Dissent in the United States* (Boston: South End Press, 1990), 95-105.

35. The pamphlet *Negro Americans Take the Lead* (Detroit: Facing Reality, 1960), written by followers of C. L. R. James, is especially lucid on this point.

36. George Lipsitz, *The Possessive Investment in Whiteness: How White People Profit from Identity Politics* (Philadelphia: Temple University Press, 1998).

37. Jill Quadagno, *The Color of Welfare: How Racism Undermined the War On Poverty* (New York: Oxford University Press, 1994), 23.

38. Rosen, "The CIO Era," in Jacobson, ed., *The Negro and the American Labor Movement,* 189-91.

39. Robinson presses this controversy under a neat disavowal: "civil rights provisions in the new constitution were not as strong as wanted by black union leaders," because a section of the constitution listed as one of the AFL-CIO's "objects" the encouragement of all to share equal benefits of union membership, and because Meany himself repeatedly attacked school segregation. Robinson, *George Meany,* 180.

40. See R. W. Thomas, "National Negro Labor Council," in Buhle, et al., *Encyclopedia of the American Left* 2d ed., 536-37.

41. See Lipsitz, *The Possessive Investment in Whiteness,* 39-40.

42. Ernesto Galarza, *Spiders in the House and Workers in the Field* (Notre Dame: University of Notre Dame Press, 1970), especially 96, 242.

43. Goulden, *Meany,* 313-14. Goulden goes on to say that Meany began to enact Randolph's previous demands, a highly imaginative reading.

44. See Julius Jacobson, "Coalitionism: From Protest to Politicking," in Hall, ed., *Autocracy and Insurgency,* 324-45.

45. The four were finally pressured into taking tests to determine their qualifications. As with Southern literacy tests for blacks voting, the questions were ridiculously difficult, requiring knowledge of various things little related to pipe fitting. They failed, but so would nearly all white union workers who reached journeyman status, not through such tests, but through on-the-job training and through the "back door." Courts later ruled that the failure was "the product of a test illegally imposed as a condition of ending a strike

illegally engaged in." Local 2 was held in violation of the National Labor Relations Act and forced to recompense the men for loss of pay.

46. Manning Marable, *Black American Politics: From the Washington Marches to Jesse Jackson* (London: Verso, 1985), 90-95. Robinson avoids Meany's opposition to the March on Washington by quoting a favorable remark made after the march had taken place. For Robinson, Meany championed the attack on discrimination, starting with the AFL-CIO's own agencies, and "construction unions adopted a program aimed at ending discrimination in employment in their own field." Curiously, these processes took so long to implement that no one working in the trades in 1963 would be troubled by the unions' traditional priority of white over non-white workers. See Robinson, *George Meany*, 237.

47. Herbert Hill, "The ILGWU Today: The Decay of a Labor Union"; Gus Tyler, "The Truth about the ILGWU," and Herbert Hill, "The ILGWU: Fact and Fiction," in Hall, ed., *Autocracy and Insurgency*, 147-200.

48. Lipsitz, *The Possessive Investment in Whiteness*, Chap. 2.

49. Hill, "The ILGWU: Fact and Fiction," 181.

50. Kevin Boyle, *The UAW and the Heyday of American Liberalism, 1945-1968* (Ithaca: Cornell University Press, 1995), 107-19.

51. R. W. Thomas, "The National Negro Labor Council," in Mari Jo Buhle et al., eds., *Encyclopedia of the American Left*, 2d ed., 536-37.

52. See James R. Zetka, Jr., *Militancy, Marketplace Dynamics and Workplace Authority* (Albany: SUNY Press, 1995), 160-62, 171, 176-78.

53. Daniel Bell, *The End of Ideology* (Glencoe: Free Press, 1960), 223-24.

54. On Richard J. Daley as a "labor candidate," see Godfried, *WCFL: Chicago's Voice of Labor*, 240-42.

55. P. K. Edwards, *Strikes in the United States, 1881-1974* (New York: St. Martin's, 1981), 216-17.

56. Boyle, *The UAW*, 122-23.

57. Robinson, *George Meany*, 182: Meany recalled "I didn't see any real need for an IUD." He nevertheless presided over its initial sessions, counting correctly on Dave Beck and others to prevent the body from becoming the dynamic center that Reuther had hoped it would be. The IUD was finally killed off in 1998, a casualty of AFL-CIO internal reorganization; the talented and energetic Joe Uehlein, the IUD's chief figure of later years and one of the few non-ideological higher-level appointments of the Kirkland regime, has since shifted to advising the new administration.

58. Best conveyed in Lichtenstein, *The Most Dangerous Man in Detroit*, 406-11.

59. The internal situation of Reuther's union at the end of the 1960s is nicely summarized in Robert Zieger, *American Workers, American Unions, 1920-1985* (Baltimore: Johns Hopkins University Press, 1995), 178-81.

60. Peter B. Levy, *The New Left and Labor in the 1960s* (Urbana: University of Illinois Press, 1994).

61. Ibid., 42-43.
62. See Robin D. G. Kelley, *Race Rebels: Culture, Politics and the Black Working Class* (New York: The Free Press, 1994), Part One, 17-102.
63. Eric Thomas Chester, *Covert Network: Progressives, the International Rescue Committee and the CIA* (Armonk, N.Y.: M. E. Sharpe, 1995), especially chap. 12-13 on the IRC and Buttinger's role in Vietnam. Only *Ramparts* magazine's exposure of the CIA backing of the American Friends of Vietnam ended its ignomious career; it was succeeded by the Citizens Committee for Peace and Freedom in Vietnam, conceived in the Johnson White House by John Roche, a former socialist turned professional policy hardliner.
64. It should be noted that *Dissent* editor Irving Howe remained on the parent IRC board until his last days, perhaps from a past sense of financial gratitude. See Chester, *Covert Network,* 201-05.
65. When student demonstrators appeared at the December 1965 AFL-CIO convention in San Francisco, making no noise but merely holding up signs to protest Secretary of State Dean Rusk speaking, Meany abruptly ordered the sergeant-at-arms to "clear the kookies out of the gallery." Halstead, *Out Now!,* 237. As Halstead notes, some of the sharpest repression was in the ILGWU, where staffers feared to voice their opposition to the war: ibid., 240.
66. Meany waited until the last moment of the Memphis garbage workers strike (during which King was killed) to offer assistance, and then did so only after a dramatic personal appeal from Jerry Wurf, a combative but safely anticommunist leader of AFSCME. The $20,000 donated from the AFL-CIO was equal to a tiny fraction of "personal" expenses for labor leaders during a swank convention. See Joan Turner Beifuss, *At the River I Stand: Memphis, The 1968 Strike and Martin Luther King* (Brooklyn: Carlson Publishing Inc., 1985), 258.
67. The head of fact-finding in the ADL, Irwin Suall, was a prominent figure in Social Democrats USA, and according to his admirers, happy to share information about the left with the House Committee on Un-American Activities. See Mira Boland, "ADL Sleuth Suall Dies at 73," *Forward,* 21 August 1998. It is not known if Suall was personally involved in the ADL scheme to offer damaging material to the FBI on Martin Luther King, Jr. But Suall's colleague Abraham Foxman moved into neoconservative circles with a new generation of leaders in institutions like the ADL, which had a mixed record of supporting civil liberties while cooperating with intelligence agencies against radicals in unions, entertainment, and elsewhere. See Robert I. Friedman, "The Enemy from Within: How the Anti-Defamation League Turned the Notion of Human Rights on its Head, Spying on Progressives and Funneling Information to Law Enforcement," *Village Voice,* 11 May 1993.
68. Goulden, *Meany,* 353-70.
69. On this bizarre notion in Humphrey's worldview and its role in his hardline hawkish politics, see Steve Gillon, *Politics and Vision: The ADA and American Liberalism, 1947-1985* (New York: Oxford University Press, 1987), 196.

70. *Proceedings of the Tenth Constitution Comnvention of the AFL-CIO* (Washington, D.C.: AFL-CIO, 1973), 15, 39.

71. Dan Georgakas and Marvin Surkin, *Detroit: I Do Mind Dying,* 2d ed. (Boston: South End Press, 1998).

72. See Kim Moody, *An Injury to All: The Decline of American Unionism* (London: Verso, 1988).

73. Quoted in Herbert Hill, "Race and Ethnicity in Organized Labor: The Historical Sources of Resistance to Affirmative Action," in *Ethnicity and the Work Force,* ed. Winston A. Van Horne and Thomas V. Tonnesen (Madison: University of Wisconsin, 1985), 54.

74. Shanker ordered seized and destroyed thousands of copies of a curriculum guide which credited Malcolm X's historical contribution. He suppressed any historical explanations which placed the black experience outside the melting pot—where all the unfortunate group traits of worthy aspirants melt in the process of a cheerful upward mobility. For background history, see Marjorie Murphy, *Blackboard Unions: The AFT and the NEA, 1900-1980* (Ithaca, N.Y.: Cornell University Press, 1900); and Celia L. Zitron, *The New York City Teachers Union, 1916-1964: A Story of Educational and Social Commitment* (New York: Humanities, 1968). Various essays in the journal *New Politics* constitute the very best guide to the internal politics of the UFT/AFT: Steve Zeluck, "The UFT Strike: A Blow Against Teacher Unionism," *New Politics* no. 25 (winter 1968); Maurice Berube, "'Democratic Socialists' and the Schools," no. 31 (summer 1969); Lois Weiner, "Cracks in Shanker's Empire," no. 44 (fall 1976), and an exchange between Albert Shanker and Herbert Hill, "Black Protest, Union Democracy and the UFT," no. 32 (fall 1970).

75. Lois Weiner, "Albert Shanker's Legacy: A Critical Perspective," unpublished paper delivered to the American Educational Research Association, April 1988.

76. Bell quoted in Rick Halpern and Jonathan Morris, "The Persistence of Exceptionalism: Class Formation and the Comparative Method," in Halpern and Morris, *American Exceptionalism? U.S. Working-Class Formation in an International Context* (London: St. Martin's Press, 1997), 17.

77. Robert Gregg, "Apropos Exceptionalism: Imperial Location and Comparative Histories of South Africa and the United States," in ibid., 293.

78. See "Herbert Hill Replies," *New Politics* no. 32 (fall 1970), 33-35. Ironically, the most articulately ferocious opponents to the UFT, the black middle class, shared this ideology to a very large extent, although with a difference. They wanted and demanded an affirmative action adjustment of available resources, exactly what the ideologues of meritocracy could never grant. Jerald Podair, "'White' Values, 'Black' Values: The Ocean Hill-Brownsville Controversy and New York City Culture, 1967-1975," *Radical History Review* no. 59 (spring 1994), 36-59. For a discussion of the impact of the Moynihan Report on a rightward-drifting liberalism, see Mari Jo Buhle, *Feminism and Its*

Discontents: A Century of Struggle with Psychoanalysis (Cambridge, Mass.: Harvard University Press, 1998), chap. 8, especially 281-85.

79. See Jack Saltzman and Cornel West, eds., *Struggles in the Promised Land: Toward a History of Black-Jewish Relations in the United States* (New York: Oxford University Press, 1997), especially Earl Lewis, "The Need to Remember: Three Phases in Black and Jewish Educational Relations," 231-56; and Paul Buhle and Robin D. G. Kelley, "Allies of a Different Sort: Jews and Blacks in the American Left," 197-230. Close watchers of the controversy about the blatantly anti-Semitic leaflet reprinted and widely distributed by Shanker's machine during the turbulent events will want to consult Earl Lewis's conclusion that the leaflet identified a non-existant group, and that no one has ever claimed credit for this leaflet; no one has yet considered seriously Lewis's provocative suggestion that, in this era of many thousands of disguised police agents engaged in disguised actions, it may well have been a COIN-TELPRO project. It would not be shocking but not surprising to learn that Shanker's office concocted the "perfect" anti-Semitic document to crystalize support for the UFT leadership. See Lewis, "The Need to Remember," 254-55, n. 51. See also Robert I. Friedman, "The Enemy from Within."

80. Joining the inner circle of George Meany's AFL-CIO cronies, Shanker, who had repeatedly declared himself for racial equality, also lobbied vigorously if unsuccessfully against any union support of the school boycotts—even those personally led by close ally Bayard Rustin; Berube, "'Democratic Socialists' and the Schools," 60. Berube argues interestingly that Shanker, the hard-nosed business unionist, was drawn into the race narrative by liberal-socialist intellectuals and in doing so had "come home" to the labor establishment, which relished its intellectual apologists.

81. The AFL-CIO's Israeli partners had meanwhile become more and more comfortable with Richard Nixon and Henry Kissinger, both of whom were attacked at home for committing war crimes of a scale unknown since the Second World War, but viewed by Tel Aviv as the best possible allies available. Reflecting the views of Prime Minister Golda Meir, Ambassador Itzhak Rabin breached all tradition by openly stating that Israel regarded Nixon the hawk as "safe" for Israel, while George McGovern the man of peace was deemed weak and untrustworthy. See Melman and Raviv, *Friends In Need,* 156-57.

82. *Proceedings of the Tenth Constitutional Convention of the AFL-CIO* (Washington, D.C.: AFL-CIO, 1973), 112.

83. Dubofsky, *The State and Labor in Modern America,* 212-217. To be more precise, Dubofsky considers the increasing disappearance of union democracy a "paradox" which allowed workers to hold their jobs more securely—while tying their hands from mounting anything more than an individual grievance. Having given up these rights, unionists found themselves less able

to combat the "takebacks" of the era following, or even to maintain the "security" that had been won at such an enormous price.

84. David Brody, *Workers in Industrial America* (New York: Oxford University Press, 1980), 244-45.

85. *Proceedings of the Thirteenth Constitution Convention of the AFL-CIO* (Washington, DC: AFL-CIO), 231.

86. Robert Zieger, "The CIO On Trial," *Labor History* 37 (spring 1996), 185.

4. The Kirkland Years

1. David Brody, "Breakdown of Labor's Social Contract," *Dissent* 39 (winter 1992), 32-41.

2. "Kirkland, (Joseph) Lane," *Current Biography*, May 1980, 21-22; see also "Kirkland, Joseph Lane," in Gary Fink, ed., *Biographical Dictionary of American Labor* (Westport, Conn.: Greenwood Press, 1984), 336; and Eric Pace, "Men in the News: Lane Krikland," *New York Times,* 29 August 1980.

3. *Proceedings of the Thirteenth Constitutional Convention of the AFL-CIO* (Washington, D.C.: AFL-CIO, 1979), 284. "Kirkland: 'We've Had Setbacks,'" *Washington Post*, 6 September 1987, an interview with two sympathetic reporters.

4. "Kirkland: 'We've Had Setbacks.'" Would the Hungarian uprising, leading to the temporary creation of egalitarian workers councils, have fallen into the hands of AFL-CIO operators? There is good reason to think that Lovestone and company would have been horrified by the success of the revolution there. See C. L. R. James, *Facing Reality* (Detroit: Bewick Ed., 1973), on the Hungarian events.

5. Quoted in "S.D. to Honor Lane Kirkland," *New America*, Feb., 1976.

6. "And I'm not kidding," Will added to drive home the point. Kathy Sawyer, "Lane Kirkland: Made in America," *Washington Post*, 15 July 1984.

7. Lane Kirkland "Crisis in Liberalism—The Revisionists," *New America*, 25 February 1970.

8. The pages of *New America* from the later 1960s offer the best evidence of the steady stream of honors bestowed upon Rustin and the small handful of other Cold War African-American unionists. A recent scandal of apparently misused funds by Freedom House president Adrian Karatnycky, a former employee of Lane Kirkland's office, sheds new light upon the assorted corporate and intelligence connections of the Cold War clique. Founded by Eleanor Roosevelt to fight fascism, Freedom House became by the 1970s a center of Cold War intrigue and official backing for terrorist "freedom fighters" such as Jonas Savimbi. Funded in part by conservative foundations along with USAID and USIA, it currently includes on its board Jeane Kirkpatrick, Max Kampelman, Reagan appointee Ken Adelman, *New Republic* savant Morton Kondracke, and *Commentary* regular (and Social Democrats USA figure) Arch Puddington; its executive committee includes assorted corporate figures

along with Norman Hill of the A. Philip Randolph Institute. A typical board member like Kampelman sat simultaneously on the board of an international arms dealer, offering more than a small clue to the planetary "freedom" that Freedom House had in mind. See "Sex, Dollars and Freedom," *CounterPunch* 5 (1-15 January 1998), 1, 5-6.

9. "Kirkland, (Joseph) Lane," *Current Biography*, 22.

10. Ibid., 23.

11. Archie Robinson, *George Meany and his Times* (New York: Simon and Schuster, 1981), 330-31, makes the case that Meany insisted Nixon resign "in the interest of national security" (in Meany's own words), but also quotes Meany slapping at Nixon as going down in history, with Leonid Brezhnev, for deserving together the "Joseph Stalin Peace Award."

12. A good summary of the AIFLD's role in Chile is contained in Fred Hirsch and Virginia Muir, "A Plumber Gets Curious About Exporting McCarthyism," in Ann Fagan Ginger and David Christiano, eds., *The Cold War Against Labor,* vol. 2 (Berkeley, Calif.: Meiklejohn Civil Liberties Center, 1987), 751-56.

13. Max Green, *Epitaph for American Labor: How Union Leaders Lost Touch with America* (Washington, D.C.: American Enterprise Institute Press, 1996), 124, 127. Later, Kirkland rewarded his Israel lobby connections by quashing Winpisinger's effort to get an AFL-CIO resolution against Israel's 1982 invasion of Lebanon. In response to Winpisinger, Kirkland declared, "Israel is catching enough hell around the world, and one of their best friends isn't going to turn on them now." Elaine Sciolino, "Kirkland Wins Acclaim for Success Abroad, but Faces Criticism at Home," *New York Times,* 14 December 1989.

14. Thus the Hatfield-McGovern Amendment, demanding Congressional approval, was viewed by those around Kirkland as a "Munich" to presidential freedom of action. "SD Opposes Any Munich Agreement," *New America*, 21 November 1973.

15. Green, *Epitaph for American Labor*, especially Chap. 8-10.

16. Lane Kirkland, "The Basic Role of Labor," *New America*, May 1976.

17. George Meany, "Labor's Goal: A Free Society Without Class Privilege," *New America*, May 1977, the text of a speech written, almost certainly, by one of Shachtman's proteges; "Kirkland, (Joseph) Lane," *Current Biography*, 23.

18. As Kathy Sawyer remarks on Irena Neumann in "Lane Kirkland," "Friends credit Irena with opening up a broader social arena to Kirkland, with her international connections. She is best friends with Nancy Kissinger, wife of Henry. . . . " Robert Reich, *Locked In the Cabinet* (New York: Knopf, 1997), 98-100, draws a funnier and almost certainly more accurate picture of the faux genteel manners and morals in an obsessively social-climbing Kirkland household.

19. Ward Churchill and Jim Vander Wall, *The Cointelpro Papers: Documents from the FBI's Secret Wars Against Dissent in the United States* (Boston: South End Press, 1990), does not cover labor issues specifically, but indicates

that part of the COINTELPRO operation against the Vietnam Veterans Against the War—mostly actions conducted after COINTELPRO had supposedly ended in 1971—involved infiltration by federal provocateurs of the United Electrical Workers and United Farm Workers, two unions on the leftward side of labor, 224. No documentation currently exists of AFL-CIO institutional cooperation with COINTELPRO or other programs; nor, of course, did AFL-CIO leaders denounce the widespread illegal activities of intelligence agencies in domestic projects. One can hope that early release of intelligence files will document the suspicions of researchers (and the private bragging of AFL-CIO staffers).

20. The pages of *New America*, organ of SDUSA in its "open" phase, especially during the middle 1970s, offer rich evidence of these clusters and are bound to provide future researchers of covert intelligence with leads.

21. Eric Thomas Chester, *Covert Network: Progressives, the International Rescue Committee, and the CIA* (Armonk, N.Y.: M. E. Sharpe, 1995), 190. With the end of the Cold War and the return of the extreme right to power in El Salvador, the IRC withdrew, its mission completed. Chester further notes that under Reagan, the National Endowment for Democracy also took up many of the tasks earlier conducted by CIA/IRC operations. Supporters of the IRC will eagerly claim, as did Shanker in his lifetime, that liberal anticommunists had played a vital role in supporting Polish Solidarity; many former members of Solidarity and their supporters would note that the real purpose of such support was to undermine the movement for workers' control no less than to undermine the Communist government.

22. See, for example, "A Concern for All," Cherne's speech on accepting the Human Rights Award from the American Federation of Teachers, *New America*, November 1977.

23. Chester provides extensive information on Cherne's background and career. See *Covert Network*, 99, 112, 118, 147-50, 157-58, 167, 181, 200.

24. James Ridgeway, "The Professor of Conspire: How a Teacher at Georgetown Helped Found the Secret Government," *Village Voice*, 4 August 1987.

25. Understandably, Cherne was one of those public figures most fervently devoted to Shanker's memory, along with Diane Ravitch and the disgraced Elliot Abrams. Jonathan Mahler, "How Albert Shanker Set the Agenda for a Generation," *Forward*, 28 February 1997.

26. Sawyer, "Lane Kirkland: Made in America."

27. "Kirkland (Joseph) Lane," *Current Biography*, 23.

28. *Proceedings to the Thirteenth Constitution Convention of the AFL-CIO*, 285.

29. George Lipsitz, *The Possessive Investment in Whiteness: How White People Profit from Identity Politics* (Philadelphia: Temple University Press, 1998).

30. Youth staffers and future staffers mounted a campaign called "Negotiations Now!", attacking the popular anti-war perspective of immediate withdrawal from Vietnam and insisting upon U.S. ground force occupation until a satisfactory

resolution could be found—that is to say, a stable non-Communist government put into place in South Vietnam. In 1970, as Irving Howe, Michael Harrington, and the *Dissent* magazine milieu abandoned this position, Meany and his supporters continued to cling to "Vietnamization," with withdrawals only as the South Vietnamese successfully held their positions.

31. Once again, assorted ideological blasts at "New Politics" in the SDUSA newspaper, *New America*, offer the most striking evidence for the 1970s.
32. James A. Gross, *Broken Promise, The Subversion of U.S. Labor Relations Policy, 1947-1994* (Philadelphia: Temple University Press, 1996), especially 247-50; Michael Goldfield, *The Decline of Organized Labor in the United States* (Chicago: University of Chicago Press, 1987).
33. Glenn Perusek and Kent Worcester, "Introduction," *Trade Union Politics: American Unions and Economic Change, 1960s-1990s* (Atlantic Highlands, N.J.: Humanities Press, 1996), 13-14.
34. Sawyer, "Lane Kirkland: Made in America."
35. I speak from personal experience. Rhode Island was one of the last "New Deal states," with strikers' unemployed benefits and similar holdover provisions. In 1984, abandoned by the state's party regulars, the Mondale machine was taken over willy-nilly by the old network of McGovernites, doggedly doing their duty. It fell to me, ironically, to help coordinate relations with the state labor leaders, including the campus rally for Mondale featuring Screen Actors Guild President Ed Asner, despised by the Meany crowd (see note 41, below).
36. Kim Moody's account of these events is excellent, with the exception of the DSA/SDUSA division over Henry Jackson as predictive of a future realignment within sections of labor. On insider intelligence issues, Moody is mostly mute: see *An Injury to All*, chap. 11, especially 262-68. On the attack upon Jesse Jackson by leading elements of the Israel Lobby, see Andy Carroll, "The Israel Lobby's Blacklist: Exposing AIPAC's Activities," *Village Voice*, 4 August 1992.
37. William Greider, *Who Will Tell the People? The Betrayal of American Democracy* (New York: Simon and Schuster, 1992), especially chap. 11, "Who Owns the Democrats."
38. Cited in "AFL-CIO's Untapped Potential Strength," *The Labor Educator* 2 (March/April, 1993), 1.
39. *Washington Post*, 9 September 1982, quoted in Max Green, *Epitaph for American Labor* (Washington: American Enterprise Institute Press, 1996), 116.
40. Thanks for a note from Emanuel Fried, labor playwright and sometime UE leader. Fried participated in the circle that brought the proposal for a march to the attention of an avid anticommunist regional functionary, who nonetheless passed on the proposal to Kirkland's office. Fried to Buhle, 7 October 1998.
41. Young staffer Kim Fellner recalls that at the end of the 1980s, when Ed Asner announced his retirement as SAG president, one of the leading figures in AFL-CIO public relations department buttonholed her in the hall, saying "We don't need bums like that in the labor movement. And don't you ever ask any

of us to help you again!" Asner, a popular speaker at labor conventions, was considered an enemy because of his active opposition to U.S. policies in Central America. See Fellner, "In Search of the Movement," in Glenn Adler and Doris Suarez, eds., *Union Voices: Labor's Responses to Crisis* (Albany: SUNY Press, 1993), 235.

42. See the many useful observations in Beth Sims, *Workers of the World Undermined: American Labor's Role in U.S. Foreign Policy* (Boston: South End Press, 1991); and Daniel Cantor and Juliet Schor, *Tunnel Vision: Labor, The World Economy, and Central America* (Boston: South End Press, 1987). See also Hobart A. Spalding, "The Two Latin American Foreign Policies of the U.S. Labor Movement: The AFL-CIO Top Brass vs Rank-and-File," *Science & Society* 56 (winter 1992-93), 421-39; and Spalding, "Solidarity Forever? Latin American Unions and the International Labor Network," *Latin American Research Review* 23 (1989), 253-65. Reporter William Serrin tells a revealing story of how labor leaders, including Albert Shanker, attempted to get ACTWU staffer Daniel Cantor fired for writing *Tunnel Vision*: "Cold Warriors Throw an Icy Reception," *In These Times*, 17-30 August 1988.

43. Green, *Epitaph for American Labor*, 73-74; and some of the better recent literature on Solidarity, such as Lawrence Goodwyn, *Breaking the Barrier: The Rise of Solidarity in Poland* (New York: Oxford, 1991), Daniel Singer, *The Road to Gdansk* (New York: Monthly Review Press, 1982), and Daniel Singer, *Whose Millennium?* (New York: Monthly Review Press, 1999), indicating how little was owed to outsiders in the overthrow of Stalinism and how much to the people themselves—as in the rest of Eastern Europe.

44. Green, *Epitaph for American Labor*, 58-61. Green notes that a disappointed A. Philip Randolph's presence at the inauguration of Ghanaian president Kwame Nkrumah in 1957 marked the last official labor delegation to Africa for more than a decade. The All African Trade Union Federation, which despite its left-wing pretentions was more like the bureaucratic AFL-CIO approach than it admitted, nevertheless wanted no part of them on grounds of self-interest: the Americans' CIA image and South African intelligence-connected allies (tied, in turn, closely to Israeli operations) had discredited them entirely.

45. Konrad Ege, "Reagan Resurrects Savimbi," *Counter Spy* 6 (November 1981/January 1982), 1-2. See also Elaine Windrich, *The Cold War Guerilla: Jonas Savimbi, the U.S. Media and the Angolan War* (Westport, Conn.: Greenwood Press, 1993), on the "selling" of a major war criminal by conservative and neoliberal sources alike. See also the social-democratic demand that the United States intervene directly to defend Savimbi: "Angola, Detente and the American Will," *New America*, January 1976. Presumably, this last essay reflected AFL-CIO views at the highest levels.

46. Ben Rathbun, *The Point Man: Irving Brown and the Deadly Post-1945 Struggle for Europe and Africa* (Montreux: Minerva Press, 1996), 328-35. This book, based in part upon interviews with high CIA officials, curiously

passed almost unnoticed—except in the *Forward,* where Brown was hailed as a great labor leader!

47. Rathbun, *The Point Man,* 348-60. Apparently speaking with a straight face, Chaikin told delegates at the 1979 AFL-CIO convention that across the third world from Asia to Latin America, Meany's "is the name, his is the voice, his is the strength . . . that has brought hope where despair has found a home. . . . " *Proceedings of the Thirteenth Constitutional Convention of the AFL-CIO* (Washington, DC: AFL-CIO, 1979), 241.

48. Debi Duke, "AFL-CIO About Face on South Africa," *Labor Notes,* January 1991; Rathbun, *The Point Man,* 376, 381.

49. Enid Eckstein, "What Is the AFL-CIO Doing in the Philippines?" *Labor Notes,* July, 1986; Kay Eisenhower, "Viewpoint: AFL-CIO Redbaiting Hits Phlippine Unionists," *Labor Notes,* April 1989.

50. Sims, *Workers of the World Undermined,* 86-87.

51. David Finkel, "Kirkland Backs Massive Escalation of U.S. Military Aid to El Salvador," *Labor Notes,* 26 January 1984. Four years later and after much controversy within the labor movement, Shanker wrote to the socialist weekly *In These Times* that he proudly and vigorously supported the contras—but only as an individual, not in his status as head of the AFL-CIO International Affairs Committee! "Letters to the Editor" (quoted by George Dartsman, a Wisconsin AFT member), *Labor Notes,* January 1988. See also Fred Hirsch and Virginia Muir, "A Plumber Gets Curious About Exporting McCarthyism," in Ann Fagan Ginger and David Christiano, eds., *The Cold War Against Labor,* vol. 2 (Berkeley, Calif.: The Meikeljohn Civil Liberties Institute, 1987), 756-58, on the AIFLD and Central America.

52. "Kirkland, (Joseph) Lane," *Current Biography,* 21-22.

53. Cantor, *Tunnel Vision,* 44.

54. For typical instances, see "Santa Clara Labor Council Calls for Action Against AIFLD in El Salvador," noting that Edwin Doherty, Jr., flew to Santa Clara to intimidate council members, *Labor Notes,* 25 September 1908; and Foss Tighe, "Union Prez Warns Against Aid to 'Wrong' Unions in El Salvador," *Labor Notes,* 29 March 1983. See also Fred Hirsch and Virginia Muir, "A Plumber Gets Curious About Exporting McCarthyism," 745.

55. "Albert Shanker's Last Stand," *Forward,* 28 February 1997.

56. Scott Dewey, "Working for the Environment: Organized Labor and the Origins of Environmentalism in the United States, 1948-1970," unpublished paper. For Biemiller's testimony: *Air Pollution—Hearings Before the Subcommittee on Air and Water Pollution of the Senate Committee on Public Works, 1963* (Washington, D.C.: Government Printing Office, 1963). Earlier, AFL-CIO legislative representative George Riley gave similar testimony for recreation and wilderness preservation, with heavy emphasis on the economic benefits of the wilderness: *Hearings before the Subcommittee on Rivers and Harbors of the*

Committee on Public Works, House of Representatives, 1958, (Washington, D.C.: Government Printing Office, 1958).

57. Resolutions at AFL-CIO conventions from the middle 1970s to the early 1990s echoed these concerns. Generally supporting the idea of environmental regulation, they unfailingly warned against "bottle bills" that might affect jobs by banning unreturnable bottles, and against "shortcomings" in Endangered Species Act regulations that might reduce jobs by sparing the northern spotted owl or native salmon. "Balance" naturally insured the loopholes the business and union leaders desired, while providing good public relations copy about intentions. See *Proceedings of the Constitutional Convention of the AFL-CIO* (Washington, D.C.: AFL-CIO, 1989), 429-30.

58. See Abby A. Rockefeller, "Civilization and Sludge: Notes on the History of the Management of Human Excreta," *Capitalism, Nature, Socialism* 9 (September 1998), 3-18.

59. Dewey, "Working for the Environment," attributes the increasing resistance against environmental legislation to declining economic conditions. A better case might be made for the conservative political offensive of the later 1970s, shared in many respects by AFL-CIO leaders themselves.

60. See the report of the executive committee to the 1975 AFL-CIO convention, *Proceedings,* 106 and resolution by the industrial union department, 148; "Support for the Endangered Species Act," 1991 AFL-CIO convention, *Proceedings,* 429.

61. At the same convention, see the resolution on "The Timber Industry" which warned against "timber harvest restrictions" now "threatened by extreme proposals to set aside vast areas of timberland," that is, to save ancient forests, ibid., 430.

62. See Kevin Phillips, *The Emerging Republican Majority* (New Rochelle, N.Y.: Arlington House, 1969).

63. Gus Tyler, *The Labor Revolution: Trade Unions in a New America* (New York: Viking, 1967), 177-78.

64. Stanley Aronowitz, *From the Ashes of the Old* (New York: Houghton Mifflin, 1998), 105-07. UNITE, energized if not noticeably democratized by the merger of the Amalgamated Clothing Workers with the ILGWU, has tried hardest to meet the problems of southern organizing. Its top leadership, however, is firmly in the hands of old guard figure Jay Mazur, unfailing supporter of the Kirkland team and its particular global enthusiasms—surely a handicap in meeting hyper-exploitation within the protégé regimes of the United States in Central America and elsewhere.

65. Barbara Kingsolver, *Holding the Line: Women in the Great Arizona Mine Strike of 1983* (Ithaca: Cornell University Press, 1989), 178-80.

66. See Christoph Scherrer, "Surprising Resilience: The Steelworkers' Struggle to Hang On to the Fordist Bargain," in Perusek and Worcester, eds., *Trade Union Politics,* 149-50. The weakness of the reform campaign did not, of course, stop

the defenders of Meanyism from attacking Sadlowski as the seventies "social equivalent of the mau-mauing black militant of the sixties," agent of a "Trojan horse" aimed at taking over the labor movement. See Carl Gershman, "Proletarian Chic, a Fad for the Seventies," *New America*, January-February 1977.

67. See Paul Buhle, "The Brown & Sharpe Strike," in *From the Knights of Labor to the New World Order* (New York: Garland Publishers, 1997).

68. The International Socialists, organized in the early 1970s, was a descendent of the Trotskyist movement and the 1940s Workers Party. The group published the weekly *Workers' Power* and devoted much of their energy to the Teamsters' struggle. Robert Fitch, "Revolution in the Teamsters," *Tikkun* 8 (March-April 1993); Christopher Phelps, "Independent Socialist Clubs/International Socialists," in Mari Jo Buhle et al., *Encyclopedia of the American Left*, 2d ed. (New York: Oxford University Press, 1998), 348-51.

69. Rochelle Gatlin, "A 'Society of Outsiders,': Union W.A.G.E, Working-Class Feminism and the Labor Movement," in Ronald C. Kent et al., eds, *Culture, Gender, Race and U.S. Labor History* (Westport, Conn.: Greenwood Press, 1993), 61-76; and Cindia Cameron, "Noon at 9 to 5: Reflections on a Decade of Organizing," in Jeremy Brecher and Tim Costello, eds., *Building Bridges: The Emerging Grassroots Coalition of Labor and Community* (New York: Monthly Review Press, 1990), 177-85.

70. Susan C. Eaton, "Women in Trade Union Leadership," in Adler and Suarez, eds., *Union Voices*, 177-79.

71. Kim Fellner, "In Search of a Movement," in ibid., 234.

72. Related well in Staughton Lynd, *Solidarity Unionism* (Chicago: Charles H. Kerr Co., 1993). See also Lynd's *Living Within Our Hope* (Ithaca: Cornell University Press, 1997), a series of reflections on his political and personal life, leading to labor activity.

73. Peter Rachleff, *Hard-Pressed in the Heartland: The Hormel Strike and the Future of the Labor Movement* (Boston: South End Press, 1993), for a lively, personal account. See also Hardy Green, *On Strike at Hormel* (Philadelphia: Temple University Press, 1990).

74. See Moody, *An Injury to All*, 327-30; and the more recent account of Watsonville Chicano/Mexicano life by Frank Bardacke, *Good Liberals and Great Blue Herons: Land, Labor and Politics in Pajaro Valley* (Santa Cruz: CNS/CPE, 1994).

75. Kenneth B. Noble, "Kirkland's Teamster Decision: Pulling a Meany," *New York Times*, 1 December 1987.

76. Serrin, "Labor as Usual," *Village Voice*, 23 February 1986.

77. According to an interview with a leader of the SNPJ (Slovenian Fraternal Benefit Society), Trumka's Croatian-American wife was a decisive factor. But the SNPJ and its sister Croatian Fraternal Union, both based in Pittsburgh and publishing weekly newspapers while handling insurance arrangements for members, had remained active in the civil rights and anti-war movements, the

leftish corners of the Democratic Party and other progressive social tendencies. Peter Elish, interviewed by Paul Buhle, 1982, in the Oral History of the American Left, Tamiment Library, New York University.

78. "Document Charges Conspiracy," *Labor Notes*, 28 April 1981; "Red Baiting Stepped Up as Church Falls Behind in Mine Workers Election Campaign," *Labor Notes*, 23 September 1982; "'Welcome to Class Struggle,'" *Labor Notes*, October 1989.

79. "Is the AFL-CIO a Monarchy?" *The Labor Educator*, January-February 1992.

80. "Report Commissioned by AFL-CIO Shocks Leaders; Changes Needed," ibid., November-December 1994.

81. See "Kirkland: 'We've Had Setbacks.' "

82. "AFL-CIO Takes a Walk as Congress Approves New Treaty," *Labor Notes*, 8 January 1995.

83. *AFL-CIO News,* Department of Information, Election Roundtable, 20 October 1994.

84. "How Kirkland Is Still Fighting the Cold War," *The Labor Educator*, May-June 1992, 3; Renfrey Clarke, "AFL-CIO Organizers in Russia: U.S. Labor 'Missionaries,' " *Against the Current*, May-June 1994, 21-24. As Clarke describes in an accompanying note, "Refounding Russian Labour Review," U.S. supporters of Russian workers set about organizing a support network, KAS-KOR, after the miners' strike in 1989, and took heart at the widening availability of sources and contacts in the early 1990s. The AFL-CIO's Russian-American Foundation for Trade Union Research determined to draw KAS-KOR under its wing, offering cash and equipment in return for loyalty. Publishers of the independent *Russian Labor Review*, refusing cooperation, were in effect sabotaged by the usual bureaucratic method.

    The new AFL-CIO leadership offered limited support for real solidarity, but funded it in part from the same suspicious source, a demonstrably unreformed National Endowment for Democracy. See David Bacon, "Solidarity Without Pay in Russia," *Nation*, 27 April 1998, 20. According to other reports, AFL-CIO representatives met with business officials and unionists in various parts of Eastern Europe during the later 1990s, leaning toward business unionism but compared to previous years, relatively ambivalent. In Bosnia, AFL-CIO reps refused to recognize the former Communist government union, placing bets instead on a weak business union propped up by U.S. sources. This was apparently an example of post-Kirkland hangover, with older figures, discredited and dismissed in other departments, still in charge of a specific program.

85. See Linda J. Cook, *Labor and Liberalization: Trade Unions in the New Russia* (New York: The Century Foundation, 1997), 59-61.

86. Ibid., 84-87.

87. Bacon, "Solidarity Without Pay in Russia." Unlike Cook's account (note 85), based mainly upon interviews with U.S. officials, Bacon's includes the perspectives of independent-minded unionists not on the U.S. clients' list.

88. Official publications ignored the recommendations of the 1994 survey and focus group gathering, and the CIO Information Department declined even to respond to inquiries about the unpleasant results. "Report Commissioned by AFL-CIO Shocks Leaders."

89. James W. Singer, "Labor Focus: A Man for All Unions," *National Journal*, 27 September 1980.

90. "AFL-CIO Convention," *Labor Notes*, 16 October 1995. Although passed without controversy, these resolutions were buried in post-convention publicity and scarcely mentioned in the *AFL-CIO News*. Labor's top leaders did not want the embarrassment of turning away from gay workers and people with AIDS, but neither were they (with a few notable exceptions) especially sympathetic. Tom Kahn and Bayard Rustin, the top-ranking gay official and gay African-American ally, respectively, of the Meany/Kirkland administations, had simply accommodated themselves, never pressing the issue for gays and lesbians unprotected by the hierarchy, not even complaining against the homophobia characteristic of the Meany office and still the rule today among Kirkland's adamant supporters, the building trades.

91. Insiders recall the late Tom Kahn calling Donohue a "Stalinoid" for his support of Edward Kennedy's Central America peace proposals.

92. Quoted from Harold Meyerson, "Mother Jones Returns," *LA Weekly*, 3-9 November 1995. This essay is the best "inside" account from the standpoint of the middle-aged DSAers who took over the speechwriting, if not the leadership itself, from the SDUSA operatives who had conducted the AFL-CIO central apparatus for decades. Both strands, as noted above, owed much to a spin on Max Shachtman's tradition, albeit the one distinctly perverse in its neoconservativsm and the other a reformist modification. From the SDUSA camp, Ronald Radosh, quoted in Jonathan Mahler, "Labor's War Winds," *Forward*, 31 October 1997, warned direly that while SDUSA members were "the intellectual mainstay of the Kirkland years," now a coalition of new leftists and others were "the intellectual brain trust for Sweeney." Kim Moody, "U.S. Labor Wars: Bottom to Top," *New Politics* 5 (winter 1996), 81-91, offers another valuable perspective.

93. My personal thanks to Arthur S. Coia for responding to communications. Within the next several years, Coia faced indictments for alleged past dealings with mob contacts of his father's, involvements that had curiously not led to charges against numerous other union leaders, prominently including noted anticommunist liberals, from the 1920s onward. Coia's LIUNA had simultaneously become known as labor's largest single donor to Democratic coffers, although LIUNA also endorsed a Republican here and there.

94. Thanks to Harry Kelber, publisher of the *Labor Educator*, for passing along "Labor Talk: AFL-CIO Convention" commentary, published in *The Labor Educator,* November-December 1995, as "My Convention Story." Kelber ran as an independent candidate for the executive council, and despite the

pressure to vote a "straight ticket" on the Unity Slate, 45 central labor councils from 24 states voted for Kelber. He was nominated by Tom Deary of Nashua, New Hampshire, who a decade earlier had courageously mortgaged his house to publish a rank-and-file newspaper for New England labor, losing home and paper in the process. Kelber recounts the story more fully in *My 60 Years as a Labor Activist* (New York: A.G. Publishing, 1996), 238-44 and 250-57. Thanks also to yet another veteran rank-and-file strike supporter, Paul Andreas Rasmussen, for passing along numerous clippings from the convention.

Conclusion

1. Sweeney's remarks hailing the formation of the new organization, Scholars, Artists, and Writers for Social Justice (SAWSJ) are partially recorded in *Faculty @ Work* (Washington, D.C.: AFL-CIO, 1998), 96.
2. "Looking Ahead After the Fast Track Victory," *Working Together,* September-October 1998; David Glenn, "Fast Track Derailed," in Jo-Ann Mort, ed., *Not Your Father's Labor Movement* (London: Verso, 1998), 189-200. "Hillary Hustling New Dems," *Forward,* 25 September 1998, outlines the DLC's hostility toward the labor movement.
3. I was a Madison TAA striker in 1970, although I left town before the first "Soglin Era" (1973-1979) and the shift of the local labor movement leftward.
4. Paul Buhle, "Lost Struggles of the 1970s: Dave Wagner and the Madison Press Connection," in *From the Knights of Labor to the New World Order: Essays on Labor and Culture* (New York: Garland Publishing, 1997), 219-38.
5. See "Labor Pumps Up Winning Election Turnout," *Union Labor News,* December 1998. Fully 30 percent of Wisconsin voters in the off-year election came from union households, and Senator Russ Feingold as well as Tammy Baldwin owed their margins to union votes. A special thanks to Madisonian Allen Ruff for keeping me up to date and making recent issues of the *ULN* available to me.
6. Joel Shoemaker, "Strikes and Solidarity in the 1990s," *Union Labor News,* March 1995, and Dexter Arnold's "Mexican Workers' Role in U.S. Labor History," ibid. Special thanks to David Newby, Jim Cavanaugh, and Dexter Arnold (the last two current and former editors of *Union Labor News*) for providing documents and insights into the story of Wisconsin labor's reinvigoration, and to Arnold especially, for reading over these passages.
7. See various features in *Working Together: Labor Report on the Americas,* including Mary Tong, "Gathering Builds Solidarity with Guatemala Workers," July-August 1996; "AFL-CIO takes strong stand against NAFTA expansion," "Crisis Not Over for Mexican Workers," and "Becker Leads Steelworker Delegation to Mexico," March-April 1997; "Victory in Phillips-Van Heuson campaign," May-June 1997; and "Contract Victory at Nicaraguan Maquila," September-October 1998. Becker, himself an interesting case, was the commander of a corporate campaign against USX during the strike in 1986,

and subsequently of solidarity efforts with Pittston miners in 1990. Perhaps most impressive was the linking of USW with non-U.S. unions on four continents during the USX campaign, setting one kind of precedent for international solidarity. Becker reputedly spearheaded the merger with the UAW and United Rubber Workers, envisioning a "SWOC II" echo of the 1930s campaign that brought industrial unionism—albeit from the top down—to steel. A strike at Wheeling-Pittsburgh Steel Corporation in 1996-1997 put Becker back into the spotlight, as delegates from a half-dozen unions pledged support. On the other hand, Becker also endorsed a political coalition with steel corporations (including several brutal non-union companies) to limit steel imports.

8. Rose Feuer, "The Staley Lockout: A View from Below," *Impact: The Rank and File Newsletter* 3 (July 1995). Issued from Youngstown, this publication reflects the decades of activity by Staughton Lynd and others.

9. Jeremy Brecher, *Strike!* (Boston: South End Press, 1997), 356-58.

10. See Steve Early, "Telephone Workers Buck Leaders, Affiliate with CWA," *Labor Notes,* August 1998.

11. Steve Early, "Membership-Based Organizing," in Gregory Matsios, ed., *A New Labor Movement for a New Century* (New York: Monthly Review Press, 1998). See also Corey Robin and Michelle Stephens, "Against the Grain: Organizing TAs at Yale," in Cary Nelson, ed., *Will Teach for Food: Academic Labor in Crisis* (Minneapolis: University of Minnesota Press, 1997), 44-79.

12. Steven Greenhouse,"Labor Party Gets to Work at its Second Convention," *New York Times,* 16 November 1998.

13. Martin Glaberman and Seymour Faber, *Working for Wages: The Roots of Insurgency* (Dix Hills, N.Y.: General Hall, 1998), 156. Glaberman and Faber were associated with the political group around C. L. R. James.

14. David Brody, "The Breakdown of Labor's Social Contract," *Dissent* 39 (winter 1992), 33.

15. See David Moberg, "Union-Busting, Past and Present," ibid., 77.

16. Michael Meeropol, *Surrender: How the Clinton Admnistration Completed the Reagan Revolution* (Ann Arbor: University of Michigan Press, 1998), chap. 11, especially 245-58.

Index

fascism, 4
Federal Bureau of Investigation, 148, 166, 184
Federated Farmer-Labor Party, 84
Federation of Trades and Labor Unions of the United States and Canada, 38
Feller, Kim, 237-38
Fiji Trades Union Congress, 228
Firing Line, 200
First World War, influence on labor, 71
Fishermen's Union, 128
Fitzpatrick John, 76
Flint, Michigan, sit-down strike, 101, 109
Foner, Philip S., 12
Food, Tobacco and Allied Workers, 128, 129
Forbath, William, 12, 41
Force Ouvriere, 140
Fortune, 8, 126, 177
Forverts (Jewish Daily Forward), 59, 60, 61
Foster, William Z., 83
Fraina, Louis C., 67, 69, 70, 71, 72
Fraser, Douglas, 199
Free Trade Union Institute (Russia), 242-43
Free Trade Union News, 226
Freedom House, 145, 209, 227
Friedan, Betty, 249
Friedman, Joel, 247
Fulbright, Senator J. William, 187
Fur and Leather Workers, 128

Gdansk Steelworks, 230
Gee, Hubert, 140
General Agreement on Tariffs and Trade (GATT), 242
General Confederation of Trade Unions (FNFR, Russia), 242-43
General Motors strike, 1945, 125
George Meany International Human Rights Award, 228
George Meany Memorial Center, 151, 255
Georgetown University, 206
Georgine, Robert, 240
Gershman, Carl, 213

Gingrich, Newt, 232
Giuliani, Rudolph, 4, 5, 250
Glazer, Nathan, 189
Goldberg, Arthur, 145, 149, 163, 166, 179
Gompers, Samuel, 7, 11, 12, 13, 15, 17, 18, 33, 39, 40, 54, 60, 71, 79, 90, 124, 252, 263
 aspirations for the Open Door, 77
 background, 40-42
 Congressional lobbying, 74
 excludes socialists from AFL representation, 53, 54
 on race riots, 80
 opposes new immigration, 49
 personal success during First World War, 75, 80, 81, 82
 political support of Democrats, 62, 64
 rise as union leader, 42-45
 role during 1920s, 105
 supports imperialism, 78
Good Shepherds, 103
Gore, Albert, 221, 250, 255
Gorman, Patrick, 162
Goulart, Joao, 153
Grace, J. Peter, 152
Green Berets, 151
Green, Max, 145, 223
Green, William, 107, 117, 123, 131, 139, 159, 263
Greer, Margolis, Mitchel, Burns & Associates, 241
Greider, William, 222
Guatemala Labor Education Project, 256
Guatemala, 144
Gulf of Tonkin incident, 183
Gutman, Herbert, 10

Harlem Renaissance, 89
Harrington, Michael, 147, 199
Harrison, George, 169
Hart, Peter D., 241
Hayes, Frank, 104
Hayes, Max, 83
Haymarket incident, 18, 38
Hearst, William Randolph, 63
Helms, Jesse, 200, 208
Helstein, Ralph, 179

Lodge, George Cabot, 152
London, Meyer, 149
Lovestone, Jay, 92, 137, 138, 139, 154, 207
Lowenstein, Allard, 149, 180
Lucker, C. H., 29
Lundeen, Ernest, 113
Lynd, Staughton, 238, 256

Madison Federation of Labor, 253
Madison Press Connection, 252-53
Magon brothers (Enrico and Ricardo Flores Magon), 78
Mandela, Nelson, 156
Marable, Manning, 172
Marcantonio, Vito, 138
March on Washington Movement (MOW), 156
March on Washington for Jobs and Freedom (1963), 156, 172, 181
Marine Cooks and Stewards union, 128
Marshall Plan, 139, 141
Marshall, Ray, 197

Martin Luther King, Jr., Memorial March (1983), 156, 224, 172
Marx, Karl, 26, 28, 33, 35
Masons, Order of, 104
Mazzocchi, Tony, 260
McBride, John, 57
McBride, Lloyd, 236
McClellan Committee, 163
McDonald, David, 134, 163
McGovern, George, 187, 210, 213, 253
McGuire, Peter J., 55, 57
McIntee, Gerald, 5, 244
McKees Rocks strike (1909), 67
McKinley, Pres. William, 53, 54
Meany, George, 9, 11, 13, 16, 17, 91, 116, 117, 130, 135, 142, 143, 144, 179, 189, 192, 196, 198, 200, 201, 215, 232, 239, 263
    influence on Kennedy administration, 145
    last years of, 200, 201
    laughing stock of press, 146
    moves unity with CIO, 132-34

on 1972 election, 187
on race and labor, 168, 169, 189
on Taft-Hartley Act, 129-30
opposes labor party, 114
personal background, 92-96
president of AFL-CIO, 134
relation to organized crime in labor movement, 159-65
relations to New Deal, 103, 111, 112, 115
role during Second World War, 122-24
role in CIA actions, 137-39
role in New York state labor of 1930s, 190-112
Meany, Michael, 93
Medicaid, 208
Medicare, 186
Meeropol, Michael, 262
Melman, Yossi, 157
Mexican Congress of Labor, 255
Mexican-Americans in labor, 102, 235
Meyer, Cord, 154
Michels, Robert, 6, 8, 202
Michigan Commonwealth Federation, 130
Midwest Academy, 245
"military Keynesianism," 2
Mills, C. Wright, 13
Minneapolis general strike (1934), 100
Mississippi Freedom Democratic Party, 180
Mitchell, John, 61, 62, 64
Modern Dance, 71
Mondale, Walter, 220
Montgomery, Alabama, 10, 35, 249
    bus boycott, 166
"Moral Economy," 20
Morgan, Lewis Henry, 66
Morison, Samuel Eliot, 79
Morrison, Frank, 116
Moscow Trials, 138
Motion Picture Association, 152
Moynihan, Daniel Patrick, 183, 189, 193, 209, 213
Muravchik, Joshua, 213
Murphy, Gov. Frank, 120
Murray, Phil, 127, 132